Reference Renaissance

Current and Future Trends

Edited by Marie L. Radford and R. David Lankes

Neal-Schuman Publishers, Inc.

New York   London

9/12

Published by Neal-Schuman Publishers, Inc.
100 William St., Suite 2004
New York, NY 10038

Library of Congress Cataloging-in-Publication Data

Reference renaissance : current and future trends / edited by Marie L. Radford and R. David Lankes.
    p. cm.
    Chapters updated from original presentations at the Reference Renaissance: Current and Future Trends conference, sponsored by the Bibliographical Center for Research of Aurora, Colorado, and Reference and User Services Association, a Division of the Ameri-can Library Association, August 4–5, 2008.
    Includes bibliographical references and index.
    ISBN 978-1-55570-680-7 (alk. paper)
    1. Reference services (Libraries)—Congresses. 2. Electronic reference services (Libraries)—Congresses. 3. Internet in library reference services—Congresses. I. Radford, Marie L. II. Lankes, R. David.

Z711.R4455 2010
025.5'2—dc22
                                               2010000229

*This book is dedicated to the vision and hard work
of reference librarians and support staff
who are the true creators of the Reference Renaissance.*

Contents

List of Tables, Figures, and Appendixes

Tables

Figures

Appendixes

Acknowledgments

The editors would like to thank everyone who contributed to the development of this book and to the planning and incredible success of the Reference Renaissance: Current and Future Trends conference. In particular, we would like to thank the conference Chair, Brenda K. Bailey-Hainer, President and CEO, BCR (Bibliographical Center for Research, Colorado) and Justine Schaffner, Library Services Consultant, BCR. Without their efforts the conference would simply not have taken place.

We would also like to thank the members of the conference planning committee, especially those who served as chapter reviewers and consultants for this book: Bill Pardue, Arlington Heights Memorial Library, IL; Kay Cassell, Rutgers, the State University of New Jersey; Nancy Huling, University of Washington; M. Kathleen Kern, University of Illinois at Urbana-Champaign; Amy VanScoy, North Carolina State University Libraries; and Lynn Westbrook, University of Texas, Austin. Nicolette Sosulski of Syracuse University also provided editorial assistance.

In addition, special recognition goes to the major conference sponsors: BCR, RUSA and Tutor.com and to these other sponsors: Compendium Library Service, OCLC, Reference Universe (Paratext), Serial Solutions and the University of Denver.

We give our thanks to each of the speakers, presenters, panel participants, and attendees, who provided an exciting conference in terms of their forward-looking vision, dedication, and enthusiasm for the Reference Renaissance.

A debt of gratitude is also due to Neal-Schuman Publishers, in particular to Charles Harmon, director of publishing and to the members of the editorial staff.

Marie L. Radford also is thankful for the love, gentle encouragement, and ever sage advice of her husband, Gary P. Radford.

Introduction

Marie L. Radford and R. David Lankes

The rumors of the "death of reference" have been greatly exaggerated. The theme of a "Reference Renaissance," the conference that serves as the foundation for this volume, was taken from the title of an editorial by Diane Zabel, in the *Reference and User Services Quarterly*, winter 2007 issue (Vol. 47, no. 2). Zable wrote of a "resurgence of interest in reference" (p. 108) and that "reference is experiencing a regeneration, a reference renaissance" (p. 109). This renaissance can be seen in the return to core values of service excellence in libraries and to the rising surge of innovative reference initiatives via virtual venues such as instant messaging, text messaging, and other emerging modes. Web 2.0 applications have presented an array of avenues for reaching tech savvy library users, including reference blogs, wikis, and library pages on social networking sites such as MySpace and Facebook. Virtual reference "desks" are also appearing in 3D digital worlds such as Second Life.

This volume demonstrates an exploration of the rapid growth and changing nature of reference, as an escalating array of information technologies blend with traditional reference service to create vibrant hybrids. It is a definitive statement that the reference renaissance continues. The march of rethinking reference that began over a decade ago with experiments with e-mail and new service models has now progressed through a spate of technological experiments, to new concepts of reference as moving beyond the desk. Through this process of refinement and invention a movement has been created, which was bonded in a series of conferences that explored the intimacies of human communication. This movement sought to not only keep reference relevant but to push forward the values of libraries in everyday life. A look over this decade shows that reference has been transformed from an area focused on resources and artifacts to one that explores a human process of questioning, contextualizing, and learning.

Reference Renaissance: Current and Future Trends was designed to capture the latest in the work of the reference movement. Its essence captures up-to-date work in reference presented at a recent conference of the same name. This highly successful conference, which drew over 500 participants, was sponsored by the Bibliographical Center for Research of Aurora, Colorado, and the Reference and User Services Association, a Division of the American Library Association. It built on the legacy of the virtual reference desk (VRD) series of seven conferences that ended in 2005. It has embraced the expanded VRD mission to incorporate the multitude of established, emerging, and merging types of reference service, including traditional and virtual reference. Updating the information presented at the conference, this volume explores all aspects of reference in a broad range of contexts, including libraries and information centers in academic, public, school, corporate, and other special library environments. It succeeded in capturing the current innovation in the field and providing a look ahead to the trends that will forge the reference future.

The chapters that follow are updated from the original conference presentations. They analyze issues, identify and describe practices, advance organizational and technological systems, propose standards, and/or suggest innovative approaches that reveal an exciting and unfolding reference landscape. Each has been rigorously reviewed by experts. *Reference Renaissance: Current and Future Trends* features three parts: "The State of Reference Services," "What Research Tells Us about Reference," and "Reference in Action: Reports from the Field."

In Part I, David W. Lewis provides his thoughts on "Reference in the Age of Wikipedia, Or Not..." in which he provides provocative ideas about the current reference landscape vis-à-vis the easy availability of information through the Internet. Next, James LaRue and Carla Stoffle provide the library directors' viewpoint, and we (Marie and Dave) put forth the library and information science faculty perspective on what is the most critical skill in reference staff, what innovative things they/we are doing to improve reference services or to improve library school education, and what are their/our predictions for the future.

In Part II, eight cutting-edge chapters grouped under topic areas of Virtual Reference; Approaches, Values, and Philosophy of Reference Services; and Innovative Service Models present research-based reports and thought-provoking essays.

Part III features eleven reports from the field that describe reference initiatives or staffing models that have already been successfully implemented or that discuss digital reference tools. These are grouped under topic areas of Virtual Reference, Search Engines and Virtual Tools, Innovative Service Models and Marketing, and Staff Development and Training.

Reference Renaissance: Current and Future Trends represents a snapshot of current reference practice as well as a glimpse into the exciting reference future we are creating. At this writing, the second Reference Renaissance conference is being planned. This event will provide yet another opportunity for researchers, practitioners, and students to exchange information, service approaches, and exciting ideas to ensure the continuation of the Reference Renaissance.

PART I

THE STATE OF REFERENCE SERVICES: AN OVERVIEW

Reference in the Age of Wikipedia, or Not...

David W. Lewis, Keynote Speaker

Introduction

The title of my talk[1] today is purposefully provocative. But it is not because I believe the reference in the age of Wikipedia is dead but rather that in the time of Wikipedia we need to be able to ask and answer the question implied by the "or not...". We all know that the old models of reference work are no longer adequate. Our challenge is to be able to affirmatively explain what it is we do and how it adds value.

I want to cover a number of topics. I'll start with a definition and move to a consideration of alphabetical order. We will proceed to a short history lesson on three revolutions. Then I will present an opening quote and an example of the world we live in. We will then move to part one of a consideration of change using the work of Clayton Christensen. After an interlude with ChaCha, we will consider change in light of the work of Clay Shirky. After that we will sample some wisdom from Paul Krugman and *Wired*, looking at "Free!" and "Better Than Free." We will finish with four questions, some answers, an uplifting quote, and a final challenge.

Definition

Renaissance [F., f. *renaître to be born again, after naissance birth: cf. RENASCENCE.*]
1. a. The great revival of art and letters, under the influence of classical models, which began in Italy in the 14th century and continued during the 15th and 16th; also, the period during which this movement was in progress.
2. Any revival, or period of marked improvement and new life, in art, literature, etc.

(*Oxford English Dictionary*, accessed 2009)

We are here to consider the proposition that reference work is in a renaissance. I am not sure if we are in a "period of marked improvement and new life," but I am confident that if we are, it is not because we are in a "great revival...under the influence of classical models." If reference is in a renaissance it is because we are finding new ways to apply the remarkable tools that are now at our disposal.

3

Alphabetical Order

In his wonderful history of reference works, Tom McArthur calls our attention to the fact that until the advent of printing, alphabetic order, though of course it existed, was not thought of as a way to arrange knowledge. As he states:

> Although some properly alphabetic works appeared before Gutenberg printed his first book, the printing press seems to have been the factor that changed everything in favor of non-thematic ordering. Compositors were constantly re-shuffling the letters of the alphabet around as small hard metal objects in trays and in composites. They and their associates—which included many writers who were wont to frequent print shops—became as a consequence increasingly at home with the convenience that the alphabet offers as an invariant series. Where scholars and copyists had previously been unaccustomed even to thinking of words and parts of words alphabetically, printers were now spending a great part of their time doing nothing else. (McArthur, 1986, p. 77)

In describing the difference between thematic and alphabetic organization McArthur goes on to say, "This dichotomy is far-reaching, however, because it operates first at a real practical level in terms of how works of reference are used and also at an ideal and theoretical level with regard to how information is best presented and understood" (McArthur, 1986, p. 80).

I think it is important as we stand at the beginning of a revolution as profound as the invention of printing that we recognize that just as alphabetical order arose as a technique to help order the vast increase in knowledge that the printing press made possible, there will be new tools, many that we can not yet imagine, that will rise to bring order to the wealth of information made possible by the Web. And just as alphabetical order was seen as crude and even offensive to the scribes and scholars of the time, so the new techniques will probably seem crude and even offensive to us. But in the end these tools, like alphabetical order, will become commonplace.

A Little History: Three Revolutions

Our brief history lesson will consider three revolutions (based on Lewis, 2006):

1. The invention of printing in the fifteenth century
2. The industrialization of printing in the nineteenth century
3. The development of the Internet and the Web in the late twentieth century

In all three cases, the capacity to reproduce knowledge increased by several orders of magnitude. Knowledge escaped the established institution and elites that had previously controlled it. And, important for our consideration, new technologies and practices to manage the increased production of knowledge were required and developed.

With the development of printing in fifteenth century, the scribal culture, which had managed and controlled access to knowledge for several millenniums, vanishes. The church could no longer control the dissemination of knowledge. New tools for managing knowledge such as alphabetical order, as discussed previously, dictionaries, encyclopedias, and scientific journals were developed to take advantage of the power of print. In this process reading and writing went from being a professional activity practiced by scribes and scholars to an amateur activity practiced by a large portion of the population.

Our second revolution was the industrialization of printing in the nineteenth century. It was made possible by the invention of the steam-driven printing presses and steam-driven paper-making machines, which made wood pulp paper. This combination created mass circulation newspapers, dime novels, and cheap schoolbooks. In most Western cultures literacy became nearly universal. The invention of the pencil and the fountain pen in combination with cheap paper made the keeping of diaries and letter writing possible for the masses.

Among the most important responses to the increase in information made possible by the industrialization of printing was the library, as we know it. Classification schemes, card catalogs, and reference assistance were all developed in the late nineteenth century, and with Carnegie funding, the public library as we know it was created. It is important to understand that this is the culture from which we all come. These tools and these approaches to service have shaped our thinking. When I started in libraries a little over 30 years ago, the most important thing that a library did was to keep millions and millions of small pieces of paper in order. We did many other things, of course, but if the pieces of paper were not in order, nothing else mattered. It is important to recognize as we face the third revolution how the previous revolution has shaped our thinking and the culture of our organizations.

The final revolution is the one happening all around us today, that of the Internet and the Web. It threatens to disrupt everyone involved in print publication and distribution, including us. In much the same way that the Gutenberg press made literacy an amateur activity, the Web makes the production and distribution of all forms of content an amateur activity. It makes possible the easy sharing and creation of content. The tools libraries created in the second revolution are not adequate to organize the huge increase in information this third revolution has created. Some of you may recall that brief period, I believe it was in the spring of 1994, when librarians thought they could catalog the Web. It was a short-lived and now humorous conceit. The successful efforts are network-level tools that track user behavior used to organize and find information. Google and Yahoo! work because they operate at network scale and because they use algorithms, not human decision making. Authority control and Boolean searching are clearly no longer adequate to the task at hand.

Opening Quote

So, finally, we come to the opening quote. It comes from Clay Shirky, who says in his very important recent book *Here Comes Everybody*:

> New technology makes new things possible: put another way, when new technology appears, previously impossible things start occurring. If enough of those impossible things are important and happen in a bundle, quickly, the change becomes a revolution. The hallmark of revolution is that the goals of the revolution cannot be contained by the institutional structure of existing society. As a result, either the revolutionaries are put down, or some of those institutions are altered, replaced, or destroyed.... Many institutions we rely on today will not survive this change without significant alteration, and the more an institution or industry relies on information as its core product, the greater and more complete the change will be. (Shirky, 2008, p. 107)

We are of course in an industry were information is core, and so Shirky's quote should give us pause. We need to recognize that if we do not alter our practice and our institutions it is likely that we and they will be replaced or destroyed, for it seems extremely unlikely that the revolution we are living through will be put down.

An Example of the World We Live In

Prominent in the promotion for the conference was the line "Rumors of the 'death of reference' have been greatly exaggerated." This is, of course, a play on the famous Mark Twain quote. You need to know that I started my library career as a reference librarian, but it has been many years since I have been an active practitioner. I thought it might be interesting to see what it would take to verify the Twain quote today. So of course I went to Google and typed in "twain quotes death." The first item returned was titled "Mark Twain quotations—Death" at www.twainquotes.com/Death.html. Clicking through to the site you find not only an explanation that there are many variations of the "report of my death" quote, but that the original note was written May 1897. A reproduction of the original letter is then provided along with a transcription. This is about as good an answer to the question as you can get—fully documented down to the note in Twain's hand. For comparison, I check some printed quotation books, and while they generally provided the correct answer, with some variation, they were not as complete, and none had the reproduction of the actual note.

This might have been a unique case, and I might have been lucky, but I think not. To me this shows clearly the power of the tools we live with. They are available to anyone with an Internet connection and can easily, in many cases, be used to find the answers people need without libraries or librarians.

Thinking about Change: Clayton Christensen

As we consider the change that is taking place around us I think it is important to look at theory. We are fortunate that a number of scholars have done good work in this area. Among the most important is Clayton Christensen. In his book the *Innovator's Dilemma* (Christensen, 2000), he provides a theoretical basis for looking at situations, as the subtitle puts it, "when new technologies cause great firms to fail." I will also draw from his second book *The Innovator's Solution* (Christensen & Raynor, 2003) and his third book *Seeing What's Next* (Christensen, Anthony, & Roth, 2004). In his first book Christensen develops "Disruptive Innovation Theory," which allows the simple, cheap, and revolutionary to overpower established firms even when these firms are well run. In the second book, Christensen refines this work with his theory of "Resources, Processes, and Value Theory," which defines the building blocks of capabilities. This theory both explains why some firms are unable to escape the trap of disruptive innovation and provides guidance on strategies to effectively deploy such innovations.

Christensen summarizes his first theory:

> Disruptive innovation theory points to situations in which new organizations can use relatively simple, convenient, low-cost innovations to create growth and triumph over powerful incumbents. The theory holds that existing companies have a high probability of beating entrant attackers when the contest is about *sustaining* innovations. But established companies almost always lose to attackers armed with *disruptive* innovations. (Christensen et al., 2004, p. xv)

A sustaining innovation improves the performance of established products along dimensions of performance that mainstream customers in major markets have historically valued. Relationships, cost structures, and organizational dynamics are unchanged, even though technology can, and often does, change radically.

Disruptive innovations bring a different value proposition to the market. Initially they underperform established products in mainstream markets, but the products improve at a rapid rate and are superior in ways that are not valued by the established market. Most often they are more reliable, easier to use, or cheaper.

Important to Christensen's theory is the notion of "performance oversupply." As he explains it, "One bedrock finding from our research is that companies innovate faster than customers' lives change. In other words, what people are looking to get done remains remarkably consistent, but products always improve. Thus, products eventually become too good" (Christensen et al., 2004, p. 12). Customers whose needs have not yet been fully met are, as Christensen puts it, "undershot." When customers are undershot they continue to pay a premium for improvements in functionality. When customers' needs are met they are "overshot," and they no longer will pay a premium for improvements, and the basis of competition changes. Companies selling to overshot customers are vulnerable to disruptive attacks. When attacked, they often move upmarket to sell to more demanding customers. High-end users don't yet value the disruptive innovation because it does not yet meet their functional needs.

For an example of how this works in our world, think of the typical first-year student who needs to write a short paper using five scholarly resources. As long as the student cannot get five good scholarly sources from the open Web, the student will need to use the library. But as soon as those five good scholarly resources can be found on the Web, it does not matter one wit to the student that the library has five hundred good resources. What matters is that it is 2:00 in the morning and the library is closed and the Web is not. The basis of competition has changed, and the library loses and the Web wins. Often the librarian's response to the loss of first-year student use of the library was to move upmarket and argue that these students weren't really our important customers; we will focus on our work with graduate students and faculty. Of course, the number of scholarly resources on the Web is growing at a faster rate than the resources in libraries, and it is only a matter of time before graduate students and then faculty will find themselves in the same situation as our hypothetical first-year student and they will respond the same way. In fact, it is likely that particle physicists and computer scientists have already reached this point.

Christensen says,

> If the technology can be developed so that a large population of less skilled or less affluent people can begin owning and using, in a more convenient context, something that historically was available only to more skilled or more affluent people in a centralized, inconvenient location, then there is potential for shaping the idea into a new-market disruption. (Christensen & Raynor, 2003, pp. 49–50)

This seems to be a perfect description of libraries today. Print libraries are centralized, inconvenient, and often require an expert's intervention to be used effectively. The technology of the Web is everywhere and easy. And as we all know, but are not always willing to admit, our historic product is being disrupted.

In considering disruptive innovation, Christensen provides some guidance:

1. Markets that don't exist can't be analyzed. The experts, including you, will be wrong. He argues for what he calls exploratory development that is learning through small-scale development projects. Libraries often have trouble with this approach. Our habit is to create a task force, do a literature search, talk to one another, and write a report. Christensen would argue that a year's experience, even with failure, is more valuable than the work of even the best task force. Remember the experts will be wrong.

2. A corollary to this is that you should not invest all of your resources on the first effort. You are likely to be wrong and will need to try a second and a third time. Again, libraries tend to have trouble with this approach.

Maybe because our budgets are often constrained, we tend to spend whatever we have on our first try.

3. Don't ask your customers what they want, rather watch what they do. Like the experts your customers will be wrong about disruptive technologies but they will adapt quickly in the ways they can use them.

4. Be impatient for profits, but patient for growth. I translate this in the library environment as be impatient for success of the pilot but patient in taking it campus-wide. This creates the right incentives for risk taking. The push on the pilot forces risk-taking, and by not being in a hurry to grow the project the risk of failure is lessened.

In explaining why established organizations have trouble seeing and adopting disruptive innovations, Christensen develops "Resources Processes Value Theory." As he says:

> The resources, processes, and values (RPV) theory explains why existing companies tend to have such difficulty grappling with disruptive innovations. The RPV theory holds that resources (what a firm has), processes (how a firm does its work), and values (what a firm wants to do) define an organization's strengths as well as its weaknesses and blind spots. (Christensen et al., 2004, p. xvii)

Resources are the entities an organization can buy or sell, build, or destroy. Customers and investors provide them and they are, by their nature, flexible. Processes are the established ways organizations turn resources into products and services. Values are the criteria by which prioritization decisions are made. Processes and values don't change easily. This allows the organization to be consistent in the way it makes decisions. In most situations consistent process and values are a key factor in an organizations success.

But when an organization confronts a disruptive innovation these same consistent processes and values become impediments to change. Since disruptive innovations bring a different value proposition to the market, organizations with established approaches cannot see the value of pursuing it, or the innovation will be "crammed" into the existing values and processes and thus will lose its potential. Christensen argues that the only way to develop disruptive innovations in established organizations is to create a separate "skunk works" that is outside the established organization and can operate with different processes and values. This will be difficult for most libraries to do.

Interlude: ChaCha

I want to talk now about ChaCha,[2] not the Cuban dance, but ChaCha the service that answers questions over mobile phones. The service is free, though standard text messaging rates and voice minutes may still apply. Answers are limited to the 160 characters of a standard text message and the "guides" who respond to the questions are relatively low-paid amateurs. ChaCha might be viewed as a challenger for established library reference services, but it is difficult to get overly concerned with a service that seems best positioned to settle bar bets. But then it is available from anywhere, at least anywhere with cell phone service, at any time. If the answers get to be good enough, can a traditional library compete? ChaCha is using a disruptive model to make money by providing answers to simple questions, but if they get better at answering questions and they start sending Web pages to G3 phones, the current limits of their capacity fall away and they could easily challenge a core part of library reference work.

Thinking about Change: Clay Shirky

Shirky (2008) discusses "organizing without organizations," exploring how what he calls the new social technologies of the Internet allow individuals to share, create, and act collectively without the organizational overheads that had previously been required. This can be thought of as the cooperation revolution. As he puts it, "The centrality of group effort to human life means that anything that changes the way groups function will have profound ramifications for everything from commerce and government to media and religion" (Shirky, 2008, p. 16). He goes on:

> We are living in the middle of a remarkable increase in our ability to share, to cooperate with one another, and to take collective action, all outside the framework of traditional institutions and organizations.... The difficulties that kept self-assembled groups from working together are shrinking, meaning that the number and kind of things groups can get done without financial motivation or managerial oversight are growing. The current change in one sentence is: most of the barriers to group action have collapsed, and without those barriers, we are free to explore new ways of gathering together and getting things done. (Shirky, 2008, pp. 20–21)

In much the same way that the invention of the printing press made literacy an amateur activity, the current Internet revolution makes content creation a mass amateur activity, and this leads to the large-scale sharing of content. To quote Shirky again:

> An individual with a camera or a keyboard is now a non-profit of one, and self-publishing is now the normal case.... This technological story is like literacy, wherein a particular capacity moves from a group of professionals to become embedded within the society itself, ubiquitously, available to a majority of citizens. (Shirky, 2008, pp. 77–78)

This creates a world quite different from the one we, as librarians, are comfortable with, and it challenges the authority of what we do. In this world, content is published first, then filtered. Shirky argues that the mass amateurization of publishing requires mass amateurization of filtering. Speaking directly to us, Shirky says, "When a profession has been created as a result of some scarcity, as with librarians or television programmers, the professionals are often the last ones to see it when that scarcity goes away. It is easier to understand that you face competition than obsolescence" (Shirky, 2008, pp. 58–59). To me this was a wake-up call.

Shirky devotes a full chapter to Wikipedia and why it is successful. I am sure that if you were to go back several years you would have found few reference librarians who were champions of Wikipedia; after all, as we said back then, "anyone can change it." Now most of us are converts, at least when it comes to answering our own questions. Christensen would explain that Wikipedia is successful because it brings a different value proposition and because it gets better quicker than competitive products. Shirky explains the social processes that produce the new value proposition and why it could get better so fast. As he explains:

> Encyclopedias used to be the kind of thing that appeared only when people paid for them, yet Wikipedia requires no fees from its users, nor payments to its contributors. The genius of wikis, and the coming change in group effort in general, is in part predicated on the ability to make nonfinancial motivations add up to something of global significance. (Shirky, 2008, p. 133)

He goes on:

> Because Wikipedia is a process not a product, it replaces guarantees offered by institutions with probabilities supported by process: if enough people care enough about an article to read it, then enough people will care enough to improve it, and over time this will lead to a large enough body of good enough work to begin to take both availability and quality of articles for granted, and to integrate Wikipedia into daily use by millions. (Shirky, 2008, pp. 139–140)

Wikipedia is successful even though "anyone can change it" because it combines both innovative technology and a new social contract. To once again quote Shirky:

> As with every fusion of group and tool, this defense against vandalism [in Wikipedia] is the result not of a novel technology alone but of a novel technology combined with a novel social strategy. Wikis provide ways for groups to work together, and defend the output of that work, but these capabilities are available only when most of the participants are committed to those outcomes. (Shirky, 2008, p. 137)

As we look to implement new tools and services, we can learn from Shirky. He argues that successful social tools require the following:

1. A plausible promise to attracts users
2. An effective tool that makes community possible
3. An acceptable bargain that creates community

I believe one of our great challenges is to create a set of social tools that will in turn create open scholarship and open information. To date we have been focused on the effective, too. This is the easy part. The hard part is the plausible promise and the acceptable bargain.

In considering open systems Shirky suggests they are successful because they accomplish the following:

1. They lower the cost, but not the likelihood, of failure—this provides the means to explore multiple possibilities and increases the likelihood of finding successful solutions.
2. They do not create a bias in favor of predictable but substandard outcomes.
3. They make it simple to integrate the contributions of people who contribute only one good idea.

Scholarship should work this way, but in a world where much scholarship has been commercialized, it does not.

Interlude: Paul Krugman

In a June 6th 2008 *New York Times* column Paul Krugman wrote:

> Bit by bit, everything that can be digitized will be digitized, making intellectual property ever easier to copy and ever harder to sell for more than a nominal price. And we'll have to find business and economic models that take this reality into account. It won't all happen immediately.
>
> But in the long run, we are all the Grateful Dead.

His point was that the current publishing models were dying and that like the Grateful Dead, who made their money in large part on concert tickets and T-shirts, authors and other content creators will need to find different models to support themselves.

Wisdom from Wired: "Free!" and "Better Than Free"

Chris Anderson, the editor in chief at *Wired*, in his article, "Free! Why $0.00 Is the Future of Business,"[3] argues that all of the feed stocks of the digital world—processing, storage, and bandwidth—are getting cheaper and that, though they will never reach zero, they will get so cheap that things that once cost money can be given away for free (Anderson, 2008).

As he says:

> In 1954, at the dawn of nuclear power, Lewis Strauss, head of the Atomic Energy Commission, promised that we were entering an age when electricity would be "too cheap to meter." Needless to say, that didn't happen, mostly because the risks of nuclear energy hugely increased its costs. But what if he'd been right?

What if electricity had in fact become virtually free? The answer is that every-thing electricity touched—which is to say just about everything—would have been transformed.... Today it's digital technologies, not electricity, that have become too cheap to meter. It took decades to shake off the assumption that computing was supposed to be rationed for the few, and we're only now starting to liberate bandwidth and storage from the same poverty of imagination. But a generation raised on the free Web is coming of age, and they will find entirely new ways to embrace waste, transforming the world in the process. Because free is what you want—and free, increasingly, is what you're going to get. (Anderson, 2008)

So in a world where most things on the Web are free, what will people pay for? This is the question asked and answered by Anderson's *Wired* colleague Kevin Kelly. Kelly begins by noting that the Internet is fundamentally a big copy machine and that the copies have become, in essence, free. He goes on:

When copies are free, you need to sell things which cannot be copied. Well, what can't be copied? There are a number of qualities that can't be copied. Consider "trust." Trust cannot be copied. You can't purchase it. Trust must be earned, over time. It cannot be downloaded. Or faked. Or counterfeited (at least for long). If everything else is equal, you'll always prefer to deal with someone you can trust. So trust is an intangible that has increasing value in a copy saturated world. (Kelly, 2008)

Kelly then goes on to enumerate the "Eight Generatives Better Than Free." I will quote him at length:

Immediacy—Sooner or later you can find a free copy of whatever you want, but getting a copy delivered to your inbox the moment it is released—or, even better, produced—by its creators is a generative asset.

Personalization—A generic version of a concert recording may be free, but if you want a copy that has been tweaked to sound perfect in your particular living room—as if it were preformed in your room—you may be willing to pay a lot.

Interpretation—As the old joke goes: software, free—the manual, $10,000. But it's no joke. A couple of high profile companies, like Red Hat, Apache, and others make their living doing exactly that.

Authenticity—You might be able to grab a key software application for free, but even if you don't need a manual, you might like to be sure it is bug free, reliable, and warranted. You'll pay for authenticity.

Accessibility—Ownership often sucks. You have to keep your things tidy, up-to-date, and in the case of digital material, backed up.... Many people, me included, will be happy to have others tend our "possessions" by subscribing to them.

Embodiment—At its core the digital copy is without a body. You can take a free copy of a work and throw it on a screen. But perhaps you'd like to see it in hi-res on a huge screen? . . . but sometimes it is delicious to have the same words printed on bright white cottony paper, bound in leather.

Patronage—It is my belief that audiences WANT to pay creators. Fans like to reward artists, musicians, authors and the like with the tokens of their appreciation, because it allows them to connect. But they will only pay if it is very easy to do, a reasonable amount, and they feel certain the money will directly benefit the creators.

Findability—Whereas the previous generative qualities reside within creative digital works, findability is an asset that occurs at a higher level in the aggregate of many works. A zero price does not help direct attention to a work, and in fact may sometimes hinder it. But no matter what its price, a work has no value unless it is seen; unfound masterpieces are worthless.

I think it is interesting to look at the eight generatives identified by Kelly and consider where the library is likely to have any chance of success when competing against network-level providers. It seems unlikely that libraries will be able to provide immediacy or personalization more effectively than network-level providers. We may have some advantages in the area of interpretation, though I believe this will be the case only to the extent that we have a deeper knowledge of our users than is typically now the case. Authenticity is still a part of the library brand and so, at least for now, we may have an advantage, but it may be hard to maintain over time. Accessibility is interesting to me because I think there is a role we can play, particularly with researchers. For them the part of ownership that sucks is the long-term management and access to the results of their old research. I believe libraries can and should fill this role. Embodiment should work to our advantage since we have the books. Patronage might work for some authors and rock bands, but I have never known it to be particularly effective for libraries. Finally, findability, once our stock and trade, is now clearly in the network realm. Authority control and Boolean searching are no match for the algorithmic solutions offered by Google.

So at best, libraries have some advantage in half of Kelly's generatives.

Four Questions and Some Answers

As we approach the conclusion, I would offer four questions to help us focus on our future as reference librarians.

1. *What happens if information skills become a mass amateur activity?* We should move upmarket and focus on high quality interactions with sophisticated users with hard questions. This will require librarians who are specialist rather than generalist. This strategy will work for a while. We should also support the teaching of information skills and provide remedial support.

2. *Can we survive with one foot in the world of proprietary content and one foot in the world of the open web?* Not well and not for long. We need to support open access and open scholarship. We will also need to create the social tools to make this possible.

3. *What is the role of institution-level services in a world of network-level tools?* We will need to accept that users will gravitate to the network level and that network-level tools don't scale down. We will be effective when we create local content that can be used by network-level tools.

4. *Do we focus our support of users in their role as information consumers or as information creators?* Yes, but the second will become more important over time.

Uplifting Final Quote

I will end as I started with a quote from Clay Shirky. This quote, though, looks not at what will be lost or changed but rather on the good that will come from the revolution.

> Emblematic of the dilemmas created by group life, the phrase "free-for-all" does not literally mean free for all but rather chaos. Too much freedom, with too little management, has generally been a recipe for a free-for-all. Now, however, it isn't. With the right kinds of collaborative tools and the right sort of bargain with users, it is possible to get a large group working on a project that is free for all. (Shirky, 2008, p. 253)

Challenge

My final challenge to you comes from Peter Senge, who said in April 2008 at Living the Future 7, "The world's knowledge belongs to the world" (Senge, 2008). For me this means that we, as librarians, must create the tools and communities for open scholarship and open information so that knowledge can be abundant in our communities, and we must do this whatever the consequences are for libraries and librarians.

Notes

1. The following is a reconstruction of the keynote address at Reference Renaissance: Current and Future Trends, August 4, 2008.

2. At this point in the presentation the video of the ChaCha commercial was played. This is available at http://answers.chacha.com/about-chacha/how-it-works (accessed March 18, 2009).

3. At this point in the presentation the video of Chris Anderson discussing "Free" was played. This is available at www.wired.com/techbiz/it/magazine/16-03/ff_free (accessed March 18, 2009).

References

Anderson, C. (2008, March). Free! Why $0.00 is the future of business. *Wired Magazine, 16*(3). Retrieved March 18, 2009, from http://wired.com/wired/16-03.

Christensen, C. M. (2000). *Innovator's dilemma: When new technologies cause great firms to fail*. New York: HaperBusiness.

Christensen, C. M., Anthony, S. D., & Roth, E. A. (2004). *Seeing what's next: Using the theories of innovation to predict industry change*. Boston, MA: Harvard Business School Press.

Christensen, C. M., & Raynor, M. E. (2003). *The innovator's solution: Creating and sustaining successful growth*. Boston, MA: Harvard Business School Press.

Kelly, K. (2008). Better than free. *The Technium*. Retrieved March 18, 2009, from www .kk.org/thetechnium/archives/2008/01/better_than_fre.php.

Krugman, P. (2008, June 6). Bits, bands and books. *New York Times*. Retrieved March 18, 2009, from www.nytimes.com/2008/06/06/opinion/06krugman.html?scp+1&sq= Bits,%20Bands%20and%20Books&st=cse.

Lewis, D. W. (2006). Alphabetical order, the Dewey Decimal System, and Google. Paper read to the Indianapolis Literary Club, February 21, Indianapolis, Indiana. Retrieved March 19, 2009, from http://idea.iupui.edu/dspace/handle/1805/556.

McArthur, T. (1986). *Worlds of reference: Lexicography, learning and language from the clay tablet to the computer*. Cambridge: Cambridge University Press.

Oxford English Dictionary. (n.d.). Retrieved March 18, 2009, from http://dictionary .oed.com.

Senge, P. M. (2008). Keynote address, Living the Future 7: Transforming Libraries Through Collaboration, April 30, 2008, Tucson, Arizona.

Shirky, C. (2008). *Here comes everybody: The power of organizing without organizations*. New York: Penguin Press.

Theory Meets Practice: Educators and Directors Talk

Plenary Panel

Plenary Introduction

"Theory Meets Practice: Educators and Directors Talk" was the title of a lively plenary session at The Reference Renaissance conference. Carla J. Stoffle of the University of Arizona and James LaRue of the Douglas County Libraries in Colorado, provided their perspectives as library directors, while R. David Lankes of Syracuse University in New York, and Marie L. Radford of Rutgers University in New Jersey shared their views as library and information science faculty members. Each speaker was asked to achieve the following in their remarks: (1) identify the most critical skill in reference librarianship, (2) explain what innovative things they/we are doing to improve reference services or to improve library school education at their institution, and (3) discuss their predictions for the future of reference. The following essays reflect the thoughtful and provocative content from these presentations.

Remarks by R. David Lankes

Introduction
My remarks are titled "Setting Sail with Map in Hand." Dr. Mervyn Susser said in 1968 that "to practice without theory is to sail an uncharted sea; theory without practice is not to set sail at all." Deep foundational concepts are essential to the continuous improvement of reference both online and off. The reference practitioner of today must understand the reference interview and indeed the whole point of reference beyond a cobbled-together set of practices and sources.

Take the reference interview as an example. One of the prime concepts in the interview is the idea of neutral questioning, explored by Brenda Dervin as part of her work on sense making (Dervin & Dewdney, 1986). Neutral questioning is a process in which the librarian asks open-ended questions that allow the user to formulate the question instead of the librarian jumping to a conclusion. Neutral questioning is itself a continuation of Robert Taylor's work on question negotiation, in which he defined the way a library member expresses a question (Taylor, 1968). Current practice is based on theory.

17

So what are the concepts and theories that can push forward our understanding and improve practice today? It begins by recognizing that reference is, at its heart, a conversation. This conversation may take place face-to-face, online, on the phone, or even through e-mail. It can be very short (a public library member asking for a known book) or very long (a PhD student consulting with a reference librarian on a thesis over years).

Concepts to Guide Practice

Conversations may sound like an informal concept, a sort of off-the-cuff exchange, yet there has been substantial work in the theories of conversation and discourse. Conversation theory, constructivism, dialectic communications theory, and even postmodernism are informing scholars and practitioners alike about the changes ahead for reference. Indeed, conversation lies at the heart of how people learn. From these conceptual sources we can draw five concepts that should guide reference practice. These concepts are explained in the following sections.

The Member Is In Control

A conversation requires at least two parties. Furthermore, these parties must be willing to participate, otherwise it becomes a simple monologue, and each must take turns sharing, listening, and absorbing. While this has huge implications for the role of librarians in the reference interview, challenging for example how neutral or unbiased you can really be in a conversation, the focus of this article is on the member.

Think about traditional face-to-face reference and ask yourself how much control the member has in the transaction. A member formulates a question, then he or she approaches a desk where the librarian sits with ready access to a computer and other resources. The member admits ignorance of a topic to the librarian and then answers questions as part of a librarian-directed interview process.

It doesn't get much better online. A member formulates a question, goes to the library Web site, fills out a form, and waits. When the library-assigned librarian comes online, it is the librarian who pushes pages and scripts at the member. It is the librarian who controls the transaction. The member, after exposing his or her name and e-mail address, is corresponding with "librarian." Really the only control the member has over the process is whether to submit or not.

Can the member share the page pushing? Can the member determine the format of the transcript or qualifications of the librarian? Can the member bring other people into the transaction? Can the member choose to pause the reference process and resume it at a later point? Who is in control of this process?

It's All About Learning

No matter what type of library you are in, all reference is learning and not simply finding artifacts (books, Web pages, etc). Why do we think our job is to get someone to a resource and not to an answer? Simply pointing to stuff is becoming less and less important, and making sense of disparate information is becoming more and more important.

Furthermore, as librarians we must always remember that the member is learning about his or her topic, not the nuances of librarianship and search strategy. In the future, learning theory tells us that librarians must become more adept teachers, understanding the motivations of the individuals and better contextualizing found information for the member's unique needs. While this may take more time, the members will wait if they get increased value in return.

Learning Is a Collaborative Conversation

Where is reference defined as a one-on-one conversation? It is nowhere to be found in definitions of digital reference. For example, take a look at this definition from the Reference and User Services Association (RUSA):

> Virtual reference is reference service initiated electronically, often in real-time, where patrons employ computers or other Internet technology to communicate with reference staff, without being physically present. Communication channels used frequently in virtual reference include chat, videoconferencing, Voice over IP, co-browsing, e-mail, and instant messaging. (Reference and User Services Association, 2004)

It is also absent in RUSA's broader definition of reference:

> **Reference Transactions** are information consultations in which library staff recommend, interpret, evaluate, and/or use information resources to help others to meet particular information needs. Reference transactions do not include formal instruction or exchanges that provide assistance with locations, schedules, equipment, supplies, or policy statements. (Reference and User Services Association, 2008)

Why can't a reference transaction have 50 people in it?

When we look at the deeper concepts of learning and conversation we see a social transaction that is iterative and often widespread in the people consulted. Rather than structuring the reference transaction after historical staffing patterns and desk space, perhaps we should design it around the form of learning interchange.

The Librarian Serves as a Facilitator

By understanding that a reference transaction is a learning event, reference staff must be aware of all the potential means of facilitating learning. Access to information (and people) is only one way. You can provide all of the relevant articles you want to a person, but if the person can't read, you have not helped him or her. So in addition to access, the reference librarians must provide contextual knowledge (the skills and understanding necessary to decode the information patrons are being given) and a safe environment (not only giving them permission to access information but pushing them to go beyond their normal boundaries with assistance), and librarians must have a keen sense of motivation (understanding why members seek information and motivating them to learn).

True Facilitation Is Shared Ownership

In a conversation, one party must always yield to the other party. I talk and then you talk. The conversation is jointly owned by librarian(s) and member(s). This co-ownership should extend to all parts of the reference endeavor. Take, for example, the construction of pathfinders, or online frequently asked questions. Can we open this process up to trusted members to help keep them current and expand them? Can we build systems that open up questions to a pool of trusted members to help answer asynchronously?

Changing the Preparation

In order to both accommodate these concepts as well as ensure the continued health of the reference function as a whole, we must look to how we educate reference librarians. Today there is a noticeable shift of innovation from the academy to the field. New ideas and tools are springing up all over the Web, not just in university laboratories. In order to accommodate this, reference must shift to a colearning environment. In this kind of class students and instructors learn together while working on real projects. Instructors can pass along the deep concepts and general approach of reference, but the means are constructed hand in hand with students.

The preparation of reference librarians needs to include communication and political skills as well as technical proficiency and values. Reference librarians increasingly need to go to the conversation instead of waiting for the member to come to them. Therefore reference librarians must know how to get into places of work, worship, and civic life. They must build bridges to the communities they serve far outside the boundaries of the library (real or virtual). Reference librarians must be cultivated to be subversive change agents.

It is nearly impossible to cover everything a starting librarian needs to know within existing MLIS programs. Serious work needs to be done to expand the educational ladder to include bachelor's, master's, doctoral, and ongoing required continuing education.

Conclusion

The best days of reference are ahead, not behind. However, it will look very different. The reference of tomorrow will be much more collaborative and focused on learning, not simply pointing. To achieve this, reference librarians must become change agents, well versed in building bridges out to the community, and identify innovation. Future reference librarians need to engage in so-called reflective practice where they not only hone their considerable skills but do so in perpetual awareness of the big picture and the underlying concepts that drive that picture.

References

Dervin, B., & Dewdney, P. (1986). Neutral questioning: A new approach to the reference interview. *Reference Quarterly, 25*(4), 506–513.

Reference and User Services Association. (2004). Guidelines for implementing and maintaining virtual reference services. Retrieved from www.ala.org/ala/mgrps/divs/rusa/resources/guidelines/virtrefguidelines.cfm.

Reference and User Services Association. (2008). Definitions of reference. Retrieved from www.ala.org/ala/mgrps/divs/rusa/resources/guidelines/definitionsreference.cfm.

Taylor, R. (1968). Question negotiation and information seeking in libraries. *College & Research Libraries, 29*, 178–194.

Remarks by Carla J. Stoffle[1]

I want to thank you for the opportunity to be here and thank the presenters over the two days of the conference. I saw very interesting work going on, people thinking about issues, and I hope that I have even incorporated some of the things that I have learned here into my remarks.

Everyone knows that library directors do not follow directions very well. It's an occupational hazard. So to start off, I do not think I can identify *one* most critical skill, although I really worked to identify just one. I thought for a while of having a one-sentence paragraph, that maybe I could work it in that way, and then I finally gave up.

When I think about critical skills for reference librarians, I think about a continual learner who is focused on the customer, who is not systems-centered or library-operations centered, which I learned in the "traditional" versus "hipster" librarians session by Rutgers University PhD student Hannah Kwon. Reference librarians need an excellent grounding in the values and philosophical framework of librarianship and an understanding of the goals of this suite of services. With these skills, we can then adapt tools or services to meet the changing information needs of our customers without fighting the "but this is how we've always done it" battle. It seems to me that the foregoing is the minimum and, actually, what we need in *every* librarian who works in a library.

Second, we obviously need more people with strong technology skills. The new "in" thing now is social networking. But the technology must be conceived as a *tool* with this continual learning creating a more flexible approach, because the technology is going to change rapidly. The technology of today is not going to be the technology of next year that you may need to be applying to the work that you do. But your work and your customers—the work you want to do for your customers—should determine what technologies you use.

We need reference librarians who understand reference writ large, as a suite of services to meet our customers' diverse information needs. As librarians, we must understand that those information needs are not static. As the needs change, we have to be flexible and adapt that suite of services or alter how those services are delivered. One of the conference sessions redefined reference, from the 1800s, which includes instruction, getting customers to what they need physically, and enabling people, as well as answering questions. It seems to me that we need people coming to our libraries who understand reference writ large, not reference as a desk or reference even as a virtual or chat environment where you are providing answers.

In academic libraries there was no reference desk on a consistent basis until the 1960s. When we define reference so narrowly that it becomes answering questions at a desk, then we are in real trouble, because we are saying that people have to come to the library or they have to approach us in some manner in order to get the benefit of what we can provide. Whether it's virtually or whether they have to physically come in, if we are wedded to that definition of reference then I do not have much enthusiasm for what our libraries will be like ten years from now. But I do have enthusiasm for what our libraries are going to be like if we take a broad approach to "what is reference?" and if we have the goal of benefitting our communities, whether it's a public library, a school library, or an academic library, and if we are helping the community achieve its goals through the knowledge, skills, values, and philosophical framework that we bring to the community information process. That is basically what we are about. So we have to get away from a very narrow definition of reference and a very narrow definition of what libraries do.

We need people with the skills to understand that we have to take the library to the customers and anticipate their needs, not require customers to know what they need and to come to us. Then we need people who are prepared to assess, not just count, but assess, impact and to monitor quality in our services and constantly be seeking this continual change and improvement and knowing what difference we make.

In terms of what are we doing at the University of Arizona, if you have heard of us, you have probably heard that we constantly restructure, and we did that again in this last year (see Center for Creative Photography, 2008a, 2008b). Some key concepts for the new structure were the following:

- "Everywhere you are, the library" (based on the customer and where the customer is)
- The library as a virtual and physical learning environment
- The idea that we would maximize the uses of our limited resources so we would seek to get the most out of everything that we have

- That we would engage in collaboration all over the place, on and off campus
- That a primary tenet of what we do is that we are going to stimulate learning and research, not wait for someone to know they need to learn or to do research

This approach requires that we think about embedding the library where the customer is. It means we need to design our work and our physical spaces to make our customers more effective rather than for the convenience of library employees.

By the way, I have been asked if I agree with labeling people "customers" and whether this affects or redefines reference desk service in an academic setting. I think that if you want to define customers only in terms of economic transactions, it probably is a problem. But, in fact, when we call people "users," we have a whole group out there that never uses libraries and that we do not put much effort into understanding or serving. Customer service is, in fact, a positive concept to think about in terms of our libraries, because these are people who, in the past, we treated as if they did not have any other option. But today they have many other options. They may not be *using* them appropriately, but they really do have other options, and we need to take that into account and think about our services in that way. We need to treat people as we would want to be treated. We have to reach out to the people who are not using us (for whatever reason) and think about them and their needs and how we can develop them into people who do use the libraries.

To address many of these issues at the University of Arizona Libraries, we restructured a number of things, ending up with (in our direct services) an Undergraduate Services Team that is not responsible for providing reference desk service but is responsible for chat and virtual reference services and for training the staff that is going to be on the desk. Undergraduate Services Team members also monitor the service. They assess quality, do usability studies, develop online instructional modules and online course modules, and (most important in the next year or two) will integrate the library into course management systems that we are using. This process will involve eliminating separate electronic reserves and building these systems to anticipate what the student in that course is going to need from the library. You do not wait for students to start. We do this in anticipation. We also help the faculty make the transition to the course management system. You would think that they are all using it, but frankly, they are not all utilizing this resource and some who are using it are doing so very, very poorly.

The Undergraduate Services Team is also developing a Course Resource Organizer that will guide faculty through the process of building customized online pages for their courses. This rich, Web-based tool will lead faculty members through the step-by-step process of identifying and selecting the library content and services that are most relevant for their course's needs. For example, a resources page might include an online tutorial on correctly citing resources, assignment information with suggestions on appropriate subject databases or search strategies to use, a link to our "Ask a Librarian" instant messenger/chat service, or tools for information fluency assessment (such as pre- and posttest quizzes). A link to each course page will be automatically generated within the appropriate course site in the course management system, allowing for convenient student and instructor access.

We need to experiment. One of the things that I would hope the Undergraduate Services Team librarians would be doing this next year is identifying faculty members in large undergraduate courses and working with them to develop online textbooks, not just electronic reserves. I want them to use content that is available out on the Web or that can be incorporated into an online textbook, to help deal with the campus textbook problem and costs. But, again, this should be part of our job, reaching out to our community and anticipating what their problems are and coming to them with solutions, not waiting for them to come to us.

The Undergraduate Services Team is also responsible for outreach to various groups on campus and to the community. So we are remote, we are out there. Our staff has developed something called LessonLink (http://lessonlink.library .arizona.edu). This LessonLink Web portal connects Arizona's K–12 teaching community to all of the helpful educational resources developed at the University of Arizona. The LessonLink database is indexed by subject, grade level, and resource type (student activities, educational content, lesson plans, field trips, professional development materials/opportunities, bilingual content, etc.). We are working to link lesson plans to Arizona Academic Standards. LessonLink also provides some social networking functions, allowing users to create favorites lists, to rank and comment on resources, and to suggest new resources. This is another way we are reaching out, anticipating, and carrying the campus outreach efforts.

The other big portion of our librarians will be in our Research Support Services group. They are going to work with faculty and graduate students. They are going to identify campus information that needs to be organized, whether it needs to be organized centrally in a main place or whether it needs to be organized locally; for example, in the science labs, where they have papers that are in filing cabinets that they use but that are not organized and accessible. We will do off-desk reference and we will move to try to create systems so that people who *do* come with a question (virtual and physically) will immediately be tracked to the person who is a specialist rather than the person who is at the desk struggling to answer those particular questions. These people will be soliciting resources for our Institutional Repository, developing tools (such as the Arizona Atlas, which is a tool that allows you to lay demographic and physical information together on a map of Arizona), and creating Rangelands West, which is a database for agriculture and for ranchers throughout the Southwest. They will also be selecting commercial information resources.

The Access and Information Services Team is serving at all of our desks. These are career staff that are not librarians but are well trained to do the work and to answer the questions that come to our service desks. Over the past several years we have worked with the university's Human Resources Department to design a new series of library job classifications. We developed a process for reclassification and implemented four new classified staff job titles. We have further worked to develop specific competency-based job descriptions, reflecting current and future competencies, which are used in the hiring and performance management of library employees. This work has helped to bring pay and job descriptions into alignment with changes in library classified staff tasks and responsibilities. This process has also allowed us to identify gaps in competencies and to have the ability to hire staff specifically for providing information services.

At the University of Arizona Libraries, we have worked to create a program where the Undergraduate Services Team coordinates the training for reference. This involves training sessions in which staff members demonstrate their competencies by passing tests. Another part of the program is desk observations, in which librarians shadow staff and provide feedback on their reference skills. As needed, we also have librarians serve on staff performance reviews so that feedback can be incorporated into a learning plan for continual progression. This programmatic approach allows the librarians to stay connected to the reference desks without consuming all of their time. This design also provides support for staff so that we ensure that the competencies are being developed and met.

In addition, our Access and Information Services Team members collect data at the desks so that we can continually monitor the kinds of questions that are coming in and how we are performing. The various survey tools we utilize allow us to stay informed about the level of service being provided and whether we are meeting the needs of our customers. We measure the desk work that needs to be done and we study usage of the desk. We address whether the questions changed, whether we need to do more advanced training, or whether we made a mistake and need librarians back. We studied for a year and a half and discovered that 85 percent of the questions that came in to our desks did not require a librarian to answer them. We were desperately short of librarians to do other outreach work on campus that needed to be done. People on the Access and Information Services Team manage the buildings and manage the building-based services so that we do not have librarians taking up their time doing things that they actually did not go to library school to do.

The future? That was an interesting exercise. In the future (and I think you have heard already what the future might be) it is less about helping people *find* information and more about helping people *use* that information. It is about creating services before the customers know they need them. It is about creating information. Traditionally, public libraries created community information databases (only they were on paper). We should be looking at the information that is not created or organized commercially, and this is something that our reference librarians should be doing.

We need to take the library to the customer. We need to be more involved and focused on assessment. We need to be heavily collaborative and not each one of us reinventing the wheel. We must respond aggressively to competition inside and outside of our institutions. We may need to change the name of "reference librarian" in order to get people to think more broadly than they currently do.

As I said earlier, we need to reach out to the community. This was some of the thinking behind our restructuring when we were sending our Research Support Services people out into the campus community to look at what the needs are, have dialogue in that community, and develop appropriate responses. Of course, this approach moves their team leaders up to another level, dealing with deans now on a dean level instead of this being the director's job. The director's job is to work at the vice president and university levels, trying to get us into the picture and be seen as supporting university goals and objectives. We cannot afford to be competing with everybody else on campus. Our goals are to help the university achieve its goals for students and for the community.

Libraries need to forge better partnerships with library schools. I have been asked about what the priorities of library schools should be. If a librarian's core skills ought to be management, leadership, communication, creativity, and flexibility, when is there time to teach classification, online searching, how databases are structured, and what reference sources are out there? Do we have to rely on on-the-job-training or continuing education to teach basic skills?

It is time to go back and think about an undergraduate degree in librarianship so that we are not trying to force everything into a year or two of graduate school. We are just touching on things lightly because this is about all we have time to do. The library profession must take some responsibility and not rail at the library schools about what they give or do not give to the beginning reference librarians. Libraries do have a responsibility to support and promote continual learning.

At the University of Arizona, I told our library school: "I want you to graduate people who are steeped in the values and the philosophical framework that librarianship has in its approach to information." Everything else is kind of gravy to me, because I can teach them most of the other stuff. My staff will probably complain, because when they hire beginning reference librarians they want someone who can come in and do the job from day one. As a profession, we do have to look at that. But what is really important for the future is to recruit people who are good communicators, who are flexible, and who understand the current situation of our libraries. When I talk to library school classes, I have people who say, "Gee, maybe this isn't the profession for me. I wanted something rather more quiet." I think it is crucial to get good people in to the profession and have them really understand what librarianship is about.

Instead of pointing fingers at each other, libraries and library schools need to collaborate on helping students develop the necessary skills. Libraries could offer more internships or graduate assistantships, and library schools could be a little bit more flexible about these field experiences. We *can* work together on this. But the long-term solution is probably thinking about an undergraduate degree and having the graduate degree really be about management, leadership, and solving some of the bigger problems in libraries, not the day one job.

Note

1. I would like to acknowledge the help of Cheryl Cuillier, Special Assistant to the Dean, University of Arizona, in preparing these remarks for publication. Ms. Cuillier is a 2008 graduate of the School of Information Resources and Library Science at the University of Arizona.

Resources

Bracke, M. S., Brewer, M., Huff-Eibl, R., Lee, D. R., Mitchell, R., & Ray, M. (2007). Finding information in a new landscape: Developing new service and staffing models for mediated information services. *College & Research Libraries, 68*(3), 248–267.

Bracke, M., Brewer, M., Huff-Eibl, R., Lee, D., & Ray, M. (2006). Finding information in a new landscape: Rethinking reference services at the University of Arizona Libraries. Poster session presented at the Living the Future 6 Conference, April 5–8, Tucson, Arizona.

Bracke, M. S., Chinnaswamy, S., & Kline, E. (2008, Winter). Evolution of reference: A new service model for science and engineering libraries. *Issues in Science and Technology Librarianship*. Retrieved from www.istl.org/08-winter/refereed3.html.

Center for Creative Photography. (2008a, April). University of Arizona Libraries and Center for Creative Photography new organizational structure—Teams and roles. Tucson, AZ: University of Arizona.

Center for Creative Photography. (2008b, June). University of Arizona Libraries and Center for Creative Photography organization chart. Tucson, AZ: University of Arizona.

Stoffle, C. J., Allen, B., Fore, J., & Mobley, E. R. (2000). Predicting the future: What does academic librarianship hold in store? *College and Research Libraries News, 61*(10), 894–897.

Stoffle, C. J., Allen, B., Morden, D., & Maloney, K. (2003). Continuing to build the future: Academic libraries and their challenges. *Portal: Libraries and the Academy, 3*(3), 363–380.

Stoffle, C. J., Leeder, K., & Sykes-Casavant, G. (2008). Bridging the gap: Wherever you are, the library. *Journal of Library Administration, 48*(1), 3–30.

Remarks by James LaRue

In theory, there's no difference between theory and practice. In practice, there is.

—Yogi Berra

I have titled my remarks "Theory Meets Practice: From Foundation to Future" and will first address the question of the skill that matters most. When I worked as a circulation clerk at the graduate library at the University of Illinois–Urbana (1980–1981), I participated in a study. Our public staff was divided into two teams: one team provided service as usual, and the other, the group I was in, was instructed to touch each patron, very lightly, even surreptitiously: a finger tap on the patron's hand, a quick palm to the forearm. The encounter was supposed to be brief and nonsexual. On the way out, the students were asked to rate the quality of the service they had received. The control group (business as usual) had largely noncommittal responses: they asked for a book, they got a book. But the students who had been touched consistently rated the service much higher.

I do not take this as permission to fondle perfect strangers. But I have generalized this insight over the years to this: we are wired for contact. Memorable service, providing meaningful service, requires that we "touch" the people we serve, a combination of behaviors that add up to the simple acknowledgment of another human being.

In the years since I got my library degree, I have seen many service transactions. The ones that were best, that left patrons with the sense that they had been well-served, were not necessarily ones in which the right answer was given but were interactions in which staff and patron connected, occupied the same mental and emotional space. The skill that matters most in reference is communication. Some of this can be taught: eye contact, open posture, smiling, and modulation of voice. Some of it, perhaps, cannot, or not as easily: the willingness to be open to another human being, to be fully present.

Here's the context of reference services at our library. Douglas County Libraries is an independent library district, encompassing an entire county of approximately 300,000 people. We are located between Denver and Colorado Springs, cities of about 500,000 people apiece. In most respects, our story has been one of growth. In 1990, Douglas County had just 65,000 residents. While library funding has been generally strong (currently at $72.64 annual expenditures per capita), the demand for our services has grown tremendously over the years. Our circulation from 2003–2007 increased by 89 percent. For the past three years, it has climbed by about a million each year. In the same period, the number of reference questions increased by over 70 percent, now comprising about 1.35 questions per capita. This demand led us to consider, then, to effect a transformation in our service model. Over the past two years, we have pulled apart our traditional circulation desks and replaced them with radio frequency identification–based self-check stations in the front and automated material handling machines in the back. These changes significantly reduced the number of people we needed to manage circulation.

We phased out the "circulation clerk" job description, and (through savings garnered through attrition) promoted our remaining former clerks into a new, paraprofessional job, one less concerned with managing circulation processes and far more concerned with building book displays, seeking out puzzled patrons, and providing a combination of reader's advisory and basic reference services. These new positions rotate among a couple of locations: a "concierge" station by the self-check stations and at our larger reference desk. The new paraprofessionals love their new jobs, which are far more interesting than their old ones and for which they receive both more pay and more patron gratitude.

At about the same time, we were taking a look at the actual questions that our patrons brought to us. A couple of studies we did determined that roughly 85 percent of the reference questions we received really did not require an MLIS to answer. But there could not be too many people merchandising our collection, and talking up books. Our intent was to build new, integrated teams of both trained librarians and the new paraprofessionals. Ultimately, we were also hoping to free up our reference staff for more outreach, which I will describe. Some of our reference staff, however, viewed this development with suspicion. Was this just part of a deprofessionalization scheme, the replacement of trained librarians with less-expensive paraprofessionals?

"Roaming the stacks" was fine, clearly an opportunity to engage patrons who were reluctant to take their questions to a service desk. But there was a service concern. Back at the desk, sometimes a reference librarian overheard a transaction between patron and paraprofessional that was not up to our usual standards of service, and the reference librarian did not know how to step in gracefully. Conversely, a paraprofessional might find it hard to admit that she or he was out of his or her depth and hand over the patron to someone better qualified to respond to the need.

This integration of service levels—and the trust and cooperation it requires among all parties—is still being developed. Many libraries have segregated their staff into stand-alone departments, trading a more holistic view of library work for greater specialization and expertise. It takes time to break down old barriers to communication, build mutual respect, and learn how to "hand off" a patron in a way that feels natural. But the dissemination of self-check, and economic pressures generally, may well result in a trend of service desk consolidation.

This quest for a seamless integration of services has another problem to solve. In many larger libraries, having a big circulation department means that most of the supervisory expertise is in the nonprofessional positions. Reference librarians are rarely hired for, or trained in, management. This has to change. I believe that the MLIS must mean more than preparation for a career of patron transactions; increasingly it will require leadership and management responsibilities, either as a mentor to paraprofessional staff, and/or as a direct supervisor. It makes sense that advanced training should mean greater responsibility for the coordination of our work.

For the past ten years or so, I have been trying to grow library market share, measured by the percentage of households with an active library card. Briefly, I believe that most public libraries, simply by opening their doors and offering the usual service array (a circulating collection, a reference service, a children's department, programming, public computers, meeting rooms, and study space), reach about 35–50 percent of their community. Adding professional public relations (one-way messages consisting of "use the library!") can grow that by another 5–15 percent. Adding thoughtful marketing (two-way communications that help libraries stay in sync with their changing communities) can grow market share by another 5–15 percent. Following this philosophy, our library has indeed gone from 51 percent market share to 84 percent over the space of a decade. But then what? At this point, the library has grabbed the folks who were already inclined to come and has reached out to those who might come if we catch them at the right moment.

To grow market share beyond the easy pickings, I believe librarians have to leave the library, and not just to passively attend meetings, march in parades, and so on. We have to demonstrate to nonusers in the most direct way that we are capable of helping them solve community problems.

My job as library director is to scout the environment in which the library operates. This means I attend a lot of community meetings. A couple of years ago, I noticed that there was a persistent concern that cut across several areas of the county: what did it take to build a strong "downtown?" The question was most urgent in one of our towns about to undertake a series of significant infrastructure changes (street widening, new sewers, plantings, street parking, etc.). In particular, a group of businessmen felt that some of the town's proposed changes actually worked against building a vital business district.

At about the same time, one of our new reference librarians, who had just gotten her degree, asked to meet me. Her name was Colbe. She had a very direct question: was there a future for reference services generally, and in Douglas County particularly? I told her I thought there was, and asked for her help to prove it. First, I introduced her to the group of businesspeople now meeting as the Downtown Development Committee, a subcommittee of the local Chamber of Commerce. I announced that the library was assigning Colbe to the group; I thought the issues that the committee was dealing with were important to the whole community. The reaction was friendly but cool, as if they had been awarded a mascot they didn't know what to do with. Colbe was all but patted on the head. After a few meetings, Colbe (and Patt, her branch manager, who was also attending) felt they had identified the key players of the committee. What next? After some discussion (we met weekly to discuss the project), we decided to do some in-depth interviews. What were the key information needs of these people before they could move forward?

So Patt and Colbe took the businesspersons out to lunch and determined that there were about four significant questions that were meaty, difficult, requiring significant research. So Patt went back and farmed them out to our professional staff, who found it far more challenging and stimulating than the usual fare at our service desks.

It quickly became apparent that just the research would not be enough. Many reference transactions consist of simply handing over some promising materials or sources to the patron. In this case it meant that the research might not be used at all. Patt asked if any of her staff had experience writing abstracts or executive summaries. One of our reference librarians did, a former special librarian, and set to the task with enthusiasm. But even the executive summary was not all that was needed. The best way to communicate the results of the research involved a presentation. Who had skills in that area?

Colbe again stepped up to the plate, and armed with her colleagues' (and her own) research attended by a professional presentation based on other colleagues' summaries, she presented the information to the Downtown Development Committee, and she wowed them. The information made a difference to their plans. It raised a host of new questions. It energized the group. They wanted to have widespread access to our research, at which point we announced our intent to post it online, through the library's Web site (see http://DouglasCountyLibraries.org/Research/iGuides/DDC). In addition to the results of our research, the iGuide became a source for tracking committee activity, with meeting minutes, planning exhibits, and more.

I mentioned that at the beginning of this process, Colbe was seen in a somewhat patronizing light. Businesspeople would say, "Oh yes, my children love the library!" But the library had no relevance to them, they thought. This changed. Committee meetings did not start until Colbe walked into the room. Some months later, Douglas County Libraries put a funding question on the ballot. I attended a Downtown Development Committee meeting to ask for a campaign contribution. But before I could open my mouth, the committee chair announced in front of the group, "We pledge to raise $20,000 for your campaign. Would that be helpful?"

For too long in our libraries, librarians have fought for status against one another or against our paraprofessional staff. This is pointless, and does nothing to affect the larger issue of our status within our communities. This overview of our "community reference question" process shows that another course is both possible and positive: if we can demonstrate our value to those who would never have dreamed of taking their problems to us, then we gain not just visibility and respect, we gain real support, measured in dollars.

I've noticed that with most significant shifts in professional expectations, staff will demonstrate three broad responses: (1) staff hail the change as precisely what they have been waiting for all their lives, (2) staff might be skeptical but are willing to give it a try (with appropriate support), and (3) some final slice of the staff does not believe in the direction and does not want to do it. The first will be the pioneers. The second group will help us grow sufficient training programs to help our people succeed. The third group, where they cannot be used to support the library's direction, will be replaced with others who can.

Given the service model of the "community reference question," ideal librarians would be willing to leave the library to attend community meetings, interview community leaders, come back to do the research, write a concise summary, and deliver it to a large audience both physically and virtually. In practice, these tasks will be shared among many librarians, as part of a team.

Finally, I have attached a graphic, "Skills for the Future of Reference," that touched on a couple of other points about the future of reference. Under the "Innovation and Education" branch I highlight economic gardening, the contact center, and our "Leadership Journey." Economic gardening—supporting the expansion of local startup businesses—is another example of a "community reference question" that affords us the opportunity to work with chambers of commerce and economic development groups. It also broadens our tax base.

The contact center is our adoption of a centralized telephone center. This department is staffed by a combination of professional and paraprofessional staff and has allowed us to do two big things: free our service desks from the interruption of phone calls and more easily track trends across the district regarding what kinds of questions are asked and how well we respond to them.

Finally, the "Leadership Journey" is our internal succession planning process. We have established a two-year course, paid for by the library, to identify and equip the next generation of staff to gain knowledge, experience, and expertise in the two stages of leadership: understanding yourself and understanding how to work with others.

These highlights may not speak, necessarily, to the future of reference. But they do speak to our attempts at Douglas County Libraries to improve reference service and library education. I believe that the future of reference work at public libraries requires being liberated from the fortresses of our service desks. First, we must

Figure I.1. Important Skills for the Future of Reference

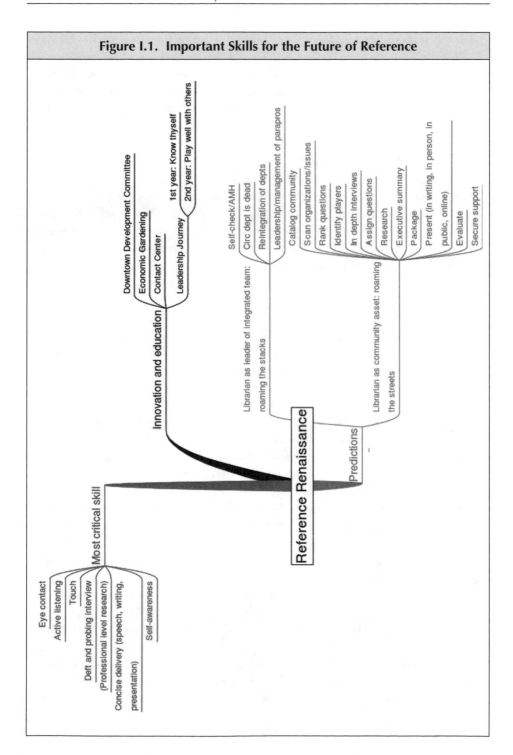

roam the stacks, merchandising our collections—and human capital—far more intelligently than we have in the past. Second, we must roam the streets, actively connecting to the people who might never have known we existed otherwise.

Our experiments to date have taught us that our community needs us. We can make a difference. But first we have to make a difference in the way we do business.

Remarks by Marie L. Radford

My thoughts on the important skills, innovative educational approaches, and the future of reference have developed across a career in which I held positions in school and academic reference and are based on an ongoing scholarly agenda that followed a passionate interest in evaluating and improving the reference process in physical as well as virtual environments. Throughout these experiences, which have involved gathering a huge volume of data on reference practice, I have come to believe strongly that rather than one critical skill for reference librarianship, there are, instead, three areas of importance.

The first of these is in the fascinating realm of human communication. An ability to effectively engage library users in the reference encounter embodies the "value-added" aspect that librarians bring to physical or virtual interactions along with their subject and searching savvy. Verbal and nonverbal communication prowess is the mark of a superior reference librarian. In order for one to be effective in today's rapidly changing reference landscape, the ability to communicate and collaborate with colleagues has become more important than ever. As user demands mount and information technology proliferates, the capacity to establish and to maintain rapport with others and to function as a team to meet increasingly diverse users' needs will largely determine one's success on the reference frontline.

Second, reference librarians need research and subject knowledge. The present and future for information professionals involve increasingly sophisticated society, sources, and systems that demand highly educated librarians who are curious, embrace change, and are committed to lifelong learning as well as to developing new knowledge and theoretical approaches. The age of reference generalists is quickly drawing to an end, as Web 2.0 technology has enabled greater and more immediate collaboration opportunities that are proliferating at a breakneck pace. In an article in the winter 2009 issue of *RUSQ* titled "A Personal Choice: Reference Service Excellence," I call for the end of "the lone ranger" approach and applaud the efforts of practitioners, administrators, and scholars who are looking at (or already implementing!) novel staffing models that leverage a team-based and/or consortial approach to reference that provides the tech savvy and deep subject knowledge that users expect and desire. Librarians are eager to use the subject specialties that they have acquired, which can be better used in the socially networked landscape. Users want subject experts to help with their queries and, in most cases, are willing to wait if necessary for assistance from someone with in-depth subject knowledge.

Finally, I contend that cognitive and behavioral skills are important to today's reference expert. Reference librarians need to cultivate what Daniel Goleman calls "Emotional Intelligence." These strategies enable librarians to seek an understanding of relational dynamics at play in the reference environment. In addition, a cognitive agility is required that means professionals are able to cope with fast change and are not merely open to new approaches but are advocates of needed changes. It is no longer acceptable to conduct the craft of reference as it was done in the 1980s or before. Passively continuing to do business as usual amid a socially networked information universe will not be conducive to sustaining relevant reference practice. To be able to lead and manage change while performing all of the ancillary tasks and engaging in the creative thinking that are required for reference work also means that professionals must cultivate their time management skills.

Priority setting and intelligent delegating of responsibilities are crucial parts of time management because there are so many conflicting and competing demands on our time. Many library professionals today want to do it all and they want to do it now. They want to go after what is new yet keep everything they have always done. The reality is that there is only a finite amount of time, so strategic planning is key to use time to the best advantage. Radical solutions are needed to longstanding problems. For example, I heard recently that one head of reference is allowing her reference staff to create their own weekly desk and virtual reference schedule. Previously this chore had taken up hours of her time every week, but now the staff cooperate and negotiate with one another. They are happier with their schedule, and the head of reference has more time to explore new endeavors. Collaboration and synergy with colleagues take time to explore and develop but can have immediate and positive results.

How can we better prepare library students in the above skill areas? At Rutgers University (RU) I have developed a number of innovative approaches in teaching reference. The first of these is to incorporate service learning into the basic reference course as much as possible. All those enrolling in reference courses at RU are involved in providing e-mail reference through the Internet Public Library (www.ipl.org, soon to also include practice in the live chat, instant messaging environment). This experience gives them real-life practice in answering reference questions in an online environment, builds their confidence, and lets them experience "the thrill of the chase" with authentic questions and for genuine people in ways that outmoded treasure hunts for assigned questions was never fully able to accomplish.

In addition, I have involved numerous RU students in project-based learning centering in participation in major research initiatives that study live chat reference and in building the Virtual Reference Bibliography (http::vrbib.rutgers.edu). Students thus get firsthand knowledge in managing an ongoing project and also cultivate their skills in research, online searching, writing, and creative problem-solving. Project-based learning is also grounded in being immediately relevant to real-world reference practice.

Turning to the question of the future of reference, I believe we are in an incredibly exciting time for reference service. At this juncture, we are only beginning to get glimpses of future possibilities. The Reference Renaissance conference has been structured to embrace a merging and morphing of all reference—not isolating traditional, face-to-face reference modes from virtual ones. I can see several emerging trends that have the potential for enormous impact on the future of reference. Among these are the following:

- Cell phone innovations, which are appearing at an incredibly rapid rate. The phone is emerging as the most important information tool of the decade. Reference initiatives such as marketing phone reference, developing text messaging service, and embedding links from library catalogs, databases, and tools to social networking sites with widgets that allow phone access are proliferating.
- Distance education growth has accelerated a merging of reference function in public and academic libraries and has prompted reference expansion in virtual arenas, including inserting reference librarians in online class environments (such as Blackboard or e-College).
- Portable wireless services will increasingly allow the reference librarian to be free of the limitations of a physical reference desk. I believe that more outreach is inevitable as reference librarians will go to where the users are through use of kiosk-type and satellite reference points. Already many creative staff members of academic libraries have set up outdoor satellites (on nice days) on the grassy quad or entrance plazas right outside of the building that are within reach of the library Wi-Fi network. Students are curious and receptive to such outreach.

I see other trends such as Web 2.0 and 3.0 networks, greater consortium involvement, and digitization of resources as additionally having lasting impact on reference futures. It seems to me that without a doubt there has never been a more challenging time for reference professionals or one that offers so much enthusiasm, exhilaration, and anticipation.

PART II
WHAT RESEARCH TELLS US ABOUT REFERENCE

C H A P T E R 1

Getting Better All the Time: Improving Communication and Accuracy in Virtual Reference

Marie L. Radford and Lynn Silipigni Connaway

Overview

This chapter reports research results from the "Seeking Synchronicity: Evaluating Virtual Reference Services from User, Non-User, and Librarian Perspectives IMLS," Rutgers University, and OCLC-funded grant. This project included focus group interviews, online surveys, and telephone interviews of virtual reference services (VRS) users, nonusers, and librarians and an analysis of a random sample of 850 live chat reference transcripts. In focus group interviews, online surveys, and telephone interviews, the users indicated they use the services because they are convenient and not necessarily because they want quick answers or are in a hurry. An analysis of the transcripts indicates that users are served in a relatively short amount of wait time. Users, who often are multitasking, are willing to wait for a subject specialist. Librarians can boost accuracy by confirming that all of the users' questions are answered before pushing a Web page or URL; by clarifying the question through asking open, neutral, and closed questions; by opening each Web link before pushing it to the users; and by closing with a follow-up question. The transcripts also were examined and coded for positive and negative aspects of interpersonal communication. Findings indicate that it is essential that the reference encounter begins and ends with a positive tone and that the librarian should tell the user when the search is going to take some time. This enables the user to decide whether to wait or to receive the answer through alternative methods, such as e-mail, etc. The findings from this research can help virtual reference librarians cultivate skills needed to understand the chat environment, to develop chat savvy, and to increase accuracy.

Introduction

Live chat reference offers a continuous challenge to reference librarians who strive to maintain a consistently high quality of information delivery and accuracy as well as interpersonal communication dimensions of service excellence. A growing base of research confirms that users and reference service providers in face-to-face (FtF) and virtual settings highly value content and information delivery along with relationship dimensions in their perceptions of success (see Dewdney & Ross, 1994a, 1994b; Nielsen, 2006; Radford, 1999, 2006a, 2006b; Radford & Connaway, 2009).

One important tool to help librarians in meeting this challenge is the verbatim chat reference transcript that is automatically generated during every reference transaction. These transcripts provide a record of reference practice and user information-seeking behavior that has never been available in FtF or phone reference settings. Transcript analysis of live chat reference encounters from the Institute of Museum and Library Science (IMLS), Rutgers University, and Online Computer Library Center (OCLC) funded project, "Seeking Synchronicity: Evaluating Virtual Reference Services from User, Non-User, and Librarian Perspectives,"[1] (Radford & Connaway, 2008) offers new insights for virtual reference service (VRS) librarians seeking to improve their precision and to build positive relationships with VR users. The project involved four phases of data collection, transcript analysis, focus group interviews, online surveys, and telephone interviews, the latter three being with VRS users, nonusers, and librarians.

In one of the initial phases of Seeking Synchronicity, a random sample of 850 transcripts was selected from 561,910 sessions from 24/7 and QuestionPoint VRS. Each month 25–50 transcripts were taken from July 2005 to November 2006. This sampling method was used to enable generalization of results to the larger transcript population. Every transcript underwent several types of analysis including both quantitative and qualitative methods (see Radford & Connaway [2008] for detailed information on research methodology).

Understanding the Reality of Time Pressure

A series of focus group interviews with VRS librarians were conducted during the selection and analysis of the transcripts (Connaway & Radford, 2007). One finding from these focus groups was that VRS librarians were often stressed over what they perceived to be heightened time pressure in the live chat environment when compared to FtF reference. To discover if these perceptions were accurate, the Seeking Synchronicity research team used the time stamps that tracked wait time and duration of the chat session to address the following time pressure concerns:

- How long do VRS users wait to be helped?
- Do VRS librarians have to hurry more than they do in FtF encounters?
- How long is the average live chat session?

Results indicate that VRS users' queries are picked up in a relatively short amount of time. The average (mean) wait time was 1.87 minutes with a median of one minute. Figure 1.1 shows that 37.2 percent of the users were helped in 30 seconds or less and 75 percent were assisted in 90 seconds or less. The shortest wait time was only 1 second, while the longest was 67 minutes. One intriguing finding from several of the Seeking Synchronicity phases was that users are willing to wait for a subject specialist. In the case of the 67 minute wait, the user was asking a law question and stayed online in the chat session in order to have his or her question posed to a legal expert.

Focus group interviews, as well as online surveys and telephone interviews from Seeking Synchronicity, uncovered evidence to indicate that users often are not using live chat because they are in a hurry but because it is more convenient and they like the familiar instant messaging (IM) format. VRS users are generally multitasking and may have several other applications open (see also Ward, 2004). Users who are impatient or rude are in the small minority. A transcript analysis by Radford (2006b) reported 10 percent of users as being impatient and

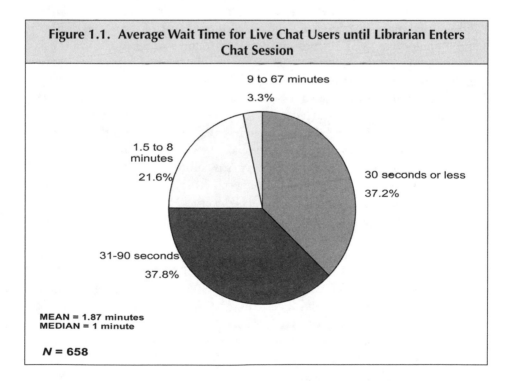

Figure 1.1. Average Wait Time for Live Chat Users until Librarian Enters Chat Session

9 to 67 minutes

3.3%

1.5 to 8 minutes

21.6%

30 seconds or less

37.2%

31-90 seconds

37.8%

MEAN = 1.87 minutes
MEDIAN = 1 minute

N **= 658**

4 percent being rude in an analysis of a random sample of transcripts from the Maryland AskUsNow! cooperative chat service. Of 372 of the Seeking Synchronicity VRS transcripts, 5 percent (14) were coded for user impatience and only 3 percent (9) of the transcripts included the use of rude or insulting remarks by the users (Connaway & Radford, 2008).

These results may be surprising to VR librarians who often feel that if they do not have a quick answer to a query users will abruptly disconnect. The finding that users are willing to wait for subject specialists leads to the recommendation that more effort needs to be made to seek ways to leverage subject experts in the queuing system. One way to accomplish this goal may be to ask users who present very specialized questions (e.g., science, medical, law) if they would like an immediate answer or if they would be willing to wait for their question to be forwarded to a subject expert to be answered through e-mail, phone reference, or, in the case of academic queues for home institutions, in an on-campus, in-library appointment. In a study of instant messaging reference at Southern Illinois University, Ruppel and Fagan (2002) found that 64 percent of these reference sessions originated within the library building, while 35 percent came from outside of the library, from an on-campus network such as a computer lab, office, or student dormitory. These results suggest that offers of in-person expert help may be welcomed more often than one might imagine.

In examining a subset of the Seeking Synchronicity transcripts Williams (2009) found one explanation for the abrupt disconnect of users that appear in approximately one-third of the transcripts. She found that when librarians asked users variations of the question "Have you already checked [the online catalog, the Business Source Premier database, etc.]?" often these users would abruptly log off. When librarians asked a less-direct form of this question, such as "Have you had a chance to get started yet?" or "Can you tell me where you have already looked so I don't repeat your search?" the users were less threatened and more likely to self-disclose. Some users would confess "I really don't know where to begin or where to look." Using these types of supportive questions may result in fewer "disappearing users" who disconnect suddenly.

As far as the length of VRS sessions is concerned, the mean average for 658 of the 850 transcripts with time stamps was found to be 12.42 minutes with a median of 12 minutes. Ward (2004) reported an average of 15 minutes for VR sessions at the University of Illinois, Champaign-Urbana. The median for FtF reference sessions in academic settings has generally been reported to be 12 to 13 minutes, so the average for VR session times is about the same length as that of FtF session times. This finding suggests that VR librarians can use many of the time management techniques that are useful for FtF encounters in the chat environment. Because VR users cannot "see" when there is a queue of users, it is important to alert them by saying "There are additional users online right now, do you have the time to wait for a few minutes, or can I e-mail you the information?" Transcripts show that some users, when the wait time is approached this way, will say "No prob, I can wait" or "Sure, I'm not in a hurry." Showing respect for the user's time commitment leads to better rapport. One strategy that is quick and effective is to use the ellipsis (. . .) or type a brief message such as "still searching" or "more" frequently, so users know their query is still being worked on and avoids getting messages like "r u there?"

Improving Accuracy

The Seeking Synchronicity project also investigated the important quality issues of how accurate live chat reference is and what can be done to increase effectiveness? The famous 55 percent rule (see Hernon & McClure, 1987) had stated that librarians in FtF settings gave correct answers only a little better than half of the time, although this methodology design has been questioned (see Durrance, 1989). With the availability of transcripts in VR, accuracy can now be checked, especially in the case of ready reference, factual questions. When an analysis of the types of questions was completed for the 850 transcripts, 27 percent (243) were found to contain ready reference questions; that is, those who had a factual answer that could usually be found quickly and be established from a single authoritative source. A careful verification that compared answers to authoritative resources found that 78 percent (141) of these were answered correctly. Closer analysis of the incorrectly answered queries determined that accuracy could be greatly enhanced through use of five strategies that are listed here (see also Ross, Nielson, & Radford, 2009).

The most important strategy to improve the number of correct answers is to always make sure that the user's specific question is answered before pushing a Web page or URL to him or her. Accuracy could have been improved from 78 percent (141) to 90 percent (168) had the librarian stopped before pushing a Web page to first check the link to make sure the requested information is present. In these 27 sessions, the librarian was asked a specific question but pushed a general Web site that concerned the broader topic and did not have the exact information requested. For example, one user asked for the longitude and latitude of the Great Wall of China and what cities were nearby. The librarian pushed a general tourist site for the Great Wall but one that did not contain the longitude, latitude, or surrounding cities.

Another valuable strategy for improving accuracy is to clarify the question through asking open, neutral, and closed questions. Research in FtF and virtual modes has determined that query clarification and the use of the traditional reference interview heightens precision across each and every different type of questions (see also Dewdney & Ross, 1994a; Nielson, 2006; Ross et al., 2009). It is important to use clarifying questions *before* the start of searching to ensure that the work will find the answer to the correct specific question, not just a description of the general topic. Additionally, increase accuracy and user satisfaction before logging off, by remembering the tried and true technique of always asking a follow-up question (e.g., Did this completely answer your question?). VR users, similar to those in FtF environments, have been shown to be most satisfied when the librarian has concluded an interaction by asking a follow-up question (see also Durrance, 1995).

One more way to boost accuracy is to open each Web link before pushing it to the user. Taking a moment to do this saves the user's time and decreases frustration. Users can be very disappointed when the librarian has found and says he or she is sending a helpful resource, but then the user clicks on the link to find an error message for a broken link. Transcript analysis showed dead links are pushed more often than might be expected. It may be that when librarians are in a hurry, they go to Google (http://google.com) or another search engine and cut and paste a good-looking link to a user without taking the extra time to check to make sure the link is live, especially if they have recently visited the site. Even popular sites can be offline at times for migration to different servers or for other technical problems.

Another mistake revealed in the transcripts occurred at times when the user asked several questions but the librarian missed one or more of these, choosing instead to focus on the first or last question. When confronted by a chat session in which the user has asked a series of questions, make sure to address each question before signing off. This type of error is also more likely when VR librarians are juggling multiple users simultaneously or they have a long line of people in the queue. Although the librarian may be in a hurry to help others in line, the original user can become impatient when obliged to log in again to re-enter one or more unanswered questions. If the situation is busy, it is better to acknowledge that there are others in the queue and to ask if it is acceptable for the user to get the answers by e-mail or to come in person to their local library, especially if the remaining question(s) is particularly complex. Using a sense of humor at these times may also work: "Oh my, I see you have loads of questions today! Which one would you like me to tackle first?" The bottom line is to end with a follow-up question like: "Did this completely answer your question?" which gives the user the chance to say, "Well, I do also need to have my question about x answered."

Improving Communication

In addition to evaluating accuracy and looking at the issues surrounding wait time and length of sessions, the 850 transcripts were examined and coded for positive and negative aspects of interpersonal communication. Codes were assigned by the research team, using and enlarging the coding scheme developed by Radford (2006a). Relational Facilitators were defined as aspects of the chat interaction that have a positive impact on interaction and that enhance communication. See

Appendix 1.1, "Radford Category Scheme for Interpersonal Communication in Chat Reference," for an outline of major themes and subthemes that were found to be facilitators. Major themes included: Greeting Ritual, Deference, Rapport Building, and Closing Ritual. Definitions for these themes can be found in Radford (2006a). To get an idea of how these facilitators operate in the chat context, closely examine the verbatim text found in Appendix 1.2, "Sample Transcript with Relational Facilitators: Mathematics in the Islamic Empire." In this transcript, one can see that both user and librarian engage in politeness rituals and make the effort to respect each other, be agreeable, and give reassurance and praise as appropriate (see also Westbrook, 2007).

On the other hand, Relational Barriers were defined as aspects of the chat interaction that have a negative impact on interaction that impede communication. Appendix 1.2 also provides an outline of major and subthemes that were found to be barriers. Major themes included: Negative Closure and Relational Disconnect—Failure to Build Rapport (see Radford 2006a for definitions of these terms). Barriers have an opposite effect from Facilitators and lead to unsuccessful interactions. Both users and librarians can exhibit Barriers, as can be seen in Appendix 1.3, "Sample Transcript with Relational Barriers: Mesopotamian Government." This transcript provides examples of negative closure (see Ross & Dewdney, 1998) in which the user obviously needs more help but the librarian refers the user to Google, and although the text has a pleasant overtone on the surface, the librarian is trying to disengage without fully assisting the user in providing the needed information.

Recommendations to Improve Interpersonal Communication in Chat

Based on the transcript analysis, Appendix 1.4 contains an updated "Checklist of Recommendations for Facilitating Interpersonal Communication in Chat Reference" (see also Ross et al., 2009). These recommendations can be seen as a reaffirmation that the basic interpersonal skills librarians use in traditional FtF and phone reference easily can be transferred to virtual encounters. It is important to remember that the user is an individual human being on the other side of the computer screen, not a passive or unfeeling automaton. When librarians are relaxed, acknowledge humor, and show sympathy (e.g., for a difficult assignment) in the transcripts, the users are seen to respond in kind, and rapport can be established quickly.

As in personal interactions at the reference desk, greetings have been revealed in this research to be extremely important in establishing a positive tone early in the encounter that will go a long way in case the going gets tough later. Similarly, it is essential to end on a positive note, avoid negative closure (Ross & Dewdney, 1998), and ask if the question has been fully answered to improve accuracy as well as to leave the user with a positive impression of the interaction. Use scripted messages sparingly in greetings and closures. If overused, these can give the user the impression that librarians are cyborgs or robots and actually can prompt rude behavior (see also Radford, 2006a). When the question looks complex, let the user know that the search is going to take awhile and ask if he or she can wait. This show of deference indicates that the user's time is valuable, and allows him or her to make the choice whether or not to wait. Presenting the alternatives to e-mail the answer, etc., further reflects cooperation and a shared responsibility for developing a positive outcome.

Much of the behaviors involved in the Facilitators can be described as common courtesy and use of "people skills." Take the cue from the user in deciding the appropriate level of formality. If the user is ultra polite and uses impeccable grammar and spelling, do the same. If they are informal and use chat speak and abbreviations, this can be "mirrored" by the librarian, as appropriate. If the librarian is uncomfortable with less formality, the user will pick up on this. It is important to adjust formality levels according to the situation of the query, using textual cues and user self-disclosure to help figure out as much context as possible. These skills are transferable from FtF experiences.

The bottom line is to be comfortable in chat, to relax and enjoy the encounter, and to expect a good experience. This research demonstrates that the overwhelming majority of live chat encounters have a positive tone and a successful ending. However, it is important to be looking for ways to improve relationships and service effectiveness in each encounter. This effort will, in turn, lead to VR users who are satisfied, who will provide recommendations to their friends to use the live chat service, and who will return confidently with future questions with expectations to be treated well and to have their queries taken seriously and answered authoritatively.

Note

1. The authors would like to extend special thanks to the members of the Seeking Synchronicity team at Rutgers University and OCLC who assisted in the transcript analysis: J. D. Williams, P. Confer, D.M. Dragos, M. A. Reilly, J. Strange, S. Sabolcsi-Boros, and T. J. Dickey.

References

Connaway, L. S., & Radford, M. L. (2007). The thrill of the chase in cyberspace: A report of focus groups with live chat librarians. *Informed Librarian Online*. Retrieved from www.informedlibrarian.com/guestForum.cfm?FILE=gf0701.html.

Connaway, L. S., & Radford, M. L. (2008). Smiling online: Applying face-to-face reference skills in a virtual environment. Presented as a Webinar (Web Based Seminar) at Online Computer Library Center, April 16, Dublin, Ohio. Retrieved from www.oclc.org/research/projects/synchronicity.

Dewdney, P., & Ross, C. S. (1994a). Best practices: An analysis of the best (and worst) in fifty-two public library reference transactions. *Public Libraries, 33*, 261–266.

Dewdney, P., & Ross, C. S. (1994b). Flying a light aircraft: Reference service evaluation from a user's viewpoint, *RQ, 34*(2), 217–230.

Durrance, J. C. (1989). Reference success: Does the 55 percent rule tell the whole story? *Library Journal, 114*(7), 31–36.

Durrance, J. C. (1995). Factors that influence reference success: What makes questioners willing to return? *The Reference Librarian, (49/50)*, 243–265.

Hernon, P., & McClure, C. R. (1987). Library reference service: An unrecognized crisis—A symposium. *Journal of Academic Librarianship, 13*(2), 69–80.

Nielsen, K. (2006). Comparing users' perspectives of in-person and virtual reference. New *Library World, 107*(1222/1223), 91–104.

Radford, M. L. (1999). *The reference encounter: Interpersonal communication in the academic library.* Chicago: Association of College and Research Libraries.

Radford, M. L. (2006a, June). Encountering virtual users: A qualitative investigation of interpersonal communication in chat reference. *Journal of the American Society for Information Science and Technology, 57*(8), 1046–1059.

Radford, M. L. (2006b). Investigating interpersonal communication in chat reference: Dealing with impatient users and rude encounters. In R. D. Lankes, E. Abels, M. White, & S. N. Haque (Eds.), *The virtual reference desk: Creating a reference future* (pp. 23–46). New York: Neal-Schuman Publishers.

Radford, M. L., & Connaway, L. S. (2008). Seeking synchronicity: Evaluating virtual reference services from user, non-user, and librarian perspectives seeking synchronicity. Retrieved from www.oclc.org/research/activities/synchronicity/default.htm.

Radford, M. L., & Connaway, L. S. (2009). CREATing a new theoretical model for reference encounters in synchronous face-to-face and virtual environments. Presented at the 2009 ALISE Conference, January 20–23, Denver, Colorado. Retrieved from www.oclc.org/research/activities/synchronicity/ppt/alise2009.ppt.

Ross, C. S., & Dewdney, P. (1998). Negative closure: Strategies and counter-strategies in the reference transaction. *RUSQ, 38*(2), 151–163.

Ross, C. S., Nielsen, K., & Radford, M. L. (2009). *Conducting the reference interview* (2nd ed.). New York: Neal-Schuman.

Ruppel, M., & Fagan, J. C. (2002). Instant messaging reference: Users' evaluation of library chat. *Reference Services Review, 30*(3), 183–197.

Ward, D. (2004, Fall). Measuring the completeness of reference transactions in online chats: Results of an unobtrusive study. *Reference & User Services Quarterly, 44*(1), 46–56.

Westbrook, L. (2007). Chat reference communication patterns and implications: Applying politeness theory. *Journal of Documentation, 63*(5), 638–658.

Williams, J. D. (2009). Friction in computer-mediated communication: An unobtrusive qualitative analysis of subjective anonymity and face threat antecedents and consequences between librarians and users. Unpublished doctoral dissertation proposal, Rutgers University, Newark, New Jersey.

Appendix 1.1. Radford Category Scheme for Interpersonal Communication in Chat Reference

I. FACILITATORS
A. Greeting Ritual
B. Deference
   1. Agreement to Try What Is Suggested, or to Wait
   2. Apology
   3. Asking for Other to Be Patient
   4. Expressions of Enthusiasm
   5. Suggesting Strategy or Explanation
   6. Thanks
   7. Polite Expressions
   8. Praise, Admiration
   9. Self-Deprecating Remarks
C. Rapport Building
   1. Familiarity
   2. Humor
   3. Hedges/Interjections (e.g., well, oh)
   4. Offering Confirmation
      a. Approval
      b. Empathy
      c. Inclusion
   5. Offering Reassurance
      a. Encouraging Remarks, Praise
      b. Enthusiastic Remarks
   6. Repair, Self-Correction
   7. Seeking Reassurance, Confirmation, or Self-Disclosure
   8. Self-Disclosure
      a. Admitting Lack of Knowledge, At a Loss as to Where to Search
      b. Explaining Search Strategy
      c. Explaining Technical Problems
      d. Offer Personal Opinion, Advice, Value Judgment
   9. Use of Informal Language
      a. Alternate Spelling, Abbreviated Single Words (e.g., Info)
      b. Lowercase
      c. Slang Expressions
   10. Re-representation of Nonverbal Cues
      a. All Caps
      b. Alphanumeric Shortcuts (e.g., l8r for Later)
      c. Asterisk (or Other Punctuation) for Emphasis
      d. Ellipsis
      e. Emoticons
      f. Phrase Abbreviations (e.g., FYI, For Your Information)
      g. Spells Out Nonverbal Behaviors (e.g., Ha Ha)
      h. Punctuation or Repeated Punctuation
D. Closing Ritual
   1. Explanation for Signing Off Abruptly
   2. Invites to Return if Necessary
   3. Makes Sure User Has No More Questions
   4. Offers to Continue Searching and E-Mail Answer

II. BARRIERS
A. Negative Closure
   1. Abrupt Ending
   2. Disclaimer
   3. Failure to Refer
   4. Ignoring Cues That User Wants More Help
   5. Premature or Attempted Closing
   6. Premature Referral
   7. Sends to Google
B. Relational Disconnect—Failure to Build Rapport
   1. Condescending
   2. Derisive Use of Spelling Out NV Behaviors
   3. Disconfirming
   4. Failing to Offer Reassurance
   5. Failure or Refusal to Provide Info
   6. Goofing Around
   7. Ignoring Humor
   8. Ignoring Self-Disclosure
   9. Impatience
   10. Inappropriate Script or Inappropriate Response
   11. Inappropriate Language
   12. Jargon, No Explanation
   13. Lack of Attention or Ignoring Question
   14. Limits Time
   15. Mirrors Rude Behavior
   16. Mistakes
   17. Misunderstands Question
   18. Reprimanding
   19. Robotic Answer
   20. Rude or Insulting

		Appendix 1.2. Sample Transcript with Relational Facilitators: Mathematics in the Islamic Empire
1	U	i need a good Web site about the accomplishments of mathematics during the islamic empire
2	L	*A librarian will be with you in about a minute.*
3	L	*A librarian has joined the session.*
4	L	*You have been conferenced with [name of service.]*
5	L	[Name], welcome to [service name]. I'm looking at your question right now; it will be just a moment.
6	L	Hi [Name]. Sorry about the delay there. This is [Name], a librarian in [City]
7	U	ok
8	L	Okay, we should be able to find something on that topic. Math and Islam. Just a minute or two while I search. Please let me know if there's anything specific in this area that you're looking for, okay?
9	U	i don't care about the delay i have plenty of time
10	L	Thanks for understanding. We just had a very busy spell on the service and I just finished up another call. Let's see. . . searching now.
11	U	i just need any certain mathematicians or the accomplishments of mathematics during the islamic Empire
12	L	Okay, to start I'm going to send you an article linked from the Math Forum:
13	L	*Page sent.*
14	L	It should show on your screen in just a few seconds. Are you able to see it? The title is Arabic mathematics : forgotten brilliance.
15	U	thank you very much
16	L	Great—glad you can see It! There was one other article. Did you want me to send it to you, or are you okay with just this one?
17	U	yes please
18	L	Okay, just a sec.
19	L	*Page sent.*
20	U	i spelled please wrong
21	L	The title of this 2nd page I just sent is "The Arabic numeral system"
22	U	thank you
23	L	No problem on the spelling. :) Typing this fast it's giong to happen.
24	L	*going*
25	L	Okay, what do you think? Will these answer your questions?
26	U	yes thank you
27	L	Great! Please do write us back if you need anything else.
28	L	Thank you for using [name of service]! If you have any further questions, please contact us again. If you provided an e-mail address, you should receive a full transcript in a few minutes. You may click the "End Call" button now.

Note: U = User; L = Librarian.

		Appendix 1.3. Sample Transcript with Relational Barriers: Mesopotamian Government
1	U	Can you find me information on Mesopotamian government?
2	L	*Please hold for the next available librarian. If you would like a transcript of this session e-mailed to you, please type your full e-mail address now.*
3	L	[Librarian Name], [X Library]. *A librarian has joined the session.*
4	L	Hello [Name] . . . I'm looking at your question . . .
5	L	it looks like your pc is not compatible with mine—we are unable to cobrowse, so I'll go to google to search. Have you looked for infomation there?
6	U	yes
7	L	well I found an excellent link on the google page . . . you can put into google's search bar: Mesopotamia +government and look at the links they provide . . .
8	U	can you send them to me
9	L	if we could cobrowse we could look at the links together . . . but you can do the search yourself, yes?
10	L	Mesopotamia +government
11	L	buhler.usd313.k12.ks.us/prosperity/meso3.html
12	L	www.kidsnewsroom.org/elmer/infoCentral/frameset/civilizations/meso/gov/
13	L	oi.uchicago.edu/OI/MUS/ED/TRC/MESO/law.html-14k-
14	U	I have already searched there and that really doesn't help me
15	L	It would be much easier for you to do the google search I showed you so you could click on the links and read the content as you go along . . .
16	L	why not?
17	L	Can you describe your needs a little for me?
18	L	[Patron Name] . . . are you there?
19	U	Well I want to know how the government ran and just a little information on Hammurabi
20	L	okay . . . let me look at one of the links I sent you . . .
21	L	The Laws of Hammurabi are the longest and best organized of the law collections that survive from ancient Mesopotamia. King Hammurabi, who ruled from . . . oi.uchicago.edu/OI/MUS/ED/TRC/MESO/law.html-14k
22	L	this link answers your questions—you need to look at this site—can you do that?
23	U	no
24	L	do you know how to use google?
25	U	yes
26	L	www.google.com
27	L	so what happens when you type in the search bar: Mesopotamis +government?
28	L	Mesopotamia
29	U	can you connect me with [Librarian2 Name]?

(Continued)

		Appendix 1.3. Sample Transcript with Relational Barriers: Mesopotamian Government *(Continued)*
30	L	hold on . . .
31	L	I don't see anyone with that name—just different libraries. You could log out and come back in again if you like?
32	U	Can you contact me with anyone from the [X Library]
33	L	I'm going to go on to another person if you don't want to continue—I need to have a little input from you . . .
34	L	I'm sorry, where is that library—in the [City A] area?
35	U	yes
36	L	I see [City A] . . . but not [City B] . . .
37	L	you can log out and come back in again . . . if you like
38	U	can you try the west valley regional
39	L	I'm going to log out now—you can request that when you come back in—I only saw [City A].
40	L	oaks
41	U	what
42	L	Try the links I sent you . . . you can get the information you need—goodbye and come again!
43	U	what
44	L	Note to staff: COMP [Librarian Name], [X Library]. User has closed this session.
45	L	*Chat Session Ended.*
Note: U = User; L = Librarian.		

Appendix 1.4. Checklist of Recommendations for Facilitating Interpersonal Communication in Chat Reference

General Notes
- Always remember that your interpersonal skills and experience are transferable to the chat environment.
- There is a general misunderstanding that interpersonal niceties are not important in chat or virtual settings. Interpersonal dimensions are present and vitally important in virtual communication.
- The large majority of time spent in virtual interactions is spent in the searching process, not in interpersonal exchanges.
- Type short sentences and hit send frequently at appropriate places to maintain "word contact." If you are going to be searching for a while, continue to send short reassurances (e.g., "Searching") so the users know you have not disconnected.

Greeting
- Give a personal greeting after the script (can be a quick "Hi!")
- Use the person's first name in your response. Younger users especially like a personal approach. This softens the anonymous environment and may head off problems.
- When reading the user's initial question, look for any self-disclosure or indications that the user is seeking reassurance ("Can you help me?") and provide an appropriate response.
- When the initial question looks complex, immediately let the user know that you think this may take some time and ask if he or she has the time to wait while you search. Users sometimes expect instant answers, as when they search Google, but often they are multitasking and may not mind waiting.
- If you can see that the user is from a geographically remote place, you may want to make a comment on this right away (e.g., "How's the weather in Florida? It's snowing here in Maryland"). This gently alerts the user that a question about local information may need to be referred.

Strategies for Building Rapport
- As appropriate, be willing to self-disclose, to provide information about yourself, to use "I" statements. This can mean the following:
  - Offer personal opinion/advice/value judgment (e.g., "I think that you will have more success if you do X" or "I have used this strategy before and it works!").
  - Admit lack of knowledge (e.g., "I don't know what you mean, could you be more specific?" or "I have not heard of this term before, can you tell me what it means?).
  - Ask for confirmation as needed (e.g., "Is this what you mean?").
- Acknowledge user self-disclosure (e.g., "I'm sorry you're not feeling well and are unable to travel to your library, let me see how I can help." Then, at the closing, "Feel better soon!").
  - Be empathetic when users self-disclose difficulty or frustration (e.g., "It is frustrating when our technology doesn't work!").
- Include user in search process (e.g., "Let's try this," "We'll look here first," "Would it be ok if we . . .").
- Indicate your approval as appropriate (e.g., "That's great!" or "Good for you!").
- Offer reassurance when users indicate that they are tentative or unsure of how to proceed. Realize that they can be fearful of your disapproval (if, for example, they have poor computer skills).
  - Use encouraging remarks, praise, and enthusiastic remarks as appropriate.
  - Use humor, as it can be reassuring, as can the use of self-deprecating remarks ("I'm not the world's best speller either!")
- Mirror the level of formality/informality of the users; if they use informal language, feel free to be less formal (as appropriate).

(Continued)

Appendix 1.4. Checklist of Recommendations for Facilitating Interpersonal Communication in Chat Reference *(Continued)*

Strategies for Building Rapport *(Continued)*
- Be deferential and respectful of all users.
  - Use polite expressions as appropriate (e.g., "please," "thanks," "you're welcome," etc.).
  - Apologize as appropriate (e.g., "sorry," "unfortunately," or "oops").

Compensation for Lack of Nonverbal Cues
- Mirror the users' style. If they use shortcuts, acronyms, abbreviations, and emoticons (smileys), feel free to do so also (as appropriate).
  - You may see more "chat speak" in younger users. Respond in kind if you are comfortable doing so.
- If you are not comfortable using emoticons, you can spell out nonverbal behaviors or use interjections (e.g., "hmmm," "oh," "ha ha," "grin").
- Use repeated punctuation for emphasis (e.g., !!, or ??).
- Use ellipsis to indicate more to come (e.g., "still searching . . .").
- Be careful when using ALL CAPS; this may seem like a reprimand or like shouting (e.g., "Don't EVER . . .").

Closing
- Always give a personal closing (can be a quick "bye!").
- In the closing, as in the greeting, be sure to respond to self-disclosure, enthusiasm, or polite expressions. (e.g., if the user says, "This is a great service!" Don't just send them the scripted closing—give an appropriate response like, "Glad you think so, thanks!").
- Avoid premature closing. Make sure you have answered users question(s) completely. Ask if they need anything else before closing.
- Look for subtle cues that the user wants more help (e.g., "Well, thanks for your help," is one example; the "well" hedge may indicate that they are settling for what you have provided, but really want more).

Relational Barriers to Be Avoided
- Avoid robotic answers.
- Avoid sending an inappropriate script (e.g., a welcome script halfway through).
- Don't ignore user self-disclosure or use of humor. If the user makes a joke (even if it is lame) respond with a ";-)" or "ha!"
- Avoid failing to offer reassurance when the user seeks it.
- Be careful not to ignore parts of questions or additional questions.
  - When dealing with a several part question, let the user know that you will take the questions in order.
  - If busy, indicate that you will start with question one, and may have to answer the others by e-mail.
- Avoid being condescending or disconfirming.
- Avoid negative closure
  - Premature closing—make sure that you have answered all questions.
  - Abrupt ending—let the user know you are going to close.
  - Disclaimer—don't indicate that the question is unanswerable or problematic before checking, many things previously unavailable may now be accessible. Provide a good referral if you are unable to answer question.
  - Never ignore cues that the user wants more help, even if it means asking him or her to wait while you help others.

(Continued)

Appendix 1.4. Checklist of Recommendations for Facilitating Interpersonal Communication in Chat Reference *(Continued)*

Relational Barriers to Be Avoided *(Continued)*

- To avoid abrupt disconnects, be careful not to ask the direct question "Have you checked X resource?" (e.g., the online catalog, the Academic Search Premier index). Instead, ask the neutral question "Have you had a chance to get started yet?" or "Can you tell me where you have already searched?"
- To avoid abrupt disconnects, do not push a general Web site quickly to hold the user's attention while you search. Tell the user you are searching (ask the user if he or she can wait if you are doing a complex search) and push a page only when you are sure it is on target for the user's request.

CHAPTER 2

Balance of Power and Negotiation of Meaning in Virtual Reference Learning Environments

Mary Kickham-Samy

Overview

Using quantitative and qualitative analyses of virtual-reference transcripts, this study examined power sharing in virtual reference environments. The quantitative statistics, generated from 250 transcripts, showed that the librarian had a much stronger presence than the student, but the statistics did not explain how this strength contributed to student learning. In order to better understand the significance of the statistical data, an exploratory reading of some of these transcripts was conducted. Using James Paul Gee's approach to discourse analysis, the researcher found that librarians were using a variety of strategies to provide students with the information and the instruction they needed to answer their research questions. In some instances, the librarian used a teacher-centered approach where the librarian delivered the instruction to the student. In other instances, the librarian created a more student-centered environment where the student and the librarian negotiated meaning and co-constructed knowledge, and sometimes the librarian used a combination of both environments.[1]

Research Problem

There is a voice among scholars in the library community that calls for a change in current practices in library instruction. They argue for an approach that is less agenda-driven and teacher-centered to one that focuses on the students. This voice argues against an objectivist approach that involves the librarian in transferring information as an object to the student. These scholars are calling for a constructivist, agenda-free, student-centered approach to teaching information literacy (Doherty, 2007; Doherty & Ketchner, 2005; Elmborg, 2006; Swanson, 2004).

Jonassen (1999) defines objectivism as the notion that knowledge is an object that can be transferred from an expert in a discipline to a novice, while constructivism is the view that knowledge is mental structures that the learners build "based on their interpretations of experiences in the world" (p. 217). In this way, the thinking is that objectivist instructional strategies involve teacher-centered activities, while constructivist activities are more student centered. Jonassen says that, while many view these concepts as "incompatible and mutually exclusive," he considers them complementary perspectives that can be applied either alone or in combination to enhance learning environments, depending on the context (p. 217). This study attempts to show that virtual reference learning environments provide a context that is conducive to the application of constructivist learning strategies.

Ellis (2004) observed that, in contrast to the more librarian-centered environment at the face-to-face reference desk, synchronous computer-conferencing environments, such as chat, instant messaging, and virtual reference, presented an opportunity for students to assume more responsibility for their own learning. In synchronous e-reference environments, students think of the librarian as an equal partner, not as an authority figure. This perspective gives the librarian the opportunity to collaborate with students in the instruction process. Westbrook (2006) urged virtual reference librarians to resist the temptation to provide quick, convenient answers for students and to become more concerned with bringing students from one level of understanding to a higher, more complete, and more accurate one. This study examines the potential that virtual reference environments offer for the application of constructivist learning strategies in which student and librarian share power in negotiating meaning and constructing knowledge.

Significance of the Problem

The purpose of this study is to provide a description of the kinds of learning and the levels of thinking taking place in the virtual reference environments so that librarians can make informed decisions on how to maximize the effectiveness of this technology. Despite the relative high cost of virtual reference, its technological glitches, and its low usage statistics, librarians persist in their efforts to provide electronic reference services to instruct students in how to use the vast amount of information that libraries are making accessible. However, more research is needed to provide librarians guidance in how best to design these environments for instruction. Lankes (2005) calls for an increased focus on research in order to build a theoretical foundation for digital reference services. He says that research is needed to guide practitioners in making effective and efficient decisions regarding their reference services and to provide evidence to support funding. The purpose of this study is to contribute to developing a baseline of research to help guide librarians in designing and participating in synchronous e-reference environments.

Literature Review

Theoretical Framework: Information Literacy and Critical Information Literacy

In 2000, the Association of Colleges and Research Libraries (ACRL), a division of the American Library Association (ALA), approved a set of competency standards of information literacy. This document defined these standards as the ability to "recognize when information is needed" and the ability to "locate, evaluate, and use [information] effectively" (American Library Association, 2000). Within the discussion in the library community on how best to teach information literacy, a movement has been growing for a more student-centered approach, one that empowers students to take ownership of their own learning. It is grounded in critical literacy theory (Doherty, 2007; Doherty & Ketchner, 2005; Elmborg, 2006; Simmons, 2005; Swanson, 2004). Critical literacy theory is an understanding that education is embedded in political, social, and cultural influences that give some learners easier access to its challenges and rewards than others. Education is not a neutral object to which everyone has equal access. Critical literacy theory is a movement away from information transfer and skills-based achievement standards to a more complex view of literacy, one that requires the educator to go to where the students are and work with them to construct knowledge (Doherty & Ketchner, 2005).

Critical Review of Relevant Research

Researchers have considered the problems librarians encountered when attempting to instruct students using real-time virtual reference. Woodward (2005) suggested that virtual reference librarians may be hesitant to instruct students and may feel pressure to provide information quickly and concisely because of "their awareness of the waiting student" (p. 207). Lee (2004) said that real-time, text-based virtual reference may not be the most appropriate environment for instruction for a number of reasons, among which was student impatience. Aware of this perception, Desai and Graves (2006) looked at whether or not students were willing to accept instruction in synchronous computer-conferencing environments. The authors gathered their data through two main sources: a survey and the reference transcripts. From the survey, they learned that as many as 92 percent of the respondents were willing to accept instruction with greater or less enthusiasm. Only 8 percent were totally "unreachable" (p. 186). One point the authors made was that many respondents wanted to learn how to find information by themselves.

Doherty and Ketchner (2005) are advocates for empowering the student with critical thinking skills. They are critical of library instruction that is librarian driven where the librarian brings to the session prescribed goals and an agenda without regard for student input. They argue that librarians "should value and build on the experiences of students" (p. 8). In this way, the librarian and the student share power in their discourse. This power sharing leads to co-construction of knowledge. Ellis (2004) says that students in online reference environments feel more empowered than those at the physical reference desk. Her position supports the idea that power sharing between the librarian and the student is intrinsic to co-constructing knowledge in virtual reference transactions.

Ward (2004) defined a "complete" virtual reference session as one that included not only whether the student found an answer to a question but also whether the librarian provided instruction in the process. The criteria Ward used to define a "complete" reference transaction consisted of four components: (1) whether the librarian asked about the number of sources required, (2) whether the librarian showed the student a useful database, (3) whether the librarian recommended search terms, and (4) whether the librarian checked that the student found the needed information. Based on this scale, the results of Ward's study showed that out of 72 transactions, 34 (47 percent) were complete sessions in that they fulfilled all four criteria (p. 49).

By using these four criteria, Ward (2004) considered "completeness" to mean more than providing the student with factual information because it also included instructing the student in how to locate similar information in the future, independent of the librarian. However, although Ward's study focused on teaching the student as opposed to providing the student with an answer, it placed the librarian in the teacher-centered tradition of instruction where the librarian controlled the session and set the agenda. Ward's definition of a "completed" session focused on the activities of the librarian and not on those of the student.

Summary of the Literature

This review of the literature revealed four main points. The Desai and Graves's (2006) study showed that, first of all, students were more receptive to instruction in virtual reference environments than librarians had previously thought, and, second, students were genuinely interested in learning how to find information themselves. Third, Ellis's (2004) research showed that virtual reference learning environments were conducive to power-sharing relationships. Fourth, Ward (2004) showed that librarians were skilled in and willing to provide the guidance students needed to learn in the virtual reference environment.

Research Questions

The focus of this study was on the level and intensity of communication between the virtual reference librarian and the student in virtual reference learning environments. The quantitative measures addressed the following questions:

1. Is there parity of participation on the part of the librarian and the student as measured by the number of turns each takes and questions each asks?

2. Does the number of questions asked during a session by the librarian, the student, or both parties combined affect the length of the transaction?
3. Does the intensity of the student and the librarian engagement as measured by the number of turns each party takes, the number of questions asked, and the number of emoticons used predict the overall quality of the virtual reference session as measured by its length or the librarian's perception of session quality?
4. Does the length of the session affect the librarian's perception of session quality?

The qualitative measures focused on what virtual reference transcripts revealed about the following:

1. The cognitive connections and social engagements that occur
2. The instructional presence librarians display

Method of Data Collection

Data Source
The source of the data for this study was an archive of transcripts of virtual reference (VR) sessions conducted via a VR software package called "Ask-A-Librarian," a product of Tutor.com. This product included not only synchronous chat but also features that allowed the participants to view Web pages. Each transcript was divided into two parts: (1) the session information and (2) the transcript. The session information contained a post-session evaluation survey with which the librarians assessed their performance as either "Excellent," "Very Good," "Good," "Fair," or "Poor." In a separate form, the librarian was prompted to state whether the session was "Completed," "Referred for Follow-up," a "Test," a "Lost Call," or "Inappropriate." The session information also stated the time of the session and its length in minutes and seconds. The transcript section contained the text of the dialogue between the librarian and the student as well as the URLs of the Web pages that the participants viewed.

Sample and Sampling Procedure
The sample for this study consisted of 250 transcripts of virtual reference sessions initiated by students attending 15 different community colleges located in a state in the Midwest of the United States. From the transcript archive, the researcher copied and pasted into Word documents purposefully selected transcripts generated during the months of January through July 2007. Transcripts were selected based on three criteria. First, only sessions initiated by community college students were selected; those initiated by a university or public library patron were deselected. Second, the sessions coded as "completed" or "referred for follow-up" were

selected, while those coded as "lost calls" due to a technical problem, "inappropriate," or "tests" were excluded from the study.

The participants consisted of virtual reference librarians and community college students. The librarians were either full-time or part-time employees in one of the 15 community colleges or in the one major research university that also participated in the service. The student participants were an ethnically, socially, and economically diverse group. Students from any of the member institutions could log into the service any time during the hours the service was in operation. Therefore, students would not necessarily be assisted by a librarian from their home institution but very likely were assisted by a librarian from another institution.

Quantitative Data Analysis

To answer the quantitative research questions, several statistical tests were conducted on eight variables: (1) session length measured in minutes and seconds; (2) the librarian's session-assessment index as measured by a five-point scale in the librarian exit form; (3) the number of librarian turns as measured by each message the librarian sent; (4) the number of student turns as measured by each message the student sent; (5) the number of librarian questions as measured by the number of question marks the librarian used; (6) the number of student questions as measured by the number of question marks the student used; (7) the strength of the librarian's social presence social presence as measured by the number of emoticons and exclamation marks the librarian used; and (8) the strength of the student's social presence as measured by the number of emoticons and exclamation marks the student used.

As for the first research question regarding "parity of participation," Pearson Correlation Coefficients were computed and descriptive statistics were generated for the six activity variables, which were turns taken, questions asked, and emoticons used by each of the two participants, the librarian and the student. The researcher also computed Pearson Correlation Coefficients to examine the second question regarding the number of questions and the length of the session. To answer the third question, the researcher conducted multiple regression tests. As for the fourth question, the researcher conducted a bivariate correlation coefficients test.

Limitations of the Quantitative Methodology

To measure the degree of engagement between the two participants in a session, the researcher used only turns taken, question marks, exclamation marks, and emoticons. Therefore, the results are conservative because the analyses do not account for all possible variables. For example, while reading transcripts, the researcher observed that in many instances the student or the librarian asked questions, as indicated by the grammar and/or context of the text, without the use of a question mark. These questions were not counted in this study because the scope of the quantitative methodology was to assess participation using only quantitative measures that could be counted objectively, without subjectivity. In addition, the researcher considered conventional uses of punctuation, such as exclamation marks, as well as the less conventional use of emoticons to be meaningful. The assumption was that, when using punctuation, including emoticons, the participants made deliberate choices that reflected their attitude toward the quality of the service and success of the session. The statistics in this chapter were an attempt to quantify this deliberation.

Results

As a first step in examining parity during a session, the researcher computed descriptive statistics for six variables that described the activities of the librarian and the student: the number of librarian turns taken, questions asked, and emoticons used, and the number of student turns, questions, and emoticons. Table 2.1 displays the means and standard deviations for these variables. On average, the librarian took 6.5 more turns and asked 3.5 more questions per session than the student did. Use of emoticons was more balanced, where the librarian used on average 1.28 emoticons and the student 1.11.

When comparing all librarians' activities to all of the students' activities, an imbalance between the two parties became more evident. As shown in Table 2.2, the librarian, who conducted an average of 23.34 actions per session, had a much stronger presence during the interaction than the student, who conducted an average of 15.14 actions per session.

Next, correlation coefficients were computed for the six activity variables. Using the Bonferroni approach to control for Type I error across the six correlations, a p value of less than .005 (.05/6 = .008) was required for significance. The results of the correlational analysis, which is presented in Table 2.3, showed that the greatest

Table 2.1. Descriptive Statistics for Participation Variables		
Participation Variables	**Means**	**Standard Deviations**
Librarian turns	18.06	15.69
Librarian questions	4.00	3.80
Librarian emoticons	1.28	2.10
Student turns	12.56	11.40
Student questions	1.47	1.67
Student emoticons	1.11	2.88

Table 2.2. Comparison of Total Amount of Participation between Librarian and Student				
Participation Variables	**Minimum**	**Maximum**	**Mean**	**Standard Deviation**
Librarian activities	1	148	23.34	19.63
Student activities	1	87	15.14	13.64

correlation was between the following three pairs of activities: librarian and student turns, $r(248) = .76$, $p = .00$, number of librarian turns and librarian questions, $r(248) = .74$, $p = .00$, and the number of student turns and librarian questions, $r(248) = .74$, $p = .00$. As for the weakest correlations, there was no statistically significant correlation between the number of emoticons the librarian used and the number of questions the student asked, $r(248) = .16$, $p > .08$. Significant bivariate correlations existed between the other pairs, but none exceeded a beta of greater than .49.

The second question looked at whether the number of questions the librarian and the student asked affected the length of the session. The researcher hypothesized that by informing the parties better, the number of questions asked would positively affect the efficiency of the sessions by shortening their overall length. The results did not support this hypothesis. The descriptive statistics showed a positive correlation between questions asked and the length of the session. A closer examination using a Pearson's Correlational Coefficients test showed a strong positive correlation between the number of questions the librarian asked and the length of the session, where $r(248) = .64$, $p = .00$. However, the number of questions the student asked did not display a high correlation with either the number of librarian questions, $r(248) = .39$, $p = .00$, nor session length, $r(248) = .34$, $p = .00$. The scatter plot in Figure 2.1 provides a visual representation of these correlations. The correlation between the length of the sessions and the number of librarian questions created a clearly delineated diagonal line from the

Table 2.3. Correlation Coefficients for Librarian and Student Activities					
	Librarian Turns	**Student Turns**	**Librarian Questions**	**Student Questions**	**Librarian Emoticons**
Student turns	.76				
Librarian questions	.74	.74			
Student questions	.38	.49	.39		
Librarian emoticons	.42	.44	.34	.16	
Student emoticons	.26	.34	.32	.40	.32

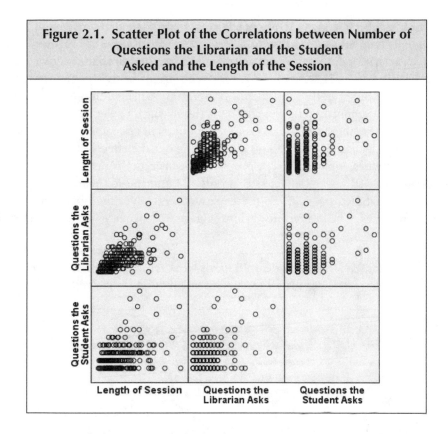

Figure 2.1. Scatter Plot of the Correlations between Number of Questions the Librarian and the Student Asked and the Length of the Session

bottom left corner to the top right, indicating a strong positive correlation. The two other correlations created strikingly vertical and horizontal lines.

The third research question asked whether the intensity of the student and the librarian engagement as measured by the number of turns each party took, the number of questions each asked, and the number of emoticons each used predicted the librarian's perception of session quality as measured by the librarian session-assessment index. The researcher hypothesized that the librarians would rate sessions that involved a great amount of activity more highly than those that did not. To test this hypothesis, two unordered multiple regression analyses were conducted. One analysis included the librarian activities—turns, questions, and emoticons, while the second analysis included the student activities—turns, questions, and emoticons.

The regression equation for the librarians' activities was significant, $R^2 = .04$, adjusted $R^2 = .03$, $F(3, 246) = 3.47$, $p < .05$. The regression equation for the student activities was not significant, $R^2 = .00$, adjusted $R^2 = -.01$, $F(3, 246) = .14$, $p = .94$. Based on these results, the librarian's activities had a greater effect on the librarian's assessment of the quality of the virtual reference session than the activities of the student. The librarians' activities predicted over and above the students' activities, R^2 change = .05, $F(3, 243) = 3.83$, $p = .01$. However the students' activities did not predict over and above the librarians' activities, R^2 change = .00, $F(3, 243) = .52$, $p = .67$. Of the librarians' activities, the emoticons index was the only significant measure of librarian satisfaction with the quality of the session. Supporting this conclusion is the strength of the bivariate correlation between the librarian emoticons and the librarian assessment of the quality of the session, which was .22, $p < .01$, partialling out the effects of the other two librarian activities, which was .20, $p < .01$. However, the betas for the librarian emoticons showed a weak effect size of only .22 and the R square showed that variable contributed only 4% to the dependent variable, the librarian session assessment index. The scatter plot below (Figure 2.2) provides a visual image of

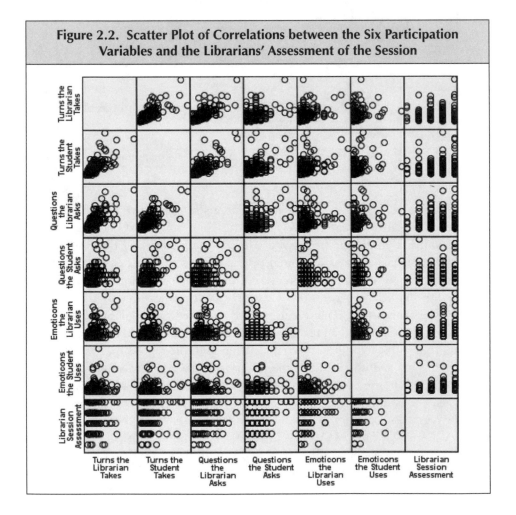

Figure 2.2. Scatter Plot of Correlations between the Six Participation Variables and the Librarians' Assessment of the Session

the lack of correlation between the librarians' assessment of a session and any of the activity variables, whether turns taken, questions asked, or emoticons used. The librarian session assessment is presented in the seventh column and again in the seventh row. The dots form completely parallel lines.

The last research question asked whether the length of the session predicted the librarians' perceptions of the quality of the session. The hypothesis was that the librarian would consider shorter sessions to be better than longer ones. To examine this question, the researcher conducted a bivariate correlation coefficients test. The test showed no correlation between the length of the session and the librarians' assessment of it, $r(248) = -.06$, $p = .37$. The scatter plot in Figure 2.3 displays a vivid representation.

Qualitative Method of Data Analysis

The method used to analyze the transcripts for qualitative evidence of power sharing was James Paul Gee's sociolinguistic approach to discourse analysis, which is based on his interpretation of "situated meanings." Gee (2005) says that "language-in-use both creates and reflects the context in which it is used." Meaning

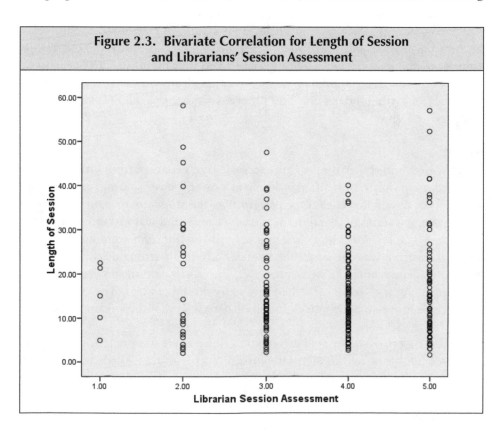

Figure 2.3. Bivariate Correlation for Length of Session and Librarians' Session Assessment

is derived from context. Gee illustrates his point with the word "coffee," the meaning of which changes depending on the context. For example, the word "coffee" in "The coffee spilled; get a mop" is very different from the word "coffee" in the sentence "The coffee spilled; get a broom" (p. 94).

Gee's approach also includes the concept of "negotiation." People negotiate meaning through their interaction with one another. Through social interaction, whole communities construct larger frameworks of meaning, which Gee calls Discourse models, with a capital "D." Therefore, when people of different communities engage in discourse, they create new meaning. Gee (2008) divides discourse into "primary" and "secondary Discourses," where the primary discourse is the language that one learns in the home while growing up, and the secondary discourse is that which one acquires outside the home through apprenticeships (p. 168).

The purpose of this qualitative section of the study was to identify the Discourse of the librarian and that of the student and then to examine where these Discourses intersected, power sharing occurred, and negotiation of meaning took place. Often the first and second year community college students are acquiring a secondary Discourse, the discourse of academia. In helping the student acquire this new discourse during a reference encounter, the librarian becomes a mentor and the student an apprentice. This study looked at this apprenticeship relationship. Gee (2005) outlined four main parts to his process. These were: (1) collection of data on an issue, (2) identification of key words and phrases, (3) relating these words and phrases to situations, and (4) validation of findings.

Results

From a preliminary reading of transcripts, five broad patterns of discourse emerged, each illustrating different levels of power, power sharing, and the construction of new knowledge. One pattern was the students' recognition of two Discourses: the vernacular and the academic. The second was instances where the Discourse of the student and the Discourse of the librarian were in alignment. The third pattern was one where the librarian asserted a strong teaching presence and the student exhibited a weak presence. The fourth pattern showed the librarian controlling the session and then gradually ceding control. The fifth pattern showed the librarian positioning himself or herself so that the student could take control of the session.

In the first pattern, the student recognized that there were two discourses and tried to align his or her familiar Discourse model with that of the librarian. An example of this first pattern is displayed in this pair of messages taken from a transcript. A student sent a message and then corrected herself with an immediate follow-up message:

Student: ty.

Student: Thank you.

The student wrote "ty" and then sent a second message in which she wrote out the whole word "thank you." The student rephrased her message to be more aligned with what she perceived to be the librarian's expectations. By conforming to a more formal, academic discourse model, the student consciously aligned her discourse with the academic discourse of the librarian.

A second pattern that emerged was the Discourse that the librarian and the student shared: the discourse of technology. For example, in many transcripts, the librarian helped a student access a proprietary database. In these transcripts, certain commonly understood words, such as "user id," "password," and "access," were repeated. Both parties used these terms fluently and seemed to be comfortable with this vocabulary. Therefore, because there was good discourse alignment, the student was able to access the database and solve the research problem.

A third pattern was the librarian-controlled session. These transcripts showed the librarian telling the student what search terms to use and which resources to search. The student was left with the opportunity to accept or reject the results of the librarian-driven search strategy.

A fourth pattern was less teacher-centered, where the librarian controlled portions of the session and ceded other portions. For example, in one transcript, the librarian initiated the research with a clear agenda. She told the student what to do and where to click. However, halfway through the session, the librarian relaxed a little and let the student share control. In the end, both the student and the librarian found many articles on the topic and began to compare their "finds." A certain parity, or balance of power, was established.

A fifth type of transcript was almost entirely student centered, where the librarian used minimal intervention. For example, in one transcript, the student asked which of two terms was used more frequently to refer to citizens of Michigan—Michiganders or Michiganians. In this transaction, the librarian and the student were using two different, parallel Discourse models: (1) the student was involved in a linguistic question and was thinking like a linguist, and (2) the librarian, thinking like a librarian, approached the question like any other reference question. Using the perspective of a linguist, the student asked the librarian which term he would use. Trained in librarianship, the librarian avoided giving his opinion but instead found Web sites for the student to study and analyze. In the end, the session was successful because the librarian provided the sources, but the student had to do the reading, make a comparison, and conduct an analysis to form her own answer. However, not for one teaching moment did the two Discourses intersect. Throughout the session they remained divergent.

Discussion of the Results

The quantitative measures showed that although librarians have a stronger presence than students, both parties participated actively in the virtual reference sessions. Librarians and students both asked and answered questions in an effort to connect cognitively and engage socially, all activities that were part of an effort to solve a research problem. However, the results of this study showed that despite these teaching and learning activities, there appeared to be very little quantitative evidence that librarians judged the quality of a session based on any of these variables. Therefore, although the literature suggested that there was a movement toward student empowerment, it could be that librarians continued to assess the quality and success of their work on the tradition of providing "an answer" to a question. Future studies should be conducted to find out what measure librarians use to assess the quality of their virtual reference sessions.

Focusing on the student activities in particular, the results showed that the student had a statistically weaker impact on the transaction than the librarian. Student questions had a relatively weak correlation with most of the factors, including the librarians' assessment of the session. Student emoticons correlated least with all of the variables. The answers to what these statistics mean cannot be addressed using quantitative measures. Rich qualitative studies are required. This chapter explored one approach that might be a useful tool in better understanding the dynamics in the relationship between the librarian and the student in a virtual reference environment.

Using Gee's approach to critical discourse analysis, an analysis of the transcripts revealed that students were willing to learn and engage in academic discourse with the librarian. This discourse included not only language on the surface level, such as grammar, spelling, and vocabulary, but also on the deeper level of higher order learning and critical thinking. It also showed that librarians were using instructional strategies where they relinquished their power to students so that the students could take on more of the responsibility for solving their research problems. The qualitative analysis contained in this chapter was only a preliminary study. More thorough analyses of the transcripts need to be conducted.

Implications for Practice

The quantitative statistics showed that the librarian had a much stronger presence than the student in the virtual reference sessions. This strength is good. A strong teaching presence is good. However, it is hoped that this chapter encourages librarians to use this strength to empower students in virtual reference environments so that they become assertive, independent learners rather than passive receptors of information. To better understand how virtual reference librarians can empower students in virtual reference environments, more qualitative analysis of transcripts needs to be done. However, the exploratory analysis in this chapter showed that some research questions were conducive to a student-centered approach that required students to search for, find, and evaluate information and then think critically to answer their research questions.

This study suggests that there are strategies and techniques that librarians can employ to guide students in taking the initiative to think through their research question. Without controlling the virtual reference transaction, librarians can use tactical scaffolding measures to nudge the students toward their goal. This chapter should encourage virtual reference librarians to develop teaching techniques that maximize the opportunities for students to participate in the learning process. One strategy to employ is for the virtual reference librarians to guide students in suggesting search terms. In many cases, the students have the best understanding of what they need in order to complete a given assignment because they have been preparing for and attending lectures and reading assignments, all of which are activities that give students access to the search terms they need. The librarian can help the students become aware of this knowledge and the way it can help them design a search strategy. In that way, both participants share in making the session a powerful learning environment.

Note

1. I want to express appreciation to Dr. Jaime Lester, Dr. Amy Adcock, Dr. Ishmail Said, Dr. Waheed Samy, and Ms. Leila Samy for their comments on my work. I would also like to thank Ann Walaskay and Debby Harris for their support and Sandy McCarthy for encouraging me to present my study at the Reference Renaissance Conference.

References

American Library Association. (2000). Information literacy competency standards for higher education. Retrieved April 22, 2009, from www.ala.org/ala/mgrps/divs/acrl/standards/standards.pdf.

Desai, C. M., & Graves, S. J. (2006). Instruction via instant messaging reference: What's happening? *The Electronic Library, 24*(2), 174–189.

Doherty, J. J. (2007, June). No shhing: Giving voice to the silenced: An essay in support of critical information literacy. *Library Philosophy and Practice*, 1–8. Retrieved from www.webpages.uidaho.edu/~mbolin/doherty2.pdf.

Doherty, J. J., & Ketchner, K. (2005). Empowering the intentional learner: A critical theory for information literacy instruction. *Library Philosophy and Practice, 8*(1), 1–10. Retrieved from www.webpages.uidaho.edu/~mbolin/doherty-ketchner.pdf.

Ellis, L. A. (2004). Approaches to teaching through digital reference. *Reference Services Review, 32*(2), 103–119.

Elmborg, J. (2006). Critical information literacy: Implications for instructional practice. *The Journal of Academic Librarianship, 32*(2), 192–199.

Gee, J. P. (2005). *An introduction to discourse analysis* (2nd ed.). New York: Routledge.

Gee, J. P. (2008). *Social linguistics and literacies: Ideology in discourses* (3rd ed.). New York: Routledge.

Jonassen, D. (1999). Designing constructivist learning environments. In C. M. Reigeluth (Ed.), *Instructional-design theories and models* (Vol. II, pp. 215–239). Mahwah, NJ: London: Lawrence Erlbaum.

Lankes, R. D. (2005). Digital reference research: Fusing research and practice. *Reference and User Services Quarterly, 44*(4), 320–326.

Lee, I. J. (2004). Do virtual reference librarians dream of digital reference questions? A qualitative and quantitative analysis of email and chat reference. *Australian Academic and Research Libraries, 35*(2), 95–110.

Simmons, M. H. (2005). Librarians as disciplinary discourse mediators: Using genre theory to move toward critical information literacy. *Portal: Libraries and the Academy, 5*(3), 297–311.

Swanson, T. A. (2004). A radical step: Implementing a critical information literacy model. *Portal: Libraries and the Academy, 4*(2), 259–273.

Ward, D. (2004). Measuring the completeness of reference transactions in online chats. *Reference and User Services Quarterly, 44*(1), 46–52.

Westbrook, L. (2006). Virtual reference training: The second generation. *College and Research Libraries, 67*(3), 249–259.

Woodward, B. S. (2005). One-on-one instruction: From the reference desk to online chat. *Reference and User Services Quarterly, 44*(3), 203–209.

CHAPTER 3

Giving Users Options for Chat Reference: Effects of QuestionPoint's Instant Message Widget on Chat Traffic

Virginia Cole

Overview

This chapter discusses the effects of adding an instant message (IM) service to an existing chat service (using full-featured chat software) at Cornell University. Implementation, staff experiences, and training are briefly discussed. IM interactions are statistically and qualitatively compared with those of full-featured chat. Initial staff reports of increased total traffic were not supported by actual statistics. In contrast to other libraries, adding IM did not increase overall traffic. Traffic remained at a consistent level, but 30–50 percent of users shifted from full-featured chat to IM. A comparative analysis of transcripts showed fewer differences between the two modes than expected. Users seemed to favor IM for briefer questions and full-featured chat for lengthy, in-depth research questions. Raising the visibility of IM on library Web pages in order to grow traffic continues to be a goal.

Introduction

This chapter will compare two modes of chat reference—full-featured chat, which requires patron login and has cobrowsing (librarian and user view and use the same Web page simultaneously) and the capability of pushing of Web pages (the Web page opens automatically for the user), and instant message service, which requires no patron login but has no cobrowse or pushing of Web pages.

In the literature and at conferences, many libraries have reported great success and increased traffic by offering an IM reference service (Kern, 2002). I was most impressed by those libraries that offered their users choices for their reference chat interaction—a vendor full-featured chat in addition to or supplemented by IM. In the past, offering IM required devising manual strategies for capturing statistics and transcripts. At Cornell, my colleagues and I were intrigued and convinced by success stories but were concerned about the additional manual labor, supervision, and staff training required to launch and maintain an IM service. In the current climate of declining reference questions, we believe accurate reference statistics are more important than ever. We've also found that ongoing routine transcript review is crucial to high-quality chat reference service. We were reluctant to divert staff time and energy to create a homegrown IM reference service.

Thus we were delighted when our current chat software provider, Online Computer Library Center (OCLC) QuestionPoint, provided us with a Meebo-like IM widget, affectionately referred to as a qwidget. Like Meebo and other IM widgets, the qwidget can easily be placed on any Web page by means of html code provided by QuestionPoint. For the user, it's immediate. It's a "see it, begin typing" approach—no login required. In addition, the Meebo-like box meant the user saw an icon, a graphic, and thus it was far more visible and eye-catching than an Ask-a-Librarian link.

Implementation

Cornell is a large academic university with 17 libraries at its Ithaca, New York, campus and approximately 20,000 students. We began offering reference services over chat in 1999 for just four hours a day Monday through Friday. Over the years, we migrated through several different kinds of software and added more hours of service. Currently we staff our chat service at least 37 hours a week and often as much as 57 hours a week. As of 2007, we were able to offer 24/7 reference service through participation in QuestionPoint's 24/7 academic cooperative. In addition to expanding service hours, we also wanted to explore adding more and different types of virtual access to reference services.

QuestionPoint made the IM qwidget available to its chat subscribers at the beginning of March 2008. At Cornell, past experience demonstrated that a phased deployment of new services works well. Consequently we launched our new IM service quietly and slowly. We first placed the IM qwidget on lower level Web pages such as our course-related guides (http://guides.library.cornell.edu) on March 10. We knew that a relatively small number of patrons would come across the IM qwidget and thus we could easily control traffic and ease into the new service.

Low visibility of the IM qwidget allowed staff to gain experience with the new service and to troubleshoot, test, and practice. The only real challenge in the first few weeks of the IM qwidget's existence was user curiosity. Users saw a box on a Web page and, wondering whether it worked, typed, "Hi is anyone there?" and then promptly disappeared. Reference staff were encouraged to test and practice with the qwidget, and they often pretended to be users to see how the qwidget worked. These practice transcripts appeared in our transcripts and had to later be manually recoded as practice or test and weeded from valid transcripts so that we could maintain accurate statistics. This was easily remedied by reminding staff to resolve, or code, IM qwidget sessions appropriately. We were happy to discover no technical issues with the IM qwidget—it was robust and problem-free for both users and staff.

After a short period of testing and experimentation, we began raising the visibility of the IM qwidget. On April 22, the beginning of the peak reference traffic season at the end of the spring semester and finals, we made the IM qwidget available on the library homepage Ask a Librarian (www.library.cornell.edu/ask). As a newer service, the qwidget option, which we called "Instant Message," was at the bottom of the page. Users had to scroll down to see it. Over the next few weeks, we tweaked the text and options on the Ask a Librarian page to raise the visibility of the qwidget. Finally at 3:12 p.m. on May 2, 2008, we succeeded in getting the IM qwidget to appear above the browser fold on all but the smallest computer screens so that it would be immediately visible to any user visiting the page. At 3:13 p.m. we received an IM qwidget.

An examination of the referring URLs, the link from which a chat or IM qwidget originated, in transcripts for the spring of 2008 shows that 98 percent of both chat and IM qwidget originated on the library homepage Ask a Librarian, 1.8 percent originated on one of the campus libraries' homepage, and only .2 percent originated on other Web pages such as course guides. Continuing to make the IM qwidget more visible on library Web pages is a goal for the future.

Chat and IM Qwidget Traffic Compared

Other libraries around the country have reported great increases in overall chat traffic when they added the IM qwidget to library Web pages (Furata, 2008; Pardue, 2008; Tomas, 2008). We did not experience quite the same dramatic increases to our overall chat traffic by adding an instant message service at Cornell. Our results were mixed. There were anecdotal staff reports that our traffic increased, a topic I'll return to in more depth in the next section. But a review of our statistics showed gains in our chat traffic came from extending our hours of service through the 24/7 cooperative, which increased our total chat traffic by 30–50 percent depending on the time of the year. At this time the IM qwidget is "open" only for local traffic, for Cornell users coming in through the Cornell queue. The IM qwidget does not feed into a cooperative queue. At times when no Cornell librarian is monitoring chat, generally weekday late evenings and weekends, the IM qwidget is not available to users and an automated message directs users to the 24/7 cooperative full-featured chat.

At Cornell, an examination of our local traffic indicates that adding the IM qwidget did not increase our traffic; our traffic remained at the same levels as before implementation. The chart below shows only Cornell users answered only

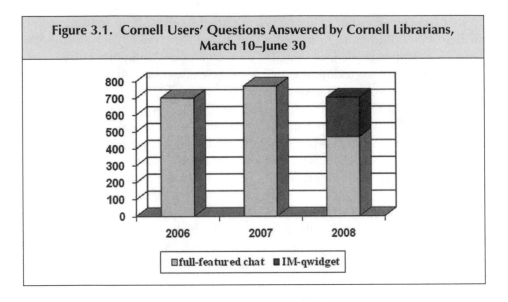

Figure 3.1. Cornell Users' Questions Answered by Cornell Librarians,
March 10–June 30

by Cornell librarians March 10–June 30, 2006, 2007, to 2008; it does not include Cornell users assisted by cooperative librarians. Thirty-three percent of our users chose the IM qwidget rather than full-featured chat.

This suggests that users who chose the IM qwidget would have used full-featured chat if it had been the only option, but, provided with choices, many users preferred the no-login ease and immediate typing of the IM qwidget.

Focusing more closely on the peak period of the last weeks of classes and finals period, April 28 to May 16, 2008, the period when we began making the qwidget more visible, even more users, 48 percent of the 167 Cornell users helped by Cornell librarians chose the IM qwidget over full-featured chat. The IM qwidget continued to slowly gain in popularity over the summer and early fall. From June to September 2008, 52 percent of users chose the IM qwidget.

Staff Experiences and the Trauma Effect

Because the IM qwidgets appear in the same librarian interface as full-featured chat, little staff training was required. Only a few key differences needed to be highlighted. The word "qwidget" appears in front of the initial user question or statement, which alerts staff to remember to tell the user to click on a link to open it rather than the link opening automatically and that the user's e-mail address is not part of the user information that the system automatically provides. Agile twenty-first century reference staff adapted to these slight differences quickly.

As mentioned previously, staff reported lots of additional chat traffic due to the IM qwidget. Accordingly, I carefully scrutinized spring 2008 traffic for traffic "spikes"—more than one chat at a time handled by the same librarian. Our spring 2008 finals were nine days long. Eight of those days experienced at least one traffic spike; three of the days experienced multiple spikes. However, it was the first day of study period, Monday, May 5, that seemed to produce what I'll term a staff "trauma effect." The day was busy, particularly in the afternoon. Seventeen chats and IM qwidgets came in between 12:00 and 5:00 p.m., ten of which were spikes: three spikes of two simultaneous—one completely IM qwidget, two mixed IM qwidget and chat, one completely chat—and two spikes of three simultaneous—one completely IM qwidget and one mixed IM and chat. Needless to say, May 5 was stressful for staff who were on chat duty. They were somewhat traumatized by the heavy traffic. Even more importantly, word of heavy IM qwidget traffic quickly spread causing anxiety and dread in those staff who hadn't been involved. The trauma lingered in the memories and gossip of staff for months. However, close analysis of traffic showed such spikes were not unusual and were not caused entirely by the new IM qwidget. During the 2007 study period, before we implemented the IM qwidget, there were also days of similar heavy traffic with similar spikes of multiple, simultaneous chats. When the results of this analysis of IM qwidget traffic was disseminated, it helped to ease staff anxiety.

User Perceptions

In order to get a sense of why users might prefer the IM qwidget over chat, I evaluated and compared transcripts from peak traffic periods in the spring of 2008. I used several different criteria to compare user behavior in full-featured chat and the IM qwidget: length of transaction, type of question, linguistic indicators of hurry and abrupt departures, openings, indicators of preference for anonymity, and satisfaction reported in an exit survey.

A common assumption among librarians seems to be that one reason users choose chat over in-person is because users believe it's quicker. A corollary of this assumption is that instant message, which has its own culture of quickness signified by its characteristic abbreviations and emoticons, is thought to be even a faster means of communication than full-featured chat. As one method of understanding user chat preferences and behaviors, I compared the length of transaction.

In neither mode was an interaction ever less than two minutes. The majority of IM qwidgets were less than 8 minutes, though many lasted 20 minutes, and a few lasted for one hour or more. In comparison, the majority of full-featured chats fell in the 12–24 minutes range. Compared to IM, more full-featured chats lasted for more than an hour. The comparison confirms that many users choose IM for shorter interactions.

A comparison by type of question asked in chat and IM qwidget provides a fuller understanding of user choices and expectations (see Figure 3.3). The chart

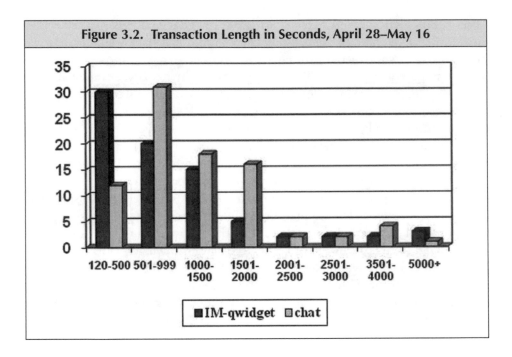

Figure 3.2. Transaction Length in Seconds, April 28–May 16

in Figure 3.3 shows type of question organized on a loose continuum—quick questions such as directional at the top, holdings and access questions in the middle, and longest questions such as instruction (cases in which the patron

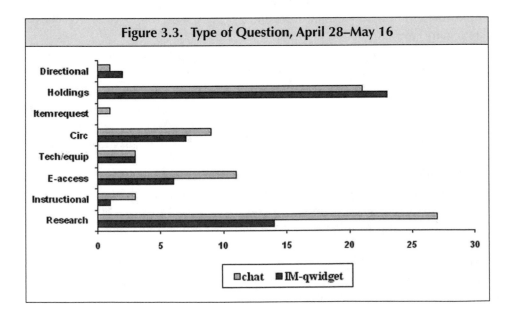

Figure 3.3. Type of Question, April 28–May 16

clearly asked for instruction using such phrases as "how do I . . . ?") and in-depth research at the bottom. Few quick, directional questions are asked either in full-featured chat or the IM qwidget. Questions about holdings, especially about issues of a particular journal in the search for a specific article, were, and continue to be, the most common type of question in both modes. There was definite user preference for using the IM qwidget for questions that both users and staff might consider quicker—holdings, item requests, circulation. While a substantial number of IM qwidget questions were in-depth research questions, there seems to be clear user preference for full-featured chat for in-depth research-related questions and other types of questions that generally take longer, such as electronic access issues and instructional.

Generally speaking, reference staff are trained to do their best to answer all questions whether they believe the mode the user chose for asking is appropriate or not for the question. Reference staff at Cornell are trained to do their best to answer, or at least get the user started, with all types of questions, from the quick to the long, from the directional to in-depth dissertation research, over whatever mode the user originally chose for asking the question. However, the two charts suggest that many Cornell users are quite savvy about the kind of question they're asking and have realistic expectations about the length of time an answer might take. They often chose to invest a bit more energy in asking their question by logging in to full-featured chat for lengthier questions.

Transcript Analysis

I examined the text of both full-featured chat and IM qwidget transcripts for other indications of user behavior and preferences. Again my sample consisted of all transcripts, 167 Cornell users answered by Cornell librarians, from April 28 to May 16, 2008, which was the last weeks of classes, study period, and finals. This was a particularly good period to sample since typically users are exhausted, tense, and stressed by the end of the long academic year. Accordingly, I looked for situational and urgency indicators in the transcripts such as abrupt departures, hurry statements, highly abbreviated language or "IM/texting-speak," openings, and anonymity preferences. I also looked at satisfaction exit surveys.

I classified abrupt departure in a transcript as no closure from the user, no thanks from the user, and/or staff saying "I haven't heard from you in a while." In my sample, 2 percent of IM qwidget transcripts exhibited such characteristics in comparison, with 1.5 percent of full-featured chat transcripts. It's hardly a statistically valid difference, but it may suggest IM qwidget users may feel slightly more pressed for time.

I looked for statements indicating user hurry in the transcripts but didn't find enough in my small sample to count. I glimpsed only occasional indications of a user's emotional state. In full-featured chat, one user said, "i can wait" when the librarian asked if the user had time. In two IM qwidget cases I saw "I have to go now" and "My rough draft is due 2morrow. Thx." Note the IM speak in lower case "i" in the chat transcript and the "2tomorrow" and "Thx" of the IM qwidget transcripts. These samples are representative of the use of IM/texting speak in our transcripts that I would characterize as slight and sprinkled throughout both full-featured chat as well as the IM qwidget interactions. Further sophisticated textual analysis might show a slight difference between the two modes, but after reading hundreds of transcripts, my sense is that our users at Cornell speak slightly more formal language to chat with a librarian than they would with friends or family, mirroring, I believe, the friendly but professional tone most Cornell chat practitioners try to adopt.

I also compared the openings between full-featured chat and the IM qwidget. After the first few weeks of staff testing and user curiosity, IM qwidget openings were in most cases not distinguishable from full-featured chat openings. Occasionally, a user still opens with "how ya doing?" in an IM qwidget, so staff have to be continually reminded to treat even the most nonchalant opening as a real question. (In this particular case, the user needed help finding sources for a research paper.)

Another somewhat common assumption by librarians is that users prefer the anonymity of IM. In my sample of transcripts, I did not find any evidence to support this assumption. Occasionally users identified themselves in an IM qwidget in their opening "I am faculty...." In other cases, users volunteered information during the transaction "Could you send me an e-mail when you find any? My e-mail is...." As part of their chat training, when an interaction in the IM qwidget becomes involved and in-depth, staff are encouraged to request an e-mail from the user in case the user gets disconnected or accidentally closes a window. In those cases when an e-mail address was requested, the request was always granted.

I also combed our transcripts for other indications of user perceptions and experiences with the two virtual reference modes. I came across a handful of interesting patterns of disconnections, when the user accidentally closed the chat or navigated away thus severing the connection between user and librarian. In my spring 2008 sample, most times when users disconnected they chose the same format to reconnect. However, in two cases, users accidentally disconnected themselves from the IM qwidget and chose to reconnect through full-featured chat. In comparison, there was only one case of disconnecting from full-featured chat and switching to the IM qwidget. Admittedly the number is small, but it suggests that users might consider full-featured chat to be slightly more technically robust.

An exit survey of five brief questions pops up at the end of every chat and IM transaction:

1. I received a better answer from this resource than I would have found on my own.
2. Was this service easy to use?
3. This is a needed service and should be continued.
4. Were you satisfied with the answer you received to your reference question?
5. The quality of the library staff service in answering this request was?

For years, our survey results have been consistently positive, and the spring of 2008 was no exception. In my spring 2008 sample, 8 percent of IM qwidget users completed the survey for a total of 11 surveys. Eight rated the staff as excellent and nine rated their answer as satisfactory. Six users wrote comments:

"Incredibly helpful!"
"It was very helpful! I was able to find what I needed so I didn't have to go to campus. Great assistance, thanks!"
"Helped me with my project!"

In comparison, users of full-featured chat completed slightly more surveys (9 percent for a total of ten surveys). Satisfaction rates were slightly higher: all ten rated staff as excellent, and nine rated the answer as satisfactory. But users of full-featured chat took the time to make only one comment. The single comment was from a repeat user "whenever I use this service, I reached a solution I need at the end of my chat...."

It's possible the slightly higher satisfaction rate with full-featured chat was due to factors such as users not being in as much of a hurry, staff being more comfortable and not feeling pressured to hurry and users having realistic expectations about the amount of time an answer might take. The number of comments suggests a different interpretation; six of the users who completed the 11 IM qwidget surveys took the time to type out comments.

In conclusion, we found the IM qwidget easy to implement and easy for both users and staff to use. Our traffic indicates many users like the fast, no-login ease of the IM qwidget. As with other reference services, visibility of the service is a key factor in success—"If they see it, they will use it." Here at Cornell, we will be working on ways to make the IM qwidget far more visible on our Ask a Librarian page, course guides, and subject guides; we will also be working to add it to more library Web pages.

References

Furata, K. (2008, August). Effects of Qwidget on traffic at University of California, Riverside [listserv]. Retrieved August 10, 2008, from http://listserv.oclc.org/scripts/wa.exe?LIST=QUESTIONPOINT-L.

Kern, K. (2002, July). Comment on University of Illinois at Urbana-Champaign IM service. Presented at the American Library Association Reference and User Services Association President's Program, "The Future of Reference," June 14–June 17, Atlanta, Georgia.

Pardue, B. (2008, August). Effects of Qwidget on traffic at Arlington Public Library [list-serv]. Retrieved August 10, 2008, from http://listserv.oclc.org/scripts/wa.exe?LIST= QUESTIONPOINT-L.

Tomas, T. (2008, August). Effects of Qwidget on traffic at Seattle Public Library [listserv]. Retrieved August 10, 2008, from http://listserv.oclc.org/scripts/wa.exe?LIST= QUESTIONPOINT-L.

Approaches, Values, and Philosophy of Reference Services

CHAPTER 4

Unconscious Cognition in the Genesis of Reference Queries

Glynn Harmon and Lynn Westbrook

Overview

Unconscious cognition is defined herein as that portion of mental content and processing unavailable to immediate awareness but that affects thought and inquiry. Up to about four-fifths of our cognition resides at unconscious levels and a fifth at conscious or awareness levels. Yet, most information professionals tend to assume that inquiry is driven by conscious cognition. Unconscious cognition plays a major role in queries that involve interplay with personal values.

Introduction

This review focuses on experimental findings about the elicitation of unconscious cognition during in-depth inquiry through the use of an information counseling approach with the aid of a programmed relaxation device (audiovisual integrator) and electroencephalographic (EEG) technology. Following multiple pilot studies, a controlled experiment was conducted on 36 participants randomly assigned to experimental and control groups. All participants first drafted a question related to a personal problem. The experimental group was subjected to relaxation entrainment via the audiovisual integrator to induce deep relaxation, which was confirmed by EEG readings (a theta or low alpha brainwave state ranging between 4-14 Hz or cycles per second). The control group had an unprogrammed interlude. Both groups then reworked their questions. The experimental group showed marked increases in intuition, insight, ideas, affect, and conceptual fluidity, whereas the control group did not. Using a single factor ANOVA, the null hypothesis of no significant difference between groups was rejected at the .05 confidence level.

Future traditional or electronic reference services, as well as embedded informationist roles, might well involve the elicitation of information needs that are deeply embedded in individual's unconscious cognition. Additionally, future reference and informationist roles could be expanded to embrace nearly all societal and research functions and endeavors.

Research Problem

The purpose of this research review is to explore the influence of unconscious cognition in the genesis of reference queries in various settings and circumstances. Its key thrust is to report on earlier and subsequent experimental findings related to the dynamics of unconscious cognition in the genesis of and transformation of queries, as such queries emerge from unconscious cognition and become explicitly recognized and consciously articulated. The basic hypothesis that drove these experiments is that unconscious cognition plays a key role in the framing of inquiry, and that its influence persists throughout the entire inquiry and research cycle. The review concludes with a discussion of implications for creating a future reference renaissance.

While many reference queries seek to obtain day-to-day factual information, others seek to help solve problems that involve the clarification of personal values that arise in personal or group problem solving. For example, value-oriented questions are those involving career direction, where to live, or various other existential dilemmas. As Robert Taylor (1968) noted in his now classic article "Question Negotiation and Information Seeking in Libraries," such value-oriented queries evolve from unconscious or subconscious cognitions that reside beneath our immediate awareness and yet affect thinking and behavior. Such queries tend to transform into negotiated, explicit question formats as they emerge from unconscious levels into consciousness or awareness.

The literature review that follows provides evidence derived from linguistic studies that about four-fifths of our cognition resides at unconscious levels, beyond immediate awareness, and about a fifth resides at conscious levels, of which we are immediately aware. The ratio of consciousness to unconsciousness is not exact, however, and can vary according to individual cognitive differences and habits, possession of domain knowledge, analytical purpose, time pressures, relaxation states, and other factors. Additionally, the notion that unconscious and conscious cognition are distinctly different and separate phenomena appears to be yielding to more recent findings that both may profitably be modeled as complementary parts of overall consciousness, and that the two can be mutually and dynamically interactive during inquiry and problem solving. Also, different basic approaches to the study of unconsciousness have developed in recent years, each of which employs different assumptions, methodologies, and terminologies. The contemporary approaches include the biological evolution of consciousness, the cognitive and computational approaches, psychodynamics, and neurophysiological approaches.

The experimental research reported herein draws primarily on studies conducted by the lead author and his doctoral student, a public reference librarian (Ballesteros, 1995; Harmon & Ballesteros, 1997). During the course of the experiments described in this chapter, it was demonstrated that if users are given the opportunity to undergo deep relaxation through the use of various methods, such as a programmed relaxation device (audiovisual integrator), their unconscious cognition becomes mobilized to help them articulate the true nature of their underlying problems and to ask the "right" questions.

For a true renaissance in reference services to occur, there is a need to acknowledge the role of unconscious cognition in the genesis of reference queries and to adjust reference interaction protocols accordingly. Perhaps a true profession of information counseling might emerge, with capability to help clientele clarify their true problems and adjust their query articulation. Future human-computer interfaces and information counseling practices might well incorporate biofeedback and other means of relaxation.

Significance of Problem

As stated earlier, unconscious cognition appears to play a major role in the genesis of value-oriented reference queries, and this role suggests some corresponding implications for creating a future reference renaissance. Throughout the history of the reference interview in library and other settings, information seekers have been reported as being unable to express their information needs in a sufficiently explicit manner for the reference or information specialist to interpret and help to satisfy those needs. One explanation for the poor formulation or even misrepresentation of underlying information needs, via specious, spurious, and vague questions (in addition to subject area unfamiliarity) might be the result of a lack of inquirers' direct access to their own deeply embedded, unconscious, information needs. If only consciously expressed needs for information are dealt with, the underlying information needs or problems may either be ignored or only partially solved. Furthermore, attempts to address only those queries that are expressed verbally may treat the symptoms of the underlying problem rather than the true problem itself. Such attempts can even give the illusion of problem resolution and hence be misleading, counterproductive, or even dangerous in some circumstances.

Nevertheless, information professionals and researchers have tended to base their study, design, and rendering of information services on the assumption that the process of inquiry resides at conscious levels of cognition—those of which we are conveniently aware. The existence and impact of a relatively large, submerged unconscious cognition, which is not quickly available to awareness and tends to be ignored or assumed away, might well be acknowledged in our reference and information-seeking endeavors. Furthermore, whether we deal with electronic or face-to-face reference or research support, the phenomenon of unconscious cognition appears to be embedded heavily in the human psyche. Unconscious cognition continues to influence our curiosity and framing of queries, our handling of acquired information, and our subsequent behavioral responses.

Literature Review

Question Negotiation

Throughout the history of the reference interview, information seekers are often viewed as being unable to express their information needs in a sufficiently explicit manner for the information specialist or reference librarian to interpret and help satisfy those needs. For example, Green (1876) noted in *Library Journal* that "the librarian should be placed at the point of first contact with the patron and from this vantage point could listen to the perhaps halting and often inchoate ramblings, and through interviewing help the patron bring some order out of his confusion" (p. 74). Eleanor Woodruff commented on this difficulty in an article published in *Library Journal* in 1897: "The famous dictum—speech was given to man to conceal thought—is often forcibly brought to mind by the ingenuity with which visitors to the reference room succeed in hiding their desires behind their questions" (Woodruff, 1897, p. 65). James Wyer (1930), writing on reference work in 1930, referred to the "invincible inarticulateness of the inquirer" (p. 100) and quoted an earlier librarian, E.V. Wilcox, as saying, "You will see that they will choke to death and die with the secret in them rather than tell you what they want" (Wilcox, 1922, p. 477). Wyer (1930) included mind reading as an integral part of the reference process and stated, "The art of mind-reading, then, is to know how to give people what they do not know they want. . . . Have you hit upon any interesting or effective methods of persuading the reader to tell you what he wants?" (pp. 101, 114).

The more contemporary writers who address the nature of reference processes and information seeking echo concerns similar to those of their predecessors. As mentioned earlier, Taylor (1968) was among the first of scholars in information studies to make explicit the presence and impact of emerging "unexpressed and visceral" information needs, even though he did not therein directly address the topic of the unconscious. Belkin (1980) proffered his anomalous states of knowledge (ASK) model to represent the underlying, inexplicit information need structures of users and discussed potential interactive retrieval system designs to map such anomalous structures. Kuhlthau (1993) demonstrated that the deeper emotional effects of uncertainty in the initial stages of inquiry could influence searching outcomes significantly. Dewdney and Michell (1997) provide a rigorous discussion about the controversial use of "why" questions during question negotiation processes. Obviously, such why questions can embarrass users who seek information about personal matters, such as medical problems, or can provoke resentment or defensiveness. These authors address cognitively embedded linguistic and psychological mechanisms at play in the reference interview and come very close to directly addressing the role of unconscious cognition. Radford (1999) addresses the in-depth dimensions of the reference encounter through critical incident and content analysis and discusses various individual and two-way psychological dynamics involved in reference transactions. These psychological dynamics include stress from time pressures and technology use; nonverbal communications; attitudes; the perceived quality of relationships; attitudinal factors; self-disclosure; emotional concomitants, such as anger and sexual attraction; and even the Hawthorne effect (to be discussed later). Bopp and Smith (2001) view question negotiation as the most important stage of the reference interview and suggest the use of several techniques for negotiating questions: encourage the user to discuss and elaborate on the query, engage in neutral questioning, listen actively and provide encouragement, and even carefully ask why the information will be needed. Nahl and Bilal (2007), among others, have extended the affective paradigm through their compilation of discussions about understanding the emotional aspects of information seeking and revised system design strategies. Fields (2006) addresses the problem of dealing with ill structured problems during the course of reference interviews. Numerous other authors advocate the use of various indirect strategies to elicit deeply embedded information needs, such as unstructured interviewing, subtle questioning, and reading the nonverbal cues of information seekers (Cassell & Hiremath, 2006). Nevertheless, within the circles of information professionalism the significant impact of unconscious cognition in information seeking continues to be unacknowledged or only partially recognized.

Perhaps a key difficulty in the resolution of question negotiation is one of context. Traditional library reference services have for the most part been located within libraries rather than embedded in usage environments of information seekers. In her remarkable but somewhat dated book, Neway (1985) advocates a greatly expanded role for information specialists as proactive members of research teams, teams that operate within offices, laboratories, industrial and service settings, corporations, medical clinics, consulting firms, legislative bodies, and other environments. Likewise, the recent emergence of the informationist concept and role in health care and research, and a variety of other areas, underscores the importance of context-embedded information services. In a landmark systematic review of 113 papers on the informationist concept, Rankin, Grefsheim, and Cato (2008) conclude that several factors contribute to success, particularly in point-of-care health settings: the context-embedded provision of services, possession of domain knowledge, and continuous learning. One implication of their review is that embedded information services can automatically provide implicit and explicit cues about information needs, including unconscious cognitive dimensions. Efforts to provide embedded information service regimes, coupled with greater attention to unconscious cognition, should contribute to a reference renaissance.

Unconscious Cognition

To deal with unconscious cognition in information professionalism, it is necessary to understand the phenomena of unconsciousness and its implications more thoroughly. Unconscious cognition appears to be deeply rooted in our biological, evolutionary history, which extends back to evolutionary antiquity. In an extensive review of the evolutionary development of consciousness, Reber (1992) concludes that unconsciousness antedates explicit consciousness, the capacity of organisms for immediate awareness and control of mental processes. While debates about the nature of unconsciousness extend back to ancient philosophers, discussions on the topic became more focused and intense during the late 1800s and throughout the twentieth century. For example, William James (1902) noted,

> Our rational consciousness, as we call it, is but one special type of consciousness, whilst all about it, parted from it by the filmiest of screens, there lie potential forms of consciousness entirely different. We may go through life without suspecting their existence, but apply the requisite stimulus, and at a touch they are there in all completeness, definite types of mentality which probably somewhere have their field of application and adaptation. No account of the universe in its totality can be final which leaves these other forms of consciousness quite disregarded. (p. 298)

A study of the history and origins of the unconscious reveals two major schools of thought. The first is often termed the *psychodynamic unconscious* as interpreted by Freud, which had its origins in primitive medicine and folk psychology (Ellenberger, 1970). The second, the experiential or cognitive unconscious as interpreted by contemporary cognitive scientists and psychologists, traces its roots back to the Greek and other early philosophers (Schacter, 1987). The concept of the unconscious cognition can be defined briefly as "those cognitive contents and processes existing in the cognitive system at some point in time and actively influencing ongoing cognition and action of which the person is not aware" (Kihlstrom, 1984, p. 155).

The two concepts of dynamic and cognitive unconscious are now being viewed within the wider framework of consciousness, which is one of the central issues in mainstream psychology. These concepts are also currently the subject of debate in anthropology, biology, cognitive science, computer science, neuroscience, psychopathology, philosophy, physics, physiology, and many other disciplines. Hampden-Turner (1981) provides 60 separate (although somewhat dated) maps of the mind that can be particularly useful in helping information counselors understand the dynamics of inquiry. To understand the interplay between consciousness and unconsciousness, Shevrin, Bond, Brakel, Hertel, and Williams (1996) synthesize numerous clinical and experimental findings. They conclude by distinguishing between psychodynamic (essentially clinical, psychotherapeutic) and cognitive (computational) approaches to the study of the *mind* and neurophysiological approaches to the study of the *brain*. The mind is said to extend throughout an individual's body and environment, while the brain refers to the body's central nervous system. Reports in *Advances in Consciousness Research* (Volumes 1–63; 1995–2007) deal with a very wide range of topics: the evolution of consciousness, imagery cognition, emotional substrates, quantum brain dynamics, the a-conceptual mind, the stratification of consciousness, individual differences, psychopathology, narrative intelligence, tone of voice and mind intonation, exploring inner experience, and higher order theories of consciousness. Additional recent findings include those of Jonides and others (2008), who provide a comprehensive review of the dynamics of human short-term memory (explicit, working memory). Short-term memory is embedded primarily within conscious cognition but interacts with long-term memory, which is embedded in unconsciousness, since we are not immediately aware of its content. Both short-term and long-term memories are used in problem-solving and decision-making tasks. Focused attention, they conclude, tends to deploy one cognitive chunk at a time. Their conclusions provide a number of implications for studying the nature of individual query formation, since initial queries tend to be pointed and vague and too brief to express underlying information needs.

In whatever way that unconscious cognition is defined, its impact on human thought continues to be regarded as crucial. An analogy initially attributed to Freud describes conscious thought as merely representing the "tip of the iceberg" of the entire realm of consciousness and that all of the rest below the waterline corresponds to the unconscious. Psycholinguistic research into "implicit knowledge," often a synonym for the unconscious, suggests that unconscious cognition may comprise a major part of total cognition. As little as 15 percent of human knowledge appears to reside in the conscious realm, with the remaining 85 percent consisting of implicit knowledge (Graesser & Goodman, 1985). Last, in addition to scientific and philosophical investigations of unconsciousness, recent popular works have served to bring about greater public awareness of unconscious influences in everyday life. Gladwell (2005), for example, provides a wealth of anecdotes within which the opaque barrier between conscious and unconscious thought can subtly but drastically impact our day-to-day attitudes, choices, and behaviors. But, as previously discussed, this 15:85 percent ratio of consciousness to unconsciousness can vary, depending on such factors as individual cognitive and behavioral differences between individuals, possession of expertise or domain knowledge, and other contingencies. Unconsciousness can be modeled against consciousness as separate phenomena, but with various kinds and degrees of interplay rather than as fixed or dichotomous entities.

Method of Data Collection

The experimental study adopted the main ideas from reference interviewing and knowledge counseling because their approach and techniques were conducive to exploring the unconscious aspects of inquiry. However, this study went farther in that it stipulated that the subject or inquirer should be in a highly relaxed mental state, one in which access to full-brain thinking (left and right cerebral hemispheres, front/back, and lower/upper brain areas) has been achieved, wherein unconscious cognition may have a greater impact on mental activity and behavior.

The principal methods used in psychology and psychiatry to probe the unconscious include hypnosis, narcosis, dream analysis, free association, biofeedback, projective techniques, and the experimental production of neurosis. Research in biofeedback technology and the psychology of consciousness has served to produce sound and light machines that can induce a "frequency following" or "entrainment" effect in the brain. The term *entrainment* refers to the tendency of the brain waves to synchronize with external stimulation, and this entrainment of the electrical activity of the brain leads to different mental states or altered states of consciousness. Different brain wave patterns have been found to be associated with different states of awareness. The theta state, in which the participant is very relaxed, lies between about 4–9 hertz (Hz), or cycles per second of brain wave activity, is especially conducive to unconscious mental activity, often in the form of reverie or imagery. For the purposes of this research, a device based on sound and light technology (an audiovisual integrator) was used to induce the appropriate state of relaxation in participants by providing sound earphones and light pulse goggles. Such sound and light pulses brought the participants' brain wave states down from full consciousness (about 14–30 Hz or cycles per second), beta state, down through alpha state (about 10–13 Hz—tranquil but not drowsy) and into theta or twilight state (4–9 Hz, a very relaxed, creative flow state).

In addition to being used for medical and clinical psychotherapeutic purposes, audiovisual integrators are also being used to induce meditation, accelerated learning, creative thinking, and problem solving. Budzynski (1991), who pioneered experimentation with light and sound stimulation technology, noted that attainment of the theta state "facilitates the emergence of repressed material as well as creative associations, and the assimilation of certain types of information... without the usual critical screening which is operative during the waking, fully conscious state" (p. 11). These devices were particularly suitable for this research: they are simple and comfortable to use and consist of a pair of headphones, stimulation goggles, and an electronic unit with built-in customized programs for eliciting the desired brain wave state and its corresponding electroencephalograph

(EEG) readings. An audiovisual integrator was used to produce deep relaxation in subjects, and a computerized EEG monitor provided readings to corroborate their corresponding brain wave states. The EEG readings effectively demonstrated that the subject was in the required mental state for the experiment. The investigation thus attempted to demonstrate how unconscious modes of inquiry differ from conscious modes in their representation, function, and structure, and what problems were encountered in the elicitation of unconscious cognition in a question negotiation or reference transaction.

But the methodology of the study did not come easily. It required preliminary trial-and-error investigation on various relaxation methods, such as deep breathing, visualization techniques, and progressive muscle relaxation, to get an idea of what might enable voluntary participants to express their information needs more clearly than they did before relaxation.

Following preliminary studies, a series of quasi-experimental, one- and two-group pilot studies were conducted over a two-year period to discover the optimal method for mobilizing the inquirer's unconscious cognitive processes during the initial stages of inquiry. It was hypothesized that subjects who reached an altered state of consciousness would have access to unconscious cognitive processes to help clarify information needs and their representations. In the first pilot study, 15 volunteer inquirers first posed and recorded a question that they were curious about and that involved a personal problem, such as where or when to apply for a position or how to deal with a difficult decision. Inquirers then used an audiovisual integrator to reach a relaxed, low alpha or theta state and again posed and recorded a reworked question on the same problem. Content analysis of the initial and relaxed queries revealed that inquirers appeared to represent their problems in a more holistic, complete, and focused way in the relaxed state, with greater degrees of affective and verbal expressiveness.

In the second pilot study, an experimental group of ten student volunteers recorded their own questions and received a five-minute deep-breathing exercise before recording their second question on the same topic. The control group of ten volunteers recorded their initial queries and then took a regular class break rather than a deep-breathing exercise before recording their second query. Content analysis and mapping on the sets of initial and subsequent queries again indicated marked differences between the first and second queries of the experimental group but not between those of the control group. Again, the experimental group's second queries revealed more completeness and focus than their initially somewhat crude representations. In contrast, the control group's first and second queries were equally vague, with little focus.

In the third pilot study, a Grey Walter Test was used on two dozen graduate student volunteer inquirers as a pretest to detect personality differences and problem-solving styles among individuals before assigning individuals randomly to experimental and control groups consisting of 12 individuals in each group. After recording initial questions, the more effective audiovisual integrator was reintroduced and used by the experimental group to induce an altered state of consciousness prior to recording their rephrased questions. The control group, unaware of the treatment, took a 20-minute break between recording their first and second queries. However, an electroencephalograph (EEG) biofeedback monitoring device was used as a pretest and posttest on both groups to confirm their brain wave states when they posed their first and second queries. While the control group remained in full beta state (full consciousness), members of the experimental group went from beta to low alpha and theta states (highly relaxed) before posing their second questions. To eliminate experimenter bias in this third pilot study, an experienced blind judge (who did not know the source of questions) was employed to contrast and compare the content characteristics of before and after questions from both groups. Again, the experimental groups' second queries were deemed to very apt, search-worthy questions. Collectively, these pilot studies served to point out the need to control for participant suitability for the experiment, to eliminate the biasing effects of individual problem-solving styles, to verify that experimental inquirers had attained a relaxed state, and to eliminate experimenter bias by using a blind judge to assess question differences.

Finally, with the results of the pilot studies, a formal experiment was devised and conducted on 36 faculty and graduate student volunteers pretested for individual differences and assigned randomly to an experimental and a control group. Both groups were asked to represent a problem of deep, authentic concern to them on two occasions as a pretest and a posttest question. The experimental group was subjected to a 20-minute deep relaxation program using the Audio-Visual Integrator (AVI), and EEG machine electrodes were attached to individual scalps to verify their attainment of low alpha and theta states between the two representations. The control group took a normal 20-minute interlude between their representations. Subsequently, individuals in both groups evaluated the differences between their individual pretest and posttest problem representations based on qualitative and quantitative criteria to identify the impact of unconscious cognitive processes. A blind judge (an experienced reference librarian) was also asked to rate the pre- and posttest questions. Again, the results demonstrated improved posttest questions from the experimental (relaxed) group but not from the control group.

Method of Analysis

Analysis of data from the formal experiment was divided into three phases. In the first phase, EEG recordings were collected to ascertain whether the experimental participants had effectively reached a relaxed, alpha/theta state. A Grey Walter Test was used to assess and normalize problem-solving styles between control and experimental group individuals. Also a McNemar Nonparametric

Test was used to verify that participants had changed from alert to relaxed states as a result of the audiovisual integrator treatment. In the second analysis phase, a single factor Analysis of Variance (ANOVA) was used to gage between and within group differences of each participant's personal evaluations of their problem representations. In the third phase, a single factor ANOVA was applied to evaluate the blind judge's evaluations of recorded question differences between and within experimental and control groups. Additionally, qualitative data was collected and analyzed to assess individual emotional reactions to audiovisual integrator experiences and the relaxed states achieved and to assess each participant's perceived quality of his or her own pre- and posttest questions.

Results

The Grey Walter Test appears to be a relatively simple and cost-effective way to assess problem solving and cognitive differences between participants in preparation for randomly assigning them to experimental and control groups. Likewise, the McNemar Test appears to be satisfactory to differentiate between alert and relaxed states of individuals to support pre- and posttest question recording for subsequent content analysis. The EEG readings were sufficiently clear to confirm the beta, alpha, and theta (and even lower delta, or sleeping) brain wave states of participants. As a result of the AVI treatment, nearly all experiment participants achieved a relaxed state of 8–10 Hz prior to generating their second question. As a result of being in a relaxed state, experimental participants rated their own inquiry states on a scale of one to seven point differences between their pre- and posttest questions. They reported having significant increases in insight and intuition, production of ideas about their problems, and production of emotions (happy or sad feelings). They noted lesser but still marked increases in expression of purpose and intention, imagination, originality, rational thinking, and overall questioning ability. In contrast, the control group perceived few differences between their original question and their second one. A single factor ANOVA, previously used to compare pilot experimental data, was applied to both groups and revealed that the differences between the two representations resulted in a high F ratio of 40.16, which easily surpassed the critical value of 4.13 at the .05 level of confidence with one degree of freedom between groups and 34 degrees of freedom within groups. Therefore, the null hypothesis (Ho) of no difference between group assessments of their own cognitive performance was rejected in favor of the alternative hypothesis (Ha). The differences in questioning performance were significant, indicating that individuals did feel that they had improved their questioning ability as a result of being relaxed.

The blind judge (an experienced public reference librarian, and career counselor) likewise found improved questioning ability among experimental participants as a result of their being relaxed. As a blind judge, she did not know which questions came from the experimental group and which ones were generated by controls. The blind judge was asked to rate the differences between the two representations with the same seven-point scale questionnaire and scale used by both groups. The resulting data were then also tested using a single factor ANOVA, with differences between representations resulting in an F ratio of 4.71 (df = 1 between groups; df = 34 within groups), which indicated a significant difference between groups at the 0.5 level of confidence. The null hypothesis of no difference was therefore rejected in favor of the alternative hypothesis. The blind judge also perceived differences between the questions generated by the experimental group individuals versus those generated by the controls, but these differences were less than those reported by the control group. The differences were apparently less because the blind judge had no contact with the individuals and had only a vague idea of the nature of the experiment. In contrast, regarding the experimental participants, she did not personally experience how initial queries had transformed into reworked queries, nor did she experience the emotional surge that experimental participants had experienced directly between their initial and reworked questions. The experimental individuals, as a function of being relaxed, reported greater insight and intuition, conceptual fluidity, originality, focus, clarity of purpose, and emotive capacity.

Experimental group participants reported what they regarded as significant relaxation and tranquility as a result of being truly relaxed. They reported that they could see their problems in broader perspective, with greater flow of ideas and new ways to focus on a problem. Specific descriptions of the altered state of consciousness included such adjectives as "stimulating," "hypnotic," "dramatic," and "fantastic." One photo-sensitive individual, however, found the audiovisual integrator light pulses to be annoying and of little help in relaxing. Some participants reported that they realized they had experienced their use of one or more psychological defense mechanisms when framing their initial query. Such psychological defense mechanisms mentioned included the following: repression (suppressing their problems and information needs), denial (not admitting they had a bothersome problem), rationalization (using untrue but socially acceptable excuses for their wishes or actions), and displacement (shifting their key problem to a different one). The role of psychological defense mechanisms in information counseling and inquiry generally apparently needs to be investigated in the future. Such defense mechanisms are discussed in most introductory and abnormal psychology textbooks.

Discussion of Results

Overall, the results of the previous experimental research reveal that participants who achieved deep relaxation did appear to generate more lengthy and "profound" questions. In the relaxed state, participants experienced a more exploratory free flow of ideas and heightened emotional and questioning capacity. They avoided premature closure on solutions to problems by seeing their problems in a broader perspective and by realizing that multiple cause-and-effect relationships tend to be involved in complex problem solving. Occasionally, participants shifted their focus of inquiry and redefined their problems in a new light. For example, one individual initially asked about what kind of house he should buy. In a relaxed state, he realized that he was avoiding buying any kind of house because he did not want to live alone. He then shifted his inquiry to how to become more sociable and find a compatible mate. The relaxed state appears to be essential to defining or redefining personal or social problems with precision and for framing appropriate questions to resolve those problems. Furthermore, relaxation might serve to weaken the inquirer's psychological mechanisms that had previously been mobilized unconsciously to preclude the effective framing of problems and their articulation in the form of questions.

Nevertheless, these positive results should be interpreted cautiously. The marked difference between the evaluations of the experimental and control group questions suggest that the higher question quality scores of the experimental group could possibly have been influenced by some extraneous variables that were not present during the experiment with the control group. One extraneous variable could, for example, have derived from the Hawthorne effect, which is famous for pointing out how the presence of an observer and the act of observation can influence those observed. In this experiment, participants in the experimental group received individual, personal attention, while the control group subjects did not, and this individual attention could have encouraged the members of the experimental group to exert more effort in discerning the differences. However, during the course of the experiments the Hawthorne effect, if present, did not appear to be a significant influence. But if a Hawthorne effect should actually be operative in reference transactions, its impact might point out the importance of having a human rather than artificial intelligence intermediaries technologically embedded in the reference process. These experimental results indicate that the human, interpersonal element plays an important role in facilitating the course of inquiry, especially in the initial stages when an information counseling approach might be the most appropriate and efficient method of eliciting unconscious cognition.

The ratings of the differences between pre- and posttest question representations by members of the experimental and control groups were compared with the ratings of the same representations by the blind judge. From this comparison, it was clear that the blind judge did not capture the subtle differences identified by the participants who had a more intimate knowledge of their own personal problems. As a result, differences in the personal evaluations of pretest and posttest question representations were much greater than those interpreted by the blind judge. A comparison of the evaluations of the differences between pre- and posttest question representations by the experimental and control groups showed an F ratio of 40.16, whereas the blind judge's evaluations showed an F ratio of

4.7. Nevertheless, in both cases, the F ratio had to surpass the critical value of 4.13 to reject the null hypothesis. In future experiments, two or more blind judges might well be used to provide a broader-based evaluation of differences between questions generated from full consciousness and those generated from relaxed states. Also, additional question analysis and concept representation mapping methods might be deployed to assess the soundness of questions that arise during the course of inquiry. It is an aphorism that when one asks the right question, a problem is half solved.

Implications for Practice

The foregoing review explores the influence of unconscious cognition in the formation and generation of reference queries. As defined herein, unconscious cognition is that which exists beyond an individual's immediate awareness but that affects conscious awareness and mentation. Queries that involve individual values, such as where to live or what occupation to pursue, tend to evoke more unconscious cognitive processing than do queries that seek factual answers. Accordingly, deeply embedded queries tend to be affected by the inquirer's pre-established mental patterns and behavioral modes that reside beyond immediate awareness. Debates about how to negotiate queries, particularly how to get clientele to be more explicit and articulate about their underlying information needs, have been published for well over a century. Contemporary discussions about query negotiation indicate a greater awareness of tacit user cognition and ways to elicit embedded information needs. But the full significance of the psychodynamics of unconscious cognition has yet to be acknowledged. The purpose of this review is to provide perspective about the nature and degree of impact of unconscious cognition in query generation and in the information counseling process.

The experimental findings reported are based primarily on a series of studies conducted by the lead author and his doctoral student during the 1990s and subsequently. These experiments were directly inspired by Robert Taylor's classic paper on question negotiation (Taylor, 1968). Following a series of pilot studies, a formal, controlled experiment was conducted, wherein 36 faculty members and graduate student volunteers were pretested for individual cognitive differences and randomly assigned to an experimental and control group. Members of both groups then formulated individual written queries about a problem of authentic, individualized personal concern. Members of the experimental group then used a programmed relaxation device for 15 minutes to achieve a relaxed state (confirmed by low brain wave frequency measurements) and were then asked to readdress their initial query. They did so by providing significantly more complete and searchable queries, queries that they felt represented their underlying problems more accurately and holistically. Experimental participants reported achieving heightened focus and clarity of purpose, a greater mobilization of creative flow and conceptual fluidity, and heightened intuition and emotive capacity. Some reported feelings of elation, and that they could reframe their problems from a different perspective. Others noted that prior to becoming relaxed they had initially used psychological defense mechanisms, such as denial, blocking, displacement, or repression of their problems and related inner conflicts, in their initial framing of problems. Still others pointed out the importance of having a human intermediary involved in the information counseling process (a possible Hawthorne effect) to help them address their true information needs and to ask the right questions. In contrast, the control group of individuals did not receive the relaxation treatment but instead were asked to take a 15-minute break and then to rephrase their initial queries. Members of the control group showed little improvement in reframing or elaborating their initial queries; their second queries tended to be still terse and less searchable, and control participants did not report increased insight into their problems or the nature of their underlying information needs.

Accordingly, a first implication of this research is that unconscious cognition is of sufficient importance in the genesis of value-oriented reference queries as well as throughout the information seeking process generally. The pilot studies and formal experiment, plus informal studies the lead author has conducted more recently, surveyed a wide variety of methods to achieve altered awareness, including the following: the use of music, systematic breathing, progressive muscle relaxation, biofeedback, dream exploration, meditation, visualization, and hypnosis. Although these studies employed the audiovisual integrator or systems device as a primary tool because of its demonstrated effectiveness, other particularly promising methods include the systematic deployment of music in work and research environments, deep breathing, and hypnotic screensavers. These methods continue to be promising because they might be economically and quickly used in any inquiry environment and they are easily learned and applied. Rhythmic breathing, in particular, is quickly available to everyone, and it continues to be almost universally applied in many counseling, learning, and therapeutic environments for a wide range of applications.

Likewise, a wide array of screensaver software exists that utilizes shifting displays, multiple colors, changing backgrounds and foregrounds, and alternative dynamics of movement, all of which make them useful to induce relaxation quite apart from their original screensaver purpose. One variety of screensaver contains subliminal suggestions that could be used to evoke relaxation. Other promising biofeedback devices feature displays on the screen that contract or change color as the user relaxes. Because the relaxation response is quite subtle and cannot be quickly discovered by most people who make inquiries, biofeedback devices can be used to capture galvanic skin response data that lie near or below the threshold of awareness. Once the information user acquires heightened sensitivity to subtle stress and relaxation triggers, this user can regulate autonomic responses associated with unfavorable stress. The information counseling environment might well include any number of these alternative tools to enable the inquirer to use a single technology or a combination of technologies geared to that particular person's individual differences and the unique nature of his or her inquiry. These various technologies should eventually serve to provide a synergistic, cybernetic loop between mind and computer, in both electronic and face-to-face reference environments.

While many information professionals might judge the deployment of relaxation techniques and technologies to be impractical, it appears to be more impractical to provide superficial or cursory question negotiation and to answer ill-formed queries. It would seem to be better to frame and ask the right question in the first place than to secure a good answer to a spurious or wrong question. Accordingly, a reference renaissance might well incorporate relaxation approaches into both electronic and physical reference settings to negotiate and better address value-oriented problems and queries. Perhaps the elicitation and fulfillment of information needs is tantamount to providing stress reduction for inquirers.

A second implication is that the presence and influence of unconscious cognition, which is permanently embedded within the minds of information seekers, will continue to exert influence well into the future. Unconscious cognition will continue to exist despite the rapid growth of electronic reference services and the ongoing deluge of new information and communication technologies with their inclusion of embedded artificial intelligence. Therefore, it might ultimately be more important from an information counseling and searching point of view to elicit deeply embedded information from the inquirer's memory in order to help them articulate and resolve their problems before providing recourse to external information sources. Systems oriented approaches to information searching continue to be strongly based on the empiricist notion that user problems are solved through the provision of electronic and print information from sources outside of the mind rather than through efficient and effective mobilization of internal cognition. In contrast, logical, rationalist, and subjective philosophical approaches place greater emphasis on the notion that individuals already possess embedded knowledge that needs to be elicited. It appears to be equally important to facilitate the extraction of information from the deeper recesses of the inquirer's mind as it is to provide information from external sources. There also appears to be a great need for information intermediaries, end users, and searching operations to incorporate direct and economical means for mobilizing deeper thought processes as a prerequisite for, and concomitant of, effective inquiry. Accordingly, information intermediaries might well become better versed particularly in the study of psychology and cognitive science. Personality theory, cognition, perception, memory, learning theory, individual differences, abnormal psychology, and counseling, among other topics, all seem applicable during the course of need elicitation and query negotiation. In particular, the use and impact of psychological defense mechanisms in information counseling and inquiry appears to fruitful topic for future investigation.

A third implication of this review is that, given the universal presence and applicability of consciousness in the conduct of inquiry, the paradigm of the reference and information counseling functions could be revised and greatly expanded to embrace the previously mentioned informationist concept, with its broader marketplace of ongoing information needs. As with education, information counseling might be expensive, but ignorance and its consequences can be more expensive, particularly in such areas as health care, industrial design or finance. Such an expanded, embedded reference/informationist paradigm could serve to extend information counseling functions to nearly all societal functions and endeavors, including research settings. One might extend the reference/informationist concept further by suggesting that informationists could become research leaders within various general and specialized areas of knowledge and even become research team leaders. By fulfilling applied problem-solving and research roles, informationists could possess the competitive advantages of knowing how to elicit the information needs of their problem-solving or research team clientele, could provide rapid access to recorded knowledge and could promote accelerated personal, professional, and scholarly learning and discovery. In an ideal reference renaissance, informationists and their information-seeking teammates should be able to convert the distress that accompanies ignorance into the euphoria that accompanies discovery.

References

Ballesteros, E. R. (1995). *Unconscious cognition in the conduct of inquiry: An information counseling approach*. Doctoral dissertation, University of Texas, Austin, Texas.

Belkin, N. J. (1980). Anomalous states of knowledge as a basis for information retrieval. *Canadian Journal of Information Science*, 5, 133–143.

Bopp, R. E., & Smith, L. C. (Eds.). (2001). *Reference and information services: An introduction*. Englewood, CO: Libraries Unlimited.

Budzynski, T. H. (1991). Clinical considerations of light and sound. In J. Isaacs (Ed.), *The science of light and sound* (p. 11). San Rafael, CA: Professional Technologies.

Cassell, K. A., & Hiremath, U. (2006). *Reference and information services in the 21st century: An introduction*. New York: Neal-Schuman.

Dewdney, P., & Michell, G. (1997, January). Asking "why" questions in the reference interview: A theoretical justification. *The Library Quarterly*, 67(1), 50–71.

Ellenberger, H. F. (1970). *The discovery of the unconscious*. New York: Basic Books.

Fields, A. M. (2006). Ill-structured problems and the reference consultation: The librarian's role in developing student expertise. *Reference Services Review*, 34, 405–420.

Gladwell, M. (2005). *Blink: The power of thinking without thinking*. New York: Little Brown.

Graesser, A. C., & Goodman, S. M. (1985). Implicit knowledge, question answering, and the representation of expository text. In B. K. Britton & J. B. Black (Eds.), *Understanding expository text: A theoretical and practical handbook for analyzing explanatory text* (pp. 109–171). Hillsdale, NJ: Lawrence Erlbaum.

Green, S. S. (1876). Personal relations between librarians and readers. *Library Journal, 1,* 74–81.

Hampden-Turner, C. (1981). *Maps of the mind: Charts and concepts of the mind and its labyrinths.* New York: Macmillan Publishing Company.

Harmon, E. G., & Ballesteros, E. R. (1997). Unconscious cognition: The elicitation of deeply embedded information needs. In *ISIC '96: Proceedings of an International Conference on Information Seeking in Context* (pp. 422–433). London: Taylor Graham Publishing.

James, W. (1902/1958). *The varieties of religious experience.* New York: New American Library.

Jonides, J., Lewis, R. L., Nee, D. E., Lustig, C. A., Berman, M. G., & Moore, K. S. (2008). The mind and brain of short-term memory. *Annual Review of Psychology, 59*(1), 193–224.

Kihlstrom, J. F. (1984). Conscious, subconscious, unconscious: A cognitive perspective. In K. S. Bowers & D. Meichenbaum (Eds.), *The unconscious reconsidered* (pp. 149–211). New York: Wiley.

Kuhlthau, C. C. (1993, December). A principle of uncertainty for information seeking. *Journal of Documentation, 49,* 339–355.

Nahl, D., & Bilal, D. (2007). *Information and emotion: The emergent affective paradigm in information behavior research and theory.* Medford, NJ: Information Today.

Neway, J. M. (1985). *Information specialist as team player in the research process.* Westport, CT: Greenwood Press.

Radford, M. L. (1999). *The reference encounter: Interpersonal communication in the academic library.* Chicago: ACRL.

Rankin, J. A., Grefsheim, S. F., & Cato, C. C. (2008, July). The emerging informationist specialty: A systematic review of the literature. *Journal of the Medical Library Association, 96*(3), 194–206.

Reber, A. S. (1992, January). An evolutionary context for the cognitive unconsciousness. *Philosophical Psychology, 5*(1), 33–51.

Schacter, D. L. (1987). Implicit memory: History and current status. *Journal of Experimental Psychology: Learning, Memory, and Cognition, 13,* 501–518.

Shevrin, H., Bond, J. A., Brakel, L. A. W., Hertel, R. K., & Williams, W. J. (1996). *Conscious and unconscious processes: Psychodynamic, cognitive, and neurophysiological convergences.* New York: Guilford Press.

Taylor, R. S. (1968, May). Question-negotiation and information seeking in libraries. *College and Research Libraries, 29,* 178–194.

Wilcox, E. V. (1922, June). Why do we have librarians? *Harvard Graduates Magazine, 30,* 477–491.

Woodruff, E. B. (1897). Reference work. *Library Journal (Conference Issue), 22,* 65–67.

Wyer, J. I. (1930). *Reference work: A textbook for students of library work and librarians.* Chicago: American Library Association.

CHAPTER 5

Systems-Centered versus User-Centered Librarianship: A Cognitive Sociological View

Hannah Kwon

Overview

Applying the framework of cognitive sociology to the library profession, this chapter considers how the "systems-centered" and "user-centered" paradigms have produced two corresponding "thought communities" (Zerubavel, 1997) with differing cognitive traditions that explain their contrasting approaches to reference and librarianship in general. Through the analysis of exemplar reference situations, the author extracts the underlying characteristics of each cognitive tradition in order to show that systems-centered and user-centered librarians have been cognitively socialized into "thought communities" with fundamentally conflicting views of the profession. The use of "thought communities" as a unit of analysis adds an additional dimension to the existing nomothetic and idiographic approaches to research in library and information science while offering a framework within which the profession can identify and address current and future changes in the values guiding professional practice.

Coexisting Paradigms in Librarianship

Recently, the *New York Times* reported that the standard stereotype of "traditional" librarians, "bespectacled women with a love of classic books and a perpetual annoyance with talkative patrons" (Jesella, 2007, para. 9) is being challenged by a new breed of "hipper librarians" who are "notable not just for their pink-streaked hair but also for their passion for pop culture, activism, and technology" (para. 12). In the heated discussions that took place on blogs and listservs in the subsequent weeks two viewpoints emerged, corresponding to the two paradigms of library and information science first articulated by Dervin and Nilan (1986): the systems-centered and user-centered paradigms. Systems-centered librarians decried the loss of librarianship's professional values, which were perceived to be under attack by the glamorization of the young, tech-savvy librarians in the article. Extending their criticism beyond the article in question, many expressed a strong disapproval of the increasing value placed by "newer generation" on user convenience, in the form of digital information and new technologies, over information quality and professional standards. Representing the perspective of systems-centered librarianship, American Library Association (ALA) Councilor-At-Large Sue Kamm (2007), criticizes the new generation's betrayal of the profession's "basic principles":

> What concerns me (and others) about the new generation of librarians is they are not being grounded in basic principles in which our profession is rooted. The queries we have had on this list displaying ignorance of intellectual freedom are appalling. The apparent belief that everything is online, what do we need books for? is disheartening.

The "newer generation" of user-centered librarians is equally critical of their systems-centered counterparts. Meredith Farkas, author of *Social Software in Libraries* (2004), draws the dividing lines between systems-centered and user-centered librarians as starkly as Sue Kamm. Gathering under the banner of "Library 2.0," Farkas and other user-centered librarians embrace the vast potential of technology and see technological fluency as a basic professional competency:

> I'm probably grossly oversimplifying this, but I think there are two types of librarians: those who embrace technology and those who are antagonistic towards it or ignore it. . . . I have been amazed that many people in my classes don't know much of anything about technology. They don't understand how search engines work, they don't know how to code in HTML or how to use [WYSIWYG] editors like Dreamweaver, and they don't have a clue about blogs, wikis, RSS, or RFIDs. These people are traditionalists. They only want to learn the skills that have been taught to librarians for decades and don't want to take classes on things they don't think they'll need to know as reference or catalog or youth librarians.

Whereas Kamm portrays user-centered librarians as lazy and lacking knowledge of basic professional values, Farkas portrays systems-centered librarians as defensive and increasingly irrelevant. Both Farkas and Kamm put forth their type of librarianship as objectively "better" than the contrasting type, creating an oppositional dynamic that seems impossible to reconcile. Both groups sincerely believe that their way is true to the essential spirit and purpose of librarianship and thus better for the user.

Those who refuse to take sides and reject the rigid arguments of both traditional and Library 2.0 librarians cling to their individuality, thus avoiding the issue entirely. From this individualistic perspective, every librarian is unique, so why bother arguing over which professional philosophy is better? Why does librarianship need a single professional identity when the individuals who comprise it are all essentially different? In explaining her frustration with the *New York Times* article, Melissa Rabey (2007) argues against both the traditional librarian stereotype and the Library 2.0 librarian stereotype:

We're exchanging one stereotype for another. Why are we so eager to be pigeon-holed into another niche? . . . When I see a group all eager to promote one way of being a librarian, I'm not going to follow that crowd. I may do all the things they do, but I don't look like they do. And that's okay, you know? For both them and me, our outward appearances don't affect the tasks we do, the service we give.

For Rabey, the stereotypes deny the individuality of librarians, who, in terms of professional identity, have only one thing in common: a commitment to serve. Rabey fails, however, to consider that any attempt to define a "commitment to serve" is likely to return us to the conflicting perspectives of the systems-centered and user-centered paradigms. Additionally, the denial of the possibility of *any* common elements in regard to professional identity, values, and practices suggests that librarianship lacks a professional identity.

Neither the rigidly held beliefs of the systems-centered and user-centered librarians nor the "anything goes" philosophy of the individualists illuminates the current tension in librarianship or offers a framework for mapping the profession's future. How can the profession reconcile the diverging philosophies of systems-centered and user-centered librarians without resorting to the total abandonment of a professional identity? By applying the framework of cognitive sociology (Zerubavel, 1997) to the current paradigmatic conflict, librarianship can avoid the pitfalls of cognitive universalism—the belief that there is one essential and objective cognitive pattern, and those of cognitive individualism—the belief in the ultimate subjectivity of cognitive patterns. A cognitive sociological approach seeks to understand the ways in which social collectives implicitly and explicitly shape the cognitive traditions of its members in order to establish inter-subjective meaning. By conceptualizing systems-centered librarians and user-centered librarians as "thought communities," the distinct professional identities, values, and practices put forth by these conflicting groups are understood as products of the paradigm shift from systems-centered librarianship to user-centered librarianship. The cognitive sociological approach thus allows the profession to appreciate and leverage the cognitive diversity of librarianship's thought communities in order to most effectively serve diverse populations.

Cognitive Sociology

Why do we eat sardines yet never goldfish, ducks yet never parrots? Why does adding cheese make a hamburger a "cheeseburger" whereas adding ketchup does not make it a "ketchupburger"? And why are Frenchmen less likely than Americans to find snails revolting? By the same token, how do we come to regard gold as more precious than water? How do we figure out which of the things that are said at a meeting ought to be included in the minutes and which ones are to be considered "off the record" and officially ignored? (Zeruvabel, 1997, p. 1)

In regard to librarianship's conflicting professional identities, we might ask, "Why do some librarians see technology as distracting from librarianship's core competencies, while others see technological skills as crucial to being a competent librarian?" Why do some reference librarians think of the physical reference desk as a beacon of help, while others think of it as a barrier? Why do some librarians consider Wikipedia as lacking true authority while other librarians consider it the ultimate authority? Why do traditional librarians insist that content is more important than format, while Library 2.0 librarians argue that format precedes content? In other words, how can beliefs and thoughts that are so essentially true for one group of librarians, be exactly the opposite of what is true for another group of librarians?

A cognitive sociological view of librarianship's conflicting professional identities avoids the traps of universalism and individualism by comparative analysis of two or more groups in order to reveal that which is conventional to each group. By approaching cognition from an intermediate perspective that complements but avoids the extremist stances of individualism and universalism, cognitive sociology reminds us that "[b]etween the purely subjective inner world of the individual and the absolutely objective physical world 'out there' lies an intersubjective, social world that is quite distinct from both of them" (Zerubavel 1997, p. 9). While people certainly think both as individuals and as human beings, they most often think as members of the particular "thought communities" to which they belong. Every individual belongs to many thought communities that are defined by profession, ethnicity, religion, political affiliation, generation, and musical and artistic taste. Membership in thought communities ranges from being deliberate and conscious to unintentional and subconscious or even involuntary. Thus, a person may willingly be a member of the thought community of opera aficionados. A person may, by default, be a member of the thought community of youngest siblings. A person may unwillingly and unknowingly be a member of the thought community of procrastinators.

At the height of its power, a thought community's conventions are perceived as the natural order and its members are not conscious of thinking or functioning as a member of the thought community (Zerubavel, 1997). Thought communities are defined both by the similarities that its members share within the group and by the differences that set them apart from all other groups. Each of these groups has an inherent language and code to its membership; being socialized into the group is the process of learning its language and code. This process of "cognitive socialization" is a rite of entry into the thought community's social world and occurs formally, often through education, as well as informally, though tacit measures such as social pressure or observation. When a child sees parents speak in a reverent tone to one person and in a disparaging tone to another, the child tacitly learns that there are different voices for different people and will proceed to mimic the parents' tones, much to their astonishment, and, sometimes, embarrassment. Once socialized, the individual views the world through the lens of the thought community, as their values and opinions, sense of humor, and even appearance (as in the "thrift-store inspired clothes and abundant tattoos" of the newer generation librarians in the *New York Times* 2007 article) reflect a common cognitive tradition. Formal and informal methods of socialization are equally normative and serve to bind the thought community together and to differentiate one community from another.

From the perspective of cognitive sociology, the professional identity crisis in librarianship can be understood as a "cognitive battle" between two thought communities: systems-centered librarians and user-centered librarians. Having been educated under different paradigms, the traditional system-oriented paradigm in library science and the alternative user-oriented paradigm that has emerged in the past few decades (Dervin & Nilan, 1986) are members of the two thought communities that have been cognitively socialized to define the profession based on two different perspectives. As librarianship transitions from a system-oriented paradigm to a user-oriented paradigm, the members of the corresponding coexisting thought communities have come into conflict over basic issues of professional identity, values, standards, and practices. These conflicting philosophies are normatively reinforced within each thought community in opposition to the other, as demonstrated by the listserv comments from librarians of both cognitive traditions.

While there are certainly librarians who value aspects of both the systems-centered and user-centered paradigms, the sociological unit of interest in the current analysis is the thought community, not the individual, which focuses attention on what is distinctly social about paradigmatic thinking. In an overview of the types of metatheories, theories, and models in library and information science, Bates (2005) identifies two major research approaches: nomothetic and idiographic. Nomothetic approaches to research aim for the discovery of general laws, while idiographic approaches are concerned with individual difference. Bates (2005) urges library and information science researchers to "maintain openness to these two positions, rather than insisting on selecting one or the other," which is "ultimately more productive and rewarding for the progress of the field" (p. 9). However, Zerubavel (1997) adds a sociological dimension to research, identifying three distinct levels of analysis, especially as it relates to cognition: individuals, social groups, and humankind. Library and information science research often neglects the social dimension of information behavior, which impedes the progress of the field, for "[o]nly an integrative approach that addresses *all* three levels, of course, can provide a complete picture of how we think" (Zerubavel, 1997, p. 6). Thus, the current analysis focuses on the *social* dimension of librarianship, as represented by the thought communities of systems-centered and user-centered librarians, in order to cast light on how the two sets of paradigmatic norms are expressed and maintained in professional practice.

> The more we become aware of our *cognitive differences* as members of different thought communities, the less likely we are to follow the common ethnocentric tendency to regard the particular way in which we ourselves happen to process the world in our minds as based on some absolute standard of "logic" or "reason" and, thus, as naturally or logically inevitable. (Zerubavel 1997, p. 10).

A comparative approach to the cognition of different thought communities serves as a form of reverse socialization, or at least a distancing from one's own thought community in order to be able to perceive others, for both professional and research purposes. By identifying the ways in which systems-centered and user-centered librarians have been cognitively socialized to think differently, the cognitive patterns of each group become not universal nor individual but social norms that exist for a collective purpose. The cognitive sociological approach to research thus offers a conceptual framework for researchers to study the social aspect of information behavior, and gives the profession a perspective from which they can see paradigmatic difference, evaluate the appropriateness of a paradigm to the situation, and anticipate future paradigmatic shifts.

Systems-Centered Reference

While differences in the cognitive traditions of systems-centered and user-centered librarians can be seen in all areas of librarianship, from cataloging to programming, library architecture to policy creation, reference is particularly well-suited to tracing the everyday practice of librarianship to its cognitive origins; it is essentially a cognitive interaction between the vastly different thought communities of information service providers and information seekers. By comparing reference scenarios as they would plausibly be conducted by systems-centered and user-centered reference librarians, we can study the manner in which the two groups have been cognitively socialized to conceptualize and actualize the provision of reference services to information seekers.

The following reference scenario is typical of reference as conducted by a traditional, systems-centered reference librarian.

A Systems-Centered Reference Scenario

A high-school-age student approaches the reference desk.

Librarian: Hello, may I help you?

Patron: Hi. I'm looking for a book about World War II.

Librarian: Okay, great. Let's look at the catalog and see what we have. Books about World War II would be under the subject heading "World War, 1939–1945." Wow, we have a lot of books in that area. We have books about aerial operations, African-Americans in WWII, the concentration camps, Jews in WWII ... what aspect of WWII are you interested in?

Patron: Umm ... the concentration camps?

Librarian: Okay, great. Here is a list of books under that subject heading, or if you'd like to browse that area, you can go to this call number. (Writes the call number down). It's in Stack 6.

Patron: Thanks. I'll go take a look.

Librarian: You're welcome. Let me know if you have any problems.

This reference scenario exemplifies the underlying cognitive traditions of systems-centered reference librarians (see Table 5.1). The librarian's trained practice of consulting the library catalog and directing the patron to a stack to look for a book reveals several of the systems-centered librarian's cognitive traditions. First, it demonstrates that the primary goal of librarianship for the systems-centered librarian is the systematic organization of materials for retrieval. Indeed, this is the defining characteristic of the system-oriented paradigm. The basic unit under the system paradigm, that which is being organized by the librarian and accessed by the patron, is the book. The goal of reference is to help users access materials from the information system. The reference librarian functions as a gatekeeper to the physical materials of the library, one who has knowledge of how the information system is ordered and who must be consulted in order to know how to access the materials in the system. The catalog serves as the main access point for the user; it is the representation of the library's intellectual content and organization, classifying discrete physical objects and thus tied to the reality of physical space—a certain number of linear feet of shelving, in rooms of certain sizes, in a building of a certain size (Weinberger, 2007). Even when library catalogs are directly accessible to the public, the user often needs to defer to the reference librarian's professional expertise and experience in order to learn the intricacies and quirks of the catalog in terms of its accuracy as a representation of the materials in the system or to learn about the physical organization of the materials in the library. In the previous scenario, the patron relies on the librarian to translate the topic of "World War II" into the subject heading, "World War, 1939–1945." While some may argue that public access catalogs and systematized subject headings are meant to provide the user with direct access to the information system, many patrons would counter that their unintuitive nature seems designed to ensure that librarians can control access rather than grant it to users.

The information seeker, in this case a high-school student, is best described as a "library patron," with its overtones of the student "patronizing" the library system and using what is being made available. It is assumed that the information seeker requires the system to fill an information need or solve a problem as

Table 5.1. Three Paradigms of Librarianship		
	Systems-Centered Librarianship	**User-Centered Librarianship**	**Knowledge-Construction-Centered Librarianship**
Goal of librarianship	To systematically organize the information system's materials to facilitate access and use	To fulfill the patron's information need	To aid the information seeker's processes of knowledge construction
Goal of reference	To help patrons retrieve materials from the information system	To deduce the user's information need	To enable the process of knowledge construction
Reference librarian as	Gatekeeper	Intermediary	Guide
Information seeker as	Library patron	Customer	Learner
Reference scenario occurs	At the library's reference desk	Wherever the user is to be found (time-bound)	Wherever the user is to be found (continuous)
Reference scenario is conducted as	A reference "interview"	A reference "interaction"	A reference "encounter"
Reference technique	Closed-ended "what" questions	Open-ended "how" questions	Continuous information feedback loops between user and information systems, as monitored and interpreted by reference librarian
Basic unit of information	Book (or other physical object)	Word or keyword	That which changes the individual's knowledge structure (Brookes, 1980)
Primary access point	Library catalog	Internet browser	No primary access point
Advantages	Promotes efficient retrieval; system and user roles are well-defined	Doesn't require users to speak in system terms; information system extends outside of the library; considers nonusers as potential "customers"	Takes a holistic and integrated approach to the information seeker's needs, behaviors, and practices
Disadvantages	Can be intellectually and culturally paternalistic; doesn't consider items outside the system; isn't concerned with nonusers	Requires high-level communication skills; access to exponentially larger amounts and types of information requires high-level technological and search skills; constant change requires continual professional development	Requires extensive personalized data mining and concurrent security measures; may require redefinition of ethics surrounding personal privacy; focus on individual personalization may repress social aspect of information needs and uses

opposed to the system requiring use by the patron. Emphasis is on the system rather than on the user's need, which may not, in fact, be met by the existing system. The entire reference scenario takes place at the library's reference desk, again highlighting the centrality of the librarian as a gatekeeper to the information and the library user's information needs as subservient to the proper functioning of the library. It is up to the patron to approach the desk, which is a symbol of intellectual authority and of the "gate" to knowledge of which the reference librarian is the "gatekeeper." Conducted as a "reference interview," directional power is in the hands of the reference librarian. The librarian asks the questions, and the user answers. Balance of power tilts heavily toward the librarian, with the user at the librarian's mercy. Utilizing closed-ended "what?" questions limits the responses that can be given by the patron. When the librarian lists a series of subject headings and then asks, "What area are you interested in?" the patron learns that the subject headings listed are the only available choices and picks one of them accordingly.

All of these underlying assumptions are the product of the cognitive tradition of systems-oriented librarians. Primary emphasis in the systems-centered perspective is on the efficient administration of the information system—the library. Reference librarians trained under the systems paradigm honor the historical legacy of early public librarianship, which sought to extend access to knowledge beyond the educated elite to the public (Shera, 1949). This access was accomplished by systematically organizing materials in the information system in order to ensure efficient retrieval; the emphasis was on democratic access to existing materials and the tools for access, open stacks, circulation and cataloging systems, and finding aids, were thus necessarily systems-centered. But the cognitive traditions that were once a legitimate basis for the professional identity are now so ingrained that they function invisibly and have attained the force of objective reality. Traditionalist librarians, having been cognitively socialized to orient to the information system, reinforce the thought community's cognitive norms through explicit means, such as systems-centered curriculum in library science courses, and implicit means, such as the systems-centered physical organization of materials in the library.

Only with the increasing perception of libraries as lacking fundamental relevance to users has the profession begun to question systems-centered librarianship's basic cognitive traditions. Libraries are no longer the only publicly accessible information system, and as patrons compare the library with low-cost retail purveyors of information and the Internet environment, many may perceive the library as the least attractive option. According to Berry (1998), new attitudes and the widespread availability of information have rendered traditional reference irrelevant and reference librarians must move into the high-risk position of "information advisors" in order to survive. The disadvantages of the systems-centered paradigm are an indication that the information space in which the profession operates has fundamentally changed and that it is time for a new paradigm that speaks directly to our increasingly technological and end-user-driven information society. This new paradigm is the user-centered paradigm, which has existed in the field's academic literature for many decades and is now growing in influence in the professional world as well.

User-Centered Reference

The user-centered paradigm does not entirely disregard information systems but acknowledges that the user's perspective should guide the organization and design of information systems. This "alternative" user-oriented paradigm, with its focus on information as something constructed by human beings (Dervin & Nilan, 1986), has gained momentum to the point of comprising a subfield (in cognitive sociological terms, a thought community) of library and information science researchers interested in information behavior (Fisher, Erdelez, & McKechnie, 2005). Librarians trained in the past two decades have begun to be exposed to user-centered values in the library and information science curriculum and are translating those values into professional practice. The translation of user-centered values into professional practice is apparent in many current trends in librarianship, such as the consideration of alternatives to the Dewey Decimal Classification System (Oder, 2007) and the transformation of reference services in light of Web 2.0 technologies (Burger, 2007). Library 2.0's ethos of user partici-pation, collective knowledge, and belief in the limitless potential of technology has attracted a group of librarians who want to empower information seekers to be transformed from consumers to producers of knowledge. While those outside of the thought community of user-centered librarians may accuse this "newer generation" of librarians of replacing substance with style and of abandoning the historical values of the profession for the lights and speed of technology, user-centered librarians are forming a cognitive tradition that is as objectively logical to its members as the traditional values are to systems-centered librarians. As the first thought community to challenge the traditional definition of librarianship, this nascent group has called into question the basic values, standards, and practices of traditional librarianship. Analysis of a reference scenario conducted by a user-centered librarian, in light of the previous systems-centered scenario, brings into sharp contrast the cognitive traditions of the two thought communities.

The following reference scenario is typical of reference as conducted by a Library 2.0, user-centered reference librarian:

A User-Centered Reference Scenario

A high-school-age student signs on to a chat reference service with a question: "can i get help finding info on wwII?" Ten reference librarians are staffing the service when the question comes in. A reference librarian with extensive knowledge of American history sees the question and picks it up.

Librarian: Hi. My name is X and I'm a reference librarian at Y. I see that you have a question about World War II—can you tell me more about what you're looking for?

Student: yeah. i'm looking for info about wwII for a school project.

Librarian: okay. what grade are you in? what class is the project for?

Student: 9th. its for english. we just read the diary of anne frank and we're supposed to write a short story as if we were in her shoes.

Librarian: so you have to write from anne's point of view about what it would be like to hide from the nazis?

Student: no it's supposed to be happening right now, not in the past. in a country where people are hiding from their government or trying to flee the country.

Librarian: OH—i think i understand. you're supposed to pick a country where there is some kind of oppression occurring right now and write as if you were a member of the targeted group?

Student: yeah exactly

Librarian: ok, so the first thing we have to do is pick a group. do you have one in mind?

Student: i saw something on mtv about darfur once.

Librarian: yeah, there's a serious genocide going on in Darfur so that would be a good place to start. hold on while i look for some info....

Student: ok

Librarian: ok, first, here are some articles that give the background on what's going on in Darfur from a database that the library subscribes to. i'll send you the links—just type in your library card number to get access. [Librarian sends the article links]

Student: cool thx. can you find anything that would give me an idea of what it feels like to be one of oppressed kids?

Librarian: definitely. there are a lot of really good Web sites from independent media outlets and nonprofit advocacy groups that have firsthand accounts (articles, short videos, audio files) by refugees who have survived the genocide. would that help?

Student: that would be awesome. can you send them?

Librarian: of course—here you go. [Librarian pushes Web sites to the user's computer screen.]

In this user-oriented reference scenario, the student leads with the same question as in the system-oriented scenario, but the process and result are entirely different. Under the user-oriented paradigm, the overarching goal of librarianship is not the use of the system but fulfilling the user's information need (see Table 5.1). This assumption results in a very different set of norms and practices for the user-centered reference librarian as compared to the systems-centered librarian. The goal of user-oriented reference is to try to deduce the information need in light of the user's anomalous state of knowledge (Belkin, 1980). This entails knowledge of the information system, which is no longer defined in physical library terms but in digital, Internet-accessible terms and in terms of the expertise required to bridge the cognitive distance between the librarian and the user. Rather than acting as a gatekeeper, the reference librarian is an "information intermediary," moving between the user in need and the information with potential to help. Rather than being a system "user," the client is a "customer." While many object to the use of this term because of its transactional connotations (Budd, 2008), it speaks directly to the shift to the user-centered paradigm, where the user is not beholden to the library but the library is beholden to the user.

Whereas the traditional reference interview takes place at the reference desk, the user-centered scenario takes place in the digital realm, where the temporal and spatial boundaries of the physical library are extended for the user's convenience. The physical library building is no longer a relevant boundary, and the reference desk is no longer the only point of service. The reference librarian seeks the user wherever the user exists instead of forcing the user to come to the library for assistance. In this digital environment, the Internet browser is the primary access point, and the unit of information is the keyword. The reference "interview" is transformed into an "interaction" that acknowledges that both parties possess equal power and responsibility in navigating the information-seeking situation. The reference librarian's use of neutral questions (Dervin & Dewdney, 1986) allows the user to speak in his or her own terms, instead of being forced to speak in the system's terms. As a thought community, user-centered librarians are cognitively socialized to focus on the user through explicit means like courses and conference presentations on customer service and social software and implicit means such as being socially connected to other Library 2.0 librarians in the blogosphere.

Embracing Cognitive Diversity

Transitional periods between paradigms inevitably produce cognitive battles between the conflicting thought communities until the emergent one becomes soundly dominant. Librarianship is currently in a transitional period, where systems-centered and user-centered librarians work side by side in the same libraries and participate in the same professional dialogues, online and face to face. Both groups see the way in which they define the profession with the objective force of reality; cognitive socialization, if effective, does not easily allow its members to allow for other ways of thinking. Others choose to withdraw from the battling by refusing to identify with any group claiming to represent the "true" professional identity. The cognitive sociological perspective opens up the middle ground between cognitive universalism and cognitive individualism in order to be able to see that each thought community is formed by the disciplinary paradigm, has its historical moment in time, and must eventually give way to the next cognitive tradition.

Thus the cognitive sociological perspective simultaneously articulates the currently existing thought communities and anticipates the next thought community and how it will define librarianship's values, standards, and practices. Just as the emergence of user-centered reference points out the weaknesses in systems-centered reference, one may look at the limitations of user-centered librarianship in order to attempt to predict what is next to come. One of the limitations of the user paradigm as its is currently practiced in the profession is the treatment of information seeking as a time- and space-bound interaction between the user and librarian rather than as an ongoing process of knowledge construction in which formal information systems, like libraries and librarians, may play a small role, or none at all (see Table 5.1). The thought community of librarians under this paradigm may define the ultimate goal of librarianship as aiding the information seeker in the process of knowledge construction and the goal of reference as enabling the process. The reference librarian would be the "guide" to the information seeker's "learning," with the reference "encounter" occurring wherever and whenever the user is to be found. Most important, reference will not be a one-time, discrete instance, but part of a continuous feedback loop of learning, driven by the collection and analysis of the limitless amounts of digital data that describes user behavior and implies learning. Cognitive sociology's comparative perspective provides a structure within which the profession can anticipate future paradigm shifts in research and professional practice and thus be better prepared for the future.

Librarianship has long realized that in order to discern and provide for the information needs of our diverse communities most effectively, the profession needs to be more ethnically, culturally, and socioeconomically diverse (Winston, 1998). In this time of paradigmatic shift, the need for diversity applies to thought communities, too. With a cognitively diverse body of librarians, librarianship will be better able to hold the waxing and waning paradigmatic perspectives in tension. One paradigm may currently be more appropriate than another, historically and culturally speaking, but there is a more fluidity and grayness than there is dominance and absolute certainty. The coexistence of multiple thought communities better equips the profession to mirror the diverse information needs and abilities of every part of the community. As the information landscape continues to accelerate, paradigmatic shifts are likely to last for shorter periods of time and occur more frequently, and traditional and Library 2.0 librarians will need to learn to acknowledge not only each other but also not-yet-existing thought communities to come.

The profession's cognitive pluralism, then, is, and will continue to be, necessary to maintain relevance to a pluralistic society of information seekers. As one listserv contributor so aptly wrote in the listserv discussion surrounding the *New York Times* article, "I would suggest that as a listserv community and as a profession we could use the motto of our nine-person reference department: "collectively we're a whole intelligence!" Folks, we're wonderful...let's fer heavens sake! not descend into internecine squabbling about who and what is important or valuable!" (Weissman, 2007). Instead of being inhibited by insular cognitive battling, by embracing its cognitive diversity, the profession of librarianship can better serve the full range of thought communities. Additionally, the cognitive sociological approach to library and information science research provides a framework for investigating the third dimension of information behavior, seeking not to understand individual differences nor general laws but that which is socially determined and enforced, which is necessary for the full picture of information behavior to emerge.

References

Bates, M. J. (2005). An introduction to metatheories, theories, and models. In K. E. Fisher, S. Erdelez, & L. McKechnie (Eds.), *Theories of information behavior* (pp. 1–24). Mendham, NJ: Information Today.

Belkin, N. J. (1980). Anomalous states of knowledge as a basis for information retrieval. *Canadian Journal of Information Science, 5,* 133–143.

Berry, J., III. (1998, May). Risking relevant reference work. *Library Journal.* Retrieved April 26, 2009, from Academic Search Premier database.

Budd, J. M. (2008). *Self-examination: The present and future of librarianship.* Westport, CT: Libraries Unlimited.

Burger, L. (2007). Transforming reference. *American Libraries, 38*(3), 5. Retrieved April 26, 2009, from Academic Search Premier database.

Dervin, B., & Dewdney, P. (1986). Neutral questioning: A new approach to the reference interview. *RQ, 25*(4), 506–512.

Dervin, B., & Nilan, M. (1986). Information needs and uses. *Annual Review of Information Science and Technology, 21,* 3–33.

Farkas, M. G. (2004, November). Tech vs. traditional in library school and libraries. Retrieved from http://meredith.wolfwater.com/wordpress/2004/11/29/tech-vs-traditional-in-library-school-and-libraries.

Fisher, K. E., Erdelez, S., & McKechnie, L. E. F. (Eds). (2005). *Theories of information behavior.* Medford, NJ: Information Today.

Jesella, K. (2007, July 8). A hipper crowd of shushers. *New York Times*. Retrieved from www.nytimes.com/2007/07/08/fashion/08librarian.html.

Kamm, S. (2007, July). Re: LibraryThing and other "free" stuff [listserv]. Retrieved from http://lists.webjunction.org/wjlists/publib/2007-July/107790.html.

Oder, N. (2007). Dropping Dewey in Maricopa. *Library Journal*. Retrieved April 26, 2009, from http://www.libraryjournal.com/article/CA6457223.html.

Rabey, M. (2007, July). Free yourself from stereotypes! Retrieved from www.popgoesthe library.com/2007/07/free-yourself-from-stereotypes.html.

Shera, J. H. (1949). *Foundations of the public library: The origins of the public library movement in New England 1629–1855*. Chicago: University of Chicago Press.

Weinberger, D. (2007). *Everything is miscellaneous: The power of the new digital disorder*. New York: Henry Holt.

Weissman, S. (2007, July). Generations of us [listserv]. Retrieved from http://lists.web junction.org/wjlists/publib/2007-July/107799.html.

Winston, M. (1998). The role of recruitment in achieving goals related to diversity. *College and Research Libraries*, *59*(3), 240. Retrieved April 26, 2009, from Academic Search Premier database.

Zerubavel, E. (1997). *Social mindscapes: An invitation to cognitive sociology*. Cambridge, MA: Harvard University Press.

CHAPTER 6

Reference Librarians' Personal Theories of Practice: A New Approach to Studying Reference Service

Amy VanScoy

Overview

Much research to date has focused on the behaviors of reference librarians and on the reactions of library users to these behaviors. An area that has received less attention is reference librarians' perceptions of their work, how they construe reference services, and their thinking, beliefs, values, and attitudes. Models of reference service addressing the mental constructs that influence both the thoughts and actions of reference librarians might help us better deal with expanding demands for reference service. A new approach for examining these thoughts and attitudes is identifying reference librarians' personal theories of practice. Personal theories of practice are the informal, often implicit theories that professionals hold about their practice. In other professions, such as teaching, nursing, and counseling, research on personal theories of practice has contributed to better understanding of work in these professions and improvements in professional education and professional development. Similar research and application in librarianship could increase understanding of reference service and contribute to professional education and professional development opportunities for reference librarians. This chapter explores the concept of personal theories of practice, describes how they have been studied in other professions, and explores the potential for such study for reference librarianship.

Introduction

Diane Zabel (2007) used the term "reference renaissance" to describe the current renewal of interest in reference services, represented by creativity and experimentation among reference librarians. There are many examples of how this renaissance has expanded reference services into new territory. In-person reference is increasingly occurring in information commons where the mission and range of questions is broader. Virtual reference is expanding from simple chat to virtual worlds like Second Life. As the activities that constitute reference service continue to expand, research into the nature and diversity of reference service is ever more important. Much research to date has focused on the behaviors of reference librarians and on the reactions of library users to these behaviors. An area that has received less attention is reference librarians' perceptions of their work, how they construe reference services, and their thinking, beliefs, values, and attitudes. Models of reference service addressing the mental constructs that influence both the thoughts and actions of reference librarians might help the profession better deal with expanding demands for reference service. Scholarship in this area could reveal the diversity of approaches that creative, experienced librarians bring to their work and contribute to the flourishing of reference services.

One such approach that has not yet been explored in library and information science is identifying personal theories of practice. This chapter explores the concept of personal theories of practice and their relevance for reference librarianship. Enlightening research on personal theories of practitioners in teaching, nursing, and counseling is described. From this research, as well as related research in library and information science, tentative suppositions are made for what the author may find in her research in the area of reference services and how these findings might contribute to the renaissance of reference services.

What Are Personal Theories of Practice?

Personal theories are informal theories about how the world works. Individuals use them to make sense of things and predict what will happen. These personal theories influence behavior whether individuals are conscious of them or not. Reference practitioners have personal theories about reference service, about their role as reference providers, and about what constitutes successful reference interactions. Examining these personal theories and naming them could have a powerful impact on personal practice as well as on the general understanding of reference service.

A variety of terms have been used to describe the concept addressed in this chapter, such as personal practical theories, implicit theories, tacit theories, and personal practical knowledge. This variety of terms is a challenge for both researchers and practitioners. Pajares (1992) recognized the challenge of studying this concept when a common terminology is not used; he argued for "beliefs" to refer to this concept. The term *beliefs*, however, seems loaded with meaning beyond the workplace context. The term *personal theories of practice* is in common use in the research literature and emphasizes both the practical (workplace-related) and personal (informal and individual) nature of the concept.

Personal theories of practice are the informal, often implicit, theories for what happens in professional work. Several decades of research on personal theories of practice in other professions have generated a number of definitions that help to explain the concept. Sanders and McCutcheon (1986) are often cited as experts in the development of the concept of practical theories of teaching. They defined the concept in this way:

> Practical theories of teaching are the conceptual structures and visions that provide teachers with reason for acting as they do, and for choosing teaching activities and curriculum materials they choose in order to be effective. They are the principles or propositions that undergird and guide teachers' appreciations, decisions, and actions. (pp. 54–55)

Cornett, Yeotis, and Terwilliger (1990) described them as "the systematic set of beliefs [theories] which guide the teacher and come from prior life experiences [personal] and classroom experiences [practical]" (p. 520). Cole (1990) stated that personal theories of practice are "informal and unvalidated (in the scientific sense) and in most case remain unarticulated; yet they are the personal foundations on which an individual's professional practice is built" (p. 203).

The concept of personal theories comes from George Kelly's (1955) work in clinical psychology. His personal construct theory has generated a half century of study, not only in psychology but in other fields, including library and information science (e.g., Crudge & Johnson, 2004, 2007; Potthoff, Weis, Montanelli, & Murbach, 2000; McKnight, 2000). The idea behind this concept is that people create hypotheses about what is going on in their own lives and then accept or reject them based on the evidence they gather from their work. These personal theories can change or they can become entrenched and resist change, despite evidence to the contrary.

A fictional example that illustrates this concept might be a librarian who has a general belief that students do not really care about their research projects and that they procrastinate, starting their research at the last minute. This belief affects how the librarian interprets information about the student and how she behaves. Thinking of this belief as a personal theory provides a new perspective. This librarian "hypothesizes" that students do not care about research. As students continue to request help at the last minute, this hypothesis is confirmed. The quality of the librarian's service and her engagement in the transaction are likely to be low, based on the theory she is using to interpret the situation. If a student does ask for research advice long before the assignment deadline, the librarian could use this new evidence to re-examine her personal theory and possibly alter her behavior.

So how do personal theories and formal theories interact? This question is addressed by two influential theorists: Donald Schön and Chris Argyris (Argyris & Schön, 1974). They argue that the formal theories that practitioners claim to use, their "espoused theories," are not necessary the same as the practitioners' "theories-in-use." Espoused theories are the formal theories that practitioners claim guide their practice. Theories-in-use are the implicit, informal, personal theories that actually influence the work practitioners do. Schön and Argyris emphasize the practitioner as an active creator of knowledge, particularly through reflection.

An illustration of espoused theories in contrast to theories-in-use might be a librarian who, when asked, will refer to the classic reference interview as the framework that guides his practice. Upon observation, however, one might discover that the librarian rarely completes the steps of the reference interview. The reference interview framework may be an espoused theory for this librarian, but his actions are guided by some other, unexamined theory-in-use.

Rando and Menges (1991) argued that both personal theories and formal theories influence behavior, but only explicit personal theories can be critically examined by the practitioner. As long as personal theories remain implicit, they influence behavior and may have unintended consequences, such as the incorrect assumptions about student motivation described in the previous example.

The Study of Personal Theories of Practice in Other Professions

There is a long tradition of examining and using personal theories in the practice of teaching, nursing, and counseling. In these professions, reflecting on personal theories and relating them to formal theories are integral parts of preservice education and professional development. These professions provide a good model for the study of reference librarians because of their similar values on helping and service. Considering its utility for these other professions, there seems to be evidence that this approach merits exploration for library and information science, and particularly for reference.

Depending on the intentions of the researchers and the study design, the personal theories reported in the research can look very different. Qualitative methodologies, especially interviews, participant observation and document review, have been used to provide thick, rich description of practitioners' personal theories of practice (e.g., Cornett et al, 1990; Radwin, 1995; Gess-Newsome, 2003). Some researchers take a less interpretivist approach, using questionnaires (e.g., Murray & McDonald, 1997) or examining student work (e.g., Levin & He, 2008). The repertory grid technique, developed by George Kelly, is yet another method used to study personal theories of practice (e.g., Hillier, 1998; Salmon, 1993). This broad diversity of approaches creates a variety of perspectives on the topic as well as challenges in comparing results across studies and across professions.

Most of the examples of personal theories of practice in this chapter are drawn from the research on teachers. This body of research is much larger than that of the other professions. In addition, counseling has established formal theories from which a student is expected to choose in developing his or her own personal theory of counseling. Therefore, most of the research on counselors, rather than exploring unique personal theories, focuses on connecting personal theories to established formal theories.

Important Concepts

Personal theories of practice can be presented as statements or lists of what practitioners' value, what they feel their role is, and how they perceive the dynamic between themselves and their students, patients, or clients. See Table 6.1 for examples of the personal theories of practice expressed by four studies on teachers. A good example from the nursing perspective is Cook, Gilmer, and Bess (2003), who found personal theories such as "nurses provide care for patients," "nursing is a helping profession," and "it involves health promotion and helping the ill regain their health" (p. 313).

Researchers interpret these statements and draw conclusions about practitioner thinking, values, and attitudes. They can also draw conclusions about what is absent from practitioners' personal theories. Cook and colleagues (2003) found that nurses' personal theories focused on "promotion of health" and "treatment of illness" with little acknowledgement of ethical, cultural, legal, and economic issues (p. 316).

Table 6.1. Examples of Personal Theories of Practice from Research in Teaching	
Theory of Practice	**Source**
• As a teacher, you are forever a student • Children should always have choices • Expectation shapes achievements • Assessments are authentic and varied	Levin and He (2008, p. 60)
• Encourage participation by students • Teach students equally • Accommodate for different student needs • Prepare for interruptions	Kettle and Sellars (1996, p. 9)
• Provide positive and successful learning experiences • Foster a desire to learn • Prepare students to be worthwhile members of society • Establish and maintain mutual trust and respect	Cole (1990, p. 207)
• Offer visual learning • Talk in kids' terms • Make science learning fun • Help students save face	Cornett, Yeotis, and Terwilliger (1990, p. 521)

Models

Personal theories of practice can resemble formal theories, showing complex interactions and relationships. Pinnegar and Carter (1990) synthesized their findings into three models of the "dynamics underlying student learning in the classroom" (p. 23). One of the models was "signalling their *respect* for students, teachers give students *responsibility* for learning. Students come to respect the teacher, in turn, and they develop a *rapport* with each other" (p. 24; italics added). They also found that teachers saw links between "confidence, trust and success" (p. 24) and "interest, honest and relevance" (p. 25).

Radwin (1995) developed a model of "knowing the patient" after studying nurses' core beliefs. "Knowing the patient" involved familiarity and intimacy; was affected by time, experience, and others' input; and employed strategies of empathizing, matching a pattern, developing a bigger picture, and balancing preferences with differences.

Typologies or Profiles

While some studies are focused on exploring an individual practitioner's personal theories, others cluster numerous participants' personal theories and develop typologies or profiles of personal theories. For example, Berman-Rossi (1988) used personal theories of teachers to develop two typologies: rational/empiricist (focused on content) or pragmatist (focused on process) (p. 52). Freire and colleagues (1992) developed typologies of teachers as traditional, experimental, constructivist, pragmatist, and social (p. 503).

Metaphors

The previous examples demonstrate a variety of approaches to studying personal theories of practice in everyday language. Another approach is to study the metaphors used by practitioners, which can reveal their thoughts, feelings, and beliefs about their work in a way that direct language may not. Clandinin (1985) felt that metaphorical "images" best capture the emotional and moral dimensions of practitioner beliefs (p. 376). Munby and Russell (1990) had originally investigated personal theories with more direct language, but later stated:

> We realized that [our] earlier work...improperly emphasized the propositional character of professional knowledge.... Our reading of the contemporary work on metaphor showed us that realities are constructed metaphorically and we realized that we could turn this around and explore practitioners' metaphors to gain insights into how they constructed their professional worlds. (p. 117)

Asking participants to share their personal theories in the form of metaphors may help to surface personal theories of practice of which practitioners were not aware. Marshall (1990) claimed that a "path to heightening teachers' awareness of their implicit beliefs systems involves focusing on the metaphors and images they use as they describe their teaching" (p. 128).

Marshall (1990) presented metaphors generated by preservice teachers, such as "disciplinarian, manager, stand-up comedian in a small loud café, wine maker, jumper cables, pillow, octopus, and decathlon participant" (p. 130). In her work with students, she tried to help them find alternatives for their problematic metaphors, such as "warden, lecturer, dispenser of information, vessel, and obstacle" (pp. 130–131). Kettle and Sellars (1996) reported that one preservice teacher described teaching as a basketball game: "It is a team effort. If you continually work at doing well or trying to achieve a goal, the results are certainly worthwhile" (p. 7).

One of Cole's (1990) teacher's used a windmill metaphor:

> I am the wind that propels the windmill. The students are the burning coals that brighten with inspiration as the wind hits them.... Without the driving force of the wind the windmill becomes stagnant and motionless. The wind gives the windmill a purpose to exist. (p. 216)

The metaphor of teacher as wind demonstrates the critical role of the teacher as perceived by this participant: the teacher gives "purpose" to the classroom. This perception is very different from the teacher studied by Kettle and Sellars who perceives himself or herself as part of the classroom "team."

Another interesting pair of contrasting metaphors are presented by Elbaz and Clandinin. Elbaz's (1981) teacher seemed to perceive an adversarial relationship between school and students. She used images such "a place to hide" to describe her subject matter, and described herself as an "ally" to help students "survive" in school (pp. 63–64). In contrast, Clandinin's (1985) teacher used the image of "classroom as home" (p. 367).

Poulou (2003) studied metaphors used by preservice school counselors to describe the role of the school psychologist: "a ship's captain, a tour guide, a politician, a coach, a conductor, a pilot, a director, a dance teacher, a leader, a shepherd, an experienced climber and an organizer of team games" (p. 382). In all of these metaphors, the school psychologist was an active member of the school. There were also metaphors that seemed to describe the psychologist as separate, but authoritative or guiding: "a Buddhist, a doctor, a grandmother, or the leader of a tribe of Indians" (p. 384).

While these metaphors are interesting in and of themselves, the ultimate goal is to use the metaphors to gain insight into the implicit theories of the practitioners. Examining the personal practical theories of other professionals raises questions about what might surface in studies of reference librarians. How might they describe their role or the principles of their practice? What profiles might be developed to describe differences among librarians? What metaphors might reference librarians use to describe their work?

What Could This New Approach Yield for Reference Services?

Reference librarians' personal theories about their practice have not yet been studied, although some scholars of reference have called for similar research. Richardson (1995) acknowledged the existence of the "private knowledge" of experienced reference librarians and stated that "a study of deep reference librarianship probably would involve motivations, desires, wants and beliefs in the reference interview" (p. 152). Bunge (1999) asserted that "the technical skills and knowledge of the helping professional seem less important to effective practice than are the beliefs and attitudes held by the professional" (p. 15).

Some reference research has taken small steps toward understanding the thinking, beliefs, and attitudes of reference librarians, including Alafiatayo and colleagues (1996), Watson-Boone (1998), Gerlich (2006), and Doherty (2007). However, these studies focus on the librarians' behaviors and on their stated beliefs. Implicit theories held by reference librarians may take more effort to surface. Although no one has probed the meaning of reference service using librarians' personal theories as a basis for understanding it, existing reference research, research on practitioners in other fields, and anecdotal evidence may provide some clues to what may result from a deliberate study of reference librarians' personal theories of practice.

Possible Themes in Reference Librarians' Personal Theories of Practice

Based on the literature, some suppositions can be made about themes that might emerge from the study of reference librarians' personal theories of practice. Librarians are likely to reveal personal theories of reference service that focus on answering questions or on instruction. Decades of debate on whether information provision or instruction is the most important feature of reference service show that both of the concepts are significant (e.g., Wagers, 1978; Nielsen, 1982). Radford's (1999) work on the importance of interpersonal relationships in reference service suggests another theme likely to surface in study of reference librarians' personal theories of practice. The literature, as well as the intuition of any experienced reference librarian, suggests that the themes of answering questions, instructing, and developing relationships will emerge. How these components interact and how they relate to reference service overall requires more study. In teaching, for example, Pinnegar and Carter (1990) were able to show how various constructs interacted to reveal complicated personal theories for teaching. In studying librarians, findings may show relationships between information provision, instruction, and relationship development. Research into reference librarians' personal theories of practice could show how these three important components of reference interact and how they are affected by contextual and situational factors.

For some librarians, one of these concepts may be more critical to what they do than others. This sort of finding could allow a typology of personal theories to emerge that show a diversity of approaches to reference service. This typology could be used to better describe and communicate about the diversity of approaches that individual librarians contribute to a reference team.

In addition to these themes, we may discover additional concepts that emerge as essential to a librarian's construction of reference work. Some studies of other professionals have surfaced themes or interactions among themes that had not previously been considered (e.g., Kover, 1995). Giving voice to reference librarians' diverse perceptions of reference service could surface new dimensions of reference service.

Possible Developmental Trends in Reference Librarians' Personal Theories of Practice

Although a typology of diverse personal theories is an attractive outcome, investigation into reference librarians' personal theories of practice may result in a more hierarchical structure. Research on teachers, for example, shows distinct developmental differences between novice and experienced teachers. Novice teachers tend to focus on their own teaching and whether or not students like them, while experienced teachers tend to focus on student learning (e.g., Fox, 1983; Samuelowicz & Bain, 2001). As librarians gain more experience and reflect on their practice, they may develop more sophisticated informal theories about reference service.

Could a trend like this exist among reference librarians? What aspects of the work, if any, change in importance from library school and field experience to early career and to expert? Might there be a shift in focus from a librarian-centered perspective to a user-centered perspective, as with teaching?

Possible Relationships between Librarians' Personal Theories and Their Behaviors

Research on how personal theories affect the behavior of reference librarians could explain behaviors that can be cryptic to managers and colleagues. If a librarian doesn't do a full reference interview, for example, it might not be that he or she doesn't value the reference interview but rather that some constraint is preventing his or her values from being implemented.

Studies show that behavior often follows from a professional's personal theories. Gess-Newsome and colleagues (2003) reported that "in all cases there is a degree of consistency between the beliefs of the instructor and the teaching practices used" (p. 758). Other studies show that constraints such as lack of resources and pressure to get through content can interfere with applying personal theories to practice (e.g., Cole, 1990; Murray & McDonald, 1997).

How do librarians' personal theories of practice affect their behavior? Do the pressures of time, limited resources, the physical arrangement of the reference desk, or the communication constraints of digital reference affect how librarians' beliefs manifest themselves? How does reflection on personal theories affect how librarians' behave? If we understood better what motivates reference librarians' behaviors, then we might be better able to evaluate and assess reference librarians' behaviors as well as create opportunities to help improve them.

Possible Sources of Librarians' Personal Theories of Practice

Another fruitful area of study about professionals in other disciplines is the sources of their personal theories (e.g., Kettle & Sellars, 1996; Levin & He, 2008). Professionals' personal theories can develop based on past experiences, professional education courses, or practica and internships. What role do basic and advanced reference courses have on librarians' personal theories of practice? How do practica, field experiences, and graduate assistant positions at the reference desk affect personal theories? How much do reference librarians' personal theories of practice change during their first years in the profession? Understanding the sources of reference librarians' personal theories of practice could help in improving professional education for future librarians and professional development opportunities for practicing librarians.

How May This Research Benefit Reference Librarianship?

Identifying librarians' personal theories of practice has a number of direct applications for improving reference service. For individual librarians, merely recognizing their implicit theories could help them reflect on their practice and make more deliberate choices in their behaviors. Reflecting on one's personal practical theories, including how they influence one's behavior and how they may be similar and different to those of one's colleagues, could provide a useful structure for professional growth and development. Several of the studies on personal theories of practice in other professions reported that participants enjoyed the opportunity to think about and talk about their practice. Some said that they seldom had the opportunity to talk about such things. For example, Levin and He (2008) report that participants were "very positive in their feedback about the value of articulating and assessing their PPTs" (p. 66). Librarians, too, might find pleasure and value in this kind of study.

For groups of librarians, such as a reference department, recognizing and discussing personal theories of practice could lead to appreciation of differences and better communication. Hunter (1997) suggested that his research could be applied to human-resources-related purposes, such as writing job descriptions, allocating work, selecting staff for project teams, identifying training needs, planning career paths, and performance appraisal (p. 79). Articulating personal theories of practice could facilitate communication between reference departments and library administration. Research into librarian beliefs could be useful not only for individual librarians but also for the library organization as a whole.

For the profession, understanding personal theories of reference librarians could lead to ideas for professional development opportunities. Many current opportunities focus on skills, such as the reference interview, database interfaces, or digital reference products. Workshops or self-evaluations that focus on personal theories of practice might provide more meaningful experiences that could be transferred from current to future reference contexts.

For professional education, integrating exploration and articulation of personal theories to the professional education of reference librarians could ease the transition into the first year of professional work and help develop reflective practice in future professionals. In counseling, courses have been developed to help students recognize their personal theories and relate them to formal theories in their profession (e.g., Spruill & Benshoff, 2000). Such opportunities could occur in reference courses, field experiences, or internships.

For the scholarship of reference, studying reference librarians' personal theories of practice could lead to the development of new models of reference service, grounded in practice. Research on personal theories in other professions has occasionally surfaced aspects not addressed by existing theory. Such research in reference services may yield new areas to explore, as well. Brennan (1973) advocated involving practitioners in adding to or generating theory: "There is a great need for experienced and competent practitioners to feed back to the universities innovative theoretical insights which they have gained through long years of testing and retesting in the action labs of practice" (p. 11). What could reference scholars learn about reference theory from watching "the action labs of practice"? Are practitioners using personal theories that might help us understand what happens during the reference encounter? Could practitioner-generated or practitioner-inspired theory help close the theory/ practice gap?

Conclusion

So what are reference librarians' personal theories of practice? What are the informal, implicit theories that guide individual's practice? Studies of librarians that have been conducted for other purposes provide some clues; however, we do not completely understand what is happening inside the minds of reference librarians, about what they think is going on in a reference transaction, what they think is important, what they think their role is, and what they think the role of library users is.

Several decades of research on practitioner beliefs suggests that this line of inquiry is fruitful and yields results that benefit scholars, practitioners, and educators. Because reference librarianship has aspects in common with teaching, nursing, and counseling, it is logical that such research into the beliefs of reference librarians would be valuable, as well.

Exploratory research into reference librarians' personal theories of practice, from basic statements of purpose to colorful metaphors, would give us insight into how reference librarians perceive their work. Qualitative methods, such as interviews with reference librarians, observation of their work at the reference desk, and review of their digital reference transcripts, or even more structured methods, such as Kelly's repertory grid technique, would be useful in surfacing reference librarians' person theories of practice.

Study of reference librarians' personal theories could show developmental changes from novice to expert and relationships between what librarians think and what they actually do at the reference desk. Research may show the sources of reference librarians' personal theories and how and why these beliefs change and develop. This information could be used to improve professional education and professional development for librarians and to add new dimensions to models of reference service or generate new theory. Study of reference librarians' personal theories of practice could have much to contribute to the renaissance of reference services.

References

Alafiatayo, B. O., Yip, Y. J., & Blunden-Ellis, J. C. P. (1996). Reference transaction and the nature of the process for general reference assistance. *Library and Information Science Research, 18*(4), 357–384.

Argyris, C., & Schön, D. A. (1974). *Theory in practice: Increasing professional effectiveness.* Jossey-Bass Publishers.

Berman-Rossi, T. (1988). Theoretical orientations of social work practice teachers: An analysis. *Journal of Social Work Education, 24*(1), 50–59.

Brennan, W. C. (1973). The practitioner as theoretician. *Journal of Education for Social Work, 9*(2), 5–12.

Bunge, C. A. (1999). Beliefs, attitudes, and values of the reference librarian. *Reference Librarian, 66,* 13–24.

Clandinin, D. J. (1985). Personal practical knowledge: A study of teachers' classroom images. *Curriculum Inquiry, 15*(4), 361–385.

Cole, A. L. (1990). Personal theories of teaching: Development in the formative years. *Alberta Journal of Educational Research, 36*(3), 203–222.

Cook, T. H., Gilmer, M. J., & Bess, C. J. (2003). Beginning students' definitions of nursing: An inductive framework of professional identity. *Journal of Nursing Education, 42*(7), 311–317.

Cornett, J. W., Yeotis, C., & Terwilliger, L. (1990). Teacher personal practical theories and their influence upon teacher curricular and instructional actions: A case study of a secondary science teacher. *Science Education, 74*(5), 517–529.

Crudge, S. E., & Johnson, C. (2004). Using the information seeker to elicit construct models for search engine evaluation. *Journal of the American Society for Information Science & Technology, 55*(9), 794–806.

Crudge, S. E. & Johnson, F. C. (2007). Using the repertory grid and laddering technique to determine the user's evaluative model of search engines. *Journal of Documentation, 63*(2), 259–280.

Doherty, J. J. (2007). *Facilitating interaction: The role of the reference librarian in online learning environments.* Doctoral dissertation, Northern Arizona University, Flagstaff, Arizona.

Elbaz, F. (1981). The teacher's "practical knowledge": Report of a case study. *Curriculum Inquiry, 11*(1), 43–71.

Fox, D. (1983). Personal theories of teaching. *Studies in Higher Education, 8*(2), 151–163.

Freire, A. M., Chorao, M. D., & Sanches, C. (1992). Elements for a typology of teachers conceptions of physics teaching. *Teaching and Teacher Education, 8*(5–6), 497–507.

Gerlich, B. K. (2006). *Work in motion/assessment at rest: An attitudinal study of academic reference librarians. A case study at mid-size university (MSU A).* Doctoral dissertation, University of Pittsburgh, Pittsburgh, Pennsylvania.

Gess-Newsome, J., Southerland, S. A., Johnston, A., & Woodbury, S. (2003). Educational reform, personal practical theories, and dissatisfaction: The anatomy of change in college science teaching. *American Educational Research Journal, 40*(3), 731–767.

Hillier, Y. (1998). Informal practitioner theory: Eliciting the implicit. *Studies in the Education of Adults, 30*(1), 35.

Hunter, M. G. (1997). The use of RepGrids to gather interview data about information systems analysts. *Information Systems Journal, 7*(1), 67–81.

Kelly, G. (1955). *The psychology of personal constructs.* New York: Norton.

Kettle, B., & Sellars, N. (1996). The development of student teachers practical theory of teaching. *Teaching and Teacher Education, 12*(1), 1–24.

Kover, A. J. (1995). Copywriters' implicit theories of communication: An exploration. *Journal of Consumer Research, 21*(4), 596–611.

Levin, B., & He, Y. (2008). Investigating the content and sources of teacher candidates' personal practical theories (PPTs). *Journal of Teacher Education, 59*(1), 55–68.

Marshall, H. H. (1990). Metaphor as an instructional tool in encouraging student teacher reflection. *Theory into Practice, 29*(2), 128–132.

McKnight, C. (2000). The personal construction of information space. *Journal of the American Society for Information Science, 51*(8), 730–733.

Munby, H., & Russell, T. (1990). Metaphor in the study of teachers' professional knowledge. *Theory into Practice, 29*(2), 116–121.

Murray, K., & MacDonald, R. (1997). The disjunction between lecturers' conceptions of teaching and their claimed educational practice. *Higher Education, 33*(3), 331–349.

Nielsen, B. (1982). Teacher or intermediary: Alternative professional models in the information age. *College and Research Libraries, 43*(3), 183–191.

Pajares, M. F. (1992). Teachers' beliefs and educational research: Cleaning up a messy construct. *Review of Educational Research, 62*(3), 307–332.

Pinnegar, S., & Carter, K. (1990). Comparing theories from textbooks and practicing teachers. *Journal of Teacher Education, 41*(1), 20–26.

Potthoff, J. K., Weis, D. L., Montanelli, D. S., & Murbach, M. M. (2000). An evaluation of patron perceptions of library space using the role repertory grid procedure. *College & Research Libraries, 61*(3), 191–203.

Poulou, M. (2003). Reflections of pre-service psychologists on the role of the school psychologist. *School Psychology International, 24*(4), 378–393.

Radford, M. L. (1999). *The reference encounter: Interpersonal communication in the academic library.* Chicago: Association of College and Research Libraries.

Radwin, L. E. (1995). Knowing the patient: A process model for individualized interventions. *Nursing Research, 44*(6), 364–370.

Rando, W. C., & Menges, R. J. (1991). How practice is shaped by personal theories. In R. J. Menges & M. D. Svinicki (Eds.), *College teaching: From theory to practice* (pp. 7–14). San Francisco: Jossey-Bass.

Richardson, J. V. (1995). *Knowledge-based systems for general reference work: Applications, problems, and progress.* San Diego: Academic Press.

Salmon, D. (1993). Anticipating the school consultant role: Changes in personal constructs following training. *School Psychology Quarterly, 8*(4), 301–317.

Samuelowicz, K., & Bain, J. D. (2001). Revisiting academics' beliefs about teaching and learning. *Higher Education, 41*(3), 299–325.

Sanders, D. P., & McCutcheon, G. (1986). The development of practical theories of teaching. *Journal of Curriculum and Supervision, 2*(1), 50–67.

Spruill, D. A., & Benshoff, J. M. (2000). Helping beginning counselors develop a personal theory of counseling. *Counselor Education and Supervision, 40*(1), 70–80.

Wagers, R. (1978). American reference theory and the information dogma. *Journal of Library History, 13*(3), 265–281.

Watson-Boone, R. (1998). *Constancy and change in the worklife of research university librarians.* Chicago: Association of College and Research Libraries.

Zabel, D. (2007). A reference renaissance. *Reference & User Services Quarterly, 47*(2), 108–110.

SECTION II.3

Innovative Service Models

CHAPTER 7

A New Route to an Old Resource: Facilitating Access to Library Research Guides for the Self-Serve Generation

Stephanie Alexander, Jennifer Gerke, and Kathryn Lage

Overview

The University of Colorado at Boulder Libraries developed a Web-based database of research and subject guides in order to improve access to the guides. This article will review the current literature and library practices, explain the database design and implementation, and analyze usage data, drawing conclusions for future enhancements. The authors discuss this new mode of access to library guides, including key lessons learned and areas identified for further research. Practical implications for improved access to library guides can be drawn from this study.

Introduction

Research and subject guides are a core element in the array of resources librarians create to assist patrons in using library materials in conducting research. They have evolved from print handouts to Web sites and from subject-specific recommended booklists into more robust guides that provide context for using all types of library resources (Vileno, 2007). Along with differences in format, new ways to provide access are emerging. No longer are the guides solely available at the reference desk; libraries now link to guides from their Web sites, repurpose them as frequently asked questions (FAQs), feature them in course management software, include them in the library catalog, and create Web-based databases to organize the guides.

At the University of Colorado at Boulder (CU Boulder) Libraries, research and subject guides are a staple of the research assistance librarians provide. Guides are available online, but until recently, access to guides was inconsistent. Responding to the changes emerging in other libraries and a perceived change in how students access library resources, the authors, three reference librarians in different departments in the CU Boulder Libraries, recently completed a project to research and redesign access to guides that resulted in a Web-based Research and Subject Guides database (http://ucblibraries.colorado.edu/research/guides/index.cfm; see Figure 7.1).

Figure 7.1. Research and Subject Guides Database Homepage

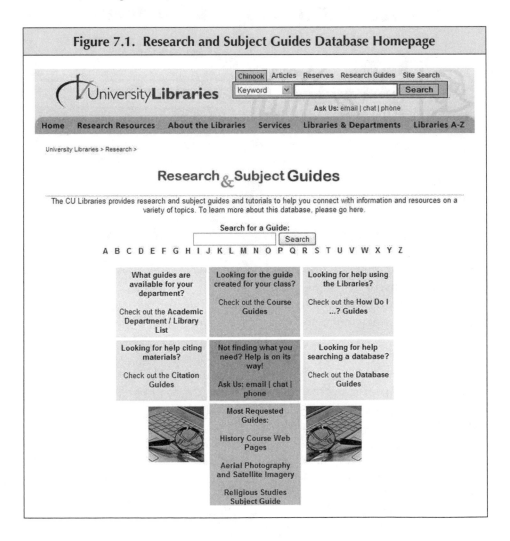

This chapter will review the current literature and library practices, explain the database design and implementation, and analyze usage data, drawing conclusions for future enhancements. Similar databases of library guides exist but have not previously been explored in the literature. The authors discuss this new mode of access to library guides, including key lessons learned and areas identified for further research. Practical implications for improved access to library guides can be drawn from this study.

Research Problem: Access to Guides

At the outset of the project, the authors hypothesized that collating CU Boulder Libraries' diverse group of guides and providing multiple modes of retrieval would increase access to the guides and expose the user to new, related, and interdisciplinary guides. In order to investigate this question, the authors examined practices at CU Boulder and other academic institutions and researched existing literature, considered user research patterns, and analyzed Web use statistics.

Local Practices

In 2006, the CU Boulder Libraries Web site had a subject guides Web page that listed 58 guides, most of which were general introductions to research in a discipline. This Web page was too long for easy browsing, presented users only with an alphabetical list of guides, and did not cross-list guides that were interdisciplinary in nature (see Figure 7.2).

The authors analyzed Web use statistics to gather information about the use of existing research and subject guides. Of the thousands of pages on the CU Boulder Libraries Web site, the previous subject guides Web page and four research and subject guides were among the top 50 most accessed Web pages for July 2006–June 2007, proving that research and subject guides were a well-used part of the libraries' online presence (see Table 7.1). However, only one of those four research and subject guides was listed on the previous subject guides Web page. A more complete inventory of the libraries' Web site revealed that many other guides were also not listed on the previous page.

The discovery that guides were missing from the previous subject guides Web page showed that users were finding other ways to navigate to the guides. While other access points may be expedient or familiar to patrons, they do not provide the user with information on related interdisciplinary guides and do not provide exposure to unfamiliar guides for research on new or related topics. The authors did not want to eliminate these alternative modes of discovery but theorized that creating a centralized point for guides would provide better access to all resources.

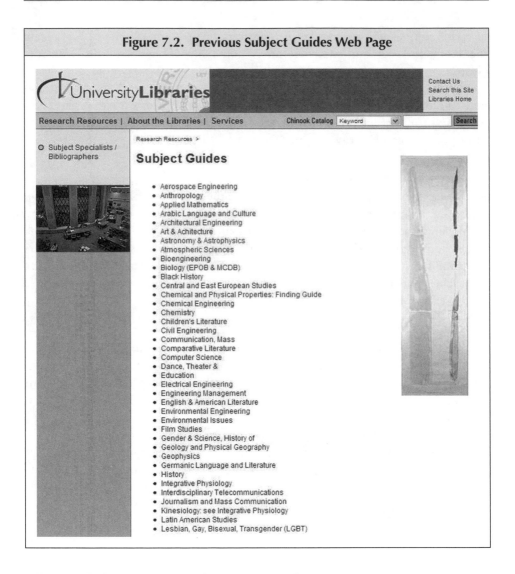

Figure 7.2. Previous Subject Guides Web Page

Review of the Literature and User Research Patterns

Literature Review and Practices at Other Academic Institutions
In a 2007 article published in *Reference Services Review*, Luigina Vileno (Vileno, 2007) presents a comprehensive review of the literature on the progression from print pathfinders to the online guides that are available from most academic library Web sites today. This review shows that much of the literature on guides examines the content of subject guides and guide creation best practices such as the necessity of using a consistent format. However, the authors were primarily interested in articles that discussed methods to bring together users and library

Table 7.1. Guides in the Top 50 Most Accessed CU Boulder Libraries Web Pages			
Guide Name	Authoring Library	Listed on Subject Guides Page	Page Rank
Subject Guides Main Page*	Norlin	*	15th
Native American Resources Guide	Government Publications	Yes	31st
Citation Guide	Norlin	No	35th
Affirmative Action Guide	Government Publications	No	36th
Public Records Guide	Government Publications	No	42nd

Source: WebTrends report for CU Boulder Libraries Web Site: June 2006–July 2007.

* Subject Guides Main Page = Previous Subject Guides Web page that listed some (not all) CU Boulder Libraries subject and research guides.

subject guides, as the central problem discussed in this article is access to guides. As Bunnell and Byerley (2000) noted, aren't the subject guides "useless if no one knows about them?" (p. 36).

The literature provides examples of five broad categories of access to guides: linking to guides from the library Web page, cataloging guides, including guides in a course management system, combining guides with a library help or FAQ site, and providing access through a searchable database. Many libraries highlight their subject guides by linking them from important library's Web pages. A study of online subject guides on Association of Research Libraries (ARL) Web sites discovered that 62 percent of libraries provided links to the guides from their homepage (Jackson & Pellack, 2004: 322). Dunsmore's (2002) study of business subject guides in the United States and Canada found that "half of the university library Websites mentioned pathfinders on their homepage, and virtually all mentioned pathfinders by the third Webpage from the library's homepage" (p. 145). Beyond including guides on the homepage, featuring the guides in additional locations on a library's Web site may be important. Reeb and Gibbons (2004) indicate that linking the subject guides from parts of the library's Web site that have "high research or coursework context to students," like the Web page that lists online databases or offers information on electronic course reserve material, could increase traffic to the guides (pp. 127–128).

Efforts to catalog research and subject guides in the library online public access catalog (OPAC) are also discussed in the literature. Cataloging guides provides access in the same place as other library resources, which "enhances the 'one stop shopping' approach many library users favor" (Nuttall & McAbee, 1997, p. 80). Cataloging guides was shown to be successful in a study done at the University of Florida. In this study, Simpson, Williams, Arlen, and Bushnell

(2005) focused on the impact of inclusion in the catalog on the Web use statistics for guides. By analyzing Web use statistics on a selected group of history guides, the authors discovered that there was an increase in traffic after records for individual guides were included in the local OPAC, and they noticed another increase after the records were added to Online Computer Library Center's (OCLC) WorldCat database (Simpson et al., 2005). Simpson and colleagues indicated that they were not expecting the user to search the catalog specifically for a guide, but instead they intended for the user to discover one when looking over results from a subject or keyword-based search (Simpson et al., 2005). They stressed that providing multiple points of access is important, a sentiment echoed in Nutall and McAbee's (1997) belief that the main benefit of having the guides available in Jacksonville State University's Houston Cole Library's OPAC was to provide an additional access point. This conclusion is similar to Wilson's (2002) assertion that the OPAC may be the best place for patrons to find the guides and may raise awareness of the guides' existence for patrons who were simply doing subject searches.

Other libraries incorporate guides into a course management system (CMS). By linking subject guides and other library resources within a CMS (such as WebCT or Blackboard), librarians aim to connect students to guides in a way that fits with their research patterns. Including guides in a CMS may help students associate the subject guide for their discipline to their specific course. A study done at Cornell University Library by Rieger, Horne, and Revels (2004) confirmed the importance of these efforts. The authors noted that "course Web sites represent effective channels for presenting students with selected library resources, e-reserve readings, and online tutorials about various aspects of library research pertinent to the course offered" (Rieger, Horne, & Revels, 2004, p. 208). The goal is to make the various library resources easy to integrate into these online course environments so that teaching faculty will be able to successfully incorporate them into the students' learning experience.

Another method many institutions are using is to create library research help sites. These libraries have co-located their guides with other library help information in order to provide a variety of resources to students. Marshall University Libraries' took their existing "subject guides, print handouts, and Library FAQs" and combined them with "learning modules and streaming video" to create a comprehensive help site designed to benefit distance and on-campus students looking for help using library resources. This help site is not searchable, but the authors noted that adding that functionality would be useful (Arnold, Csir, Sias, & Zhang, 2005). Libraries at the University of Pennsylvania and the University of Minnesota have both developed searchable Web-based FAQ databases to provide answers to commonly asked research questions. The business librarians at the University of Pennsylvania's Wharton School developed a business FAQ database of over 500 question and answer pairs that can be accessed by keyword searches or topic/subject browsing. The FAQ was developed to "meet the patrons where they are, giving them a customized, interactive, always-on database of questions and answers that can be searched or browsed for useful, succinct answers to their most pressing questions (Anello & Bonfield, 2007). Similarly, the FAQ database at the University of Minnesota Libraries can be browsed by table of contents or index or searched by keyword to find answers to commonly asked questions about doing research in the library (University of Minnesota University Libraries, n.d.).

An FAQ database can be an inclusive site for resources to answer common questions, but it does not provide the more comprehensive and complex assistance of a traditional library research or subject guide. Guides database projects at the University of Michigan (UM) (University of Michigan Libraries, n.d.) and the University of North Carolina (UNC) libraries (University of North Carolina University Libraries, n.d.) combine the flexible approach of an FAQ site with the content-rich library guides model. These two libraries developed databases to provide access to their guides. Both databases offer keyword searches of guide metadata. This metadata include related guides. Neither database supports Boolean searching, and both appear to treat multiple word searches as if they had an OR operator between the search terms. The UNC Libraries database can be browsed by subject and alphabetically by title and highlights the most requested guides. The UM Libraries database can be browsed by title, library department, or subject. The subject browsing is broken down into browsing by guide type: citation or style guides, guides to online databases, subject guides, and technology guides. The UM Libraries database offers an RSS (Really Simple Syndication) feed of new guides. By giving users the choice to browse by different criteria or search for guides by keyword, these database-driven alternatives give users access to traditional library guides through a new model.

User Research Patterns

Changes in Academic Research Methods

Changing academic research practices are resulting in fewer in-person reference interactions. There has been a steady decrease in the number of reference transactions in ARL libraries. This decrease is mirrored at CU Boulder (see Figure 7.3). A recent study of undergraduate research behavior at the University of Rochester characterizes today's service paradigm as containing few interpersonal service interactions. "The student model of service is self-service" (Fried Foster & Gibbons, 2007, p. 75). Library users who expect self-service may no longer come to the reference desk for help doing research, but they still need assistance finding and utilizing library materials. Many of the "Net generation" or "millennial" students found on college campuses "often find library-sponsored resources difficult to figure out on

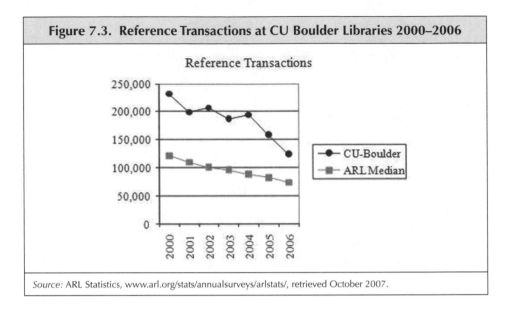

Figure 7.3. Reference Transactions at CU Boulder Libraries 2000–2006

Source: ARL Statistics, www.arl.org/stats/annualsurveys/arlstats/, retrieved October 2007.

their own" (Lippincott, 2005, p. 13.2). Given this reference climate, librarians need to assess how access to research and subject guides is provided.

CU Boulder Libraries users are accessing subject guides when the reference desk is open and when it is closed. The reference desk in Norlin Library (the main humanities and social sciences library on the CU Boulder campus) provides 60 hours of reference services per week during the fall and spring semesters. During the hours when librarians are not available for research assistance, the Libraries' Web site serves as a substitute for this in-person assistance. However, as the authors of the study at the University of Rochester assert, the student model of self-service means that students use the Web site even when in-person research help is available. Nearly 59 percent of all visits to the CU Boulder Libraries subject guides and over 57 percent of visits to the libraries' Web site (University of Colorado at Boulder Libraries, 2007) occur between the hours of 9:00 a.m. and 8:00 p.m., showing that many users are accessing the guides even when in-person desk assistance may be available (see Table 7.2).[1]

Different Approaches to Research
Students and librarians have very different approaches to research and perceptions of the research process. Veldof and Beaver (2001) call this the "clash of the mental models" (p. 12). During their usability testing of the University of Minnesota's library tutorial, they discovered that while "students tend to view library research as a means to an end, librarians tend to teach research as if it is an end in itself" (Veldof & Beavers, 2001, p. 10). A student starting a history paper may want information on how to use a database to find a peer-reviewed article and

Table 7.2. Subject Guides Visits by Hour of the Day				
Hour	**# of Hits**	**% of total hits**	**# of visits**	**% of total visits**
00:00–12:59	11,587	4.65	2,034	2.97
1:00–01:59	10,956	4.40	1,844	2.69
2:00–02:59	9,514	3.82	1,762	2.57
3:00–03:59	8,826	3.54	1,741	2.54
4:00–04:59	4,245	1.70	1,719	2.51
5:00–05:59	3,585	1.44	1,815	2.65
6:00–06:59	3,887	1.56	1,896	2.77
7:00–07:59	3,895	1.56	2,091	3.05
8:00–08:59	6,118	2.45	2,585	3.77
9:00–09:59	8,870	3.56	3,153	4.60
10:00–10:59	9,772	3.92	3,465	5.06
11:00–11:59	10,806	4.34	3,962	5.78
12:00–12:59	14,360	5.77	3,959	5.78
13:00–13:59	15,517	6.23	4,181	6.10
14:00–14:59	14,180	5.69	4,244	6.19
15:00–15:59	12,550	5.04	4,016	5.86
16:00–16:59	12,654	5.08	3,853	5.62
17:00–17:59	11,962	4.80	3,388	4.94
18:00–18:59	13,489	5.42	3,175	4.63
19:00–19:59	13,219	5.31	3,017	4.40
20:00–20:59	12,146	4.88	2,888	4.21
21:00–21:59	12,001	4.82	2,852	4.16
22:00–22:59	12,027	4.83	2,692	3.93
23:00–23:59	12,617	5.07	2,204	3.22
Total	248,783		68,536	

Source: WebTrends report for subject guides directory: September 2006–June 2007.

may be less concerned about how to "correctly" start his or her research. Librarians, on the other hand, may want to guide a student through the research process, from brainstorming keywords for better Boolean searching to finding background information on his or her topic in reference sources.

In addition to having a different approach to research than librarians, studies show that students do not frame their research process using a discipline-based model and therefore do not associate their information need with discipline-based library guides (Reeb & Gibbons, 2004: 124). Reeb and Gibbons' (2004) work, "Students, Librarians, and Subject Guides: Improving a Poor Rate of Return," discusses students' lack of a conceptual understanding of the discipline-based organizational model due to the increasing emphasis on interdisciplinary learning and research. They conclude that students' "mental model is not well suited to library subject guides that require an understanding of disciplines" (Reeb & Gibbons, 2004, p. 126).

Students want to be able to search for library resources much in the same way they are used to searching the Web. Studies demonstrate that people searching the Web (in the United States) are not doing complex searches using Boolean operators. Jansen and Spink (2006) note that from 1997–2002 "the usage of query operators on the US-based Web Search engines varied from 11% to 20%" (p. 257). Additionally, 73 percent view only the first page of results (Jansen & Spink, 2006). In support for translating Web searching trends to the design of access to library resources, Nichols and Mellenger's (2007) examination of the usefulness of library portals for undergraduates at Oregon State University found that "millennials have a mental model of putting keywords into a search box" (p. 481). Similarly, the University of Rochester study concluded that "giving [the students] Google-like simplicity in the library interface...certainly would be desirable" (Fried Foster & Gibbons, 2007, p. 77).

Development of the CU Boulder Libraries Research and Subject Guides Database

After reviewing different models for access to guides and considering current student preferences in Web searching, the authors developed the Research and Subject Guides database. The database allows browsable and searchable access to the large number of guides created by the CU Boulder Libraries. The flexible mode of access caters to the user who prefers a self-service model.

Before deciding to create a database, the authors considered cataloging guides so they would be accessible through the CU Boulder Libraries' catalog, as the University of Florida and other libraries have done. Cataloging all of the guides would not be advisable in the CU Boulder Libraries setting, given that the libraries have over 500 guides, some that need to exist for only a semester (such as a guide to a specific class) and others that may change so much that the cataloging would need to be revised. Instead, a decision was made to include a link to the main guide for each academic department or library from "Find Articles & More," the libraries' Web page that lists electronic databases by subject.

Database Design

The Research and Subject Guides database was implemented in late August 2007. As of October 2008, the database includes over 500 guides, versus the 58 guides that were listed on the previous subject guides Web page. In designing the database, the authors partnered with staff from the CU Boulder Libraries' Systems Department, who provided technical knowledge and programming expertise. The Web-based database uses MySQL and ColdFusion and allows users to search for guides by keyword or browse to locate guides. The database contains and searches only the metadata for the guides, not the content of the guides themselves. Research and subject guide Web pages continue to be stored in various departmental or branch library directories on the Libraries' Web server, allowing guide creators to control the content and update schedule of their guides.

The Research and Subject Guides database provides access to many types of library guides. It includes metadata for research, citation, course, database, and How Do I? guides. Research guides provide an introduction to research on a particular subject or material format, citation guides give assistance citing resources using different style manuals, course guides are created for the research needs of a specific class, database guides provide in-depth instruction on using individual databases, and How Do I? guides provide quick answers to commonly asked questions about doing library research.

The Research and Subject Guides database is prominently linked from the CU Boulder Libraries' homepage, as one of the featured research links. It is also interconnected to the libraries' other research resources. The database is included as one of nine featured resources presented at the bottom of the libraries' catalog and linked from the bottom of the electronic databases page. There is a record in the catalog for the Research and Subject Guides database. In addition, many guide creators have included links to the database from their individual guides.

Searching

The database search uses the MySQL function "LIKE" with wildcard characters to perform simple pattern matching on search terms found in the title, description, keyword, and academic department or library metadata fields for each guide (MySQL AB, 2008). Multiple search terms are assumed to be a phrase and the use of Boolean operators is not supported. When the database was initially deployed, the keyword search was programmed to look for any characters before or after the search term. After analyzing the keyword searches executed during the first month, the project team decided to change the function to search for characters only after the search term to reduce the frequency of false hits.

Search results are presented alphabetically by guide title, which is linked directly to the guide itself. A description of the guide and a link to the metadata (denoted by an "i" icon) appear after the title. When a search generates zero results, the user is given basic tips for a more successful search, such as searching a single word or phrase. The user is notified that Boolean searches are not supported and browsing options are suggested (see Figure 7.4 for a sample keyword search).

Browsing

Users can browse the database for guides in three main ways: by viewing an alphabetical list of all guides, reviewing guides of a certain type (research, citation, course, database, or How Do I?), or browsing by academic department or library (i.e., discipline; see Figure 7.5). All browse options display guides listed by title followed by the description and a link to the metadata, consistent with the search results display. The option to browse for guides by academic department or library displays a tabbed list of all guides associated with the selected department or library. The research tab lists the primary guide for each department first; the rest

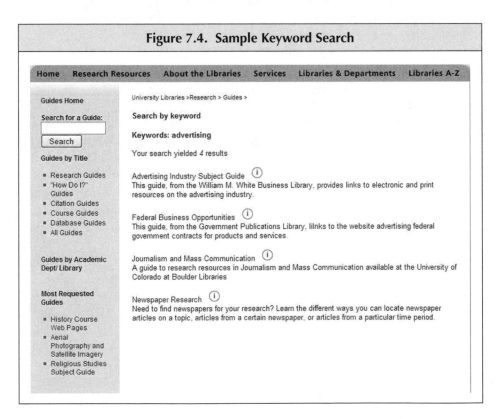

Figure 7.4. Sample Keyword Search

Figure 7.5. Sample Academic Department or Library Browse Display

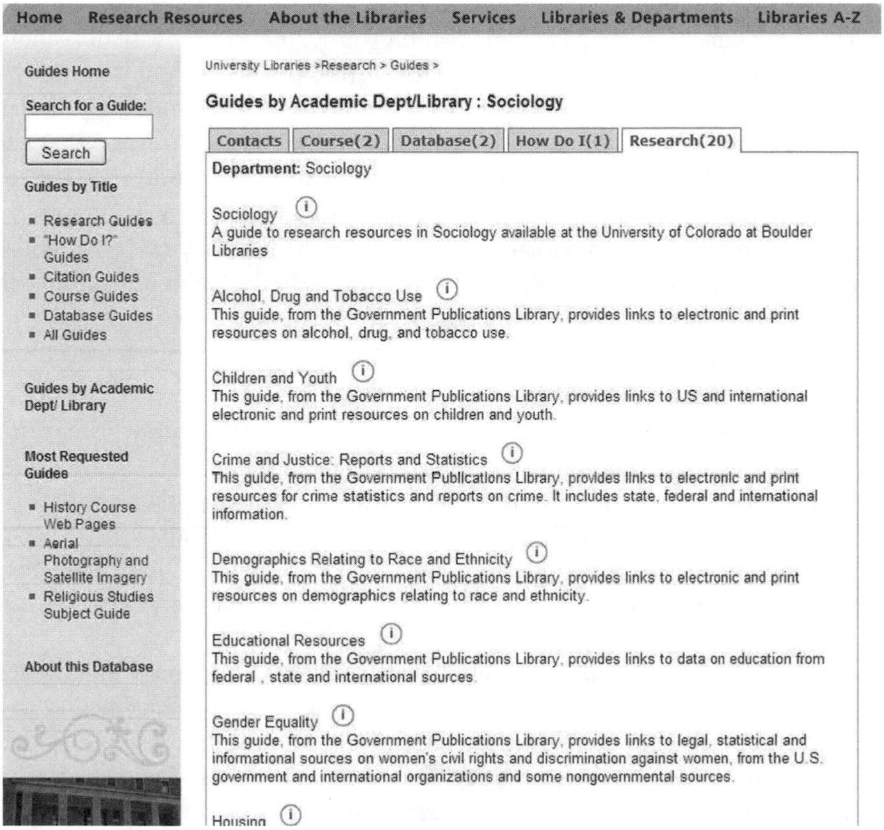

of the associated guides appear alphabetically. Tabs for other categories of guides (citation, course, database, and How Do I?) display if there are guides of that type associated with the chosen department or library. Another tab displays contact information for the bibliographer and/or instruction librarian for each department.

Database Implementation

The Research and Subject Guides database was populated with metadata for all Libraries guides over two weeks in August of 2007. The responsibility for adding metadata for the guides was placed on the guide creators. This short timeframe was made possible by the Web-based input form that prompts guide creators to enter metadata (title, description, keywords, URL, etc.) for their guides. Creators also select a guide type and choose academic departments or libraries and related guides to associate with their guide. In general, the process of adding the metadata went smoothly and the authors were available to assist creators as necessary. Since the initial release of the database the authors have made instructions available on how to add or modify guide metadata.

The input guidelines for metadata creation were minimal. For ease of scanning alphabetical lists, guidelines suggested that the title of the guide not start with, "Guide to" but rather with the topic of the guide itself. Controlled vocabulary for keywords was not used to allow guide creators to easily respond to user needs. The metadata includes a "last updated" field that lets both the creators and users know the date the guide (not the guide metadata) was last edited. Changes to existing guide metadata may be made through a Web-based update form. As new guides are created, guide creators are responsible for adding the metadata for the new guides to the database.

Data Collection and Assessment

Articles in the current literature have decried the lack of usage data when creating or working with subject and research guides (Hemmig, 2005). The authors recognized that it was important to collect as much data as possible in order to determine whether or not the Research and Subject Guides database is successful in improving access to the guides created by the libraries. The project team decided to use two main sources of data collection: internal database reporting and Web use statistics software.

Internal database reporting incorporates a keyword log and a guide query log. The keyword log stores information based on the last occurrence in each search, the number of times it has been conducted, the last date it was executed, and the number of guides the search retrieved. The guide query log records every time a guide is accessed from within the database. These two logs can be viewed as date-ordered lists, sortable JavaScript tables or raw data that can be downloaded for further manipulation and analysis. The authors also used Web-use statistics information that was already being gathered by the CU Boulder Libraries. The libraries have WebTrends software that utilizes the Web server log files to provide reports related to user activity on Libraries' Web site.

Data on Navigation Method Selection

Data on the use of the Research and Subject Guides database reflects student preferences for keyword searching as discussed previously. To determine how users are choosing to locate guides in the Research and Subject Guides database, the authors looked at the Web use statistics report that shows how many visits were recorded for the keyword search versus the combined visits for all of the different Web pages for browsing (alphabetical, academic department or library, citation, course, database or How Do I? guides). The keyword search option is used over 95 percent of the time (see Table 7.3).

Table 7.3. Navigation Method Selection		
Type of navigation	# of visits	% of total
Browse	18,444	4.45
Keyword	395,785	95.55
Total	414,229	

Source: WebTrends report for subject guides directory: September 2007–June 2008.

Data on Browsing

To determine how users are browsing for guides, the authors looked at the Web use statistics that show how many visits were recorded for each of the browsing Web pages (alphabetical list, academic department or library, citation, course, database, and How Do I? guides). The alphabetical list Web page is the most popular, accounting for 36 percent of all browse Web page visits. Users show an equal preference for browsing by academic department or course—each option account for approximately 17 percent of visits to the browse Web pages. The choice to browse by academic department or library most closely mimics the organizational structure of the previous subject guides Web page. The fact that users like to browse by course guides is not a surprise, considering that research done at other libraries has shown that undergraduates tend to "connect their research needs with specific courses rather than with a college or discipline" (Nichols & Mellinger, 2007, p. 487). As shown in Table 7.4, the rest of the browsing Web pages, in descending order of popularity, are the pages for database guides (13 percent), How Do I? guides (9 percent) and citation guides (8 percent).

Table 7.4. Browse Page Visits			
Page Name	Description	# of visits	% of total
Guidesall.cfm	Alphabetical list	6,730	36.49
Guidescourse.cfm	Course guides list	3,088	16.74
Guidebydept.cfm	Academic department or library list	3,077	16.68
Guidesdatabase.cfm	Database guides list	2,490	13.50
Guideshdi.cfm	How Do I? guides list	1,573	8.53
Guidescitation.cfm	Citation guides list	1,486	8.06

Source: WebTrends report for subject guides directory: September 2007–June 2008.

Data on Keyword Searching

As of October of 2008, over a half a million searches have been executed from within the database. The usage data show that 98.7 percent of searches in the Research and Subject Guides database are successful. A search is successful if it retrieves at least one guide with a metadata record that includes the user's search terms. A little under 2 percent of the searches in the database are conducted only once, implying that users are searching for similar resources in this database.

In order to investigate users' search strategies, the authors analyzed the 5,000 most common search terms used in the database (University of Colorado at Boulder Libraries, 2008). Most searches are one word or short phrases. Only 12 of the most common 5,000 searches included the use of the Boolean operator AND. None included the operators OR, NOT, or AND NOT. This lack of operator use in the database mirrors the Web search behavior shown in the Jansen and Spink study (Jansen & Spink, 2006).

Users of the Research and Subject Guides database search for resources on a wide variety of topics. The list of the ten most common keyword searches (from the keyword log) provides a snapshot of these topics (see Table 7.5). These results demonstrate that users are searching for general assistance, using keywords such as "sources" and "statistics" as well as looking for more specific resources on topics such as "island nation" and "middle east." "Biography" also appears in this list, providing support for the inclusion of the "How do I?" type guides in the database.

The keyword log also shows which keywords generate the greatest number of results (see Table 7.6). The most common search with the greatest number of

	Search term	# of searches	# of results
Table 7.5. Ten Most Common Searches			
1	statistics	963	150
2	war	680	28
3	Sources	608	441
4	UN	594	331
5	Middle East	571	23
6	Island Nation	535	37
7	environment	521	32
8	census	511	10
9	Reference	504	38
10	Biography	504	3

Source: Database Keyword Log, retrieved October 2008.

results is a blank search, which returns a list of all guides in the database. Many of the searches included in this list are common words or prefixes, such as "pro" and "for" and "un." Common research terms such as "sources" or "resources," which are included in the descriptions for many guides, also appear on this list.

Analysis of searches with zero results, as documented in the keyword log, has led to changes to guide metadata and the creation of new guides. For example, failed searches for the phrase "English Literature" indicated that metadata for the "English and American Literature Guide" lacked this phrase, rendering it undiscoverable through the current keyword searching algorithm. The Government Publications Library significantly expanded its offering of guides to country information after review of the keyword log showed many searches for foreign countries with no hits in the database.

Data on Guides Accessed from Within the Database

Data collected from the internal guide query log shows how many people are visiting guides from within the database. The authors compiled a list of the ten most frequently accessed guides, which provides insight into what type of resources users are accessing the database to find (see Table 7.7). Four out of the five types of guides available in the database are represented in this list: research, citation, course, and database. Course guides are popular with users: the History Course Web Pages is the most popular guide; two other course guides also appear

Table 7.6. Searches That Generate the Highest Number of Results			
	Search term	# of searches	# of results
1	[blank]	483	532
2	sources	595	436
3	pro	334	415
4	Resources	242	391
5	for	377	371
6	government	323	342
7	government publications	315	341
8	publications	260	341
9	UN	571	328
10	Information	234	258

Source: Database Keyword Log, retrieved October 2008.

Note: Searches executed less than 100 times were excluded because most were searches on an individual letter or contained typographical errors.

Table 7.7. Ten Most Frequently Accessed Guides			
	Guide title	**# of queries**	**Type**
1	History Course Web pages	2690	Course
2	Religious Studies Subject Guide	2245	Research
3	Aerial Photography and Satellite Imagery	2228	Research
4	MLA Style	1380	Citation
5	WRTG 3030: Writing on Science and Society	1352	Course
6	RIOT—Research Online Tutorial	1305	Course
7	ECON 4999: Political Economy in the Middle East	1302	Course
8	APA Style	1288	Citation
9	Citation Guides	1282	Citation
10	LexisNexis Congressional Database	1188	Database
Source: Database Guide Query Log, retrieved October 2008.			

in the top ten list. Citation guides account for three of the ten guides on this list. Two research guides appear on the list, with only one focused on a particular discipline (religious studies). In tenth place is the guide created for the LexisNexis Congressional database. Each guide in this list has been accessed over one thousand times since the implementation of the database.

Using data from the guide query log in conjunction with Web use statistics information gathered through WebTrends reports, the authors were able to compare traffic to a subset of the guides in the three years prior to the Research and Subject Guides database implementation and the year after the database became available. WebTrends data was used to collect the total number of visits to guides in the "/subjectguides" directory for September–June of 2004–2008.[2] The guide query log was used to show how many visits from the 2007–2008 year (post–database implementation) originated from within the database. Visits to these guides varied widely over the four years studied. Visits were up 36 percent between 2004–2005 and 2005–2006, down 40 percent the following year, and then up 48 percent the year after the database was implemented. Of the visits to the guides in 2007–2008, 45 percent originated from within the database. The authors do not know what other factors may have caused the wide swings in number of visits to the guides year to year. Additionally, there is not enough data available postimplementation to know whether or not the database has had a true positive or negative effect on the number of visits each guide receives. This is an area for further research over the life of the database (see Table 7.8).

Table 7.8. Guide Use Over Time					
Guide Name	2004–2005	2005–2006	2006–2007	2007–2008	hits in database
Music	616	995	793	2877	958
Anthropology	1415	1775	823	1672	678
Education	1454	1302	1152	2150	1025
History Course Web Pages	972	1242	1293	2398	2202
Religious Studies	1755	2363	1717	3102	1905
Chemistry	1792	2037	1392	2367	742
English and American Literature	1639	1917	1539	2589	1030
Germanic Language and Literature	1090	1506	805	1353	750
Children's Literature	921	1349	744	1221	788
Comparative Literature	1085	1493	812	1285	752
Film Studies	1432	2242	1139	1706	744
Philosophy	1698	2175	1233	1840	980
History	3783	3827	2402	3469	965
Journalism and Mass Communication	1598	2188	1304	1859	722
Women and Gender Studies	1651	2470	1230	1689	684
Theater and Dance	1116	1929	1089	1490	638
Sociology	1848	2426	1414	1896	758
General Medicine	2202	2355	1564	2088	674
Psychology	3359	4485	2690	3439	937
Biology	3008	2721	1877	2392	740
Spanish and Portuguese	1934	2197	1146	1358	710
Integrative Physiology / Physiology	1238	2207	1289	1527	269
Central and Eastern Europe	1304	3349	1556	1158	981
Linguistics	542	3081	1285	900	784
Averages	**1644**	**2235**	**1345**	**1993**	**892**
% Increase/Decrease		**35.94**	**–39.80**	**48.12**	

Source: WebTrends reports for subject guides directory: September to June for years listed, Database Guide Query Log (for hits in database, August 2007–September 2008).

Note: Data were collected for guides for which four years of data were available (excludes some files in the subject guides directory that lack four years of data).

Issues and Future Improvements to the Database

While the usage data show that the Research and Subject Guides database has been an overall success, the data have also exposed aspects of the database that are undesirable or need improvement. The authors have identified many of these issues and are considering refinements and additions to the database in order to improve its functionality.

Search

The authors identified the search functionality of the database as an area that needed improvement and, as mentioned earlier, they adjusted the MySQL search function shortly after the database was implemented. However, there are still a number of issues the authors would like the address in future releases of the database. As discussed in the data on keyword searching section, keyword log analysis shows that patrons are not using Boolean operators in their searches. Adding this functionality to the search would not be beneficial. However, the keyword log does provide evidence of many phrase searches that would benefit from the automatic "AND" search (as is present in common Web searching functionality and in the CU Boulder Libraries' catalog). This modification would have eliminated the need to update the "English and American Literature" guide metadata as previously discussed.

The automatic truncation feature, while helpful in searching for plural occurrences of a word or variant word endings, creates a problem with common prefixes for words. For example, a search for "pro," a common search, displays 418 search results for guides with metadata records that contain the words "provides" "probability" "properties" and other words beginning with the letters "pro."[3] The database also returns too many results from other common search terms, such as "resources," with 395 search results.[4] Words like "resources" often appear in the description field in the guide metadata. The search functionality could be altered so that when these common words are searched, the results screen could suggest the use of more specific terms. Alternatively, the metadata guidelines could be revised to encourage guide creators to avoid these common terms in their descriptions.

Given that studies demonstrate that Web searchers look only at the first page of results (Jansen & Spink, 2006), the Research and Subject Guides database results display could be modified to better meet user needs through relevance ranking or weighting certain metadata fields. Search results are currently displayed alphabetically by title. For example, a search for "RefWorks" returns 16 results and the guide to using RefWorks appears last, alphabetically, in the list, after guides titled "Applied Mathematics" and "Environmental Engineering," which mention RefWorks in their metadata.[5] However, one would assume that a user searching for "RefWorks" would most likely want to access the main guide to using RefWorks. Similarly, "statistics," the most popular keyword search, returns 150 results, and the guide to finding statistics shows up far down the results page (under "S").[6] These two examples demonstrate how relevance ranking or weighting the title field of the metadata could improve the results display.

Metadata

For ease of setting up and managing the database, guide creators are allowed to associate a guide with only five departments and three related guides. As guide metadata has been added to the database, anecdotal evidence shows that these restrictions are unnecessarily limiting, and there are valid reasons for needing to associate a guide with more departments or related guides. In addition, the metadata structure allows a guide to be designated as only one type (research, course, etc.). In some instances, it would be beneficial to allow multiple designations. For example, a user might browse for a guide to the bibliographic management software RefWorks in the citation, database, or How Do I? categories. In addition, the project team has received comments from internal users asking for a method to easily identify tutorials in any format (videos, Web, PDF, etc.) by the addition of a separate tutorial guide category or an icon to indicate a tutorial in a list of results.

Integrating the Research and Subject Guides Database with Other Resources

As discussed in the section addressing the development of the database, the main guide for each subject area is included on the "Find Articles and More" Web page that provides access to electronic databases by subject. The authors plan to incorporate reciprocal links from the Research and Subject Guides database to all electronic databases by subject through the addition of a tab in the results display for guides associated with a department or library (see Figure 7 "Sample Academic Department or Library Browse Display"). The tab display would be automatically populated using the locally developed, discipline-based terms by which electronic databases are listed in the library catalog.

In order to integrate the Research and Subject Guides database with the CU Boulder resources outside of the library, the authors plan to investigate including the Research and Subject Guides Database in the campus classroom management system. Enhancing the database by using Web 2.0 technologies is also under consideration; specifically, allowing for social tagging and the creation of tag clouds as an alternative discovery method for guides.

Ongoing and Future Research

The authors will continue to collect and analyze usage data to identify potential guide changes and additions and assess and evaluate the effectiveness of the database. In addition to analyzing usage data, the authors also want to collect data from guide creators. A short survey was sent out to library staff. The survey generated a very small response set, so statistically valid conclusions could not be drawn. However, the authors were able to explore some findings from the survey. The survey showed that respondents were confused about how to access usage data; in fact, no one had used the data. Based on this feedback, the authors provided additional training and documentation on accessing and using the data for the creation and modification of guides and guide metadata. The authors plan to continue gathering information from guide creators, such as input on additional metadata modifications and features for the database.

As the project team discusses and works toward new enhancements to the database, the importance of studying users of the database will be paramount. This examination will come in the form of usability studies, surveys, and other tools in order to gather information on user behavior in regard to guide discovery.

Conclusion

This article has discussed research on access to library guides and the CU Boulder Libraries' project to develop a Web-based database for research and subject guides. With the implementation of the Research and Subject Guides database at the CU Boulder Libraries in August of 2007, over 500 guides created by the libraries are now available in one central location. The database was designed to offer keyword searching and various methods of browsing to accommodate different approaches to research. External literature, practices at other institutions, consideration of user research patterns, and analysis of local Web use statistics supported this approach.

The database had been searched over a half a million times as of October 2008, and data show that all types of guides available in the database are being used. These usage data have also enabled the libraries to create new guides, refine existing guides and guide descriptions, evaluate the search function, and identify areas for improvement. Future developments to improve search functionality and integrate the database with the CU Boulder campus and library research offerings are under consideration. The research conducted by the authors has had practical implications for access to guides at the CU Boulder Libraries and can be employed by other libraries planning on improving access to guides. Library users often do not know about and are unable to locate the wealth of instructional material created by libraries, essentially rendering it useless. The Research and Subject Guides database provides a new mode of access that centralizes and simplifies access to research help.

Notes

1. Some of this use of the Web site during open hours is library staff usage. The authors were unable to determine how much since current data collection methods do not

allow for separation between librarian and patron usage. Norlin Library's main reference desk is open from 9:00 a.m. to 8:00 p.m. Monday to Thursday, 9:00 a.m. to 5:00 p.m. Friday, and 1:00 p.m. to 5:00 p.m. Saturday and Sunday.

2. The "/subjectguides" directory was used for this analysis because it contains the largest group of guides on the CU Boulder Libraries Web server, and most guides in this directory have been present over the four years studied.
3. Search conducted on October 19, 2008, in Research and Subject Guides database, http://ucblibraries.colorado.edu/research/subjectguides/index.htm.
4. Ibid.
5. Ibid.
6. Ibid.

References

Anello, K., & Bonfield, B. (2007). Providing reference service in our sleep: Using a FAQ database to guide users to the right sources. *Reference and User Services Quarterly*, *46*(3), 28.

Arnold, J. M., Csir, F., Sias, J., & Zhang, J. (2005). Does anyone need help out there? Lessons from designing online help. *Internet Reference Services Quarterly*, *9*(3–4), 115–134.

Bunnell, D. P., & Byerley, S. L. (2000). Creating and maintaining Web-based subject resource guides for small academic libraries. *College and Undergraduate Libraries*, *7*(1), 33–40.

Dunsmore, C. (2002). A qualitative study of Web-mounted pathfinders created by academic business libraries. *Libri*, *52*(3), 137–156.

Fried Foster, N., & Gibbons, S. (Eds.). (2007). *Studying students: The undergraduate research project at the University Of Rochester*. Chicago: Association of College and Research Libraries.

Hemmig, W. (2005). Online pathfinders toward an experience-centered model. *Reference Services Review*, *33*(1), 66–87.

Jackson, R., & Pellack, L. J. (2004). Internet subject guides in academic libraries. *Reference & User Services Quarterly*, *43*(4), 319–327.

Jansen, B. J., & Spink, A. (2006). How are we searching the World Wide Web? A comparison of nine search engine transaction logs. *Information Processing and Management*, *42*(1), 248–263.

Lippincott, J. (2005). Net generation students & libraries. In D. G. Oblinger & J. L. Oblinger (Eds.), *Educating the Net Generation* (pp. 13.1–13.15). Boulder, CO: EDUCAUSE. Retrieved January 28, 2008, from www.educause.edu/educatingthenetgen/5989.

MySQL AB. (2008). MySQL 3.23, 4.0, 4.1 Reference manual. 11.4.1 string comparison functions. Retrieved January 28, 2008, from http://dev.mysql.com/doc/refman/4.1/en/string-comparison-functions.html#operator_like.

Nichols, J., & Mellinger, M. (2007). Portals for undergraduate subject searching: Are they worth it? *Portal: Libraries and the Academy*, *7*(4), 481–490.

Nuttall, H. D., & McAbee, S. L. (1997). Pathfinders on-line: Adding pathfinders to a NOTIS on-line system. *College & Undergraduate Libraries*, *4*(1), 77–101.

Reeb, B., & Gibbons, S. (2004). Students, librarians, and subject guides: Improving a poor rate of return. *Portal*, *4*(1), 123–130.

Rieger, O. Y., Horne, A. K., & Revels, I. (2004). Linking course Web sites to library collections and services. *Journal of Academic Librarianship*, *30*(3), 205–251.

Simpson, B., Williams, P., Arlen, S., & Bushnell, P. (2005). Accessing locally created subject guides via the library's catalog. *Collection Management*, *30*(4), 31–42.

University of Colorado at Boulder Libraries. (2007). Webtrends default report: FY 06–07 site report (with exclusions). Retrieved October 2008 from http://libnet.colorado.edu/webstats/fy0607.

University of Colorado at Boulder Libraries. (2008). Keyword log from research and subject guides database. Retrieved October 2008 from http://ucblibraries.colorado.edu/research/guides/about.cfm.

University of Michigan Libraries. (n.d.). UM library: Library guides and tutorials. Retrieved October 3, 2007, from http://lib.umich.edu/guides.

University of Minnesota University Libraries. (n.d.). Library frequently asked questions. Retrieved October 3, 2007, from http://faq.lib.umn.edu/public/PubAccess.pl.

University of North Carolina University Libraries. (n.d.). Subject guides-subject guide search. Retrieved October 3, 2007, from www.lib.unc.edu/guides.

Veldof, J. R., & Beavers, K. (2001). Going mental: Tackling mental models for the online library tutorial. *Research Strategies*, *18*(1), 3–20.

Vileno, L. (2007). From paper to electronic, the evolution of pathfinders: A review of the literature. *Reference Services Review*, *35*(3), 434–451.

Wilson, P. (2002). Perfecting pathfinders for the Web. *Public Libraries*, *41*(2), 99–100.

CHAPTER 8

Meeting Users' Needs through New Reference Service Models

Kay Ann Cassell

Overview

The reference model has undergone considerable change in the past three decades. Librarians realize that all users cannot be served by merely having a reference desk. A variety of new models have emerged beginning with tiered reference service and roving reference. New configurations of the reference desk have also evolved while some libraries choose not to have a separate reference desk at all. Libraries have also moved beyond their walls to reach users in other locations. Virtual reference has taken a larger role in serving users who prefer to communicate with the library using e-mail, chat, IM (instant message), and SMS (short message service). Social software such as Facebook and MySpace are also being used to reach new users.

Introduction

Reference service began in 1876 at the Worcester Free Public Library when Samuel Green, the library director, decided that providing more service to the public would increase the use of the library's collection and would show the city officials the value of the library. Thus the reference desk was born, and through the years libraries have continued to provide user service from the reference desk. Many in recent decades have begun to question whether the reference desk model should continue to be the primary model. In 1988 Barbara Ford called for a re-examination of the reference desk model, stating, "As long as the reference desk model is uncritically accepted, librarians are not challenged to respond creatively to changes in materials, formats, and research opportunities for our users, and users are not challenged to use any of a variety of printed or computerized sources or aids" (Ford, 1988, p. 580). Yet most libraries and librarians were content to stay with this model.

Reference Models

Tiered Reference Service
In the 1990s libraries began to experiment with other models. Virginia Massey-Burzio at the Brandeis University Library developed a tiered reference service. In

this model there is a desk staffed by paraprofessionals who are responsible for answering frequently asked questions. Users with questions that require more extensive assistance are referred to a consultation area where librarians are available to assist them with more complex questions and projects. This model was designed to make the best possible use of librarians (Massey-Burzio, 1992). Other libraries developed a three-tier model with the first tier being an information desk at the front door followed by the second tier with a desk for frequently asked questions and the third tier with a consultation area. The County of Los Angeles Public Library has developed a tiered model in which tier one answers frequently asked questions and tier two answers e-mail, chat, and tough questions or more research-oriented questions.

Roving Reference

Roving reference is one of my favorite models. There is both passive roving where librarians roam the library waiting to be approached and active roving where librarians approach users and ask them if they are finding what they need. Roving reference enables the librarian to talk with users who do not approach the desk since not every user feels comfortable approaching the reference desk. Many users sitting at computer stations need help and don't want to leave their computer to find a librarian. With the roving model librarians can talk casually with users wherever they are in the library using the reference interview techniques including follow-up questions, summarizing the question, and nonverbal communication such as smiling, nodding, and looking at the user (Reference and User Services Association, 2004). In order to work with users in different spaces, librarians have to learn how to approach them comfortably as well as identify users who may need help. The idea is to help users at the "point of puzzlement."

Martin Courtois and Maira Liriano (2000) wrote of their experiment with roving at the George Washington University Library in *College & Research Libraries News*, documenting earlier experiments by Adreane Bregman and Barbara Mento at Boston College and Eileen H. Kramer at Utica College. The authors had developed their roving project to help students who were using computers and needed assistance.

The King County Library System in suburban Seattle, Washington, has developed various scheduling models for roving. Staff is asked to rove for at least 15 to 20 minutes during a one-hour shift on the reference desk. The staff document roving transactions using a standardized form to generate statistics. A dedicated rover is scheduled during selected hours when the library is very busy. He or she can either rove or take reference desk questions if the librarian at the reference desk needs assistance. Staff is also given a list of possible tasks on the floor so they have something to do when they are not helping users such as restocking display books, reshelving reference books, restocking flyers, etc. (Pitney & Slote, 2007).

New Configurations for Reference Desks

Many librarians think that reference desks are not even needed at least as a separate entity. But most agree that at a minimum a reference desk should be smaller since it is less intimidating and does not take up so much space. Fewer materials are now needed at the reference desk since many ready reference materials have been replaced by Web sites so libraries can minimize storage space in the desk area. Smaller reference desks encourage the librarian to move around and not remain seated behind the desk and limit the amount of staff work brought to the desk. Desks can be structured so that librarian and user can sit down and look at a screen together with dual monitors and dual keyboards and mice. The Westerville Public Library (OH) has a small "Ask Here" desk equipped with wireless headsets and tablet PCs that access the online catalog and the library's databases. They are hoping to upgrade their technology so that they can check out books on the spot, thus making it easier and faster for the user (Pierce, 2006). The King County Library System (WA) has been trying new reference desks models including using small kidney-shaped desks "allowing patrons a feeling of spaciousness and giving a more intimate, friendly feeling to our assistance points" (Pitney & Slote, 2007, p. 60). At Indiana State University, a new octagonal-shaped desk was installed toward the front of the library with a neon sign with the word ASK followed by a question mark. Users can approach the desk from all sides and sit down to talk to a librarian (Frey & Kaiser, 2008).

At the University of California at Merced Library there is no separate reference desk. The library believes in "just in time reference," which could be drop-in reference, reference appointments, chat reference, or text messaging. Students, faculty, and staff may contact librarians wherever they happen to be—in their offices, at conferences, in the classroom, or walking around the building (Davidson, 2008).

Consolidating Service Points

Another model is that of consolidating service points. An example of this is at the University of Arizona where circulation, photocopy, and reference were combined and staffed only by paraprofessionals after multifaceted training. The library had observed that students were often confused and did not understand the difference between the various service points. This new service provides a one-stop service point for library users. Since librarians no longer staff this desk, the library staff member can either call another desk or subject specialist to assist in answering the question or can fill out an online form and send it to a subject specialist who will get back to the user (Bracke, Chinnaswamy, & Kline, 2008). Public libraries such as the Warren Newport Public Library in Illinois have combined their reference service into one desk where they serve all ages, preschoolers through senior citizens. The reference desk has two heights to accommodate a variety of users (Brattin, 2005).

Reference Outreach

Outreach is not a new concept, but libraries have been putting a new spin on it. We need to be where the users are if we want them to know about reference service. Therefore, we have to find ways to introduce our users to the vast array of resources in the library. If users know about library resources and services, they are more likely to use them; it is often just a matter of seeing that the library really does have more than Google. In an academic library librarians can set up office hours in academic departments to assist faculty and students. In a public library librarians can visit local government offices, Chamber of Commerce, local organizations and institutions, etc. Libraries have also developed portable wireless kiosks that can be placed in busy areas such as malls and train stations to meet user information needs. Libraries can also use the library's Web site as a way to reach out to users and make the services of the library readily accessible from the homepage.

Rutgers University Libraries reported on an outreach project in which the Outpost Services Team developed a pilot to investigate the need for library services at campus centers. The pilot provided traditional reference services using electronic resources. The number of reference questions was small, which the reference staff thought was due to the newness of the service. But they felt that it was worthwhile since the response of the users was positive (Kuchi, Mullen, & Tama-Bartels, 2004).

The University of Montana librarians called their outreach project "outpost reference." They visited dorms and then the student union. The librarians found that academic hangouts produced the best results and that visiting the student union produced better results than visiting the dorms. The results of their study indicated that having a consistent and reliable location and schedule was very important and that their visits often focused on public relations rather than research assistance (Hines, 2007).

Virtual Reference

Virtual reference is an important addition in the development of new reference models. Librarians can use e-mail, chat, and IM to reach users who cannot or choose not to visit the library or need assistance outside of library hours. These are not in place of face-to-face but rather another means of communication with users. E-mail, chat, IM, and SMS (also called text messaging) are new models for reaching users who may not visit the library

E-mail reference enables the librarian to have time to research the query and provide a more thorough response. Libraries can contract with companies for virtual reference (chat) such as OCLC's (Online Computer Library Center) QuestionPoint or can use Meebo, which is available for free. Many libraries join a consortium so that they can share the cost of virtual reference services and also not be completely responsible for staffing it. Virtual reference can be 24/7, accommodating users who need assistance outside of library hours. The advantage of chat reference and instant messaging is that the librarian can use the reference interview techniques to clarify the user's question. In these forums some of the personality of the librarian comes out, and there is a chance to ask follow-up questions and be sure that the information provided is what the user wants.

Use of New Technology for Reference

Libraries use a variety of technology in the library to make reference work more seamless to the user. One such case study is the Salem-South Lyon District Library in Michigan that is trying a variety of new technology. They have an LCD (liquid crystal display) screen for the user at the reference desk so the user can see what the librarian is searching. They have integrated tablet PCs (personal computers) into their reference service so that the librarians can carry the tablet PC with them to help the user when they are in the stacks. The librarians can check the catalog, databases, or other Internet sites from any location. This library also has Voice over Internet Protocol (VoIP) so the staff can communicate with one another within the library when they have a question or need the assistance of another librarian. The librarians also have AOL (America Online) Instant Messenger accounts that enable users to contact them. Their AIM (AOL Instant Messenger) handles are on their business cards and on other public relations materials. Some librarians also have Yahoo! Messenger, MSN (Microsoft Network) Messenger, and ICQ accounts as well (Hibner, 2007).

Seattle Public Library's new central building has many different floors and many different departments. The library's central reference space is called the Mixing Chamber. Here librarians answer questions on all subjects. But since staff and collections are in different parts of the building, the staff needs to communicate with one another in order to identify material or information needed by a user. Their goal is to deliver the information or material to the user rather than the user having to move around the building. For this the library uses a wireless communications system from Vocera Communications. In this way they can minimize the amount of time it takes for users to get their information or material (Bourne, 2005).

Social Software

Social software has also made it possible for libraries to provide information services in another space. Libraries have provided access to their online catalog, their chat service, and to groups of users. Some have been particularly active reaching young adults and students who use this social software regularly. Applications include using blogs, wikis, Twitter, and sites such as Facebook, MySpace, and Second Life, among others. A number of libraries provide information services through Facebook and MySpace. Libraries using Facebook include the Hennepin County Library and the University of Massachusetts Library. Those using MySpace include Brooklyn College Library and the Denver Public Library.

Prescriptions and Recommendations

Not all reference models are fully developed; many need more research. But these new models are slowly being refined. The tiered reference model depended on well-trained paraprofessionals who would be able to determine when to refer the user to the next level. This was sometimes the weak link in the system since the paraprofessionals often failed to do the proper referrals and tried to meet the users' needs even if the question was too complex to answer at the reference desk. Although there are problems with this model, it is still a viable model and is used by both college and public libraries.

Courtois and Liriano (2000) advised training staff on roving techniques, wearing a nametag to identify them as a member of the staff, scheduling times for roving, following up with users to check on their progress, and being mobile and not spending too much time with any one user. A good reference interview is necessary, which uses welcoming behaviors, addresses the user face to face, and includes a neutral opening line such as "Are you finding what you need?" or "How are you doing?" It is usually obvious which users do not need assistance and need not be approached. Librarians should work together referring questions to the reference desk or to the rover. Librarians doing roving should keep statistics just as is done at the reference desk. Although roving seems such an ideal way to assist users, many librarians are reluctant to move away from the reference desk.

The reconfiguration of the reference desk has many possibilities. New furniture available through library vendors can give the librarian ideas for changing the service. The change to either a smaller desk or even no desk at all is a matter of evaluating the library and its users' needs. The type of library as well as its users can determine whether a reference desk is still needed. But redesigns can create a more friendly environment for users with less barriers to service. Even the name "reference desk" can be off-putting and perhaps using the name "service point" or "assistance" will be more welcoming (Pitney & Slote, 2007, p. 60).

Consolidating service points can produce economies while providing the users with a one-stop service. The key to consolidation lies in cross-training staff so that all staff can respond to the wider variety of range of questions and requests for service. The University of Arizona makes a continuous effort to upgrade their paraprofessionals' skills and knowledge.

E-mail reference is asynchronous. It depends on a well-designed electronic form so that enough information is collected to be able to answer the users' query. Although e-mail is slower than other virtual reference options, it allows the librarian to take time to research the question and provide a more thorough response. Chat reference is synchronous; it allows the librarian to either cobrowse or provide URLs. Chat reference provides a transcript of the session. IM reference is also synchronous. It allows for short messages only but can provide the beginnings of a reference session that can be followed by e-mail, fax, or perhaps by a visit to the library.

Virtual reference services require a great deal of marketing. The library must mention it on each page of the library's Web site. It is impossible to do too much publicity.

Future Directions

Two factors are changing the way reference service is delivered. First of all, as the usage of libraries has changed, libraries have moved beyond the reference desk. In academic libraries fewer users come to the library, while in public libraries there is still a great demand for face-to-face service (Academic Libraries, 2008). Second, library budgets have in many cases diminished, resulting in the need to rethink their staffing patterns. As a result libraries are evaluating and analyzing their own situations and trying out new arrangements and new technologies that will better meet the needs of their users and deal with their own budgetary limitations. Librarians understand that one model does not fit all users and that they must be flexible in order to meet user needs. Some users have more complex needs that require a consultation session with the librarian. On the other hand, many users need to have an answer immediately and want to communicate with the library by e-mail, chat, or instant messaging. But the good news is that many models are now being tried. It is essential that libraries continue to experiment with new organizational models and new technologies.

References

Academic Libraries. (2008). Statistics. Retrieved from www.nces.ed.gov/surveys/libraries/academic.asp.

Bourne, J. (2005). Reference by design: Technologies enhance a new service model at Seattle's Central Library. *Library Mosaics, 16*(3), 10–11.

Bracke, M., Chinnaswamy, S. & Kline, E. (2008, Winter). Evolution of reference: A new service model for science and engineering libraries. *Issues in Science and Technology Librarianship*. Retrieved from www.istl.org/08-winter/refereed3.html.

Brattin, B. (2005). Reorganizing reference. *Public Libraries, 44*(6), 340–346.

Courtois, M., & Liriano, M. (2000). Tips for roving reference: How to best serve library users. *College & Research Libraries News, 61*(4), 289–290, 315.

Davidson, S. (2008). Reference services. Presented at Machine Assisted Reference Services (MARS) Program, American Library Association Conference, June 2008, Anaheim, California.

Ford, B. J. (1988). Reference service: Past, present, and future. *College & Research Libraries News, 49*(9), 578–582.

Frey, S. M., & Kaiser, A. (2008). Still evolving or facing extinction? Reference-as-place. *Indiana Libraries*, 27(1), 42–45.

Hibner, H. (2007). Reference on the edge. *Public Libraries*, 46(1), 21–22.

Hines, S. S. (2007). Outpost reference: Meeting patrons on their own ground. *PNLA Quarterly*, 72(1), 12–13, 26.

Kuchi, T., Mullen, L. B., & Tama-Bartels, S. (2004) Librarians without borders: Reaching out to students at a campus center. *Reference & User Services Quarterly*, 43(4), 318–325.

Massey-Burzio, V. (1992, October). Reference encounters of a different kind: A symposium. *Journal of Academic Librarianship*, 18, 276–286.

Pierce, J. B. (2006). Where reference librarians do rove. *American Libraries*, 37(2), 39.

Pitney, B., & Slote, N. (2007). Going mobile: The KCLS roving reference model. *Public Libraries*, 46(1), 54–68.

Reference and User Services Association. (2004). Guidelines for behavioral performance of reference and information service providers. Retrieved from www.ala.org/ala/mgrps/divs/rusa/resources/guidelines/guidlinesbehvioral.cfm.

PART III
REFERENCE IN ACTION: REPORTS FROM THE FIELD

Virtual Reference

Apples and Oranges: Creating a Hybrid Virtual Reference Service with Proprietary Chat Reference Software and Free Instant Messaging Services

Lorrie Evans, Nina McHale, and Karen Sobel

Overview

Many libraries see the choice between in-house and consortium-based virtual reference as an either/or situation. The debate over which provides better service to academic populations is familiar to many librarians. However, with its unusual user base of students from one community college, one four-year college, and one university, staff at the Auraria Library in Denver, Colorado, chose to investigate all possibilities for virtual reference. The final decision combined usage of AskAuraria, a new in-house instant messaging (IM) service, and continuation with AskColorado, a statewide Web-based chat consortium. This article discusses detailed considerations related to users, technology, and staffing.

Introduction

During a spring 2008 evaluation of public services, a task group at the Auraria Library determined that adding IM reference services to the library's repertoire of services would help bring the library up to date with current reference practices. While the Auraria Library had long participated in AskColorado, a statewide collaborative virtual reference service, librarians had discussed adding an IM service expressly for their own campus and community users as well. This eventually led to the creation of AskAuraria. Web-based proprietary chat and IM have long been pitted against one another (see Houghton and Schmidt, 2005). Once the reference department had decided to implement AskAuraria, they had to decide whether to use this as a replacement for AskColorado or to combine the two. The final decision was to keep both services, creating a hybrid virtual reference service out of the existing AskColorado and newly created AskAuraria. This chapter outlines the process of making that decision and creating a hybrid service in hopes of guiding other libraries that are making similar choices.

The Auraria Library serves an unusual user population that often defies the common assumptions made about information-seeking behaviors of college students. The library is based on the Auraria Campus in downtown Denver, Colorado, which is home to three schools: the University of Colorado Denver (UCD), Metropolitan State College of Denver (MSCD), and the Community College of Denver (CCD). Thus, the library serves students in programs ranging from engineering to welding. There are many returning and older students, and the average age of the student population is 28. The UCD has an enrollment of approximately 13,000 students, including graduates and undergraduates (University of Colorado Denver, 2008). MSCD has approximately 22,000 undergraduate students, many of whom attend school part time (Metropolitan State College of Denver Office of Institutional Research, 2008). Notably, MSCD has begun working toward gaining status as a Hispanic-Serving Institution, which would mean that at least 25 percent of the student population would be Hispanic, and at least 50 percent of the Hispanic students would have low incomes (Metropolitan State College of Denver, 2007). CCD serves 8,000 students, over 60 percent of whom belong to minority groups (Community College of Denver, 2007). CCD holds Hispanic-Serving Institution status. Part-time enrollment is common at all three schools. Many students at the latter two schools in particular do not own computers. Reference staff note anecdotally that these students frequently demonstrate unfamiliarity with such basic Web skills as attaching files to e-mail and navigating with browsers. The Auraria Library also serves a large number of public users.

History of Virtual Reference at Auraria

Prior to 2008, virtual reference service at the Auraria Library had been provided exclusively through AskColorado. Staff believed that this reference service, offered 24/7 in English and Spanish, was appropriate for the Auraria Campus's student population, which is primarily a commuting population and includes many bilingual students. However, throughout the history of Auraria's involvement, reference staff had two major concerns with participation. First, the software used to operate AskColorado, Tutor.com's AAL (Ask a Librarian), presented a host of technical difficulties. The complex software often crashed both user and librarian computers. Also, although AskColorado allows librarians and users to access a limited number of databases together, academic librarians and users coming from different institutions often cannot both access a database the user needs. Finally, some librarians voiced concerns about the relatively high proportion of questions that came from children in primary and secondary schools. Many of these questions were either perceived as pranks or required resources that academic librarians do not have access to or are not familiar with.

Due to these concerns, Auraria Library suspended AskColorado for the two academic years from 2004 to 2006. During this time, limited staffing—two volunteer hours per week—were provided to the consortium by the distance education librarian. All promotion of the service was stopped, and the links to AskColorado were removed from the Library's Web site. It became apparent, however, that Auraria students were still using the service in spite of the lack of official participation. During the 2005–2006 academic year, 297 questions came from Auraria users. After AskColorado instituted an academic queue, largely to address the previously mentioned concerns, Auraria Library reinstated full participation and program marketing for the fall 2006 semester. Usage has continued to increase, with 341 Auraria-based questions during the 2006–2007 academic year, and 486 questions during the 2007–2008 academic year.

However, by the spring 2008 public services task force evaluation, in-house service, generally using IM software and services, had become an accepted standard for providing virtual reference. Librarians involved in the public services evaluation believed that help available immediately and directly from the library's homepage in the form of a chat widget would prove more beneficial than the more complex AskColorado, at least during the statistically high-traffic Web hours of late morning and early afternoon. Under the guidance of the library's Web Advisory Committee (WAC), the recommendation from the public services task group grew into a pilot project. Initial discussion of creating an IM chat service began late in the spring 2008 semester. A testing phase was planned for summer, with launch planned for release with a slightly revised (new color and graphics) homepage for fall.

Reference staff decided that, since the VR (virtual reference) service would be designed with academic aims in mind, public users' needs would not be specifically included in planning. However, they did choose to refrain from noting anything such as "students and faculty only" anywhere on the IM chat interface.

The reference staff generally expressed dedication to participating in AskColorado. The requisite ten hours of staffing AskColorado are a moderate strain on staff. However, participating in AskColorado assures support of a service that supplies Auraria students with 24-hour access to reference, which the Auraria librarians obviously cannot provide alone. Hence, giving ten hours of service per week in exchange for 24 hours of reference availability was considered a point in favor of AskColorado.

Instant Message Product Selection

The Web Advisory Committee had planned on using Meebo (www.meebo.com), which, based on conversations with staff at peer institutions and a brief literature review, seemed to be the most popular software option. Criteria cited by libraries in their IM product selection included ease of use, support of multiple services, price, and privacy (Foley, 2002; Ciocco & Huff, 2007). Meebo held a number of advantages as a chat reference platform: it was free, required little in terms of computing resources from an operator's workstation, and, most important, it interacted smoothly with many popular instant messenger services. Lorrie Evans, Head of Library Instruction, had begun experimenting with it by embedding a Meebo widget into her existing course pages. Chat boxes on her pages allowed students who had attended one of her information literacy sessions to chat with her on her personal account. While she appreciated the functionality, she received relatively few messages that were not from her teenage sons. This likely resulted from the limited number of hours she was signed into her account as well as the relatively low profile of the chat widget in the library's Web space. While this rather flawed experiment on the use of IM for instructional support was not successful, the literature does support both IM and chat as facilitators of teaching moments (Desai & Graves, 2006; Desai & Graves, 2008). One additional concern was privacy; students' screen names appeared during chat sessions and could be connected with individuals with little effort. However, these concerns seemed minor compared with the potential benefits of in-house chat reference.

Just as formal plans for the chat pilot project were taking shape, Reference and Instruction Librarian Karen Sobel discovered Libraryh3lp (http://code .google.com/p/libraryh3lp). Created by programmer Eric Sessoms and librarian Pam Sessoms, (of Nub Games, Inc., and the University of North Carolina at Chapel Hill, respectively), Libraryh3lp addressed the Auraria librarians' concerns and provided additional benefits as well. One particularly attractive additional feature was the possibility of creating multiple queues, which could direct specialized questions to particular librarians or circulation inquiries to a library staff member in the circulation department. Also, each queue allowed multiple librarians to monitor queues simultaneously, which has proven invaluable during busy periods. Simultaneous monitoring was not available with Meebo, which was designed for use with individual rather than group accounts.

Implementation of the Libraryh3lp Instant Message Service

Implementation of the Libraryh3lp IM chat service proceeded quickly and was completed in-house in June 2008 by Nina McHale, the Web Librarian. Libraryh3lp is a hosted service, meaning that the magic happens in their server space—no installation or maintenance on library servers is necessary. In fact, establishing service on the Libraryh3lp server is alarmingly easy. One creates an account for the library, creates the number of desired queues, and creates operator accounts for staff who will be monitoring IM queues. Users are then added to queues as appropriate. This work was completed in one evening.

Like the proprietary Tutor.com AAL software, Libraryh3lp operators require software installation on the chat operators' workstations. Unlike most proprietary Web-based chat software, however, Libraryh3lp requires only a very lightweight Jabber/XMPP client (Erickson, 2007). Since Auraria implemented Libraryh3lp, a Web-based chat, which requires no local client software, has also been developed. While these options have fewer features than the proprietary software used in many commercial Web-based chat applications, these programs do not present as steep a learning curve or require as much configuration or training. The Libraryh3lp developers had done most of their testing with and developed a Libraryh3lp plug-in for the Jabber client Pidgin, so the Auraria team implementing the new IM pilot chose it (Robbins, 2008). While Pidgin runs on Windows, which was exclusively what the Auraria staff would be using to monitor chat queues in the library, an option for Mac users who expressed interest in staffing the service from their Macs at home is Adium (www.adiumx.com). This contrasts to the platform limitations of Tutor.com's AAL software, which currently cannot run for operators on Macintosh workstations. The Web Librarian received assistance from other members of the Systems Department to speed the Pidgin installation so that chat could be integrated into the Library's Web pages as soon as possible.

With Pidgin and the Libraryh3lp plug-in installed on operator (and potential operator, as many who had not previously participated in AskColorado queue monitoring expressed interest in the new IM program) workstations, the final piece to put in place was incorporating the widget into the library's existing Web pages. On the library's homepage, a "My Account" login to the OPAC (online public access catalog) that had never quite worked correctly due to a security issue with Internet Explorer was replaced with a chunk of HTML code that would display appropriate content, such as the chat widget, when a member of the library staff was monitoring the main queue (see Figure 9.1). When the chat widget was not available, a list of all other means of receiving reference help appeared. The other options that were presented were the Reference Desk phone number, a link to the E-mail Reference service form, and AskColorado (see Figure 9.2).

Creating the code that displays the chat widget was made easy by Libraryh3lp's "Design Public Services" tool, which allows librarians to dynamically generate HTML and JavaScript necessary for displaying a chat widget on the Library's Web pages (see Figure 9.3). For the mid-June 2008 soft launch, the chat widget was embedded in the library's home page, with plans to include the widget code in the new templates that would be used to update the entire library's Web site during the fall semester.

Successes and Challenges

The successes and challenges of maintaining the hybrid VR service hinge on further developing AskAuraria to provide immediate service, as staffing and other considerations for AskColorado service have not changed. A very early sign of the success of AskAuraria lies in the sheer volume of questions asked. Seven hundred six chat sessions have been logged in the first five months, as compared to the 468 Auraria user questions answered through AskColorado during the entire 2007 calendar year. This is with limited catch-as-catch-can staffing. No marketing or promotional considerations were made; the best advertisement has thus far proven to be the prominent placement of the chat widget on the library's homepage. Librarians staffing AskAuraria have received positive comments about the service from students. Some have even inquired as to whether it is available on the weekends, which, at the time of this writing, it was generally not.

The cost of maintaining both services is not prohibitive. Depending on the library's size, participation in AskColorado is currently $300 to $1,500 annually. Auraria tends to the higher side of this range as it is a larger library, but the amount is planned into the annual budget. While Libraryh3lp began as a free service, its creators are now asking for an annual fee to defray the cost of maintaining the resources necessary for hosting the service. However, the annual fee is quite modest; for academic institutions, the pricing model is currently $1 per 100 full-time enrolled students. Development of the Libraryh3lp product is done in the creators' own time. Once the Libraryh3lp service is established in a library, very little technical support from library systems is necessary.

Balancing two chat services may not be the most efficient service model in terms of staffing, yet each type of service provides a different appeal for students. The IM reference service is informal, anonymous, highly accessible, and consistent with many aspects of student life and culture. The typical undergraduate student is multitasking: writing the paper, searching databases, talking on the phone and on IM, sending questions to the reference librarian. The high visibility and simple question box is no different than the IM services most students have been using for years to communicate on a daily basis.

By its nature, AskColorado is more complex than IM reference. Cobrowsing allows librarians to lead users through the intricacies of database searching, whereas with IM, librarians and users can pass only hyperlinks back and forth. The spontaneous question is not as likely since the access point is two levels below the homepage, and a short sign-in page is required. This sign-in removes some of the perceived anonymity for the user but can provide the librarian with useful demographic information. Furthermore, Ward and Kern (2006) concluded of their study of their own hybrid service at the University of Illinois at Urbana-Champaign that "there is sufficient evidence from [the] pilot project to indicate that this [hybrid] approach should be continued, as it provides a good method for attracting different types of users" by having two tools available (p. 427).

Anyone can post a question to IM reference since there are no posted policies or separate queues for public users, as offered by AskColorado. Any behavioral transgressions must be dealt with by the librarian. To date, this has not presented a problem, likely because most individuals using the IM reference service are accessing it through the homepage and are Auraria students. The greatest benefit AskColorado offers is 24/7 access. Currently, Auraria librarians can staff IM reference only during regular business hours.

Staffing the AskAuraria service has proved the biggest challenge. During early discussions on how to staff the IM reference service, one main option emerged. The Auraria Library's reference department uses a staffing model in which either one or two librarians or trained paraprofessionals are on the reference desk, and an additional person is on call in his or her office. It was decided that the person who was on call would staff the IM reference service. Since multiple librarians can sign on to the IM software, additional staff who were particularly interested in providing virtual reference could sign on as well. This staffing issue is not unique to Auraria; in their survey about librarian perceptions and misunderstandings about IM, Steiner and Long (2007) note that "[t]here are presently no quick cures for a lack of staffing, the most frequently cited problem" of their survey respondents (p. 45).

In practice, however, the Auraria staffing model has proved somewhat problematic. The person who is on call frequently has to move to the reference desk because of a high volume of questions or because one of the desk staff is ill. Thus the staffing model is a work in progress; more time and training will likely need to be devoted to supporting the IM service. Since many members of the reference staff had not used IM for either reference or social purposes in the past, considering staff training needs is particularly important. Concerns over the quality of reference service that chat provides have arisen as well; however, this is also not unique to Auraria reference staff. Only 10 percent of Steiner and Long's (2007) survey respondents stated that they had "no concerns" about using IM as a reference tool.

Assessment

The Auraria Library's blended virtual reference service has not gone through formal assessment as of yet. Analysis of both chat and IM use, user types, time of day, and question type/question subject distribution along the lines of Ward and Kern's (2007) study could be conducted. Members of the public service task force have suggested examining usage statistics for AskAuraria's first semester of operation day by day as well as gathering transcripts of representative transactions for analysis. Reference staff members most involved with AskAuraria plan to present these statistics and transcripts to their colleagues to stimulate discussion of future plans. Similar statistics on Auraria students' usage of AskColorado, as well as sample transcripts, will be presented as well. While the final verdict on the success of the hybrid service will likely not be reached for several months, all signs point to success. Only modifications to staffing and hours may prove necessary.

In addition to a more robust staffing model, other future plans include creating accounts on popular IM services such as America Online Instant Messenger (AIM), MSN (Microsoft Network) Messenger, Yahoo!, Google Talk, and Meebo. Many early adopters of IM technology in libraries approached launching an IM service in this way, prior to the advent of the chat widget. Plans to conduct survey on user use of technology may inform ways chat services could be expanded. Libraryh3lp allows multiple queues and transferring questions between queues, which raises possibilities for the other public service desks. For example, a renewal question could be routed to a circulation queue, and a reserves question to a reserves queue. Many libraries are using IM chat software for these purposes and also internal communication already; it seems wise to evaluate these applications and put the software to use.

Further integration into Web pages, to include OPAC screens, is planned as well. A new three-column template for library Web pages includes the chat widget in the rightmost column. Regarding chat in the OPAC, Meier (2008) suggests, "A great example of service at the point of need is a chat widget appearing after an unsuccessful library catalog search" (p. 48). Experimentation with inserting the chat widgets into Blackboard, which is one of the course management systems in use by UCD, has been successful, and librarians have heard anecdotally from teaching faculty that this would be a highly desirable feature to offer within their Blackboard course pages. Finally, a recommendation has been forwarded to library administration that includes further development of IM (and other modes of communication as they become available) in the library's strategic planning documents.

Conclusion

While proprietary Web-based chat and IM chat are different products—apples and oranges—with different strengths and weaknesses, in the case of the Auraria Library, creating a hybrid chat comprised of both types of service has proved, on first blush, quite successful. To a great extent, the common criticisms of both types of service are cancelled out when offering both in conjunction. The AskAuraria chat widget on the library's homepage provides users immediate access to Auraria Library staff when they are available yet rolls over to AskColorado as a backup for users who would prefer chat as a mode of receiving assistance, with the added benefit of it being a 24/7 service. Further transcript and statistical analysis in the vein of Ward and Kern's (2007) study of their own hybrid reference service and feedback from Auraria students about the quality of the service will guide future developments of Auraria Library's hybrid virtual reference service.

References

Ciocco, R., & Huff, A. (2007). Mission im-possible. *Computers in Libraries*, 27(1), 26–31.

Community College of Denver. (2007). Key college data. Retrieved October 1, 2009, from www.ccd.edu/main.aspx?CID=10.

Desai, C. M., & Graves, S. J. (2006). Instruction via instant messaging reference: What's happening? *Electronic Library*, 24(2), 174–189.

Desai, C. M., & Graves, S .J. (2008). Cyberspace or face to face: The teachable moment and changing reference mediums. *Reference & User Services Quarterly*, 47(3), 242–254.

Erikson, B. (2007). XMPP. *Computers in Libraries*, 27(4), 22.

Foley, M. (2002). Instant messaging reference in an academic library: A case study. *College & Research Libraries*, 63(1), 36.

Houghton, H., & Schmidt, A. (2005). Web-based chat vs. instant messaging: Who wins? *Online*, 29(4), 26–30.

Meier, J. J. (2008). Chat widgets on the library website: Help at the point of need. *Computers in Libraries*, 28(6), 10–13, 48.

Metropolitan State College of Denver. (2007). Dr. Jordan's remarks: HSI launch: Thursday, April 19, 2007. Retrieved October 1, 2009, from www.mscd.edu/president/assets/docs/hsi_speech041907.pdf.

Metropolitan State College of Denver Office of Institutional Research. (2008). Metropolitan State College of Denver 2004–2008 census fall student profiles. Retrieved October 1, 2009, from www.mscd.edu/facstaff/oir/PDF%20Files/OIR/Census%20Student%20Profiles/Fall_Student_Profile.pdf.

Robbins, L. P. (2008). Pidgin. *The Charleston Advisor*, 9(4), 38–39.

Steiner, S. K., & Long, C. M. (2007). What are we afraid of? A survey of librarian opinions and misconceptions regarding instant messenger. *The Reference Librarian*, 47(1), 31–50.

University of Colorado Denver. (2008). Institutional research, planning and analysis: Enrollment reports: Downtown Campus. Retrieved October 1, 2009, from http://wilbur.cudenver.edu/admin/ir/reports/enrollment_reports/FY0809/Headcount_DDC_FA08C.htm.

Ward, D., & Kern, M. K. (2006). Combining IM and vendor-based chat: A report from the frontlines of an integrated service. *portal: Libraries and the Academy*, 6(4), 417–429.

CHAPTER 10

California's AskNow Law Librarian Service

Ralph Stahlberg and Mary Pinard

Overview

California's AskNow Law Librarian Service coordinators trace the history of their service and discuss the challenges in providing virtual legal reference service. The work of the California Council of County Law Libraries (CCCLL) and their collaboration with the California Judicial Council in marketing and making the service successful is discussed. The service has grown from a project answering a few questions a month to one that assists over 18,000 users a year with 11 of California's county law libraries participating in live chat and e-mail follow-up. The distinction between legal advice and information is covered along with the changing nature of public law library users. The article concludes with a review of the coordinators' efforts to ensure both user and librarian satisfaction with the service. The project has increased the visibility of California's county law libraries and has helped improve the delivery of legal reference services to the residents of California.

California's AskNow Law Librarian Service

California's AskNow virtual reference service is a project of the Metropolitan Cooperative Library System, supported by Federal Library Services and Technology Act (LSTA) funding and administered by the California State Library. AskNow is a statewide project, which is part of the nationwide 24/7 Reference Cooperative. Over 100 California public and special libraries participate in this project, providing virtual reference service to users via live chat and e-mail. Among the special libraries participating in the AskNow project are public law libraries from 11 counties throughout the state. The law librarians serve two functions in this project: law-question experts, accepting legal reference questions transferred from public librarians, and first-tier reference providers, with patrons directly accessing the law librarians from links on a variety of law-related Web sites. This collaboration has greatly increased the visibility of California's county law libraries and has helped the law libraries achieve their mission of providing public access to legal information.

History of California's County Law Libraries

California statutes require every county in the state to provide the public with access to legal information (California Business and Professions Code [CBPC], 2003, §§ 6300-6364). Larger counties often have one or more county law libraries, while smaller counties may have a collection of law books at the public library or a computer terminal at the library or courthouse that provides access to legal research databases such as Westlaw or Lexis. Each county must provide facilities and related services for its law library (CBPC, 2003, § 6361) and a portion of civil court filing fees fund the libraries' operations (CBPC, 2003, § 6321). A board of law library trustees governs each county law library (CBPC, 2003, § 6348.2).

In the 1970s, the directors of these county law libraries formed a professional group, the California Council of County Law Libraries, to promote county law libraries with the state legislature and local governments. The group also provides mutual support and works together on projects to ensure public access to legal information.

History of the AskNow Law Librarian Service

In September 2000, Susan McGlamery from the Metropolitan Cooperative Library System (MCLS) approached CCCLL about the new 24/7 Reference Project she was heading, which was funded by an LSTA grant. Ms. McGlamery invited CCCLL to explore the software she was using and to evaluate if it could be used in the county law libraries.

Over the next year, the CCCLL libraries discussed the expansion of reference services to the Internet. As with everything else, an ever-growing number of patrons were turning to the Web to find legal information. Many CCCLL librarians advocated expanding our reference services to the Internet, where more of our patrons would find us. The group agreed that providing chat reference was a natural extension of the reference services already provided both in person and through e-mail. In the fall of 2001, CCCLL agreed to serve as law question experts for the 24/7 Reference Project. In exchange, the law libraries received free access to the software and training for the participating librarians. In January 2002, the librarians began a three-month training period, and the service went live to the public in April of that year.

CCCLL and the participating libraries made efforts to market this new service to the public and legal community. CCCLL put out press releases, published articles in professional journals and newsletters (David, 2002, 2003a, 2003b), and placed links on law library Web sites and the Judicial Council's California Courts Self-Help Web site (www.courtinfo.ca.gov). Despite these efforts, the AskNow Law Librarian Service was not heavily used. By December of 2002, law librarians were answering only about 100 chat and e-mail questions per month. Most of these questions were transferred to the law librarians by public librarians.

In the early months of the project, the link to AskNow from the Judicial Council's Web site was buried in the "other free services" section of the site, making it unlikely that patrons would stumble across the service. During this time, the law librarians worked with the Judicial Council on its Web site redesign, hoping to make the AskNow link more visible. As part of this redesign, an "Ask the Law Librarian" icon was prominently added to every page of the Self-Help Web site. The newly redesigned site was launched January 2, 2003, and the law librarians immediately saw an increase in usage. The number of questions rose from five per day to five per hour. In the first month after the Web site launch, the law librarians fielded 921 live chat questions and received 1,124 e-mail questions. By March, the law librarian service had to close the e-mail queue to all questions but those transferred in by the public librarians. There were too many questions for the law librarians to handle, and the backlog was growing rapidly.

Calls for more volunteers brought in several more county law libraries to assist in answering chat and e-mail questions. Scripted answers for recurring questions were written and shared. These scripts were Microsoft Word documents that were easily copied and pasted, with minor customizations, into e-mail responses and chat sessions. The scripts allowed librarians to send more e-mail responses and to handle more chats per staffing period because they had to do less research while the patron was waiting. The combination of increased staffing and scripts enabled the law librarians to quickly catch up and resume accepting e-mailed questions. Over the next year, adjustments were made to the chat staffing schedule to provide fuller coverage and double-staffing during peak hours.

In August 2004, OCLC (Online Computer Library Center) acquired the 24/7 Reference Cooperative, which provided the software used by the AskNow project. Hybrid software, QuestionPoint 24/7, was introduced in October 2005. New QuestionPoint software was again introduced in March 2006, which required extensive training and practice for the participating librarians. Unfortunately, technical adjustments interrupted service for much of April, May, June, and July 2006.

In July 2006, LSTA funding expired for the statewide coordinator for the AskNow project, and it was believed that LSTA funding for the software would expire July 1, 2007. By this time, many law librarians had begun to lose interest in the project, largely due the technical problems, the loss of a statewide coordinator, and the impending end of the project. Despite these problems, CCCLL still believed that virtual reference was valuable to our patrons and advocated the continuation of the service. CCCLL saw the end of the statewide project as an opportunity to establish its own virtual reference service.

In October 2006, the CCCLL Virtual Reference Task Force was created to explore this possibility. The Task Force thoroughly assessed the existing service, researched alternate options, and presented a report to the CCCLL Board in March 2007. Among the recommendations were to:

- continue using the QuestionPoint software;
- pursue grant funding for a CCCLL Virtual Reference Coordinator; and
- modify the staffing so that the larger county law libraries commit to staffing the chat more hours per week.

Luckily, a new LSTA grant was awarded in July 2007, funding the software for an additional two years. CCCLL decided to continue in the AskNow project rather than pursue its own virtual reference service.

Current AskNow Law Librarian Service

The Task Force's activities led to a renewed interest in the project. Several additional libraries volunteered to answer chat and e-mail questions. The chat staffing schedule was revised to provide better coverage. In 2007, there were several gaps in staffing during the busiest hours, between 10:00 a.m. and 4:00 p.m., and several double-staffed sessions outside of these busy periods. The revised schedule eliminated double-staffing. Additionally, several libraries volunteered for the previously unstaffed periods. The current schedule includes no gaps in service during the busiest hours and provides full coverage during normal business hours.

Currently, live chat service is available to patrons 43 hours per week. Nine of the participating libraries staff the chat service, and all 11 participating libraries answer e-mail reference questions. The expanded hours of chat and increased participation in e-mail reference allow the law libraries to provide better virtual reference service to patrons and to assist more patrons than ever before.

In 2008, the law librarians provided chat and e-mail assistance to 18,233 patrons. The law librarians had an average of 1,530 chat requests per month and were able to accept an average of 976 (64 percent). The law librarians also sent an average of 540 e-mail answers each month. These numbers represent a nearly 65 percent increase in service since 2006.

Virtual Reference and the Unauthorized Practice of Law (UPL)

California's AskNow law librarians have unique challenges in providing virtual reference service. When assisting their users, law librarians always need to be aware of the distinction between providing legal reference assistance and giving legal advice. The latter is the unauthorized practice of law (UPL) and is prohibited both under California law (CBPC, 2003, § 6125) and by the American Association of Law Libraries Ethical Principles (American Association of Law Libraries, 2007).[1] Dealing with the differences can be challenging for law librarians providing virtual reference service.

Much has been written in law librarianship literature (Brown, 1994; Mills, 1979) about the distinction between giving legal advice and providing legal information. Nearly every meeting of the American Association of Law Libraries has a program that touches on the issue or an aspect of it. Still, law librarians do not always agree on the distinction. But most law librarians agree on the following: we cannot interpret the law and we cannot give specific guidance on a legal issue. What we can do is guide our users to print and electronic resources that discuss the different options available and that contain practice checklists, procedural guidance, and filled-in examples of forms. Librarians can also explain the legal process in general, stressing the often complex nature of legal actions.

Many law libraries deal with the UPL concern by posting written statements. California's AskNow law librarians have a legal advice statement on our welcome page (AskNow, n.d.).[2] A UPL script is also available for the librarians to use, but the coordinators encourage the librarians to be positive and focus on the services that we can provide for our users rather than on what we are not allowed to do.

Changing Nature of Law Library Patrons

The users of public law libraries are changing. In the past, most law library users were attorneys, court personnel, and law students. In recent years, the court system has seen a growing number of litigants representing themselves. A 2004 California Judicial Council Statewide Action Plan for Serving Self-Represented Litigants (SRLs) found that over 4.3 million of the state's court users are self-represented, and close to 70 percent of initial family law filings are by SRLs (Judicial Council of California, 2004). Many of these litigants are coming to public law libraries either in person or via virtual reference seeking assistance with their cases and legal problems.

The California Courts and Legislature have responded to the growth in SRLs. As the statistics indicate, many SRLs are handling family law matters. In 1996, the California Legislature enacted the Family Law Facilitator Act (California Family Code, 2004, § 10000 et seq.). It established facilitator offices in each California County with staff to assist with family law matters. The AskNow law librarians often refer patrons to their local facilitator offices for further information and guidance.

The California Judicial Council created an Online Self-Help Center at www.courtinfo.ca.gov/selfhelp. The Web site contains a great deal of useful information and has prominent links on all of its pages to the "Ask the Law Librarian" service. Our librarians are very familiar with the information on the Web site. While many of our virtual reference questions come from links on the Web site, the answers to the patrons' questions are often found on the site's pages with guidance from the participating librarians.

Many reference questions come from SRLs. Patrons have questions about forms and court procedures. The librarians are careful to provide legal information and research guidance as opposed to giving legal advice. Sometimes both the users and librarians are frustrated. Our librarians have said "I can't answer these questions," which is sometimes true, but they can provide research guidance, referrals to county law libraries for further research beyond what is available online, and referrals to agencies that can provide more specific help. A good example of this is patrons requesting forms to use in their cases. A common question on our service is "I have been served with a summons and need to respond. What do I do?" The librarians cannot recommend specific forms. Many legal situations require not just one form, but a series of forms or a choice among several different forms. The librarians frequently refer patrons to their local county law libraries with citations to self-help and other practice guides. The law librarians help users make educated choices in handling their legal actions.

California's AskNow law librarian service is a good public relations tool for California's County law libraries. Many users are unaware of our system of public law libraries and virtual reference connects them to the resource.

Patron and Librarian Satisfaction

Patron and librarian satisfaction are important gauges of the success of a virtual reference service. California's AskNow law coordinators work to ensure both patron and librarian satisfaction. For the patrons, we try to ensure that our posted hours are staffed. We have a listserv and ask the librarians to post messages if they are unable to staff assigned hours. The librarians handle a significant amount of follow-up. Because of the large numbers, we cannot always send specific individual replies. Instead, we have created a scripted response that directs patrons to several legal Web sites and to their local county law libraries, so all users get a response.

For the librarians, the California AskNow law coordinators work to ensure satisfaction with periodic statistical reports and updates. We encourage communication among the participating libraries for staffing and other issues. We have enabled Question Point's survey feature and are getting many positive responses, close to an 81 percent positive rate, with nearly 93 percent responding they would consider using the service again. We review the survey results to identify issues and use the information to add or modify our scripts.

The most common patron complaint is about the wait time to connect with a librarian, not the quality of information given. The nature of legal research requires lengthy reference interviews and continued interaction with a librarian through the research process. Our average chat length is nearly 15 minutes, well above the average 12 minutes reported by other virtual reference services (Radford, 2007; White, Abels, & Kaske, 2003). With high patron demand and only one librarian staffing chat, it is common to have several patrons in the queue, with an average wait time of 9 minutes, which is also well above the average wait time of under 2 minutes reported by other virtual reference services (Radford, 2007).

California's AskNow legal reference service is a useful and valuable service for the legal information consumers of California and an important public relations and outreach tool for California's public county law libraries. Our stable and dedicated group of participating librarians find staffing the service both challenging and rewarding.

Notes

1. "We acknowledge the limits on service imposed by our institutions and by the duty to avoid the unauthorized practice of law."
2. "It is unlawful for librarians to interpret legal information or advise an individual how the law might apply to one's situation. This kind of service would constitute the unauthorized practice of law. If you need further help to solve your legal problem, we recommend that you consult an attorney."

References

American Association of Law Libraries. (2007). Ethical principles. In *AALL Directory and Handbook 2007–08* (p. 434). Chicago: American Association of Law Libraries.

AskNow. (n.d.). Get help from the librarian in real time. Retrieved April 14, 2009, from http://www.247ref/org/portal/access_law3.cfm.

Brown, Y. (1994). From the reference desk to the jail house: Unauthorized practice of law and librarians. *Legal Reference Services Quarterly, 13*(4), 31–45.

California Business and Professions Code. (2003). *West's annotated California codes*. St. Paul, MN: West Group.

California Family Code. (2004). *West's annotated California codes*. St Paul, MN: West Group.

David, S. (2002, June 20). Catching the 24/7 reference wave. *San Francisco Daily Journal*, p. 12.

David, S. (2003a, May 15). 24/7 Reference update: Legal reference services to the public. *San Francisco Daily Journal*.

David, S. (2003b). California residents find their other public libraries: 24/7 reference and Q&A café programs catch on. *State, Court & County Law Libraries News, 29*(2), 18.

Judicial Council of California. (2004). *Statewide action plan for serving self-represented litigants*. San Francisco: Judicial Council of California.

Mills, R. K. (1979). Reference service v. legal advice: Is it possible to draw the line? *Law Library Journal, 72*(2), 179–193.

Radford, M. (2007). Creating chat connections: E-valuating virtual reference transcripts. Retrieved April 14, 2009, from www.oclc.org/research/projects/synchronicity/ppt/acrl-delval07-radford.ppt#287,5,VRS Session Times.

White, D. M., Abels, E. G., & Kaske, N. (2003). Evaluation of chat reference service Quality. *D-Lib Magazine, 9*(2). Retrieved April 14, 2009, from http://webdoc.sub.gwdg.de/edoc/aw/d-lib/dlib/february03/white/02white.html.

CHAPTER 11

Expanding Service and Enhancing Learning: Preliminary Report on a Novel Virtual Reference Collaboration

Andrea Wright and Feili Tu

Overview

To address both the need for virtual reference service (VRS) training in library education and expansion of a VRS program, a novel collaboration was developed between the Association of Southeastern Research Libraries' (ASERL) Ask-a-Librarian (AAL) consortium and the School of Library and Information Science at the University of South Carolina (USC-SLIS). The hours of service for ASERL AAL were expanded for the 2007–2008 school year, and these new evening and weekend hours were covered by master's level library and information science students or recent graduates of USC-SLIS competitively selected to participate in the program. This chapter describes the project in detail, including information on student training and supervision.

This project also created the opportunity to explore several research areas. Three important questions are: What specific knowledge and skills learned in USC-SLIS coursework help students provide VRS? Is this VRS practice beneficial to students' careers? Can libraries benefit from utilizing the skills and knowledge of select master's level USC-SLIS students and recent graduates? Data was collected by interviewing with student workers and ASERL AAL management. Further information was gathered by analyzing transcripts for information on communication skills, reference interview skills, searching and information-finding skills, and technology skills. Overall, the assessment of this project for Fall 2007 indicates a mutually beneficial relationship for the students relating to their skills and future careers, USC-SLIS in providing a unique learning opportunity to its students, and the libraries for their ability to expand service without requiring more time from librarians.

Introduction

In February 2004, the Association of Southeastern Research Libraries created a virtual reference service consortium that would allow participating institutions to share in the purchase of Virtual Reference (VR) software and coverage of a VR desk. The members of and software used by this Ask-a-Librarian group would fluctuate over time. The AAL service allowed users from any participating institution to engage a librarian in real-time chat during any of the standard service hours (see Table 11.1) while requiring institutions to provide coverage for only a few hours a week. This service model provided 61 hours of coverage. Librarians could (and did) cover additional hours, but this coverage was inconsistent, unscheduled, and did not necessarily include users from all institutions.

This expansion project took place during the 2007–2008 academic year when there were eight institutions participating in the ASERL AAL consortium (see Table 11.2) and used SirsiDynix's Docutek VRLplus software.

Table 11.1. Standard AAL Service Model	
Day of the Week	**Coverage Time**
Monday–Thursday	9:00 a.m.–9:00 p.m.
Friday	9:00 a.m.–6:00 p.m.
Saturday	1:00 p.m.–5:00 p.m.
Sunday	None

Table 11.2. AAL Participating Institutions, 2007–2008			
Institution	**Location**	**Type**	**Enrollment**
College of William & Mary	Williamsburg, VA	Public, 4 Year	7,625
Mississippi State University	Starkville, MS	Public, 4 Year	17,039
University of Alabama	Tuscaloosa, AL	Public, 4 Year	25,580
University of Central Florida	Orlando, FL	Public, 4 Year	48,699
University of Memphis	Memphis, TN	Public, 4 Year	20,379
University of Mississippi	Oxford, MS	Public, 4 Year	17,323
University of North Carolina at Charlotte	Charlotte, NC	Public, 4 Year	22,388
Virginia Commonwealth University	Richmond, VA	Public, 4 Year	31,907

The School of Library and Information Science at the University of South Carolina is the only American Library Association (ALA)–accredited program in South Carolina. The school offers bachelor's, master's, and doctorate degrees utilizing a combination of in-person, satellite, and Web technologies for instruction and extracurricular activities. USC-SLIS serves students not only throughout South Carolina but the entire country, as the school provides cohort programs in Maine, Virginia, and West Virginia.

The ASERL AAL consortium sought a way to increase the hours of VRS without requiring more hours from the institutions' librarians. The ASERL selected USC-SLIS to support AAL Online Chat Extended Reference Service in 2007–2008. The AAL service model would be expanded to include late night and weekend hours (see Table 11.3). This expansion meant that VRS would be available to faculty, students, and staff of all eight institutions for nearly 100 hours a week.

Feili Tu, PhD, MLIS, a faculty member of the USC-SLIS, was the primary investigator (PI) for this project, which was designed as a paid internship and practicum program. The PI oversaw the project development and implementation of procedures. MLIS candidate Andrea Wright was the project coordinator and handled the day-to-day operational needs. The project coordinator's responsibilities included scheduling training, supervising student staff, facilitating trouble-shooting on the use of Docutek VRLplus software, scheduling meetings, serving as a liaison to the steering committee of the ASERL AAL project, and helping the PI conduct the project evaluation research.

Eight master's level library and information science students and recent graduates were recruited for the student staff each semester. Potential student staff members were required to have completed a majority of their coursework and to have taken Introduction to Information Services and Sources, an introductory course on reference resources and services. The staff selection process was highly competitive. A copy of the application is available in Appendix 11.1. The application packages were reviewed by the PI and project coordinator. Students had the choice of participating in a paid practicum or a paid internship. The

Table 11.3. Expanded AAL Service Model	
Day of the Week	**Coverage Time**
Monday–Thursday	9:00 a.m.–Midnight
Friday	9:00 a.m.–Midnight
Saturday	1:00 p.m.–Midnight
Sunday	Noon–Midnight

practicum offered a stipend based on an hourly rate for virtual desk coverage. The internship offered the same hourly rate for virtual desk coverage. However, students were required to enroll in Internship in Library and Information Science under the supervision of the PI to earn course credits.

Value of the Project

Integrating real-world library operations into the curriculum is one of the goals of library and information science (LIS) education, and VRS training is now part of many programs. Therefore, to enhance the education of reference librarians, this real-world VRS internship or practicum was established in the USC-SLIS. Two important research questions associated with this project are the following: What specific knowledge and skills learned in LIS coursework help students provide VRS? Is this VRS practice beneficial to students' careers (finding jobs, getting promotions, being given responsibility for special assignments)?

A research component for project evaluation was built into this collaborative initiative. The research protocol was designed by the PI, and the research processes were conducted by the project coordinator. These aspects of the study were of particular interest:

- The quality of students' services, as evidenced by application of knowledge and skills learned from the curriculum of the LIS education program and how well students provided these services
- Training provided by ASERL AAL and its effectiveness, as evidenced by how well the student staff used Docutek VRLplus for the provision of VRS
- The availability of a real-world internship and if it facilitated qualitative changes in student learning
- Evaluation of the effectiveness of VRS services provided by the students from the ASERL AAL management

The project evaluations helped in assessing whether students had acquired from their coursework the knowledge and skills needed to provide professional-level services and whether LIS programs should offer this type of real-world experience.

Review of Literature

Technology has made fundamental changes in the services provided by libraries and librarians. Users' demands on services have made a lot of magic happen (Tu, 2004), but it is the Internet that has caused the most sweeping changes in library services (Francoeur, 2002). VRS, which is also known as digital reference, is basically computer-mediated reference service (Lipow, 2003).

VRS was introduced more than a decade ago. The service models include all electronic methods by which libraries fulfill patrons' information needs, such as e-mail, online forms, interactive chat, and Web-browsing software (Janes,

Carter, & Memmott, 1999). The best known of the early efforts was the Internet Public Library (IPL; www.ipl.org), a service launched in 1995 by the University of Michigan's School of Information and Library Studies (Boss, 2004; Janes, 1998). Janes (1998) describes the online reference help provided by the IPL: "Despite the desire to do real-time reference, it seemed obvious that using email as the medium made sense, but that meant that reference interviews would be difficult or at least asynchronous and therefore time consuming" (Janes, 1998, p. 60).

Janes points out that (1) there are limitations to what can be done online and that (2) certain skills are required for VRS. Lankes discusses the digital reference research agenda and indicates that one of the central questions in digital reference is "how can human expertise be incorporated effectively and efficiently into information systems to answer information seekers' questions?" (Lankes, 2005, p. 322). One of the research questions in the same article is related to the necessary VRS staffing levels, expertise, and training.

In 2004 the Reference and User Services Association (RUSA) of the ALA published practice guidelines for implementing and maintaining VRS. Even though the guidelines contain no clear definition of the core competencies for providing VRS, the descriptions of service behaviors present some basic information related to the provision of VRS. As Lankes (2005) said:

> To ignore the truth that LIS research is testable is to ignore reality.... [A]ny research hypothesis in digital reference, no matter how abstract or conceptual, should be able to be tested in libraries. Practice without research, on the other hand, risks constant reinvention and avoids economies of scale that build communal knowledge across organizations. (p. 324)

The concepts mentioned previously were used to design the research component of the project evaluation. The intent was to collect evidence from the students' services and then use it to fill the knowledge gap related to the effective provision of VRS by LIS graduate students and potential entry-level librarians.

Project Details

The ASERL AAL management requested double-coverage for shifts late on Sunday and Monday through Thursday evenings. This double-coverage increased the student coverage time to 53 hours per week, meaning each student would cover approximately 7.5 hours per week. Students were assigned shifts on a weekly basis by the project coordinator.

Prior to the start of coverage, students were provided with in-person and online training. The training was conducted over two days. The first day (Friday) consisted of a live, afternoon Webinar with a trainer from SirsiDynix on the Docutek system. The second day (Saturday) was a full day. Bridgette Sanders, a librarian at University of North Carolina–Charlotte, helped introduce students to the ASERL AAL program. Her presentation included tips and insights into the Docutek system and providing service from an experienced point of view. ASERL AAL policies and standards were covered, and a brief review of important reference topics and points specific to VR was given. The day ended with a hands-on practice session where students could log into the system and practice using the software with one another, both as librarian and user.

To support the ASERL Institutional Policy Pages and to provide material relevant to the students' work, a del.icio.us account was created. This account provided tagged links to ASERL policy pages, important Web pages for each institution (such as the library catalog and online databases), online tutorials for popular databases, and links to Web sites on best practices and standards for VR. These links are still available from the account at http://delicious.com/slis_aal/. A project Blackboard account was also created and accessible to all students. This account included links to recordings of the training sessions, the policy pages, the del.icio.us account, and the Docutek VRLplusManual.

Assessment

This project created an opportunity to explore several research areas. Three important questions were the following:

1. What specific knowledge and skills learned in LIS coursework help students provide VRS?
2. Is this VRS practice beneficial to students' careers?
3. Can libraries benefit from utilizing the skills and knowledge of select master's level LIS students and recent graduates?

The research component was built into the project and the methodology was ethnographic research. The sample was comprised of USC-SLIS student staff and the ASERL AAL management. Interviews were conducted near the end of the semester with both student staff and ASERL AAL management. Session transcripts were downloaded from the Docutek software and analyzed using an instrument developed by the PI to rank for communication, reference interview skills, searching and information-finding skills, and technology skills (see Appendix 11.2).

Student Interviews

Fall semester student staff members ($n = 7$) were interviewed during early November 2007 using Adobe Connect meeting software. Students were asked a series of questions that covered topics such as the SLIS curriculum, program training, and the actual VRS practice. Interview questions and results are provided in the following sections.

Please describe the specific knowledge and skills you learned from the SLIS courses that helped you provide chat-based virtual reference service.
All students identified the reference interview as a specific skill learned from USC-SLIS that aided in their provision of VRS. Another topic mentioned frequently was knowledge of reference sources ($n = 6$).

Please list the SLIS courses you have taken that provided adequate knowledge and skills for you in providing VRS.
All students indicated SLIS 703: Introduction to Information Services and Sources. Also mentioned was SLIS 740: Online Information Services ($n = 4$), along with a variety of courses ranging from government information to children's literature to a digital preservation course.

Several questions were asked regarding the training, including the most useful aspects, the least useful, and what was not adequately covered. All of the students found the hands-on portion of the training to be useful. Several ($n = 3$) students indicated that the training provided by Docutek was not as important as the separate training on Saturday. Students indicated that dealing with problem users was an important topic not covered during the training.

In your opinion, what is the valuable experience you have gained?
Students indicated that one valuable experience was working live reference with real users.

In your opinion, is this VRS practice beneficial to your career development?
All of the students indicated that this experience was beneficial to their career development. One student noted that it was a "clearly positive experience that I can cite when I apply for full-time library positions." Another stated that, "I hope to become an academic librarian, so this is truly invaluable experience that I . . . believe will give me an advantage in finding a job."

In your opinion, what are the strengths and weaknesses of the current AAL service model?
Providing service to eight institutions was seen by the student staff as both a strength and a weakness. Students believed that it was more efficient than coverage by a single institution. At the same time, workers could not access all online resources owned by an institution and had to deal with issues that only specific institutional staff could help with. The software was also named as both a strength and a weakness as it had positive aspects (such as an easy interface) and negative aspects (such as regular technical glitches). Cobrowsing was a favorite, useful tool of the students—when it worked correctly.

When rating their overall experience in the ASERL AAL/USC-SLIS project, all students indicated a 7 out of 7 rating (excellent).

ASERL AAL Management Interview

An interview of Ros Lett, ASERL VR coordinator, was conducted by the PI using Adobe Connect on December 18, 2007. The interview included questions pertaining to the VRS provided by the SLIS student staff and AAL Management Issues. Questions about training were not posed as Ms. Lett was unable to attend the fall training session. Interview questions and results are provided in the following sections.

Overall evaluation of VRS provided by SLIS/USC student staff on a 1–7 scale.
7 (Totally Satisfied).

Overall rating of program on 1–7 scale.
7 (Excellent).

In your opinion, what are the strengths and weakness of the current AAL service model?
Ms. Lett noted several strengths of the new expanded hours model, including increased coverage without requiring increased service by librarians, the hands-on experience for student workers, and the good communication and sharing among the consortium. She also noted program weaknesses, such as delays in updating the ASERL AAL Web site because it is handled by an outside group. Ms. Lett also noted that, because the VRS is covered by a consortium, some transactions take longer because a question may be specific to an institution but the answering worker is from a different library.

Should ASERL continue to partner with USC/SLIS?
Ms. Lett indicated that ASERL should continue to partner with USC-SLIS on this project, noting that USC-SLIS created a successful, structured model for the extended hours program.

Documentation Analysis

Session statistics were gathered using reports generated by the Docutek system. Transcripts of all sessions held by student workers were downloaded from the Docutek system and analyzed using an instrument developed by the PI (see Appendix 11.2).

USC-SLIS students covered the ASERL AAL VR desk from Sunday, September 16, 2007, through Friday, December 7, 2007. During that time, the service handled 3,068 total sessions. Of those, 1,091 (36 percent) occurred during the expanded hours. A comparison of a similar time frame for fall 2006 (Sunday, September 17, 2006, through Friday, December 8, 2006) shows 2,117 total sessions, with 535 (25 percent) occurring in what would become the expanded hours. Thus, the service saw an increase of 45 percent in total traffic between fall 2006 and fall 2007. Furthermore, the expanded hours accounted for 35.6 percent of all sessions during the above time frame for fall 2007. Of the 1,091 sessions handled by student workers, 874 contained legitimate transactions. The others included "ghost" users from previous sessions, users leaving before a transaction could begin, or other technical glitches that prevented complete worker/user interaction.

The Docutek VRLplus software includes several special features: prescripted replies, pushing Web pages into a user's browser, cobrowsing, and transferring a user between staffers. Of the 874 sessions, student workers utilized at least one special feature in 225 (25 percent) sessions (see Figure 11.1). It is worth noting that cobrowsing requires both worker and user to be using a PC and Internet Explorer along with other system requirements. Even when these conditions were met, the cobrowse feature was not always successfully connected.

There were 730 sessions that required a resource to answer the question (see Figure 11.2); other transactions involved referrals to a user's home library for further assistance. Of those 730 sessions, 152 (21 percent) involved accessing two or more resource categories.

The library Web site was a very popular resource as many questions dealt with library hours, policies, and services such as interlibrary loan. Subscription databases were also popular resources, even through student staff workers could not search along with user unless cobrowsing was initiated and successful.

Internet searches and results were generally avoided by the student staff except when necessary, such as locating a specific citation style online. Even when limited to free online resources, student workers were able to recommend authoritative sites such as Purdue's OWL Web site (http://owl.english.purdue.edu).

The transcript analysis instrument ranked each session based on areas such as resources, interpersonal communication, the reference interview, information

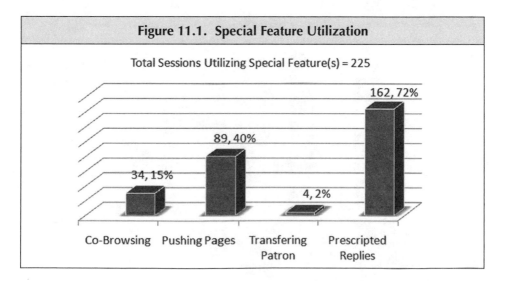

Figure 11.1. Special Feature Utilization

Total Sessions Utilizing Special Feature(s) = 225

162, 72%

89, 40%

34, 15%

4, 2%

Co-Browsing   Pushing Pages   Transfering Patron   Prescripted Replies

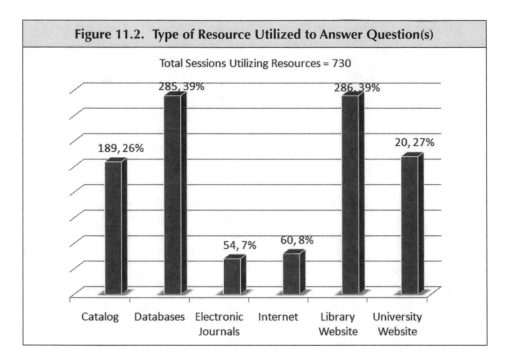

Figure 11.2. Type of Resource Utilized to Answer Question(s)

Total Sessions Utilizing Resources = 730

- Catalog: 189, 26%
- Databases: 285, 39%
- Electronic Journals: 54, 7%
- Internet: 60, 8%
- Library Website: 286, 39%
- University Website: 20, 27%

retrieval, and online instruction. All areas were ranked on a 7-point scale, with 1 being Totally Unsatisfied, 5 being Reasonably Satisfied, and 7 being Totally Satisfied (see Figure 11.3).

Student staff workers were very strong in selecting appropriate resources, retrieving accurate and authoritative information quickly, and communicating

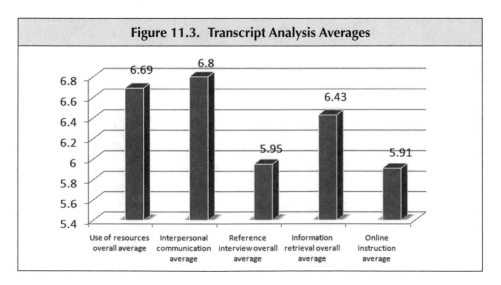

Figure 11.3. Transcript Analysis Averages

- Use of resources overall average: 6.69
- Interpersonal communication average: 6.8
- Reference interview overall average: 5.95
- Information retrieval overall average: 6.43
- Online instruction average: 5.91

with users professionally, politely, and regularly. Reference interviews and user instruction were good, though not as strong. These areas seem to be more difficult to conduct thoroughly in an online environment, especially when ASERL policy recommends limiting transactions to 20 minutes. Overall, the student sessions were quite successful. Sessions were rated on a scale with 1 representing poor service quality, 4 indicating average service quality, and 7 representing excellent service quality (see Figure 11.4). Overall rating of sessions averaged 5.78 on the 7-point scale. Many of the midrange rating resulted from questions that could not be answered by an outside librarian or in some cases by any librarian over VR (both of which were referred to the user's home library), not the worker's ability or conduct.

Discussion

This project had a positive impact on the student workers. It essentially offered students the chance for paid professional development with the additional opportunity to earn course credit. Students will be able to draw on real experiences with academic users in a virtual environment as they apply for and interview for professional positions. This project also improved student confidence regarding reference transactions and VR skills.

For USC-SLIS, this program presented not only an excellent learning opportunity for students but also a chance to verify student learning outcomes and transference of skills and theory to real-world experience. This project also

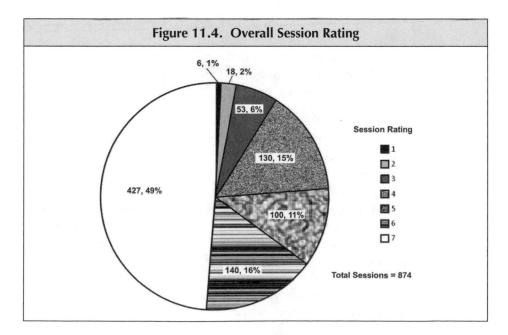

Figure 11.4. Overall Session Rating

demonstrated the competency of new USC-SLIS graduates to librarians at other institutions.

Previously, the ASERL AAL program had tried working in a less formal setting with other LIS graduate students. This setup had not been a beneficial experience for the consortium as students needed additional reference training, were not providing professional-level service, and had no accountable supervision. The model described herein rectified these problems by offering training both before service began and throughout with online support, by careful screening of participants through a selective application process and by creation of the project coordinator position. By joining with USC-SLIS to create a standardized, rigorous model for the expanded-hours project, ASERL AAL libraries were able to expand service with the comfort that students would be online during their scheduled hours, that they would provide users with professional-level service (that often included direction to subscription library resources), and that appropriate referrals would be made back to the home institution.

Conclusion

Overall, the assessment of this project for fall 2007 indicates a mutually beneficial relationship for all involved. Ratings according to the transcript analysis instrument indicate that master's level students are able to provide professional-level VRS. Student interviews show that they gain hands-on skills and confidence in their abilities. Participating libraries are able to confidently expand their hours without requiring more coverage by their librarians, as noted by the ASERL AAL management interviews. And USC-SLIS was able to offer a unique learning opportunity to students in the master's program.

The success of this program is rooted in the rigorous model developed by the PI and project coordinator. The following are five main points of this model that we feel were critical to the program's success:

1. Student workers were selected by a competitive application process. There were 11 applications for the 8 student spots in fall 2007. The number of applications increased to 16 for the 8 student spots in spring 2008. This increase allowed the PI and project coordinator to carefully screen workers based on coursework, previous experience, and references.
2. Student workers must have completed coursework in reference, with preference for upper-level reference coursework and experience. In fall of 2007, a new curriculum began at USC-SLIS, and though the introductory reference course was no longer required in the curriculum, it was still required for consideration in this project.
3. The students had thorough training and review of the VR software and reference skills prior to their service. All-day training included not only

instruction on the software and procedures but also on AAL policy and a review of reference skills and resources.

4. Ongoing training and support was available to student workers online throughout the semester. Students were able to access the del.icio.us account with links to important library pages, AAL pages, best reference practice information, and information and tutorials on specific databases. Blackboard software was available to all students for sharing questions, concerns, and answers.

5. The project included accessible supervision of student staff. The project coordinator was in regular communication with student workers regarding scheduling, coverage, paperwork, transaction questions, and software technical issues.

This project was very successful, as it was beneficial to the participating libraries, the student staff, and USC-SLIS. This model, however, should not be limited to this particular situation. The critical aspects of the model described previously could be replicated at an individual institution or within a new collaboration of libraries. While having a consortium of libraries involved did allow for maximum benefits to all involved, a single institution could work with a smaller number of LIS students to expand their own virtual reference hours. Also, because the VR software allowed for remote login, the student workers were able to work from a variety of locations. This opens up this model of VRS to institutions that are not geographically close to a LIS program. Furthermore, because one the greatest benefits to the LIS students was experience and confidence, an unpaid internship or practicum could still attract excellent student workers.

The data available from this project is copious and offers the chance to investigate a number of issues in VR. Transcripts have been downloaded for the spring 2008 semester and will provide further data regarding student ability and benefits to all involved. All of the transcripts include potentially useful data not yet analyzed, such as late night and weekend traffic patterns, types of questions received in extended hours, and types and frequency of technical issues. Further mining and analysis should make the conclusions herein stronger and offer unique insights into VRS and its integration with LIS education.

The grant funding of this project lasted an academic year. The termination of the project was due to the dismantlement of the ASERL AAL consortium. Although the scope of this project is limited, this study is a step toward a better understanding of how to prepare LIS master's students in the provision of effective chat-based VRS. The PI and project coordinator firmly believe that this is a sustainable business model for providing LIS master's students with stipends and real-world experience. Both of these factors are pluses in students' résumés. LIS educators and information professionals need to work together to figure out how to develop entrepreneurial models to promote these types of services. In addition, LIS educators can be proactive in marketing the real-world professional services that can be provided by LIS master's students. Ultimately, the goal is to ensure that librarians and information professionals will be able to design and deliver effective, customized VRS in today's fast-paced and challenging information environments.

Related Web Sites

- ASERL AAL Web site (via Internet Archive Wayback Machine): http://web .archive.org/web/20070304122500/http://www.ask-a-librarian.org
- Docutek: www.docutek.com
- SLIS AAL del.icio.us account: http://delicious.com/slis_aal

References

Boss, R. W. (2004). *Virtual references*. Chicago: American Library Association. Retrieved July 31, 2008, from www.ala.org/ala/mgrps/divs/pla/plapublications/platechnotes/virtualreference.cfm.

Francoeur, S. (2002, August). Digital reference. *The Teaching Librarian*. Retrieved October 8, 2003, from www.teachinglibrarian.org/digref.htm.

Janes, J. (1998). The Internet public library: An intellectual history. *Library Hi Tech*, 16(2), 55–68.

Janes, J., Carter, D., & Memmott, P. (1999, Winter). Digital reference services in academic libraries. *Reference & User Services Quarterly*, 39, 145–150.

Lankes, R. D. (2005, Summer). Digital reference research. *Reference and Users Services Quarterly*, 44(4), 320–326.

Lipow, A. G. (2003). *The virtual reference librarian's handbook*. New York: Neal-Schuman.

Reference and User Services Association. (2004). *Guidelines for implementing and maintaining virtual reference services*. Chicago: American Library Association. Retrieved April 23, 2009, from www.ala.org/ala/mgrps/divs/rusa/archive/protools/referenceguide/virtrefguidelines.cfm.

Tu, F. (2004). Virtual reference services and the school library media specialists. *School Library Media Activities Monthly*, 20(7), 49–51.

Appendix 11.1. The University of South Carolina ASERL "Ask-a-Librarian" Internship or Practicum Application

THE UNIVERSITY OF SOUTH CAROLINA

School of Library and Information Science

ASERL "ASK-A-LIBRARIAN" INTERNSHIP OR PRACTICUM APPLICATION

NAME: _____ DATE OF APPLICATION: _____

CURRENT ADDRESS (Campus or Mailing Address): _____

_____

TELEPHONE NUMBER: _____

E-MAIL ADDRESS: _____

PERMANENT ADDRESS & TELEPHONE NUMBER: _____

_____

Are you currently enrolled in SLIS? Please list the courses (numbers and titles) that you have completed.

_____

_____

_____

_____

CUMULATIVE GPA: _____   # of A's: _____   # of D's and F's: _____

ANTICIPATED/ACTUAL GRADUATION DATE: _____

Within librarianship, what is your major of interest? School, public, academic, special, medical? Public services or technical services?

_____

_____

In one paragraph (4-6 sentences), please briefly describe your understanding of virtual reference service via an online chatting system and how to provide this type of service

_____

_____

_____

_____

(Continued)

Appendix 11.1. The University of South Carolina ASERL "Ask-a-Librarian" Internship or Practicum Application *(Continued)*

Please list the colleges/universities you have attended, the dates of attendance, degree received, major, and GPA.

_____

_____

Please list any foreign languages you know and indicate those that you can read and speak well.

_____

Please list previous work experience; include volunteer experience if in a library:

_____

_____

_____

Are you able to type? _____ Words per minute _____

Are you able to use a personal computer? _____ If yes, with which software are you familiar?

_____

_____

_____

AVAILABILITY (*Circle all that apply*):

	Monday 9 pm – midnight	Tuesday 9 pm – midnight
Wednesday 9 pm – midnight	Thursday 9 pm – midnight	Friday 6 pm – midnight
Saturday 5 pm – midnight	Sunday noon – midnight	Sunday 7 pm – 11 pm

Are you presently employed on or off campus? _____

If so, please list the following: Name of Department/Business: _____

Hours: _____

Please list the names of three persons qualified to recommend you for this internship/practicum. These references do not necessarily have to be people at Carolina – they may be anyone you have known who would have knowledge of your work ethic.

Name	Address (Home or Business)	City/State	Phone

Please include a one to two paragraph statement about your interest in this internship/practicum and any relevant experience or classwork you have completed and email to:

Andrea Wright
Project Coordinator
Re: ASERL "Ask-A-Librarian" Internship

Appendix 11.2. Docutek: Communication, Reference Interview Skills, Searching and Information Finding Skills, and Technology Skills

Transaction Number	
Student Worker Number	
Date and Time	
Reviewer	
Patron Institution	
Queue Wait Time	
Chat Duration	

Use of DocuTek Software
 	
Please describe how well/poorly the student staff member uses Docutek VRL-Plus during the chat-based virtual reference service (VRS) transaction(s).
	Overall evaluation:
	∞ Is the subject familiar with the available software features?
	
	        Yes No No opinion
	Comments:
	∞ Is the subject capable of using the available software features?
	
	        Yes No No opinion
	Comments:
	∞ Is the subject using any specific software features during VRS transactions? Please describe the features (e.g., sending pre-scripted messages) used during the transactions.
	
	        Yes No No opinion
	Comments:

Use of resources for problem-solving	Overall evaluation:
	  1 2 3 4 5 6 7
	Totally ⟵ Reasonably ⟶ Totally
	Unsatisfied Satisfied Satisfied
	Please record the resources used by the subject for problem-solving.
	
	           Print Electronic Both
	Title(s) of the resources used:
	Comments:
	∞ Is the resource (or are the resources) used by the subject appropriate for the problem-solving?
	
	        Yes No No opinion
	Comments:
	∞ Is the subject capable of using the resources from a specific institution to answer the question posted by a user from that specific institution?
	
	        Yes No No opinion
	Comments:

Time management	Overall evaluation:
	  1 2 3 4 5 6 7
	Totally ⟵ Reasonably ⟶ Totally
	Unsatisfied Satisfied Satisfied
	∞ Does the subject manage the transaction(s) efficiently?
	
	        Yes No No opinion
	Comments:

Interpersonal	Overall evaluation:

(Continued)

Appendix 11.2. Docutek: Communication, Reference Interview Skills, Searching and Information Finding Skills, and Technology Skills *(Continued)*

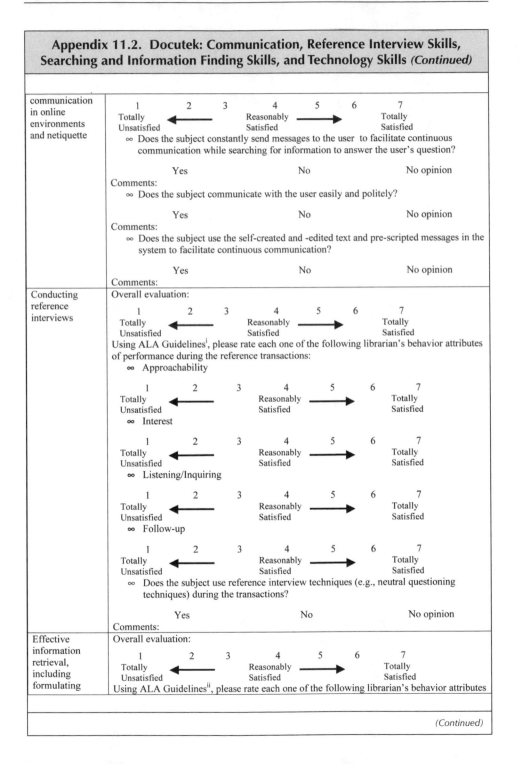

communication in online environments and netiquette	1 2 3 4 5 6 7
	Totally Unsatisfied ⟵ Reasonably Satisfied ⟶ Totally Satisfied
	∞ Does the subject constantly send messages to the user to facilitate continuous communication while searching for information to answer the user's question?
	
	    Yes No No opinion
	Comments:
	∞ Does the subject communicate with the user easily and politely?
	
	    Yes No No opinion
	Comments:
	∞ Does the subject use the self-created and -edited text and pre-scripted messages in the system to facilitate continuous communication?
	
	    Yes No No opinion
	Comments:

Conducting reference interviews	Overall evaluation: 1 2 3 4 5 6 7 Totally Unsatisfied ⟵ Reasonably Satisfied ⟶ Totally Satisfied Using ALA Guidelines[i], please rate each one of the following librarian's behavior attributes of performance during the reference transactions: ∞ Approachability 1 2 3 4 5 6 7 Totally Unsatisfied ⟵ Reasonably Satisfied ⟶ Totally Satisfied ∞ Interest 1 2 3 4 5 6 7 Totally Unsatisfied ⟵ Reasonably Satisfied ⟶ Totally Satisfied ∞ Listening/Inquiring 1 2 3 4 5 6 7 Totally Unsatisfied ⟵ Reasonably Satisfied ⟶ Totally Satisfied ∞ Follow-up 1 2 3 4 5 6 7 Totally Unsatisfied ⟵ Reasonably Satisfied ⟶ Totally Satisfied ∞ Does the subject use reference interview techniques (e.g., neutral questioning techniques) during the transactions? Yes No No opinion Comments:
Effective information retrieval, including formulating	Overall evaluation: 1 2 3 4 5 6 7 Totally Unsatisfied ⟵ Reasonably Satisfied ⟶ Totally Satisfied Using ALA Guidelines[ii], please rate each one of the following librarian's behavior attributes

(Continued)

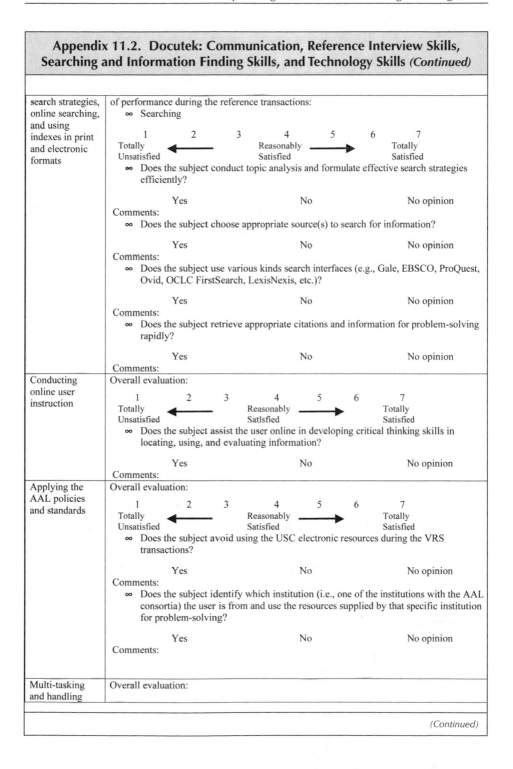

Appendix 11.2. Docutek: Communication, Reference Interview Skills, Searching and Information Finding Skills, and Technology Skills *(Continued)*

search strategies, online searching, and using indexes in print and electronic formats	of performance during the reference transactions:
	∞ Searching
	
	1 2 3 4 5 6 7
	Totally ◄——— Reasonably ———► Totally
	Unsatisfied Satisfied Satisfied
	∞ Does the subject conduct topic analysis and formulate effective search strategies efficiently?
	
	    Yes No No opinion
	Comments:
	∞ Does the subject choose appropriate source(s) to search for information?
	
	    Yes No No opinion
	Comments:
	∞ Does the subject use various kinds search interfaces (e.g., Gale, EBSCO, ProQuest, Ovid, OCLC FirstSearch, LexisNexis, etc.)?
	
	    Yes No No opinion
	Comments:
	∞ Does the subject retrieve appropriate citations and information for problem-solving rapidly?
	
	    Yes No No opinion
	Comments:

Conducting online user instruction	Overall evaluation: 1 2 3 4 5 6 7 Totally ◄——— Reasonably ———► Totally Unsatisfied Satisfied Satisfied ∞ Does the subject assist the user online in developing critical thinking skills in locating, using, and evaluating information? Yes No No opinion Comments:

Applying the AAL policies and standards	Overall evaluation:
	
	1 2 3 4 5 6 7
	Totally ◄——— Reasonably ———► Totally
	Unsatisfied Satisfied Satisfied
	∞ Does the subject avoid using the USC electronic resources during the VRS transactions?
	
	    Yes No No opinion
	Comments:
	∞ Does the subject identify which institution (i.e., one of the institutions with the AAL consortia) the user is from and use the resources supplied by that specific institution for problem-solving?
	
	    Yes No No opinion
	Comments:

Multi-tasking and handling	Overall evaluation:

(Continued)

Appendix 11.2. Docutek: Communication, Reference Interview Skills, Searching and Information Finding Skills, and Technology Skills *(Continued)*

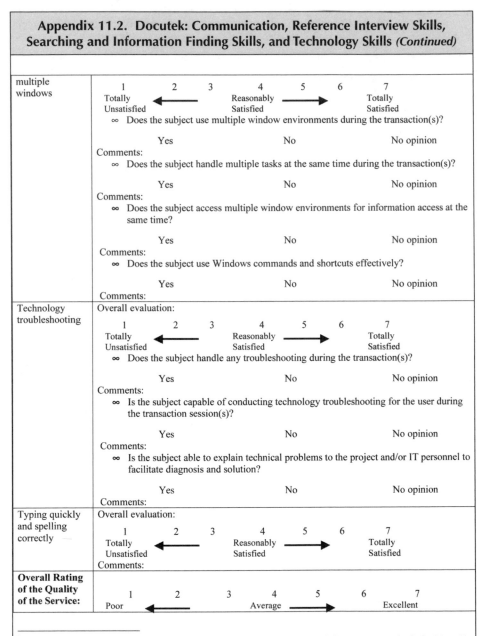

multiple windows	1 2 3 4 5 6 7 Totally ⟵ Reasonably ⟶ Totally Unsatisfied Satisfied Satisfied

∞ Does the subject use multiple window environments during the transaction(s)?

	Yes	No	No opinion

Comments:

∞ Does the subject handle multiple tasks at the same time during the transaction(s)?

Yes   No   No opinion

Comments:

∞ Does the subject access multiple window environments for information access at the same time?

Yes   No   No opinion

Comments:

∞ Does the subject use Windows commands and shortcuts effectively?

Yes   No   No opinion

Comments:

Technology troubleshooting

Overall evaluation:

1   2   3   4   5   6   7
Totally ⟵ Reasonably ⟶ Totally
Unsatisfied   Satisfied   Satisfied

∞ Does the subject handle any troubleshooting during the transaction(s)?

Yes   No   No opinion

Comments:

∞ Is the subject capable of conducting technology troubleshooting for the user during the transaction session(s)?

Yes   No   No opinion

Comments:

∞ Is the subject able to explain technical problems to the project and/or IT personnel to facilitate diagnosis and solution?

Yes   No   No opinion

Comments:

Typing quickly and spelling correctly

Overall evaluation:

1   2   3   4   5   6   7
Totally ⟵ Reasonably ⟶ Totally
Unsatisfied   Satisfied   Satisfied

Comments:

Overall Rating of the Quality of the Service:

1   2   3   4   5   6   7
Poor ⟵ Average ⟶ Excellent

[i] MOUSS Management of Reference Committee. (2004). *Guidelines for behavioral performance of reference and information service providers.* Retrieved August 16, 2004 from http://www.ala.org/ala/rusa/rusaprotools/referenceguide/guidelinesbehavioral.htm

[ii] MOUSS Management of Reference Committee. (2004). *Guidelines for behavioral performance of reference and information service providers.* Retrieved August 16, 2004 from http://www.ala.org/ala/rusa/rusaprotools/referenceguide/guidelinesbehavioral.htm

Search Engines and Virtual Tools

CHAPTER 12

You Virtually Can't Miss Us: Harnessing Virtual Tools to Enhance the Quality of Our Reference Services

Judy Ng, Ivy Lee Huey Shin, and Yit Chin Chuan

Overview

Customers' lifestyles and expectations are changing rapidly in today's wired world. The National Library of Singapore repositioned its Reference and Information Services to meet changing needs by leveraging on technological innovations, which results in increased access to content and services. The new initiatives require librarians to acquire new skills as well as adapt to new working environment and habits. This means rethinking traditional reference services and adapting it to our users' lifestyles.

Three service objectives are articulated in the design and delivery of the National Library of Singapore's Reference and Information Services:

1. Service within reach—providing services wherever, however and whenever customers need them, with any device they have at hand.
2. Service as a lifestyle—making services available within the social space that customers are comfortable in, e.g., Google, Yahoo!, or MSN, without them having to leave their space in order to find the library's content.
3. Service as a team—providing services by leveraging on the collective wisdom and knowledge of the library community. Through an online collaboration platform, librarians from anywhere can come together digitally to collaborate in real time, discuss and simultaneously work on one enquiry using their respective e-mail systems.

Description of Library Context
Lee Kong Chian Reference Library is the reference arm of the National Library of Singapore. The library was named after a famous philanthropist in Singapore who has contributed generously to its existence since the 1950s. Subsequently, a foundation that he had set up continued to sponsor the building of the new National Library in 2004 (National Library Board Singapore, accessed 2009a). The National Library's main target users are residents of Singapore aged 12 and above. It aims to service the reference and research needs of the researchers, practitioners, and general populace in many broad areas of topics with specific focus on Singapore and Asiatic content.

Detailed Description of Reference Initiatives
To support the National Library Board's plans as outlined in the Library 2010 report (National Library Board Singapore, 2005), three service objectives were articulated in the design and delivery of our reference services:

1. Service within reach—providing services wherever, however, and whenever customers need it, with any device they have at hand.
2. Service as a lifestyle—making services available within the social space that customers are comfortable in, such as Google, Yahoo!, or MSN (Microsoft Network), without them having to leave their space in order to find the library's content.
3. Service as a team—providing services by using the collective wisdom and knowledge of the library community. Through an online collaboration platform, librarians from anywhere can come together digitally to collaborate in real time and discuss and simultaneously work on one inquiry using their respective e-mail systems.

These three service objectives were realized through the initiatives described in the following sections.

Short Messaging Service Reference Service
In Singapore, there is widespread ownership of handphones and other handheld devices as well as high utilization of the short messaging services (SMS, or more commonly known as "texting") using these devices (Infocomm Development Authority of Singapore, 2008). In April 2008, we had 1.06 billion message transactions with about 6 million subscribers, which works out to an average of 177 messages per month per subscriber. With the prevalent use of handphones, personal digital assistants and Blackberries, many customers are now able to access the Internet via their handheld devices. We saw a good opportunity to provide convenient reference and information services using SMS.

Short messaging services were used by several academic libraries to provide answers for simpler direct inquiries while referring complex inquiries to e-mails or chat reference services due to the character limitation in text messages. The National Library of Singapore overcame this hurdle by providing replies to complex inquiries using a unique URL link sent to the user's handheld device. The user then has the option to open the URL link directly if his or her handheld devices have Internet access or to view the personalized answer page later from a computer with the URL provided at their convenience. Using SMS as a channel for our reference service allows our customers to reach us anytime and anywhere they like, via a handheld device that is kept close to them most of the time.

To achieve this, we had to create various infrastructure elements and amend some work procedures. First, we set up an SMS server, which receives the SMS messages sent by users to the library. This converts the received text into an e-mail that feeds to our regular reference point service (National Library Board Singapore, accessed 2009c). Our staff then makes use of an input template (see Figures 12.1 to 12.3) to create a personalized answer in the form of a Web page for the user. This tool enables staff to add citations from our online public access catalogue (OPAC) system, the Google search engine, and some electronic databases.

Upon completion, the input template system will automatically send the URL information to the SMS server if the reply to user's questions is lengthy or send

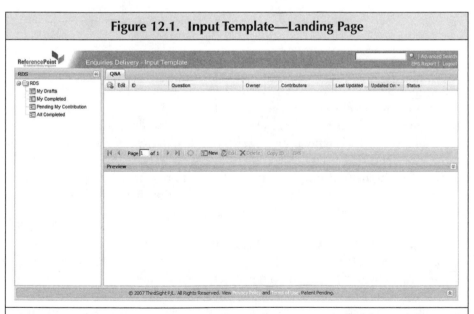

Figure 12.1. Input Template—Landing Page

This is the portable workspace that allows staff to access inquiries and collaborate on answers, all in one online platform. Staff can opt to create a new document, work on existing ones (saved in My Drafts) or work on documents created by other colleagues who asked for help (saved in Pending My Contribution). Staff is able to search All Completed to see if there have been answers to related inquiries.

Figure 12.2. Input Template—New Document

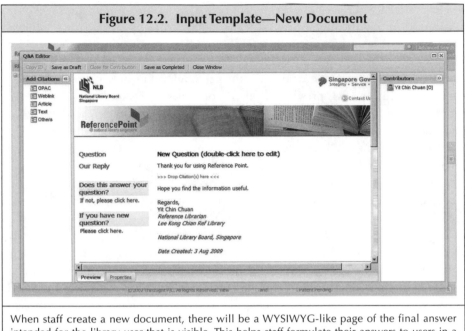

When staff create a new document, there will be a WYSIWYG-like page of the final answer intended for the library user that is visible. This helps staff formulate their answers to users in a more structured and organized manner—we have also provided tools to add citations from OPAC (our library catalog), Weblink (via Google Search), Articles (from Serial Solutions Search), etc. Staff only need to drag and drop these commonly used tools into the document to activate search.

the text information to the SMS server if the reply is short so that a reply can be sent from the server to the user who sent us the question.

The library receives an average of 10 to 15 SMS inquiries daily. Users receive an automatic acknowledgment message within 10 minutes that also informs the user of the operating hours of the service. As far as was possible, librarians responded to inquiries within the day itself. For more complex inquiries, library users were notified of the need for a longer research time. Almost all inquiries are closed within three working days (Ng & Lee, 2008).

Providing Access to Reference Collections through Google, Yahoo!, and MSN

With more people using popular search engines like Google, Yahoo!, and MSN to start their process of seeking information (Burns, 2008; Online Computer Library Center, 2005), it becomes critical for libraries to ensure that their rich electronic reference content can be located directly by Google, Yahoo!, or MSN. Using encyclopedic articles on Singapore written by librarians, which we called Singapore Infopedia (National Library Board Singapore, accessed 2009d), as samples, the library leveraged on search engine optimization techniques (Spencer, 2008) and

Figure 12.3. Input Template—End Product

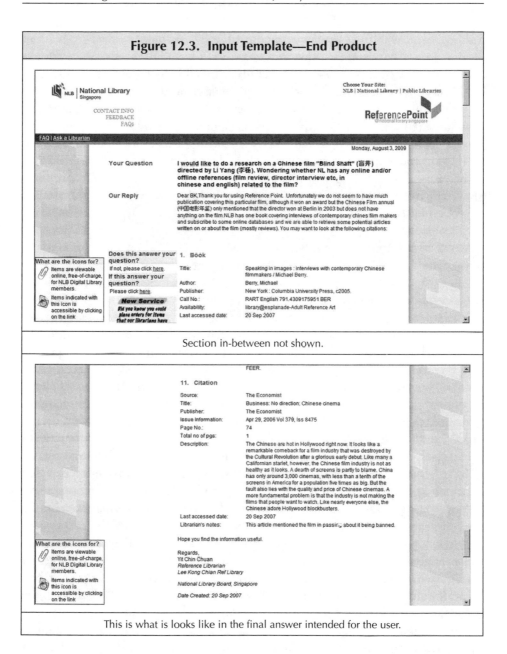

Section in-between not shown.

This is what is looks like in the final answer intended for the user.

redesigned its Website's architecture to enhance discovery of our electronic content via Google, Yahoo!, and MSN. A comparison of pages viewed before and after our experiment showed a 2,290-fold increase in usage, from 400 hits per month to more than 916,000 hits a month (monthly average for January to June 2008, see Table 12.2). Reconfiguring our Web site to enhance discovery via Google,

Yahoo!, and MSN is rewarding for both the library and its users. This has resulted in an increase in the value of the library's content as the articles are created once and accessed many times. Being easily searchable by Google-Yahoo!-MSN, the library's content is found "incidentally" by users at their point of need.

To encourage conversations with the general public, especially Singaporeans with stories to share about the history of Singapore, a copy of Singapore Infopedia was also put up as a blog format that we call InfopediaTalk (National Library Board Singapore, accessed 2009b). The blog format allows our readers to comment on our articles and add information, stories, and interesting anecdotes about the topic and encourage conversation and discussion among the readers interested in the topic itself.

Collaborative Reference Network

In the past, reference librarians are often left on their own to handle complicated inquiries, unless they already know who they can seek help from. There is no effective means for a community of librarians to share and collaborate to answer challenging inquiries. Discussions in librarian forums for "stumpers" inquiries are available, but consolidating the information from different parties can be difficult.

Taking advantage of technological innovations, the library has put in place a collaborative platform where communities of librarians can share their knowledge and help one another to answer difficult inquiries more effectively. Anyone who uses this platform can tap into the intrinsic knowledge of the communities and discover new knowledge. The platform, also known as the Network of Specialists (Figure 12.4 shows a sample screenshot), allows reference librarians to broadcast their inquiries to a community of subject librarians without needing to know the e-mail addresses of these librarians. This allows librarians to broaden their network of contacts to include people with whom they may be unfamiliar. Subsequently, e-mail discussions are captured in a threaded format and can be viewed in either blog or HTML form for the librarians to easily package an answer to the inquiry they were working on. Alternatively, participating librarians can contribute to the inquiry directly via a template that uses the principles of "wiki," which allows the initiating librarian to collate all contributions effortlessly, followed by the ability to send the completed answer as a Web page to the original inquirer directly. The platform not only allows for simultaneous collaboration within the knowledge network, it also tracks and acknowledges contributions by participating individuals. Through sharing and collaborating, the library is able to enhance the quality of its services for users. Besides enhancing the quality of reference and information services, the platform has been well used by our junior librarians as a learning aid.

The challenge for the library was not to simply introduce another platform for use by our staff; what we did was to create a means for our staff to continue

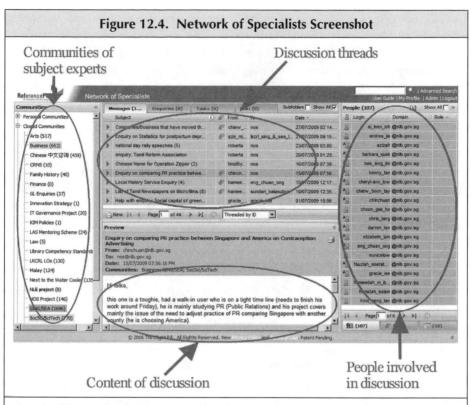

Figure 12.4. Network of Specialists Screenshot

Threads of discussion related to topic of inquiry are tracked and organized by the software and staff who are interested to see the whole flow of discussion can make the system generate all the related e-mail discussions into a flat HTML Web page or a Blog page.

Operatively, participants of the NOS continue to operate in their normal platform (which is commonly the e-mail). There is no change in usage behavior; staff simply reply with history to an e-mail from their colleague seeking assistance, and the system will organize their e-mail discussions into a discussion thread. We have found additional value in that such threads become a way to trap some of the tacit knowledge transfers that are usually transpiring between staff speaking with one another. Some of our librarians found it educational to read some of the discussion threads.

to use the platform that they were most familiar with (which was the e-mail) and make use of a software to collate and organize the relevant exchanges together.

Assessment of Initiatives

Short Messaging Service Reference Services

The SMS Reference Service has served as an additional channel for our users to use library services. The experience of our library in using the service to handle more complex inquiries demonstrates an attempt to extend the use of SMS beyond handling directional and "simple" inquiries. The service achieved the objective of "service within reach" by providing reference and information service wherever, however, and whenever customers need it, with any device they have at hand. The challenge is to continue to publicize this channel to encourage its usage.

Moving our answers to a Web page embedded with a feedback form had an additional advantage: we observed a tenfold increase in the number of positive feedback received for our answers (see Table 12.1).

Singapore Infopedia

For Singapore Infopedia, we made used of a Web statistic tracking tool called Awstats (the product information is available at: http://awstats.sourceforge.net) and have observed significant increase in the visitors and access to our contents. Table 12.2 shows the data for January to June of 2008, and Figure 12.5 compares the monthly visitor statistics from 2007 to 2009.

Network of Specialists

The Network of Specialists (NOS) has served as a collaborative platform where librarians can help one another answer inquiries more effectively by tapping on the collective wisdom and knowledge of community members. Staff can turn to communities of subject specialists established within the Network of Specialists

Table 12.1. Percentage of Positive Feedback Received	
Operation Model	**Percent of Positive Feedback over Total Inquiries Handled**
Original operations	2
New operations	20
New operations (inquiries handled with assistance from communities in Network of Specialists)	40

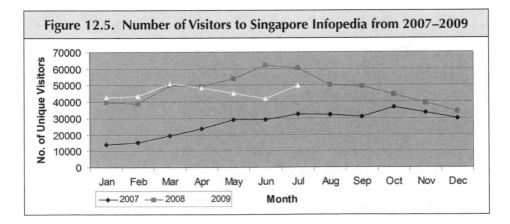

Figure 12.5. Number of Visitors to Singapore Infopedia from 2007–2009

Table 12.2. Web Access Statistics for Singapore Infopedia			
Month	**Unique Visitors***	**Number of Visits****	**Number of Hits**
January 2008	39,688	56,172	1,186,247
February 2008	38,610	54,071	976,630
March 2008	49,724	67,837	744,336
April 2008	49,452	69,161	821,279
May 2008	53,937	74,104	880,196
June 2008	62,147	85,089	887,468

* Unique visitors are defined as new visitors with unique IP addresses visiting our Web site.
** As a comparison, pre-implementation of search engine optimization, our monthly average was around only 300 per month (before year of 2007).

environment for inputs, regardless of where the specialists are located. To date, there are

- more than 200 members now working in collaboration on reference inquiries;
- 18 subject communities formed;
- an average of 350 postings per month;
- over 1,211 discussion threads; and
- a record of over 2,249 reads (logins by staff to read the postings for self-learning).

The benefits of the platform were determined as described in the following sections.

Efficiency Improvement
On average, the time taken for a reference librarian to respond to a challenging reference inquiry is five workdays. By escalating the inquiry to the NOS platform, staff were able to respond to customers within three workdays. This has increased turnaround time by 40 percent when replying to our customers.

Quality and Service Improvement
The system facilitates the depth and breadth of knowledge sharing. It allows not only sharing of explicit knowledge but also intrinsic knowledge. As a result, librarians are able to improve the quality reply to library customers' inquiries.

Customer Satisfaction and Compliments
We have observed a doubling of positive feedback on inquiries that have the backing of the service (see Table 12.1) and have received numerous compliments from library customers on the substantial list of recommended resources sent to them. The following are some examples of inquiries that were answered and the compliments received:

I am very happy and grateful for the answer given the knowledge imparted and the time taken to put it together. I am surprised at the speed and excellence of the service and everyone involved with this service should be very proud of themselves.

I'm pleased and surprised by the speed. Thank you very much once again. I'll definitely use this service again.

Really appreciate the library's help and efforts to find out the answer to my question. Although the answer is not a straightforward one, I think the library has done a great job. Pls continue to keep up the good work and provide this very useful service!!

Staff Satisfaction
The following are some positive comments gathered from staff:

Thanks also to everyone for your invaluable inputs, suggestions and advice! This NOS system is great :-)

I am really impressed with the sharing and willingness to give their time from our fellow colleagues, without whom I would have no clue on how to handle this inquiry. The NOS spirit and the equation "1 + 1 > 2" :-)

Learning Tool
The platform captured both explicit and tacit knowledge of the communities. It serves as a good learning tool and knowledge repository for librarians, especially the new staff.

Learning Experience of New Staff
A trend observed for the past few months is that the top two readers were consistently new librarians. This is evidence that the platform is helpful to them as a self-learning tool. A new business librarian, who has been providing quality contributions to the platform, was observed to have been studiously studying discussions between other librarians for several months.

Learning Points
Like all projects, the project team faced some initial barriers and hurdles, but with strong management support, the team was able to overcome them and in the process learned valuable lessons. The following sections offer a summary of our learning points (Chow, 2008).

Changing Conservative Mind-Sets
Although generally the librarians are open to sharing and not afraid to ask for contributions/assistance via the collaborative platform, there are some who are not accustomed to sharing on an open discussion platform. These librarians are usually those who are not in the habit of blogging or participating in online forums, Yahoo or Google groups, or Wikipedia. We noticed that such behavior is brought to the collaborative platform. In order to help librarians change their mind-set and the working behavior that they had been accustomed to, the project

team conducted regular communication sessions and involved most of them in the project planning stage. This made them feel part of the initiative and hence they developed a certain degree of responsibility to make it work.

Getting Strong Management Support

Management support has been instrumental to the success of the project. Management talked to staff directly about their roles in making the initiative a success, encouraged them in its usage, and provided general directions on how the success of the initiative would impact the organization.

Gathering Useful Feedback

Two separate surveys and focus group discussions were conducted with participants of the system to ascertain their satisfaction and reception rate for the product and to address staff concerns. Measures were implemented promptly to address concerns raised during these sessions. For instance, staff mentioned that they would be more eager to participate if their contributions are acknowledged and linked back to their work performance. As such the project team ensured that the system tracks individual contributions and used it to provide statistical data of individual staff performance.

Adopting a Personalized Approach

Project team members also made an effort to talk to staff individually. We approached every staff member whenever opportunities arose and through informal chats were able to glean hidden thoughts about the system that were not raised in official meetings.

Improving User Acceptability

Due to the relative complexity of the system, staff shared that they could not remember how to use certain functions. The project team took the initiative to send weekly tips of key functions in the system to staff via e-mail. The logic behind this exercise was to break down the tools into digestible portions so staff would not find it so overwhelming when they were taught how to use the system.

Identifying Champions

Despite the continuing efforts put in by the project team to encourage usage, there were still a few librarians who have yet to use the system in their reference work. It is hoped that as more people join the collaborative platform, their interest will be aroused by the vibrant discussions and they see the benefits of the system through testimonies from other librarians. On hindsight, the team realized that obtaining earlier buy-ins from librarians who are more senior could have helped garner more staff support and participation as such staff are regarded as "leaders" among the librarians.

Conclusion

The various initiatives have enabled the National Library of Singapore to extend the reach of its services and content to the users as well as facilitate knowledge sharing among librarians to provide higher quality reference and information service. The library will continue to explore new virtual tools and media to further enhance its services to meet the changing needs of the users.

References

Burns, E. (2008, February 5). U.S. search engine rankings, December 2007. *Search Engine Watch*. Retrieved April 2, 2009, from http://searchenginewatch.com/showPage .html?page=3628341.

Chow, W. H. (2008). Knowledge sharing platform for practicing librarians: A case study from the National Library of Singapore. In S. N. Kan (Ed.), *Knowledge management: Singapore perspectives 2008* (pp. 95–106). Singapore: Information and Knowledge Management Society.

Infocomm Development Authority of Singapore. (2008). Statistics on telecom services for 2008 (Jan–Jun). Retrieved April 2, 2009, from www.ida.gov.sg/Publications/ 20080212114723.aspx.

National Library Board Singapore. (2005). *Library 2010: Libraries for life, knowledge for success*. Singapore: National Library Board Singapore. Retrieved April 2, 2009, from www.nlb.gov.sg/Corporate.portal?_nfpb=true&_pageLabel=Corporate_portal_page_ publications&node=corporate%2FPublications%2FL2010&commonBrudCrum= Library+2010+Report&corpCareerNLBParam=Library+2010+Report.

National Library Board Singapore. (accessed 2009a). *History of the National Library*. Singapore: National Library Board Singapore. Retrieved April 2, 2009, from www.nl.sg/NLWEB.portal?_cn_nodePath=NL%2FAboutNL%2FHistoryOfNLS&_nfpb =true&_cn_bookLevel=1&_cn_bookTitle1=Abt+NL&_pageLabel=NL_CMSPage1& _cn_pageTitle=History+Of+NLS.

National Library Board Singapore. (accessed 2009b). InfopediaTalk. Retrieved April 2, 2009, from http://infopediatalk.nl.sg.

National Library Board Singapore. (accessed 2009c). *Reference Point@national library Singapore*. Singapore: National Library Board Singapore. Retrieved April 2, 2009, from http://nl.sg/NLWEB.portal?_nfpb=true&_nfls=false&_pageLabel=NL_ASK.

National Library Board Singapore. (accessed 2009d). Singapore Infopedia. Retrieved April 2, 2009, from http://infopedia.nl.sg.

Ng, J., & Lee, I. (2008). Repositioning our information services in the digital age: A study of the National Library Singapore strategy. In *Proceedings of the fourth Shanghai International Library Forum* (pp. 27–35). Shanghai: Shanghai Kexue Jishu Wenxian Chubanshe.

Online Computer Library Center. (2005). *Perceptions of libraries and information resources* (2005). Dublin, OH: OCLC. Retrieved April 2, 2009, from www.oclc.org/ reports/2005perceptions.htm.

Spencer, S. (2008). Best-kept secrets for search marketing success: The art and the science. Retrieved April 2, 2009, from www.web2expo.com/webexny2008/public/schedule/ proceedings.

CHAPTER 13

Google 2.0:
Benefits and Burdens

Wayne Bivens-Tatum

Overview

Despite its clean appearance, Google is obviously much more than a search engine these days. Through its creation or purchase of tools such as Maps, Blogger, YouTube, and Sites, as well as through its productivity suite of office products, Google makes it easier than ever for people to explore the world of Web 2.0 products. Google users can easily find information and organize it, create wikis or spreadsheets or other documents, and connect with other people for social or productive purposes. Give Google everything, and they will make your online life easier. The major downside to relying extensively on Google is the loss of guaranteed privacy, because the ease of use is the end of privacy.

According to their Web site, "Google's mission is to organize the world's information and make it universally accessible and useful." The information they want to organize includes Internet sites, but also *your* information: your e-mail, your appointments, your documents, even your credit card information if you let them. Google was first known for search, and probably still is for the majority of people who never dig below the Google surface. Besides search, the clean layout was one reason so many people liked Google. It wasn't cluttered like Yahoo! and others. It's still clean, but these days this cleanliness masks the wealth of tools Google makes available. In the beginning, it was just about search. They wanted you to *find stuff*. They still do, but now they're trying to be One-Stop Shopping 2.0.

Google has a lot going on these days. Here is part of a list from their "Even More" page: Alerts, Blog Search, Book Search, Checkout, Google Chrome, Custom Search, Desktop, Earth, Finance, Goog-411, Health, Images, Map, News, Notebook, Patent Search, Product Search, Scholar, Toolbar, Video, Blogger, Calendar, Docs, Gmail, Groups, Knol, Orkut, Picasa, Reader, Sites, Sketchup, Talk, Translate, YouTube, Mobile—and there's a lot more. I'm going to discuss just highlights from their offerings, or this could be a book-length manual about using Google, which might even be more boring than an article about Google. The list just keeps on going, and there's even more than this if you go the Web Search Features or the Labs page.

One might ask why we should bother exploring Google more thoroughly at all. I suggest three reasons. First, keeping up with Google more or less means keeping up with Web trends in general, because Google is almost always either pushing ahead or racing quickly behind many of the latest trends. Even if you normally do not use social software or networking tools, as a librarian you should be aware of these tools and how they work. Google allows you to explore such tools on one site. Second, awareness of these tools and their easy availability in one place makes it easier for us as librarians to use them for our own work. Group documents, shared calendars, or wikis are all easy to create, and staying within one Web site that many people are already familiar with and trust might make it easier to implement the professional use of some of these tools among librarians who might otherwise be resistant. Finally, if library users want to learn about these tools, being able to point them to one place where they can find a wide variety of useful Web tools might make it easier to help them.

The products available in what we might call "Google 2.0" provide us with a lot of useful tools to find and organize information, but this usefulness does come with a price. For this report, I'm going to focus on a few useful features that will help you find stuff, organize stuff, create stuff, and connect to other people. I will also discuss potential dangers a heavy reliance on Google exposes us to. The more we use Google, the more useful Google becomes, but we also become more dependent on a single company, and this company knows a lot about us.

Find Stuff

Obviously Google wants you to find stuff, but not just Web sites: weather, stock quotes, movie showtimes, local restaurants, flight information, anything. You can Google a shipping number and track packages. You can Google *pizza* and your zip code and find pizza places near your house, complete with a map to help you find them. You can even do all this from your mobile phone. The following sections describe a few especially useful search tools.

Google News

This was created after 9/11 by a Google engineer who wanted frequent news updates. The news page automatically searches hundreds of online news sites around the world and presents the results based on the most popular stories. Click on a story and you can see links to other stories on that topic. You can set up news alerts, create specialized local pages, view pages for foreign countries, and many other options. There's even a news archive search that will lead you to news content from the eighteenth century on. Not all of this content is freely available, but the archival search does help identify news articles that exist.

Google Video

Google Video used to be limited in use and was not much competition for YouTube. This may be why Google bought YouTube. Video started out just searching Google hosted videos because they didn't want you to leave their site. Now, in addition to adding all of the content from YouTube, they have a general video search that searches their content as well as video content from around the Internet, thus eliminating the need to go to video search sites like AltaVista, which used to be superior in many ways.

Google Maps

They also want you to find your way about. There was already Mapquest, but if you go to Mapquest, you have to leave the Google Site, so Google developed its own map feature. Once inside Google Maps, you can get a live traffic view, a satellite view, and for a growing number of citics a street view that shows actual images of the city at street level, complete with whoever was passing by when Google had their cameras going.

Google Books

Google has scanned millions of books from libraries around the world. Until now the copyrighted content has been searchable, but not fully viewable. With the settlement of the publishers' lawsuit against Google, this should change at some point, making everything viewable through libraries for an undetermined fee. (This settlement is itself the subject of much controversy; if you want to find out more, search "Google book settlement" in—what else—Google.) Google Books, like everything else Google, undergoes constant tweaking and improvement. For example, the use of metadata to enhance searching has improved dramatically since Google Books was launched (Jackson, 2008). The Advanced Search page allows for most of the search options we might expect in an OPAC (online public access catalog).

Google Scholar

Google Scholar finds scholarly books and articles and works best when libraries cooperate with Google. "As Google acknowledges, Google Scholar succeeds only because libraries have provided access to their resources via the Google Scholar interface" (Potter, 2008, p. 6). Though I still usually find more relevant scholarly literature in traditional indexes, this service works quite well for many topics and provides users with the familiar Google interface. Google Scholar is great for those obscure or cross-disciplinary topics poorly covered in traditional indexes. It works best if your library actually subscribes to most of the journals and works with Google, because the links then go directly to the articles. According to a recent study by some digital librarians at the University of Michigan, only 44 percent of a sample group of deep-Web pages from scholarly archives showed up in Google searches, so we should educate users to not consider this the end of their research, even if it might be a good beginning.

Google Shopping

Google Shopping provides comparison shopping within thousands of online sales catalogs. With Google Checkout, you can give them your credit card information and purchase products directly through Google. Don't ever leave Google. They don't like it. The shopping site works well for comparison shopping. Search by "relevance" and find a toaster oven for $49.99. Or you can search by price and find one for $59,000. Either way you get a long list of items from a range of retailers to choose from.

Organize Stuff

Now Google wants to help you organize stuff as well. You can organize your time with the Google Calendar and your e-mail with Gmail, plus plenty more.

iGoogle and Google Gadgets

The main Google page is uncluttered, but you can clutter it up with iGoogle and Google Gadgets. Now you can create your own completely personalized homepage with iGoogle (see Figure 13.1). The best thing about the iGoogle page is that wherever you log in, you have the same homepage, whether you're at home, at work, or traveling. It's always the same. You can even create your own gadgets. Google Gadgets are HTML and javascript applications that let you embed Web content in into small boxes that can be added to your iGoogle page and moved around to create a customized look. My homepage isn't very clean anymore, but I have gadgets for my Google Bookmarks, Reader, Gmail, and Calendar. I can search OpenWorldcat or the Wikipedia straight from the page or know what the weather is at a glance.

The iGoogle page allows tabs within the page, so you can organize different types of gadgets and avoid scrolling down one long page. For example, I have a tab dedicated to news sites that gather a dozen or so news-related gadgets. The gadgets are all RSS feeds from news sites, which can be added to the iGoogle page as gadgets as well as to Google Reader. For any Web site with an RSS feed you can turn the feed into a Gadget. At a glance I get the top headlines of the *New York Times*, the *Wall Street Journal*, the *International Herald Tribune*, the *Times of London*, the *Daily Telegraph*, and *BBC News* without even scrolling for more news. I also have a tab dedicated to games like blackjack, chess, and backgammon.

Google Calendar

This works much like Outlook or some other calendaring program and makes it very easy to share calendars and create group calendars with anyone who has a Google account. My reference department has used Calendar effectively to

Figure 13.1. Example of iGoogle Page

organize several group calendars, all of which can be viewed simultaneously depending on your settings. Google tools such as this work to replace Microsoft products with free Google products.

Google Bookmarks

Google Bookmarks works just like the "favorites" or "bookmarks" feature standard on Internet browsers, the main difference being that the bookmarks are available wherever you log into your Google account. Like all of the best Web 2.0 applications, this feature releases you from using a particular computer or a particular browser. You can import all of your old bookmarks from Internet Explorer or Firefox into this as well. Is this better than del.icio.us? It depends. Del.icio.us is a social bookmarking site that allows you to do much the same thing. Google Bookmarks are private, not shared like bookmarks on del.icio.us. Google Bookmarks is better understood as making your old browser bookmarks accessible where you happen to log in to the Internet. It also works very well with the Google Toolbar.

Google Toolbar

The toolbar works with Internet Explorer and Firefox, but not so well with some other browsers (and does not work at all on Google's own browser Chrome). The toolbar allows Google searching and easy access to your Gmail and Bookmarks, but has some other very useful features. Autofill will, at a click of a button, fill in name and address and even credit card information requested on Web sites. Also, any Web site with a search box can be turned into a search button. Right click on a search box (e.g., on Amazon.com or the IMDb), and you see a command to "Generate Custom Search." Click that and a new button appears on your toolbar. If you put a term in the search box and click the button, it searches that site. If there is no search term, the button acts like a link to the site.

Google Reader

Organize your RSS feeds with Google Reader. It allows you to put them in folders, star the most important ones, and share them with other Google Reader users. Bloglines already worked well, but if you go to Bloglines, you must leave Google. Google's products do not necessarily work better than comparable products (though personally I prefer the Google Reader interface to Bloglines or other RSS readers). The advantage is having everything in one place. There are disadvantages that I will discuss in the conclusion.

Picasa

Picasa helps you organize digital photos. Compare this to the very popular Flickr site. Again, Google has created a useful product modeled on other popular products.

Create Stuff

Google always helped you find Web content. With the tools described previously, they help you organize that content in customizable ways. In the past few years, Google has made an active effort to allow even novice Internet users to create content as well. Some of these tools work better than others, and some are poor substitutes for more expensive software products, but they all are free and easy to use.

Blogger

Don't have a blogging program? Buy one! Google did. They want to make it easier for everyone to have a blog, and now everyone does. Of the programs I've tried, I consider Blogger the easiest to use but not necessarily the most robust. Blogger is an obvious choice for the novice blogger who might, for example, just want to share vacation updates with relatives and won't need anything more powerful. Blogger also makes it easy to create a blog using another domain name if you happen to have one, which you might if you use Google Apps (more on that later).

Google Docs

Microsoft had a near monopoly on document creation programs, but Google is trying to compete. They bought Writerly and integrated it within the Google universe. It includes documents, spreadsheets, and PowerPoint-like presentations. It isn't nearly as powerful as the Microsoft products, but most people probably don't use even 20 percent of Word's offerings. It does make it easy to both create and share the documents, facilitating group commentary, if that sort of thing appeals to you. Also, it's free.

Google Page Creator

And of course Google has a Web page editor with free hosting. It's very primitive compared to programs like Dreamweaver, though. For example, I made a page with a table and bullet points and had to handcode the HTML. This is unlikely to make it appealing to people desiring robust Web sites, but for novices who just want to put some information online or people who do not have access to more expensive programs it can work well. It won't exactly give Dreamweaver a run for its money, but it is free and the Web sites created can be immediately published.

Google Sites

For a long while the main 2.0 tool missing from Google was a wiki, but once again they purchased another company (in this case, Jotspot) and integrated it into their platform. Google Sites provides an easy to use wiki program that creates public or private wikis.

Sketchup

And there's SketchUp, a 3D modeling application. SketchUp is one instance where Google is not competing with other free and popular Web 2.0 products. Autodesk and Bentley have systems that do this, but they are definitely not free.

Google Apps

You can bring everything together into one site with Google Apps. The basic Google Apps is free, and for a small fee you can get more storage space and use Apps for small business Web sites. They help you get a domain name as part of the signup. Google Apps integrates chat, page creator, groups, e-mail, calendar, docs, and the wiki. The Web site can have your domain name. You get 200 e-mail accounts and 200 megabytes of storage. Sites can be publicly available or can be part of a private suite of resources. If you want to use Google to create an entire online presence or help users to create such a presence (for a small business or organization, for example), this is the tool to use.

Only Connect

Google doesn't just want you to find and organize and create stuff. They want to connect you to other people. I've mentioned how one can share Google documents or selected RSS feeds with others. This is only part of what Google can do.

Gmail

Everyone knows about this, but I thought I should include it anyway. In my experience, it's the best free, online e-mail system available, maybe even the best overall. Plus, it comes with about 7,500 megabytes of storage space that keeps increasing every day. Save all the messages, because there's plenty of space. From within Gmail, you can access Google Talk as well as AOL (American Online) Instant Messenger.

Google Talk
Talk is Google's instant messaging program. It works within Gmail or through its own downloadable application. With other Talk users you can have voice over IP (Internet protocol) conversations and video chat, thus eliminating the need to leave Google and go to Skype.

Google Groups
There's Google Groups, which let you create a community space. Members can post various kinds of content, have discussions, etc. As an example of how this might be used, my neighborhood association has a Google Group site that allows us to keep up with news about the neighborhood.

Orkut, or Facebook for Brazilians
Orkut is a social networking service similar to Facebook. The problem with social software is that it needs a critical mass of users to be effective. As far as I can tell, Orkut doesn't have this, at least in America. I don't know anyone who actually uses Orkut, but I've read it's very popular in Brazil. There are definitely American users, but it doesn't generate the buzz of Myspace or Facebook. I've yet to hear anyone use Orkut as a verb, as people frequently do with Facebook. In fact, rarely do I meet anyone who has even heard of this service. This seems to be one of Google's few failures to attract a lot of (North American) attention. Of all the Google tools, this might be the one that for most of us would serve only an educational function.

Lively, or Second Life Light
Lively was an even bigger failure, since it is now deceased. It was supposed to be a virtual online playground like Second Life, but it was around for such a short time that I never got a chance to play with it. I downloaded it, but the whole first page of "virtual spaces" seemed to be about sex, and since I was at work at the time I thought it best not to go into one.

Knol for Knowledge
And now they're taking on another big Web sensation, trying to create an encyclopedia. Somebody at Google probably got sick of Wikipedia results coming up first in just about every Google search. They'll show Wikipedia! And this one's going to be authoritative, because we don't have any other authoritative encyclopedias to choose from. Scott Jenson, for example, is a leading authority

on buttermilk pancakes, or so I hear from Knol. I wouldn't be surprised if this shared the fates of Orkut or Lively.

Google Chrome

I wasn't sure where to put Google Chrome. It doesn't help you connect to people, but it helps you connect to the Internet. Chrome is a slick new Internet browser from Google. It loads very quickly, and has a minimum of toolbars and a maximum amount of space dedicated to the Web site being viewed. So far, it doesn't allow the Google Toolbar, though. It is the latest application that shows Google wants all of your Internet attention.

Conclusion

Unsurprisingly, Google has created a number of useful, functional applications, as I hope this brief tour has shown. Not all of them are equally useful or popular. For every Google Reader, there's an Orkut, for every Google News, a Lively. The Google engineers dedicate part of their time to just playing around with new ideas, which has created the abundance of applications Google offers. You can go to the Google Labs page to see what they're playing with at the moment. At the time of writing, the following were listed on the Labs page:

- Google Moderator: Collaborative Q&A for group events
- In Quotes: Compare some quotes and help save the world!
- Google Audio Indexing: Search what people are saying inside YouTube videos

With time we will see if they share the fate of Lab graduates like Reader and Scholar or end up on the scrapheap of Google history like Lively.

Google wants to be everything Web 2.0 to everyone. This has many advantages. If you want to keep up with what's going on with social software and Internet search, Google provides a useful toolbox to play around with. If you want to bring together a group to work on documents or create wikis, Google can help. Anyone with a Google account can use and share and connect. Some of these tools are excellent and provide an easy way to organize your online world so that it is just like you want it anywhere you log in. Whatever computer I use, I have access to the same pages: the iGoogle page, the Google Gadgets I have created or found, my bookmarks and RSS feeds and e-mail.

However, there are disadvantages to using so many Google tools. If you use all of the Google products, you easily get locked into an excessive dependence on their site, which is fine as long as nothing ever happens to the site. There are also serious privacy concerns. Google Street View would probably include a very clear picture of your house, and possibly of you if you were standing outside it. But according to Google, your complete privacy is impossible so you should get used to it (Zeman, 2008). Nevertheless, people worry about their loss of privacy with Google cameras snapping pictures of everything (KJCT News, 2009). There's the danger of Google hacking (Long, 2004; Tatli, 2008), where hackers use Google's sophisticated search engine to identify sensitive personal data.

The latest privacy brouhaha as of this writing is a rumor that Google will buy Twitter, thus combining all of the information people enter into both. Consider this analysis of some of the privacy issues:

> Researchers have found that when anonymous data is aggregated from multiple social networking sites, people's true identities and their activities can be reconstructed, even when the data has been scrubbed of personally identifying information. The BBC reports that researchers at the University of Texas at Austin were able to take completely anonymous data from Flickr and Twitter, run an algorithm on it, and from that reconstruct people's real names and addresses. They were able to do that to a third of the people who used both social networks. Now add Google information to the mix, and you can imagine how easy it would be to personally identify people, and then match them not just to their interests and surfing habits, but actual conversations and what they do in their everyday lives, as revealed by Twitter. (Gralla, 2009)

And this concerns only the anonymous information gathered by Google every time you use it, without even considering all of the information that you give them yourself.

There are concerns over the safety of all of the information people willingly hand over to Google. This is especially serious with something like Google Health Records, but in general, for Google applications to work well and do a lot for you, they ask for and collect a lot of information about you, which for a heavy Google user would include everything from your credit card information to every search you have ever done on Google through your account. How safe is this information? What could Google do with it? How dangerous is it to have so much information gathered into one place?

Google in this case is merely a microcosm of the 2.0 Internet, though admittedly an enormous microcosm (if this makes sense). There's nothing special about the Google gathering information about you. Every Internet application you use does this. The issue is concentration. Google can help you organize everything from your e-mail to your health records. It can help you find restaurants and discover useful scholarly articles. It can, in short, pull your online life together into one relatively manageable package and give you the benefit of all of the tools I have described and more.

All you risk in return is having one company—Google—know where you live, what you shop for, what you search for, how you schedule your time, where you travel, what your tastes are, who you e-mail or IM, what you say to them, the contents of every document you create, what you invest in (or at least the stocks you follow), your credit card numbers, your passwords, and more. The ease of use is the end of privacy.

References

Gralla, P. (2009). Google + Twitter = end of privacy. Retrieved April 18, 2009, from http://blogs.computerworld.com/google_twitter_end_of_privacy.

Jackson, M. (2008). Using metadata to discover the buried treasure in Google Book Search. *Journal of Library Administration, 47,* 165.

KJCT News. (2009, April). New Google feature raises privacy concerns among locals. Retrieved April 18, 2009, from http://www.kjct8.com/Global/story.asp?S=10184282.

Long, J. (2004). Google hacking mini-guide. Retrieved April 18, 2009 from www.informit .com/articles/article.aspx?p=170880.

Potter, C. (2008). Standing on the shoulders of libraries: A holistic and rhetorical approach to teaching Google scholar. *Journal of Library Administration, 47,* 5–28.

Tatli, E. (2008). Privacy in danger: Let's Google your privacy. In K. Rannenberg, D. Royer, & A. Deuker (Eds.), *The future of identity in the information society* (pp. 51–59). Boston: Springer.

Zeman, E. (2008). Google says privacy doesn't exist, get used to everyone knowing everything about you. *Information Week.* Retrieved April 18, 2009, from www.information week.com/blog/main/archives/2008/07/google_says_pri.html.

Stayin' Alive in the Google Age: Adding Custom Search Engines for Better Internet Results

Lilia Murray

Overview

While libraries' "Internet Resource Guides" are increasingly ignored, lying in the virtual dust, more and more students are turning to the ever-popular Google for their research needs. How do reference librarians stay relevant and provide useful finding tools for authoritative, reliable, and appropriate Web sites? Rather than dismissing Google, Murray State University (MSU) librarians in western Kentucky integrated this search engine via the company's Custom Search Engine (CSE) application. Currently in 2008, MSU Libraries offer 34 different subject-related Google Custom Search Engines. CSEs have enhanced the traditional static guides by allowing users to search all librarian-recommended sites at once, saving user time and frustration. This chapter explores the creation and customization of one's own CSE as well as the advantages and disadvantages of this Google service.

Introduction

For many reference librarians, one of the most significant effects of the Internet has been our bypass as intermediaries for information (Bates, 2006). According to the Association of Research Libraries (ARL), statistics reveal a sharp decline in reference transactions from a median value of 155,336 in 1996 to a median value of 67,697 in 2006 (Kyrillidou & Young, 2008). This decline is mirrored in Murray State University's reference statistics, with a drop from 12,177 in 2004 to 8,878 in 2008. A significant reason for this downward trend is student reliance on the Internet as the main source of information when doing research (Graham & Metaxas, 2003). Rather than asking information professionals for help or guidance, students want to find their answers electronically and on their own (Bates, 2006).

Since the advent of the Internet, Murray State University (MSU) reference librarians have created "Internet Resource Guides." These sites listed Web sites that were considered authoritative, reliable, and relevant, and were organized by subject area. Although patrons had a list of quality resources, student comments indicated that the guides were rarely used since they were extremely unwieldy and difficult to read (e.g., see Figure 14.1). In addition, there was no comprehensive search function to make them easier to use. These shortfalls and overall lack of use motivated the reference librarians at Murray State University to investigate other methods for providing guidance for Internet resources.

University Background

Murray State University is a state-funded university with a 2008 enrollment of approximately 10,000 ful-time students and 400 faculty (Muscio, 2008). This medium-sized regional institution is comprised of five academic colleges, a school of agriculture, and nine residential colleges. The Murray State University Libraries consist of Waterfield Library, which houses the main collection, Pogue Library, which houses Special Collections and Archives, and Overby Law Library, which houses the law collection. MSU Libraries provide leadership to the university community in accessing and using information resources for learning, research, and teaching. Although the MSU Libraries primarily serve students, faculty, and staff, as a public institution they are also open to the local community. Waterfield

Figure 14.1. Example of MSU Internet Resource Guide

Internet Resource Guide - Chemistry

- **MSU Department of Chemistry**
- **arXiv.org** - The premier pre-print site in physics, engineering physics, computer science, mathematics and related fields. PLEASE NOTE: this site is included in Google Scholar and can best be searched using Google's domain-limited searches. A sample search for publications on genome uses of quantum dots might be – "quantum dots" genome site:.arxiv.org.
- **Bio.com** - Bio.com is the most reliable and up-to-date information resource for those working in the life sciences and associated industries. Our editorial focus is on the technology of the life sciences. To that end, we publish daily news, information and research tools for life science professionals and students.
- **Chemistry.org** - First stop for chemists and students; exhaustive site with access to full-text journal indexing-some accessible without subscription, extensive web directory, government sites, industry sites; use the Educators and Students link for more information.
- **Chemdex** - From the University of Sheffield, England; exhaustive annotated chemistry web directory especially useful is the "Chemistry and the WWW" section which includes a comprehensive list of web tools for chemists and students.
- **Chemfinder** - Largest single chemistry web directory with information in several areas; working from a single master list of chemical compounds, Chemfinder claims to have eliminated most errors found on general WWW searches and is capable of including both physical property data and 2D chemical structures; crosslisted on every other chemistry web directory.
- **CHEMINFO** - Maintained by Indiana University and produced to assist their students; Chemical Information Sources is a resource designed to help people find and learn how to use Chemistry information resources on the Internet and elsewhere; a search results in hyperlinks to other websites or databases.
- **Chemistry: Patent Information** - Maintained by Syracuse University; provides patent tutorial, index by date, links on a variety of subjects including patent coverage in ChemAbstracts
- **Chemistry Central** - Peer-reviewed, open access research in chemistry, including articles from *Geochemical Transactions, Beilstein Journal of Organic Chemistry, BMC Chemical Biology,* and others.
- **CHEMWEB** - Established in 1997, this site bills itself as the largest chemistry community on the Web. Registration is required, but is free. Provides access to a very wide range of resources. Those of special interest to the university community are Chemistry Pre-Print Server, journal database search for tables of contents and abstracts, chemistry bookstore, and career and job information.
- **Material Safety Data Sheets** - Searchable index maintained by Cornell
- **The National Academies** - Comprised of the *National Academy of Sciences,* the *National Academy of Engineering,* the *Institute of Medicine* and the *National Research Council,* the National Academies makes available science news, publications, current projects and research information.
- **Public Library of Science** - PloS is a nonprofit organization of scientists and physicians committed to making the world's scientific and medical literature a freely available public resource through open access.
- **PubChem** – PubChem provides information on the biological activities of small molecules. It is a component of NIH's Molecular Libraries Roadmap Initiative. PubChem is organized as three linked databases within the NCBI's Entrez information retrieval system. These are PubChem Substance, PubChem Compound, and PubChem BioAssay. PubChem also provides a fast chemical structure similarity search tool. More information about using each component database may be found using the links above.
- **PubMed** - PubMed is a service of the U.S. National Library of Medicine that includes over 16 million citations from MEDLINE and other life science journals for biomedical articles back to the 1950s. PubMed includes links to full text articles and other related resources.
- **Science Niche** - Nicely done portal to information in all branches of science. Very useful site.
- **Web Elements and Periodic Table** - From the University of Sheffield, England; designed for students at universities and schools, includes thousands of graphics showing elements structures and periodic properties

This page contains links to sites related to the listed subjects. If you know of a link that you think should be added, or if you find a problem with one of the links, please send your suggestions to reference@murraystate.edu

Library attracts approximately 3,000 visitors daily—nearly a third of the student population.

Google Custom Search Engine

In the summer of 2007, MSU reference librarians introduced a more dynamic solution to the static "Internet Resource Guides" in the form of a custom search engine (CSE). A CSE allows "users to identify the sites and/or search strategies that they know will retrieve high relevance, high quality content to match the interests of their user communities" (Quint, 2007). In other words, a CSE is a search engine tailored to the *user's* needs and interests (Google Co-op, 2008). Authors choose which Web sites are included in the index. Thus, rather than searching billions of Web sites, a CSE searches only the sites it was told to search. It eliminates junky sites from the results list and places authoritative, reliable, and relevant sites on the first page of results.

There are many CSEs available, including Gigablast Custom Topic Search, Rollyo, and Yahoo! Search Builder. However, MSU Libraries chose Google's CSE, having found it more user-friendly and with more customized options. Among its many advantages are its price (it's free) and its simplicity (there are no complicated codes to learn). Furthermore, unlike other CSEs, Google's CSE does not have a restricted upper limit to the total amount of Web sites that can be included. As of October 21, 2008, the author's History CSE indexed 648 sites (Murray, 2008a). Once a CSE is developed, multiple search boxes tied to the CSE can be embedded in appropriate Web pages.

Setup

Due to Google's spartan homepage (www.google.com), it can be a little difficult to locate the setup page for the CSE application. Unfortunately, even hitting the "more" link from the top toolbar doesn't list the Custom Search Engine. One must click "more," scroll down, and then click the "even more" link in order to access the CSE function (www.google.com/cse). Another hurdle is that in order to begin creating a Google CSE, one must have a Google Account. If an account already exists, one can simply sign in. However, if an account is needed, one must click the "create an account now" link found below the password sign-in box and fill out the account form. The steps to create this custom search engine are shown in Figure 14.2.

Once signed in, the setup is quite simple. Filling out convenient boxes, CSE authors can give a CSE a name, description, and keywords. The latter choice is very important since keywords not only describe the contents of a CSE but they also help weight its search results. At MSU, reference librarians selected keywords from their liaison department program titles. For example, the keywords chosen for the Theatre CSE include acting, costume design, directing, play analysis,

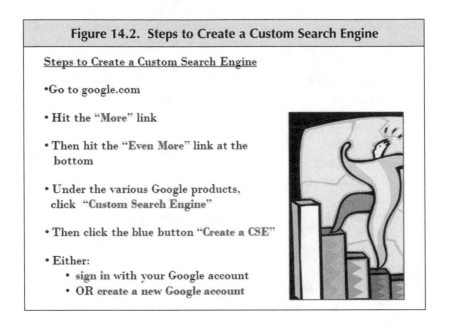

Figure 14.2. Steps to Create a Custom Search Engine

Steps to Create a Custom Search Engine

•Go to google.com

• Hit the "More" link

• Then hit the "Even More" link at the bottom

• Under the various Google products, click "Custom Search Engine"

• Then click the blue button "Create a CSE"

• Either:
   • sign in with your Google account
   • OR create a new Google account

stagecraft, and theater history (http://tinyurl.com/theatre-cse). These will allow the search results to focus on Web sites that directly concern MSU students. Words such as "drama" and "theater" could accurately describe the CSE but would be too broad to effectively rank results. In addition to the name, description, and keywords choices, there is also a language selection option that can be very useful for language liaisons.

In the "What Do You Want to Search" area, searches can be limited in one of three ways: to only those sites that one has selected, to the entire Web but emphasizing sites that one has selected, or to the entire Web. The MSU reference librarians chose to limit the CSEs' searches to only sites they had selected. This ensured the authority, reliability, and relevancy of the resources.

Selection of Sites

Immediately below the "What Do You Want to Search" area is the "Select Some Sites" section where the list of searched Web sites is entered. Since one can edit, add to, and delete these sites later, there is no need to have all of the Web sites chosen at this stage. Clicking on the Tips link to the right explains the only formatting that is needed. It covers tips on the four things that can be included in a CSE: (1) an individual page, (2) entire sites, (3) parts of sites, and (4) entire domains.

These tips include the proper placement of asterisks, which serve as truncation and wildcard symbols. As seen from Figure 14.3, one would simply type the URL when including an individual page. For instance, entering www.usa.gov

would include only this homepage; the CSE would search only this site's one individual page. However, for an entire site, one would enter the URL followed by a slash and an asterisk (URL/*). Thus, the same URL with a slash and asterisk at the end (www.usa.gov/*) would include the entire Web site. This is perhaps the most common code that would be utilized since most users would want their CSE to search an entire site, not just one Web page. Using asterisk quotes around a word in a URL (URL/*word/*) would include just certain parts of a site. For example, www.usa.gov/*about* would include only files on www.usa.gov that have *about* in their name, such as www.usa.gov/visitors/about.shtml. Finally, an entire domain would be included using *.domain/*, as in *.gov/*.

Besides the formatting, perhaps the most difficult part of creating a Google CSE is the selection of Web sites that would be most useful to one's community. However, this challenge was partially met by using the contents of the static "Internet Resource Guides" already in existence, which provided the initial load of Web sites for CSE creation. To those, the reference librarians at MSU added more sites via professional resources such as listserv announcements, Scout Report alerts, and the Librarians' Internet Index.

This leads to another issue: the continuing time commitment to not only add but also correct any URL changes that might have occurred in the included site lists. One solution might be to simply create CSEs that search a small number of sites. However, in order for a CSE to be truly useful, one must include a variety of Web sites for semicomprehensive coverage. Therefore, a small number of Web sites could lower the CSE's productivity, which may result in lower use. Web sites providing information and coverage for some disciplines, particularly those in business and the sciences, tend to be fee-based, limiting the number of sites that can be included in a CSE. For instance, the MSU Accounting CSE indexes 22 sites; since September 2007 its statistics show an overall usage of 53 queries (Waterfield Reference Librarians, 2008). The History CSE, on the other hand, indexes 648 sites; since July 2007 its statistics indicate an overall usage of 1,119 queries (Murray, 2008a). Yet, the larger the site index, the more URLs need to be maintained. A possible solution, however labor intensive, may be to be employ student workers with the task of checking URLs.

A variety of items can be included in the Google CSE, such as hand-selected Web sites, lecture transcripts, online textbooks, PDFs, syllabi, or Wikipedia entries. The latter resource can be a controversial issue for both librarians and professors—some allow it as an acceptable resource for their discipline, others do not. A convenient CSE option is the ability to exclude certain sites. If a CSE was allowed to search the entire Web but emphasize sites that one has selected, then excluding http://en.wikipedia.org/* might be an important preference. However, if a librarian or professor felt a *specific* Wikipedia entry was acceptable, the CSE creator would enter only that unique URL. No other Wikipedia site would be searched if the CSE was limited to only those sites that one has selected.

Since a CSE could easily support one point of view, librarians must be careful to create a balanced CSE including numerous standpoints on controversial subjects. For example, a political CSE could consist of only those sites that support Republican platforms, or a Religion CSE could contain only Christian tenets. Building a search engine should be no different than any other form of collection development: it should be fair and unbiased, presenting a balanced set of information.

Edition
Next, creators choose which CSE edition they would like: standard or business. While the standard edition is free, it requires accepting the Google ads that accompany the results pages. For some, this online advertising may be a drawback. On the other hand, the business edition offers ad-free results pages starting at $100 per year (Google Custom Search, 2008). Yet, many libraries may not have the funds to pay $1,000 for ten ad-free CSEs every year. The good news is that the standard edition offers a version for nonprofit organizations, universities, and government agencies that is exempt from the ad requirements. Academic, public, and government libraries can select this option; unfortunately, many special libraries cannot.

Customization
Once the edition has been chosen and the terms of service have been accepted, creators can try their new search engine and examine search results via the preview function. For further fine-tuning or addition of Web sites, users click "Finish" and are directed to their "My Search Engines" page (see Figure 14.4). This page lists all of one's created CSEs and includes links to their homepages, control panels, statistics, and an option to delete the CSE completely.

Figure 14.4. Example of "My Search Engines" Page

To access a CSE's homepage on Google, simply use homepage link. Here one can see its specific URL address and share it with others; unfortunately, the Google CSE URL's are very long and difficult to remember. For example, the URL for the MSU Music CSE is www.google.com/coop/cse?cx=0015174123075 33037157:d_e77qewpte, and the Art & Design CSE is www.google.com/coop/cse?cx=00151741230753303 7157:39q0wo_cpsm. However, this can be easily remedied by using a Web service that provides short aliases to redirect long URLs, such as TinyURL.com.

Another option is to simply embed the CSE on a Web site, providing convenient access for users. In the lower right-hand corner of the search engine's homepage are links to add the CSE on one's blog, Google homepage, or another Web page. Simply click on the appropriate link and make any width, height, or border adjustments and preview the changes. If satisfied, hit the "Get the Code" button and copy and paste the HTML to include the CSE on a Web page. At MSU, CSE search boxes were added to the Library on Blackboard pages, the library's integration in the university's Blackboard course management software (see Figure 14.5). The author added the CSEs she created to her iGoogle page by hitting the Google homepage option. This provided an easy means of accessing and updating all of her CSEs.

Control Panel
The control panel is very important since it allows further customization options. These options are grouped under a top toolbar and include "Basics, Sites, Indexing, Refinements, Look and Feel, Code, and Collaboration." "Basics" allow the CSE author to alter the original setup information, such as the search engine's name,

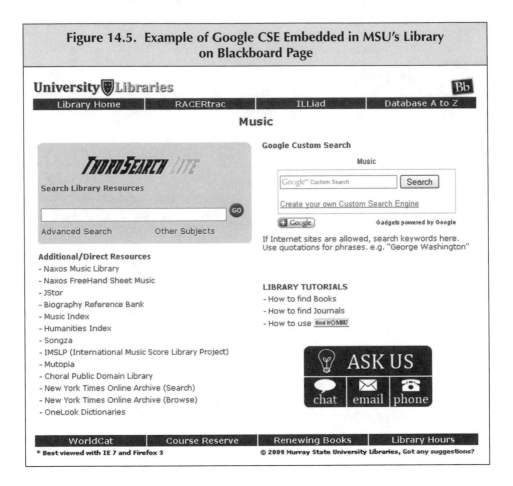

Figure 14.5. Example of Google CSE Embedded in MSU's Library on Blackboard Page

description, keywords, and language. "Sites" is the section whereby authors can add, edit, delete, or exclude other sites. To see how many pages are indexed in one's CSE, click the "Indexing" link. The number can be quite impressive; for example, although 378 sites are listed in the MSU Theatre CSE, 338,000 pages are actually indexed (Murray, 2008b). The "Refinements" option lets creators apply labels to the added Web sites. These labels are seen as a row of links above search results and suggest to users a means of narrowing their query. Clicking a refinement label link reorders the search results so that the labeled sites are listed first in the results.

In addition, one can control the look and feel of the CSE, changing its appearance via the customization of branding and colors. This is especially useful if one is trying to match the search engine with an existing institutional Web site. Not only can one select a branding style for the search box, one can also choose the color of the border, title, background, text, links, visited links, and cached links. Adding a logo or image to the results page is a very easy process. Again, no complex code is needed; one simply enters the image URL in a box and hits "Save Changes." At MSU, an image of the main library, Waterfield Library, was added to the homepage and result pages, marketing the library's contribution to this resource (see Figure 14.6).

The "Code" link within the Control Panel offers the same embedding choices as the links found in the lower right-hand corner of a CSE's homepage. However, this access point allows one to customize the setup and location a bit more. For instance, if one prefers to host the CSE on his or her Web site, the user can choose between an iframe layout, which requires two pages (one for the search box and the other for the results), or an overlay format, which requires only one page and shows results in a modal overlay. One can even specify the URL for a site, where the search results should appear, and where the advertising should be placed: right, top and right, or top and bottom. Of course, the location of ads is relevant only for those who chose the Standard Option and who weren't a non-profit, university, or government agency.

Also in the Control Panel section, there is a "Collaboration" feature whereby users can view current contributors and invite other people to volunteer by e-mailing an invitation. Although they would be given limited access to the search engine, they would provide a more social search by being able to add sites and apply refinement labels via tagging or annotating content for the CSE. However, if not careful, the addition of volunteers may jeopardize the integrity of the search engine. To handle this dilemma, MSU contributors were limited to either other library or departmental faculty.

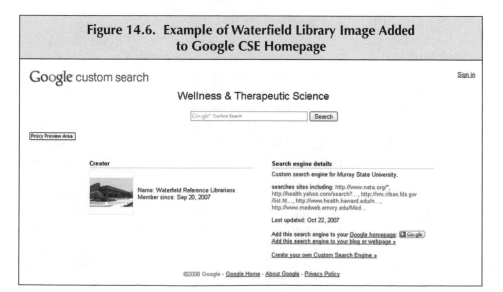

Figure 14.6. Example of Waterfield Library Image Added to Google CSE Homepage

Assessment: Statistics

To access usage statistics, creators must return to their "My Search Engine Page" and click on the statistics link. Reports are shown for the current day, week, and month; in addition, an overall report can be viewed that lists the total number of queries as well as the total number of distinct queries. This is a helpful tool in determining its effectiveness compared to the traditional Internet Resource Guides. For the past year, MSU usage statistics have been high; from July 2007 to October 23, 2008, the MSU custom search engines have received 9,369 total queries. That is approximately one query per MSU student. The CSEs were marketed in several ways, including being featured on the library on Blackboard pages as well as in library monthly newsletters.

Searching

Google Custom Search Engines work just like the regular Google Simple Search. Users type one or more terms into the search box and click Enter; there is no need to use the Boolean "AND" between words since Google does that by default. To search for a phrase, such as *primary sources*, one would enclose it in quotes: "primary sources." If a word has more than one connotation, users would put a minus sign in front of the term(s) to ignore. For example, a search for *mustang-horse* would return results pertaining to the car. A search limited to a specific domain would be entered site colon dot domain (site:.edu). The full range of Google's advanced search operators are available in these refinements. The negative is that there is no Advanced Search link or option. The Google Custom Search Engine provides only the one search window to enter one's query. This means in order to use a CSE most effectively, users will need to know the various search tips such as those mentioned previously.

Conclusion

For years, Murray State University librarians created Internet resource guides with the intention of directing students toward authoritative, reliable, and relevant Web sites. However, these static sites were rarely visited because they were difficult to read due to their frustrating, bulky layout. Furthermore, visitors had to click on Web site by Web site and scroll within them in order to access the information they needed. This was a very time-consuming process and led many patrons to just "Google" it.

Since Google ranks the importance of pages via PageRank—a technology containing more than two billion terms and an equation of 500 million variables, users often got distracted by nonrelevant sites when using a regular Google search (Pemberton, 2000). However, the human influence provided by creating a Google Custom Search Engine offered more relevance than Google's pure algorithms (Kopytoff, 2006). Shashi Seth, the Product Lead for the Custom Search Engine explained,

"We are trying to shore up our algorithms with the wisdom of the crowds. We know we are not always the expert in every topic in every domain" (Sherman, 2006).

Future plans at MSU include creating course-specific CSEs, further tailoring the relevance of the sites indexed. In addition, the reference librarians are exploring CSEs' possible utilization in the university's new Enterprise Resource Planning (ERP) system, which will integrate the data and processes of MSU into a unified system. The development of CSE mobile applications is also being discussed.

By creating CSEs tailored to their liaison departments, the reference librarians at Murray State University basically helped build a better Google. In addition, improving the search engine increased the number of people visiting this "Internet Guide" since patrons could search just the area they were interested in. It allowed users to search all previously recommended sites at once, saving time and frustration. Implementing Google's Custom Search Engines provided not only immediate results but also an engaging means of guiding users to quality Web resources.

> **Partial List of Custom Search Engines Created by Reference Librarians at Waterfield Library, Murray State University**
>
> Accounting: http://tinyurl.com/accounting-cse
>
> Art & Design: http://tinyurl.com/art-cse
>
> Chemistry: http://tinyurl.com/chem-cse
>
> Government, Law, and International Affairs: http://tinyurl.com/glia-cse
>
> History: http://tinyurl.com/history-cse
>
> Modern Languages: http://tinyurl.com/mola-cse
>
> Music: http://tinyurl.com/music-cse
>
> Nursing: http://tinyurl.com/nurs-cse
>
> Theatre: http://tinyurl.com/theatre-cse

References

Bates, M. E. (2006, September). The information drought. *EContent*, *29*(7), 29.

Google Co-op. (2008). Welcome to Google Co-op. Retrieved October 9, 2008, from www.google.com/coop.

Google Custom Search. (2008). Create a custom search engine. Retrieved October 17, 2008, from www.google.com/coop/manage/cse/create/1.

Graham, L., & Metaxas, P.T. (2003). "Of course it's true; I saw it on the Internet!" Critical thinking in the Internet era. *Communications of the ACM*, *46*(5), 70–75.

Kopytoff, V. (2006, October 24). Google offers custom search: Web site operators can narrow results to more specific topics. *SFGate*. Retrieved March 6, 2008, from http://www.sfgate.com/cgi-bin/article.cgi?f=/c/a/2006/10/24/BUGJOLUK881.DTL.

Kyrillidou, M., & Young, M. (2008). ARL statistics 2005–2006. *Association of Research Libraries*. Retrieved October 7, 2008, from www.arl.org/bm~doc/arlstats06.pdf.

Murray, L. (2008a, October 17). History. Retrieved October 23, 2008, from http://tinyurl.com/history-cse.

Murray, L. (2008b, October 9). Theatre. Retrieved October 9, 2008, from http:// tinyurl.com/theatre-cse.

Muscio, F. (2008, February). 2007–2008 fact book. Retrieved October 13, 2008, from www.murraystate.edu/oir/factbook2007.pdf.

Pemberton, J. (2000, May/June). Google raises the bar on search technology. *Online*, *24*(3), 41–48.

Quint, B. (2007, July/August). A great idea!! *Searcher*, *15*(7), 4–6.

Sherman, C. (2006, October 24). Google launches custom search engine service. Retrieved October 7, 2008, from http://searchenginewatch.com/showPage.html?page=3623765.

Waterfield Reference Librarians. (2008, July 16). Accounting. Retrieved October 17, 2008, from http://tinyurl.com/accounting-cse.

Innovative Service Models and Marketing

CHAPTER 15

Innovations from the Inside Out

Lisa A. Ancelet and Lorin Flores Fisher

Overview

Albert B. Alkek Library at Texas State University–San Marcos has implemented several methods to respond to the challenge of managing constant change and the fast pace of technology. A new approach to service execution and staff training can revolutionize service implementation and bring your library reference services into the twenty-first century. Large institutions must go through a vetting process for new services and often the process takes months or longer. However, emerging trends in Web 2.0 applications and constant changes in the technology require a new method in order to stay fresh and relevant to today's library users.

History of Library and Context of Initiatives

Albert B. Alkek Library is the primary library serving the campus of Texas State University–San Marcos, a major multipurpose university with a diverse student body of 29,125. Alkek Library operates within a hierarchical management structure typical of major organizations. Although this type of management model works well in large institutions, with a structured hierarchical model in place, new services often have to go through a longer approval process, delaying implementation. The ever-changing and fast-paced world of technology requires libraries to rethink their management model and approach to keeping up with the changes in order to remain relevant to their users and to offer innovative services.

Although the management model in 2003 was solidly hierarchical, there was a sense of autonomy among the reference librarians without the hindrance of micromanagement. However, it was still difficult for the department to pilot a new initiative or service without going through a formal review and approval process. The process was long and involved multiple stages for a service to gain official approval and implementation. After many years of applying the traditional service model, an opportunity to change to one more responsive to rapidly developing technologies presented itself when a new head of Reference and Instructional Services was hired in early 2004. Expectations were high for the new department head to lead the reference department into the twenty-first century, especially in areas of service and technology.

The Honeymoon Period

The department was going through a transitional period after many years without major departmental changes. The Honeymoon Period, a term coined by the new head of reference was the first year when the excitement surrounding the hiring of the department leader helped to set into motion many new initiatives and services. The first major service implemented was the Ask- a-Librarian Live service. Preparation to offer virtual reference (VR) service included researching the service, evaluating commercial products, and developing a pilot to begin by August 2004, the beginning of the fall semester. In part, this was accomplished in six short months by the VR task force, one of multiple task forces, or informal working groups, created by the new department head. Task forces as management tools were relatively new at Alkek Library.

The System

Alkek Library, in common with other academic libraries, has a very traditional structure for dealing with change and introducing new services. In this model, impetus for change comes from the top. Generally a committee is formed of persons appointed by the department head to investigate new services or tools. If this hierarchical model was conceptualized in a diagram, it would resemble the tines of a pitchfork facing downward with management on top and staff at bottom.

However, there are distinct disadvantages to this type of approach. The time-intensive nature of this process is particularly ill-suited to the accelerated lifespan of products and trends that can be new to obsolete within months or even days. In fact, this is a major criticism of the "pitchfork" system and makes it unsuitable for rapid deployment of new products and services in an ever-changing climate. (Owens, 1999).

The Total Quality Management (TQM) model was the norm at Texas State University going back to the mid-1990s. Advocates of TQM put forth this method as an alternative to traditional hierarchical management structure. Although TQM began as an alternative model, the TQM model requires a more formal approach to teams and committees with very specific rules and procedures. In comparison, the task forces that were deployed were much more informal. Task Forces at Alkek became a "work around" to the TQM formality and were made up of reference department staff to investigate and pilot new services.

Another factor that contributed to the use of task forces as opposed to TQM teams is that often TQM teams are "closed" in terms of flow of information and communication. Those who are not on teams are generally out of the loop so to speak, and there can be a lack of staff buy-in or enthusiasm since the project information and decisions are made by the team members without much consultation or input from other staff members. We felt that buy-in was critical for staff to want to implement additional new services that would inevitably change their workload, job duties, and service to the department. Working in informal task forces enabled more staff members to be involved in the decision making process directly or indirectly. This tended to increase staff buy-in and support for the new services being implemented.

Timing was also a factor in the adoption of our alternate task force working model. Timelines were much shorter due to the informality of the process. Due to the semi-autonomous nature of the task forces, decisions could be made by the task force without the review and approval process from the library administration. The Head of Reference gave broad direction and general goals, but the teams were allowed latitude to develop projects.

At this time, the hierarchical structure and TQM was still in place, but the barriers of this management model and time constraints were beginning to come down. All in all, the informal workings of the task forces fostered a less structured and better service implementation process that in some sense defied the TQM model. Abundant examples of alternate management approaches and also criticism of the traditional approach exist in relevant professional literature in both the business and library disciplines.

In some respects, the task forces bear striking similarities to the self-managing work teams (SMWT) composed of "empowered clusters of employees possessing the required skills...to efficiently accomplish a well defined project or task" as described by Castiglione (Castiglione, 2007). Another concept associated with SMWTs is "organizational democracy" (OD), which implies more of an open, collaborative approach to managing change as well as complementing the current climate and influence of collaborative projects and social networking. More important, one of the pertinent tenets of OD is that every employee is a leader, a concept that has had significant applications in our environment (Castiglione, 2007).

The SMWT approach assumes employees possess the skills needed to be leaders in self-directed semiautonomous teams. However, one of the challenges we faced at the beginning was getting staff to a baseline level of knowledge and comfort with new technologies. We also wanted to encourage an underlying mindset of continual learning. The "Learning Organization" approach to management in libraries appears in the literature dating from the mid to late 1990s as an effective way to manage change, but it also postulates a method for management and staff to embrace new ways of thinking in their organizations. Specifically this approach emphasizes continual learning, both individually and in teams. Creative thinking is another important part of this approach, as is looking at existing processes differently (Worrell, 1995; Riggs, 1997).

In short, the sheer number of projects and services we wanted to implement would have completely overwhelmed us if we had stayed with our usual hierarchical "pitchfork" model or had alternatively formed a TQM team. Ultimately a method evolved incorporating the various management influences mentioned previously that enabled us to expedite the introduction of numerous concurrent initiatives. It should be strongly emphasized that this new approach did not supersede the original model. Rather, it allowed us to move freely around, within, and through the system.

Interest/Investigation Stage

The first stage of the process would begin with a staff member who was interested in a new service or tool. The interested person would launch an investigation of the new process/tool and then generally communicate their interest with the head of reference at this point. During this first step, the department head would give verbal permission to proceed to the next step, though occasionally the interested person or small group of interested people might prepare a working model first and then present it to the head of reference for approval.

Working Test Model Stage

If no working model had been prepared during the interest/investigative stage, the interested person would prepare a proof of concept to show that the new idea/service/tool could work. The proof of concept would be shown to the head to review and approve. We found this stage also very valuable to test new workflows and hone new skills and to familiarize ourselves with new software and tools. Also, we found it very helpful in some cases to have a model for demonstration purposes. It is often quite difficult to envision how a new service or tool would work in the wider scheme of things, especially when dealing with an audience unfamiliar with what is being presented or skeptics.

Informal Pilot Stage

Once the working model had been seen and approved, then permission to begin an informal pilot was granted. Usually the interested person would be the pilot organizer, often setting up training for other interested staff and undertaking scheduling duties. An informal pilot would normally last for a semester. Other interested staff might also participate in the informal pilot and an introductory informal training might also occur to prepare pilot participants. Data would be collected during this period for the assessment stage and any necessary adjustments undertaken.

Assessment Stage

At the end of the informal pilot period, the head of reference and pilot organizer would then meet to assess how the pilot went and whether the pilot was successful enough to continue as a part of regular department services. The assessment often took the form of a narrative report with included statistics, which was then distributed to upper levels of management.

Incorporation Stage

If the pilot appeared to be successful then it would advance to the incorporation phase, being absorbed in the appropriate departmental units. Often the responsibility would also shift from the interested person (who might be from a different unit) to fit in with the organization of the department. Also at this point there would be more training to prepare other staff who were not directly involved in the pilot.

Informal Leaders

One of the great strengths of this approach was the tendency for those who had been involved in the pilot phases of projects to become "informal leaders" serving as guides, tutors, and support for other staff, especially during the incorporation phase. These groups or individual informal leaders also had opportunities to give in-house staff workshops at monthly department meetings and other scheduled staff workshops. Generally other staff felt more comfortable learning from their peers. In addition, the influence of other peers helped spread ideas, encourage innovation, and create a state of constant reinvention. This same network of informal leaders has served us well in our current period of transition.

The Buzz about 2.0

Paralleling changes in the Reference Department were the rapid changes in technology. Beginning with the O'Reilly Web 2.0 conference in 2004 and then followed by "Library 2.0" making its debut at the Internet Librarian conference in October 2005, "2.0" was the buzzword in both the tech world and the library world. Librarians were already discussing Library 2.0 in library literature, at conferences, and on their blogs by 2005. Stephen Abrams noted in his article "Web 2.0—Huh? Library 2.0, Librarian 2.0" that "we have the ability, insight and knowledge to influence the knowledge to influence the creation of this new dynamic and guarantee the future of our profession. Librarian 2.0 now" (Abrams, 2005). Our institution saw this as a call to action for libraries and librarians to remain the leaders in an information world and embrace the Web. Another paper that generated a great deal of discussion about the relevancy of libraries in the Web 2.0 world was "Do Libraries Matter? The Rise of Library 2.0." The white paper asked the question and provided suggestions for libraries to remain relevant by moving "beyond the notion of libraries without walls" to a more pervasive library; one integrated and visible and without boundaries (Chad & Miller, 2005). Others noted that Web 2.0 was more than a buzzword; Web 2.0 is the Web in constant evolution for the benefit of the online user (Stephens, 2006).

By early 2006, the term had made it to the consciousness of Alkek reference librarians. The excitement generated by the 2.0 buzz was the impetus for the department to address the rapid changes in technology and the excitement Web 2.0 tools was generating among some of the librarians. Reference staff attended Library 2.0 Webinars and conferences during 2005 and 2006 and reported to the department head how these tools and services could be implemented at Alkek Library. The new working model was a perfect mechanism to stay abreast of emerging technologies.

Another approach Alkek used to deal with change was the formation of a cross-departmental group to investigate emerging technologies. The Emerging Technologies Committee began in November 2006. The committee was formed to tackle technology head on. Members were volunteers from different departments, with varying levels of technology comfort, expertise, and ages represented. This wasn't a governing board. All members took part in the evaluation and investigation of different technologies and how the technologies could impact the library and/or improve public services, outreach, marketing, and instruction. Many of the technologies moved from the committee into the Interest/Investigational Stage of our model and continued on the path toward implementation.

Accomplishments and Assessment of the Initiatives

The Ask a Librarian Live virtual reference service began in 2004, incorporating chat with cobrowse and e-mail reference using a commercial virtual reference product. The pilot ran the fall 2004 semester and the preliminary report was prepared for library administration at the end of the semester. Usage of the service has grown each year and survey responses are overwhelmingly positive. Eighty-nine percent of the surveys taken after a chat session reflect a good user experience, with the e-mail surveys even higher. We piloted the instant messaging (IM) component in fall 2005 and added it to the existing service. IM is managed using the Pidgin multiprotocol IM client so multiple accounts can be created and statistics can be logged. In addition to the basic AIM (America Online Instant Messenger), MSN (Microsoft Network), and Yahoo! accounts, Alkek Library added a Gmail and Meebo account this past year. With the launch of the new library Web site in January 2008, the Meebo Me widget was added to Web pages so that users can contact us from multiple locations in addition to having access to a variety of chat options. The decisions to add the new components to the Ask-a-Librarian service were based solely on the success of the service from the beginning and because the new management model enabled a quicker implementation time.

The library blogs followed VR in 2005. The Alkek Library Reference and the Information Literacy (IL) blogs both started in August 2005. The Reference blog has since evolved into the Alkek Library News blog and is pushed out to the library community by a Feedburner script placed directly on the library homepage. The blog reports about library events, added resources, research tips, and more. The number of visitors to the blog tripled with the placement of the feed directly onto the library homepage. The IL blog focuses on IL related topics and has found a wide audience. Both blogs have been a successful addition to services at Alkek Library.

In 2006, we partnered with the library's IT department to host the IL wiki. The IT department was initially a little skeptical about this pilot because of the server space and setup time involved in hosting the Media Wiki platform. However, it has proved to be a successful collaboration between IT and the Reference and Instruction departments. The IL wiki hosts IL resources for librarians and faculty, subject research guides, IL class outlines, and other resources. Based on feedback from faculty and students, the wiki has been successful. One professor wrote, "I just wanted to thank you again for a great class last Thursday. My students said to say thanks too, especially for the wiki page, which they found extremely helpful on their research" (Bayless, R., personal communication, March 12, 2009). Another student stated, "I plan on frequently using this site (e.g., wiki class outline)...thanks again!" (Spidle, C., personal communication, January 31, 2009.

Alkek Library is also supporting other Library 2.0 initiatives implemented using the new model. When the library Web site was being redesigned, the Web team created a community space for the promotion of social networking tools such as Alkek's Facebook, Myspace, and del.icio.us sites and the library YouTube channel. The permanent location of the "Community" and "Ask-a-Librarian" navigation on all of the library Web pages has helped market the services in a way that promotes visibility, access, and success of the services and or initiatives brought about by the new model. The innovative approach to service implementation has won over the library administration, and our process has become the norm for keeping up with changes in services because of technology.

Caveats and Lessons Learned

Our situation was helped by a supportive Reference Department Head and Assistant Vice President. Trust and support may not be so easy to obtain in other institutions and situations. Those who wish to attempt this sort of system, even in a very supportive environment, must be in constant communication with administration to keep him or her/them informed of the various projects being developed.

For those who cannot get the support or leave of their higher-ups, advancing to the working test model stage may prove to be difficult. Even if the working test model was the only achievable product, it would still prove useful as a learning exercise and also as a selling point to perhaps demonstrate and persuade skeptics. One of the great advantages of many emerging technologies and Web 2.0 applications is that most of them are very simple to use, cost nothing (or next to nothing) to use, and can be set up very quickly. The most valuable and enduring part of the whole process is the development of informal leaders sharing their knowledge with their peers formally and informally, ultimately strengthening morale and teamwork among colleagues, even if implementation is not possible.

Lessons one can take away from this process are during the Assessment Stage modifications to the service may be needed. Libraries must continuously work to improve the services or initiatives in addition to adding new ones. When the blogs first started, users had to find a link on the Web site in order to read the posts. Pushing out the information with eye-catching headlines creates more visibility and guarantees more patrons will get the information. Allowing comments on blogs also generates conversation with your patrons. In addition, we realized that although the media wiki platform is great for developing a wiki, for the research guides, it was not the best choice. We wanted to add the Meebo Me widget to our research guides for patrons to contact us directly. Unfortunately, the script used for the chat widget isn't compatible and does not show up on the guides. Currently we are in the process of moving the research guides into the university content management system where the chat widget does work.

Finally, if nothing else, we have learned that change is always constant. In January of 2008 our Reference Department Head resigned. Our experience with building a network of "informal leaders" seems to have benefited us, especially during this transitional period, as we continue forward with new innovations. We have continued to implement and develop new projects using the method outlined previously in tandem with our more traditional committee-based model. Examples include an IL pilot that "embeds" a librarian into the course management system for the IL classes taught. The librarian creates a wiki research guide for the assignment, adds relevant library links, and places a Meebo Me chat widget into the course for students to have a follow up contact after the IL class. Also new are reference desk office hours in the virtual world Second Life. Texas State University's Second Life campus called Bobcat Village includes the library. Volunteer librarians started both pilots in fall 2008. As a final note, this spring the library administration recognized the leadership among the reference librarians enough to internally post and fill the Head of Reference Services position.

References and Further Reading

Abrams, S. (2005). Web 2.0—huh?! Library 2.0, librarian 2.0. *Information Outlook*, 9(12), 44–46.

Abrams, S. (2006). 25 technologies in 50 minutes. Retrieved March 1, 2008, from www.sirsidynixinstitute.com/seminar_page.php?sid=69.

Barnard, S. B. (1992). *A draft model for adopting total quality management in a research library*. Washington, DC: Association of Research Libraries.

Blowers, H. (2007). Learning 2.0: 23 things you can do to become web 2.0 savvy. Retrieved March 1, 2008, from: http://plcmclearning.blogspot.com.

Bradley, P. (2005). Internet Q & A. *Library & Information Update*, 4(12), 10.

Bradley, P. (2006). Web 2.0 a new generation of services. *Library & Information Update*, 5(5), 32–33.

Casey, M., & Savastinuk, L. (2006, September 1). Library 2.0: Service for the next-generation library. *Library Journal*. Retrieved March 1, 2008, from www.libraryjournal.com/article/CA6365200.html.

Castiglione, J. (2007). Self-managing work teams and their external leadership: A primer for library administrators. *Library Management*, 28(6/7), 380–393. Retrieved April 10, 2009, from Academic Search Complete.

Chad, K. (2005). Library 2.0. *Public Library Journal*, 20(4), 11–12.

Chad, K., & Miller, P. (2005). Do libraries matter? The rise of Library 2.0. Retrieved December 1, 2009, from www.talis.com/applications/downloads/white_papers/Do LibrariesMatter.pdf.

Donohue, N. (2005). Library 2.0: What's next in tech. *ILA Reporter*, 23(6), 18–19.

Internet Librarian Conference. (2005). Internet librarian 2005. Retrieved March 1, 2008, from www.infotoday.com/il2005.

Owens, I. (1999). The impact of change from hierarchy to teams in two academic libraries: Intended results vs. actual results using Total Quality Management. *College and Research Libraries*, 60(6), 571–84. Retrieved March 1, 2008, from Wilson OmniFile Full Text Mega Edition.

Peek, R. (2005). Web publishing 2.0. *Information Today*, 22(10), 17–18.

Riggs, D. (1997). What's in store for academic libraries? Leadership and management issues. *Journal of Academic Librarianship*, 23(1), 3–8. Retrieved April 10, 2009, from Library, Information Science & Technology Abstracts with Full Text.

Sociallibrary.com. (2006). Five weeks to a social library: The first free, grassroots, completely online course devoted to teaching librarians about social software. Retrieved March 1, 2008, from www.sociallibraries.com/course.

Stephens, M. (2006). Creating conversations, connections, and community. *Library Technology Reports*, 42(4), 6–7.

Worrell, D. (1995). The learning organization: Management theory for the information age or new age fad? *Journal of Academic Librarianship*, 21(5), 351–357. Retrieved April 10, 2009, from Library, Information Science & Technology Abstracts with Full Text.

CHAPTER 16

Neoreference: Looking for New Models in Response to Disjunctive Change

Susan Beatty and Helen Clarke

Overview

This chapter examines the current situation of reference and discusses a future where a new reference service can emerge. We have two choices: we can be traditionalists—we can maintain our roles with ever diminishing numbers and use social tools available to us to seek out that vanishing species of users who still need "help" with simple tasks, or we can expand into new territory, mastering a higher level of skill and far more complex tools. This chapter proposes three vectors for exploring this new space: aggregation, complexity, and creation. We also reflect on the impact such a change will have on traditional structures, staffing, and collection development. The purpose of our chapter is not to define one model of neoreference but rather to offer up some thought-provoking ideas to get people thinking about the future.

> [W]hen a profession has been created as a result of some scarcity, as with librarians...the professionals are often the last ones to see it when that scarcity goes away. It is easier to understand that you face competition than obsolescence. (Shirky, 2008: 59)

Perhaps it is a cliché to note that reference is changing, or that technology is the driving force behind this change. However, despite general acknowledgement of a new environment, academic libraries still struggle to understand how far we need to evolve to survive. This chapter explores the magnitude of ongoing change in reference collections and services as we move toward a learning space environment and a learning support service model. From looking at how reference sources are changing we go on to discuss the impact this will have on the nature of reference service delivery in academic libraries.

Our concern for the future of reference is rooted in our experience at the University of Calgary, a four-year medical doctoral institution with 23,000+ full-time equivalent students. The opening of our Information Commons in 1999 was accompanied by the rapid expansion of digital resources. Since then, we have seen users become increasingly sophisticated and independent in using and acquiring information. As reported at other academic reference desks, quick reference requests (short facts) seem to be disappearing, while more complex questions along with the "how do I" and "where is" questions are increasing (LaGuardia, 2003). This leads us to believe that many users still experience difficulty using specialized interfaces and that the addition of increasingly sophisticated resources results in a need for guidance on how to access, discover, and critique information.

Disjunctive Change

Evidence of change is captured in falling reference statistics coupled with rising use statistics for electronic resources. According to ARL statistics (2008), from 1996 to 2006 the average number of reference queries reported by Canadian members of the Association of Research Libraries fell from 180,221 to 118,254—a 35 percent reduction. Conversely, at the University of Calgary, we saw an increase in use of electronic resources from 498,593 in 2001 to 3,174,406 in 2006—a sixfold increase (University of Calgary Library, 2009). The juxtaposition of these two trends is not a coincidence. They are related. The independent user operates quite happily in the digital library without the need for frequent expert mediation. What then of the future of reference?

By stepping back to examine the forces of change we can come to a better understanding of the new relationship between the user and the reference librarian. With the advent of Web based distribution and wide scale digitization of information resources we have achieved a transformation in academic libraries whereby a formerly scarce commodity requiring considerable control and support has become abundant and easily obtained. This is a disjunctive change that requires fundamental rethinking of how and where libraries allocate resources. Buckland (2008) notes that in responding to this new environment we have placed emphasis on empowering librarians and have not properly considered the consequences of an independent, empowered information user. Buckland believes that a renewed attention to bibliographic access and a more holistic view are needed.

Mann (2008) also addresses the question of the impact of information technology on reference, and while his articulate defense of traditional librarian user interactions may seem at odds with our position, it is important to note that he bases his defense on valuing complexity and centering help where it is needed. In this at least we agree with Mann.

Emergence of Learning Spaces

Currently the University of Calgary is planning a new facility, the Taylor Family Digital Library, which will replace the current central library. Scheduled to open in fall 2010, the Taylor is being designed for the twenty-first-century scholar, with new partners (art gallery, museum, archives, learning support) and a focus on using digital resources for learning. "More than a building with books, it is a place to learn, to study, to talk, to work together, to research, and to get help with learning and research" (www.Taylor.ucalgary.ca). Resources will include traditional library materials as well as archives, artifacts, special collections, original art, and digital media. Classrooms and group study spaces will coexist with large presentation spaces and individual carrels. There will be new ways of learning: experiential, active, collaborative, and multidisciplinary and new ways of getting help. This complexity of space and resources will demand new ways of interacting with the user. The heart of the building will not be the reference desk but rather the learning spaces. While we anticipate a high degree of interaction with users, we recognize that people will strive for independence and the provision of resources and design of the space should support this desire. At the center will be learning, not a desk.

The services and resources currently offered from a traditional desk are no longer relevant to a growing number of users. Writers who have examined this issue emphasize the need to tease out from accepted tools and practice what actually remains as necessary and useful. Buckland (2008) warns against models that seek to sustain the user-librarian power relationship; we must accept that new technologies empower users who experience ever greater levels of success without the intervention of librarians. Landesmann (2005) notes that even though librarians may be able to provide more sophisticated tools and service, users prefer their independence and will not seek out assistance. Finally, Bennett (2006) alerts us to the fundamental change in which a foundational view of knowledge becomes less relevant as users are able to successfully navigate vast information resources. Users no longer need to memorize either individual facts or texts, as these are very findable, nor do they need to rely on librarians to help with complex navigational methods in the simple "just Google it" world.

Taken together these trends pose a key question. Does reference service continue to need to exist? Any answer to this question needs to move past simply migrating traditional services to the digital realm. We believe that users have changed their behavior because digital information is fundamentally different from print and that their move away from librarian intervention is a sensible, well-grounded response.

Equivalency may be the greatest trap to avoid in planning a future for reference. Equivalency holds that the change in user behavior is related to trivial motivations or ignorance and that we need to make only minor changes in delivery to re-engage with users. Chat services, for example, are particularly vulnerable to this criticism. While low uptake is often noted in discussion of chat services, there is less speculation as to why these services prove unpopular. Dee and Allen (2006) propose a combination of usability and poor promotion. Naylor, Stoffel, and Van der Laan (2008) conducted a focus group study to discover why students do not make more use of chat reference. They found that promotion is an issue, but surprisingly students gave more value to personalized reference service, and chat is seen as very impersonal. We believe that the relatively low uptake of chat service in comparison to face-to-face reference is also evidence of a lack of need for quick information assistance. The types of quick answers best given through chat are not needed by users who are happily independent of what were once the bread and butter of reference service.

Two key areas of reference where equivalency is a particular challenge are the reference collection and the reference desk. In their traditional physical manifestations these two concepts circumscribed the boundaries of reference, creating a visual signifier for both staff and users.

Impact of Digital Formats on Reference Collections

At the University of Calgary Library information technology made its first forays into reference through citation tools for articles or patents. Dialogue and other online search services were the exclusive domain of librarians. Because cost included time spent on searching, the user-librarian power relationship was maintained. In these early days the presence of online sources increased the status of the librarian. Librarians with expert skills in searching were an important factor in controlling cost. The migration from these early days to the present situation where users independently seek and retrieve citations from a wide range of commercial and open access sources is being mirrored in the transformation of other types of reference sources, including tools that provide basic facts, introductory descriptions, physical properties, enumerations, or tools that describe processes and techniques.

Ritchie and Genoni (2007) surveyed Australian libraries to assess sources used to answer information queries. While their study is library focused, looking at reference worker behavior rather than user behavior, they still concluded that use of electronic sources would increase, and this raised important questions regarding downgrading/deskilling of reference services. We believe this change is grounded in the fundamentally different nature of electronic sources.

The changes we are experiencing in reference collections can be conceptualized as operating along two vectors: first, a progression from the need for mediation to user independence, and second, a transformation from presenting information in small specialized units toward aggregating sources into generalized databases. These vectors and the types of collections that sit on the extremes of the different axis are illustrated in Figure 16.1, the Reference Collection Matrix. The four quadrants of the matrix represent the past, present, and future of reference collections.

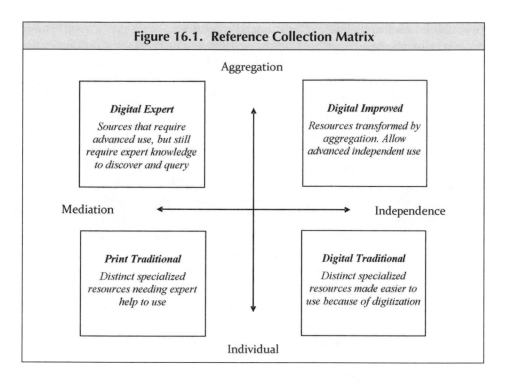

Figure 16.1. Reference Collection Matrix

Aggregation

Digital Expert

Sources that require
advanced use, but still
require expert knowledge
to discover and query

Digital Improved

Resources transformed by
aggregation. Allow
advanced independent use

Mediation ←————————→ Independence

Print Traditional

Distinct specialized
resources needing expert
help to use

Digital Traditional

Distinct specialized
resources made easier to
use because of digitization

Individual

In the matrix the Print Traditional reference collection represents the historic norm in many academic libraries. This is a highly mediated collection made up of a multitude of discrete units of information. This type of collection required librarian intervention to answer what were often conceptually very simple questions. Librarian expertise lay in knowing how to navigate the variety of print sources, but it did not lie in any significant level of subject expertise. Where subject expertise was needed, services and collections were often segregated into physically separate areas.

The first stage of development for digital reference collections is represented as the Digital Traditional collection. Here, digital versions of traditional reference tools have an immediate impact because they increase user independence, freeing consultation from the physical confines of the library and easing searching by being open to more natural inquiry. The Oxford English Dictionary Online is many levels of convenience and usability beyond the print OED. For example, the print lacks wildcard capabilities, which are an important feature for the spelling challenged. Independence allows users to make queries within their own time frame and also makes recursive querying over an extended period more convenient and likely to happen.

The Digital Improved collection introduces the quality of aggregation, meaning that separate sources can be brought together and treated in a unified manner.

Aggregation may be the most critical change digital formats bring to information. Examples of aggregation include Credo Reference, which brings a variety of distinct sources together under one search interface; Google, which harvests data to create a single index; and Wikipedia, which provides a central framework under which an unlimited range of information is gathered. Aggregated content allows discovery without predetermining a specific source and it allows users to frame complex, individually crafted queries. Aggregated content also supports concurrent use of a variety of sources, building in a level of independent user verification.

The common concern librarians express regarding the accuracy of reference sources, a question Buckland (2008) characterizes as trust, is rethought by aggregation, which provides variety, rather than relying on the accuracy of the single source. While this variety can arise from the crowd sourced nature of Wikipedia entries we would add that it is important to understand the role of Wikipedia in the information strategy of users. Concern with Wikipedia accuracy compared to more traditional sources is valid (see Rector [2008] for an example of a study into this question). However, Wikipedia results are part of the larger information ecology of the Internet, and concerns about overreliance should be balanced against the knowledge that users are easily exposed to a variety of sources for comparison. This is an aspect of aggregation that we can easily overlook in evaluating nontraditional, Internet-based sources.

The final vector along which reference collections may develop is the Digital Expert collection. Here we rediscover the need for expert help, but at a higher, more conceptually complex level. An example of this type of development is the digitized versions of definitive editions of key thinkers and writers created by Intelex Past Masters. Previously, editions such as this required scholarly knowledge and intent to discover and an extended time commitment to review. The digitized version, with improved searching, becomes a reference tool. For example, a researcher may wish to know dates when Coleridge visited with Charles or Mary Lamb. With a digital version of Coleridge's correspondence, what was a research question becomes a suitable reference query, with the librarian not only able to point the patron to a likely source but able to perform a search and provide results directly to the user. The librarian becomes an expert by combining knowledge of sources with the ability to map the client's needs to those sources in novel and unexpected ways. It is this in-depth subject and source knowledge that distinguishes help given with these types of resources from the more basic navigational assistance given with the traditional print reference collection.

Neoreference Collections in the New Learning Space
Accepting that reference collections are fundamentally changed poses challenges for their care and development. Some challenges are familiar from traditional experience, but the difficulty and emphasis we put on different areas change as

we move from considering the reference collection as a discrete physical entity to viewing it as any array of sources, mostly digital, that can be brought to bear on reference queries.

The first challenge of the neoreference collection is the familiar one of provision, making sure patrons have access to the information they need. A key change in assuring the provision of information is the need to acknowledge the role of open access sources. We need to honestly assess the utility of tools such as Wikipedia, Google, and the array of lovingly and expertly created tools available freely on the Web. We do not need to re-create these tools through purchasing commercial equivalents, particularly where open access sources prove themselves through ease of discovery and use. Part of this honest assessment is moving beyond the view that there is a distinct divide in reliability or quality between formally published materials and open access sources.

The new academic library/learning space will emphasize help with resources that are complex. Conceptually simple tools that answer straightforward questions will be replaced by digitized and aggregated resources that can be used independently. Reference in the digital realm requires the ability to mine information sources through a deep understanding of structure and content. Census data, digital texts, georeference data, and financial statistics are all examples of information sources that can be used to answer reference queries but that require an expert level of knowledge to use successfully.

The learning space as it is envisioned for the Taylor will be a creative site focusing on new and innovative investigations and experiences with an emphasis on learning through inquiry. Librarians with advanced subject and resource knowledge will be well placed to adopt a role in designing and building new reference sources. These may be specific to certain research projects and places, or they may be of wider application.

A final collection challenge in this new environment is preserving the refindability of information. In the past we could rely on standardized metadata and a limited range of resources to support refindability. Now, we can predict that helping users locate and verify previously found information will grow in difficulty. Scholars have always used resources gathered from sources outside of the library, many of which were informal unpublished materials. However, with the advent of Web-based distribution this information is easier to find and acquire, and while open access information is increasingly mainstream, much of it is ephemeral and poorly documented. Early responses to this issue included attempts to capture metadata, cataloging, and describing the full range of resources. It is more likely that solutions to the problem will be found in a combination of responses ranging from formal local archiving through third-party collaborative archives and finally by supporting the maintenance of portable, stable customized collections of data and information.

In providing support for information resources in a new model of reference we need to be certain to put thought into our evaluative role, our ability to master a higher level of complex information skills, the creation of new resources, and finally making information refindable and stable.

Reference Service in a Learning Space

The learning needs of the user in the digital age are transforming the core activities of the library. We are "self-consciously and resolutely designing it for learning" (Bennett, 2006). Tools and resources will be physical and virtual and formats should easily migrate between digital and physical. Learners will express their learning through physical and digital creations. This space will be designed for the learner while librarians and other experts will be visitors in the space. In this design, what is the role of reference? This section will attempt to provide a framework for future thinking. There are no real answers at the moment but perhaps there are a few hints at what a neoreference model would look like.

One way of planning for changes in reference is to consider the physical and virtual as one space. The learning space of the Taylor truly is the whole building. Multiple and varied student spaces are within a high technology environment where learners have access to three-dimensional modeling, video editing, collaborative software, and an array of primary and secondary resources both digital and print. The Taylor is planned as a studio where new knowledge is created. The learning space will be a creative space where tools, resources, and experts are immediately available (White, n.d.).

Three Vectors for Change in Service Delivery

Reference services in a learning space are affected by three forces previously identified as affecting the future of reference collections: aggregation, complexity, and creation. Aggregation refers to the ease with which disparate sources can be linked and how the independent user can search, extract, and combine information from multiple aggregated sources. Aggregation yields new complexities and interpretations, requiring specialized knowledge and expertise on the part of both the learner and the librarian. The opportunities of digitization combined with the increased complexity of sources results in the need for the librarian to create new research tools and services for the learner.

At the center of the vectors of aggregation, complexity, and creation is a user who is technologically skilled and sophisticated in understanding his or her needs: customization, flexibility, ease of access, just-in-time information, and ubiquity. However, this user is naive about information resources, whether they are open access sources such as Wikipedia or complex tools such as Intelex Past Masters or a national census. Users operate within this matrix of technology and aggregated resources until the matrix reaches a critical mass of complexity, the breaking point, when his or her current skills and knowledge no longer work. It is at this point of need that the librarian has to provide help with the learning experience. Dede (2005) refers to the "neomillenial" learning style has being typified by "co-design of learning experiences personalized to individual needs and preferences." While he was referring to faculty interaction with the learner, there is no reason why customization and personalization for effective and directed assistance developed with the learner rather than for the learner should not be part of the new reference model. Cocreation and collaboration could include the development of new tools or the creation of customized resources or posting a guide for learning. A basic of reference services is the librarian and the learner working jointly to resolve an information need.

A Future Scenario

Consider the example of a student arriving at the Taylor needing to create a video to provide "proof of learning" on the Peloponnesian War. What type of service model can we follow that will integrate information and learning into this activity? Students may know how to use video editing software but not how to integrate knowledge. They may know about the topic but not necessarily what graphics or other resources are available. Posting a technical assistant at the service desk to help with the software is an easy answer and follows a popular model in information commons. But this model will fall short in the Taylor. It confuses the need to understand and manipulate complex software with the fundamental mission of the librarian and the learning need of the user. The current role for the librarian is to open up the information and make it accessible to the user. A future role will include not only making resources accessible but enabling the translation of information to the learner's environment.

For the librarian to assist this student, he or she needs to understand the concept of "proof of learning." The librarian will need to have expertise in the resources and the subject and he or she will need to be able to collect resources and make them available for the student in such a way that the student can store and refine them. We need information expert librarians who have technical skills and a large ability to learn. Although we say complexity, we are also talking about simplicity, in that we have a responsibility to ease the path for the learner. Traditionally this has always been the responsibility of the reference librarian.

How do we help someone create evidence of new learning in the digital environment? Our problem is not just learning how to use the software but understanding how the user may use the tools and resources to create new knowledge and what our role is in that creation. We therefore need to spend more time with our users, investigating their learning needs and their goals so that we can best devise the appropriate intermediation that works for them. We need to develop new literacies.

New Literacies for Librarians

To live and thrive in this new environment we need to focus on integrating the new complexity of information with the users' need to create new knowledge. We know how to evaluate, acquire, and make accessible collections. As we work with publishers to break down the mind-set of digital "book" and move toward the creation of manipulable aggregates of information, the result will be complexity and the need for more specialized knowledge and expertise on the part of both user and librarian.

For example, we will have to learn how to put information together for the unique user in a precise and specific way and then reorganize for the next user(s). In the process we will create new tools designed to meet user needs and with an understanding of how users learn. This is the most important new knowledge we can acquire. To become learning literate, librarians will have to understand how the users learn. In the Taylor we will need to be where the user is, learn the skills of instruction and instructional design, organize our physical and virtual space for the learner, and understand that there is not one approach for all. Being flexible, responsive, and proactive will require a greater degree of involvement and collaboration as well as a higher level of knowledge and skills.

The Taylor provides the University of Calgary Library with the perfect opportunity to be creative, but while a new building is a catalyst, the changes coming to reference will happen for all libraries. There are certain key actions that will carry us through the turmoil of new resources, expectations, and services. By interacting with users and understanding more of their learning needs we will be able to identify new tools and new ways to be involved. We should organize and describe information to suit the user, designing systems that allow users to contribute knowledge. We should open libraries up to the participation of multiple experts, not only librarians, seeking out collaborators who will enhance the learning experience of the user. We must talk to software designers, resource providers, and learning experts pushing for the creation of tools and functionalities not found in current offerings. Others may be surprised by the library involving itself in learning, but the library has great knowledge and expertise to share. For example, the National Library of Singapore (www.nlb.gov.sg) has created a tool to aggregate and organize e-mail exchanges, which enables collection knowledge, knowledge management, and collective learning. It is a very creative tool meant to enhance the reference service and the users' learning (Ng, Shin, & Chuan, 2008). They have created this tool by acquiring new literacies. They have learned to understand the learning needs and processes of their users. They have worked with experts in technology, software design, and knowledge management. They have listened to the user and applied their creative knowledge toward making a new learning tool that enables the users to be independent and to share their learning with others. This is true reference.

In the future the new learning space must be a creative space where tools, resources, and experts are immediately available. In the Taylor Family Digital Library new knowledge will be created by both the librarian and the learner.

Conclusion

Change is pervasive and disjunctive. Future collections will not be about volumes but about information organization and functionality. Future staff will be experts at learning as well as knowing about learning. Reference service will evolve as a multilayered, helping, ubiquitous service in which reference as a discrete service will disappear. We will see the librarian growing in his or her understanding of the complexity and interrelatedness of information, working with new tools that are complex and flexible, such as customized aggregation and providing digitization on demand, creating a digital library beyond the current mind-set. Whatever the new service model is, it will be proactive, anticipatory, creative, individualized and flexible, personal, and expert. There will be new relationships where the librarian is directly involved in the learning outcomes of the academy.

In summary, we believe that there is no discrete reference collection in the digital age; it is all of the resources. The future of reference is that there is no discrete reference service but service that focuses on learning needs and creative responses. The main focus of reference—to ease the path of the learner—has not changed; it has simply moved to a new matrix. The mould has been broken. Step away and see what you can do.

References

ARL Statistics. (2008). Interactive edition. Retrieved November 5, 2008, from http://fisher .lib.virginia.edu/arl/index.html.

Bennett, S. (2006, January). The choice for learning. *Journal of Academic Librarianship*, 32(1), 3–13.

Buckland, M. K. (2008, June). Reference library service in the digital environment. *Library & Information Science Research*, 30(2), 81–85.

Dede, C. (2005). Planning for neomillenial learning styles: Implications for investments in technology and faculty. In D. G. Oblinger & J. L. Oblinger (Eds.), *Educating the net generation*. Retrieved August 5, 2009, from www.educause.edu/educatingthenetgen.

Dee, C., & Allen, M. (2006, January). A survey of the usability of digital reference services on academic health science library Web sites. *Journal of Academic Librarianship*, 32(1), 69–78.

LaGuardia, C. (2003). The future of reference: Get real! *Reference Services Review*, 31(1), 39–42.

Landesman, M. (2005). Getting it right—The evolution of reference collections. *Reference Librarian*, 44(91), 5–22.

Mann, T. (2008). The Peloponnesian war and the future of reference, cataloging, and scholarship in research libraries. *Journal of Library Metadata*, 8(1), 53–100.

Naylor, S., Stoffel, B., & Van der Laan, S. (2008). Why isn't our chat reference service used more? *Reference and User Services Quarterly, 47*(4), 342–354.

Ng, J., Shin, I. L., & Chuan, Y. C. (2008). You virtually can't miss us: Harnessing virtual tools to enhance the quality of our reference services. Paper presented at Reference Renaissance: Current and Future Trends, August 4–5, Denver, Colorado.

Rector, L. H. (2008). Comparison of Wikipedia and other encyclopedias for accuracy, breadth, and depth in historical articles. *Reference Services Review, 36*(1), 7–22.

Ritchie, A., & Genoni, P. (2007). Print v. electronic reference sources: Implications of an Australian study. *The Electronic Library, 25*(4), 440–452.

Shirky, C. (2008). *Here comes everybody*. New York: Penguin.

University of Calgary Library. (2009). Library database access statistics. Retrieved November 5, 2008, from www.ucalgary.ca/lib-old/analog_old/analog3/statistics/stats.html.

White, P. (n.d.). Introducing the Taylor Family Digital Library. Retrieved April 13, 2009, from http://lcr.ucalgary.ca/tfdl-teams/communication.

CHAPTER 17

Drawing in the Community for Reference Services at Wilkinson Public Library in Telluride, Colorado

Sarah Lawton

Overview

This report from the field details an innovative approach to reference services implemented at Wilkinson Public Library (WPL) in Telluride, Colorado. Demonstrating the power of reworking reference programs to match the needs of the community, WPL staff has taken practical steps to reposition the library as a community focal point for education and entertainment. Exemplary service practices combine with focused programs such as BookMatch to showcase the ways that libraries may enhance visibility of reference and reader's advisory resources, train clients in the use of electronic resources, and promote community engagement with reference staff. This report is an attempt to illustrate the guiding principles behind the kinds of programs and service practices that have been established and tested at WPL and can be replicated within other institutions.

> The ends of information, after all, are human ends. The logic of information must ultimately be the logic of humanity. For all information's independence and extent, it is people, in their communities, organizations, and institutions, who ultimately decide what it all means and why it matters. (Brown & Duguid, 2000, p. 18)

A new kind of society requires a new kind of library. As we move into a global information paradigm, where expectations for instantaneous access collide with the availability of inconceivable quantities of raw information, we must embrace a new model of reference librarianship. Instead of the keepers of the books, we must become community-based information resources, linking our clients with the tools they need to improve their lives and their neighborhoods. Taking on this role means positioning ourselves as visible public figures and taking every opportunity to demonstrate the services we offer. In Telluride, Colorado, at the Wilkinson Public Library, we have developed a new approach to reference service that serves as a model to those seeking to bridge the gap between the library and the community.

261

Wilkinson Public Library (WPL) is a medium-sized library serving a small resort community high in the San Juan Mountains of Colorado. With a library service area population of 5,500, WPL boasts 9,500 library card holders and a staggering 37 annual circulations per capita (Library Research Service, 2007). While many libraries have seen the use of reference services fall in recent years, WPL has experienced a steady rise in reference inquiries over the past five years (Library Research Service, 2007). In fact, since the inception of the programs and practices detailed in this report, reference interactions have doubled (Library Research Service, 2007; Wilkinson Public Library, 2008). In 2007, WPL boasted 3.52 reference questions per capita, the second highest in the state of Colorado (Wilkinson Public Library, 2007). In a national climate of shrinking library budgets and increased demands on staff time and training, WPL has used its unique position to develop an innovative model for reference service that reinvents people's perceptions of the library and our role in the community. This report is an attempt to illustrate the guiding principles behind the kinds of programs and service practices that have been established and tested at WPL and can be replicated within other institutions.

Reference Is Ready

Traditionally, the role of reference librarians within the public library has been primarily focused on the management of library collections and effectively locating information for our clients. Yet with the introduction of electronic resources and the Internet, we are no longer in control of the resources that our clients wish to access. This change in physical access to information has fundamentally shifted our role from information provider to information intermediary. Instead of selecting resources for our clients, we are increasingly helping them navigate resources and substantiate the information that they can find on their own.

It used to be that reference librarians were seated at desks, awaiting questions. Now we have a variety of new models for service delivery: roving reference, 24/7 virtual reference, instant messaging, social networking Web sites. Instead of waiting for the questions to come to us, we are learning to be proactive educators seeking to provide quality service to our communities. We are in the process of defining the role of the public library in society as a public service institution and an effective space for building and strengthening our communities. Clearly, this goes beyond the ready reference paradigm.

Yet there is much within our professional history that sets the tone for the innovations generated by a reference renaissance. A deep commitment to personal service, a value imbued in reference librarianship a century ago by pioneers like Samuel Swett Green, remains the bedrock of our profession (Swett Green, 1876). As we seek to enhance our appeal by integrating innovations derived from marketing and business models, we must remain true to our public service tradition and our professional integrity.

At WPL, we have embraced professional practices that define our role by the services we provide. We focus on developing information literacy skills through service, taking on the role of educators and community resources. We engage our clients in the world of books and other media as well. We establish the continued importance of the library as a central hub of information in the community. And, finally, we provide a space, both physical and conceptual, where people can come together to learn and participate in community dialogue. As reference librarians, we are the public figures that represent these goals. It is up to us to use ingenuity and leadership to draw in our communities for lifelong learning.

From Service Goals to Practices and Programs

The emphasis of public librarianship on developing information literacy provides a wonderful opportunity for repositioning the reference service model. Recognizing the shift in client use of libraries and in their orientation to information more generally, WPL has developed a series of information literacy programs that seek to educate as they entertain. The philosophy behind these programs is simple: our patrons want and need to learn skills that will help them thrive within information society, but effective learning occurs within a social context, where people are encouraged to actively engage with the material and its applications. Telling someone how to access computer databases does little to promote his or her fluent use of the electronic resources the library has to offer. Demonstrating the ways that resources can be utilized within a specific social context can have lasting impact on people's perceptions of what is available. Just as simply knowing the meanings of words does not imply comprehension of a language, information literacy requires that learners have the ability to apply their knowledge to novel situations that require critical thinking and reciprocal communication (Breivik & Gee, 1989).

These principles of effective learning provide a point of departure for the design of new methods in assisting our clients, through community programs and service at the reference desk. At WPL, we asked ourselves the following questions: How can we provide instruction but taper it in such a way that our clients are receptive? How can we fulfill our clients' need for meaningful social activity as we achieve our goal of fostering lifelong learning and developing literacy skills? We looked for the answers to these questions through the introduction of new programs and a tireless commitment to service. We sought to develop programs that featured titles that communicated the content of the program and the value to the patron as well as identifying tools and services offered by the library. Respecting the value of our clients' leisure time, we focused on programming that is casual and fun, encouraging active involvement and building relationships within our community.

We also integrated this paradigm in our interactions at the reference desk. Using a dual computer monitor system, service staff has developed a habit of actively involving the client in our search process, accompanying the patron in accordance with key recommendations on searching contained within the 2004 Reference and User Services Association (RUSA) Guidelines for Behavioral Performance of Reference and Information Service Providers (Reference and User Services Association, 2004). Instead of working on a reference question out of view of clients, we are able to switch on a second monitor that allows them to follow along as we navigate the catalog or electronic databases. Broadcasting the reference process in this way serves to demonstrate our thought processes and to expose clients to the breadth of resources the library has to offer.

This paradigm shift instigated a makeover of many classic library programs and services. The author reading became a social event built around the authors or the broader subjects of their works, providing fertile ground for partnerships with other organizations within the community. We began to formulate a series of professional networking sessions aimed at various demographics within our community, such as nonprofit organizations, to replace the classic model of the general library tour or the database instruction session. Reader's advisory service was bolstered by BookMatch, a high-profile approach to reader recommendations that will be discussed in greater detail in this chapter. These programs are geared toward building relationships of ongoing reference assistance as we establish a core group of savvy library clients who are actively spreading the word about our electronic databases, our friendliness, and our commitment to service.

BookMatch

Reader's Advisory (RA) has a long history at the reference desk (Saricks & Brown, 1989). Often the most visible public liaison, the reference librarian occupies a key position in the task of helping clients select a book suited to their interests and taste. Yet many library clients remain unaware of the expertise available to them. At WPL, we recognized a shift from reading-related reference questions to inquiries focused on technology and research. We felt that it was vital to demonstrate our willingness to talk about books and to promote the library as a social forum to discuss reading. We also noticed that attempts to approach clients for RA can be uncomfortable for both librarian and client and must be carefully navigated. These observations led to the introduction of monthly RA sessions that aimed to increase awareness about new books and reference staff's eagerness to assist clients in deciding what to read next. We also wanted to promote electronic resources that aid in reading selection by demonstrating their utility to clients during RA sessions.

The program born of these objectives was BookMatch, held on a monthly basis in the main lobby of the library to spotlight our RA services. We chose the title BookMatch to imply a casual and fun matchmaking process that would be easily understood and unintimidating. While sessions were promoted in advance as a special program, our intent was to offer the service to anyone who came by, casually offering to show clients a selection of new books and to help them find a perfect match. Seated at a card table, staff was equipped with a portable display of new books, bestseller lists, and a laptop computer. In addition, we created a form that clients could fill out if they preferred or if they were short on time.

The form that we developed for BookMatch was inspired by the approach to RA articulated by Nancy Pearl. In her lecture titled "Doorways to Enjoyment," Pearl describes RA as the process of combining appeal and interest to formulate an appropriate recommendation (Pearl, 2007). First, the librarian must encourage clients to talk about a book that they have read and enjoyed. It need not be clients' favorite book, nor must they endorse it wholeheartedly. In fact, instead of critiquing the book, it is preferable if clients describe the book, in the process betraying the elements of the work that had the greatest appeal for the them. The concept of the appeal of a book as a basis for RA dates back to Joyce Saricks and Nancy Brown's seminal exposition on *Reader's Advisory Service in the Public Library* (Saricks & Brown, 1989). In suggesting that RA has more to do with the interpretive experience of reading than specific subject matter, Saricks and Brown grounded contemporary RA in the translation of reading styles to writing styles. Pearl extends this work, identifying four elements that people generally use as "doorways" to access their reading. Story, character, setting, and language provide a framework for thinking about how a reader tends to engage with the books that they read (Pearl, 2007). Based on the way that clients describe the book, whether they felt connected to its characters or couldn't put it down or found it "beautiful," a librarian may match clients to other books that display similar prominent doorways. This approach does not require personal experience of the books that the librarian is recommending, rather an ability to categorize books based on presumed doorways indicated by knowledge of genre, author, or style. This is not to say that subject matter or areas of interest are irrelevant to RA, rather that a focus on appeal can lead the reader in new directions and toward greater satisfaction.

In the spirit of merging appeal with tangible factors that can narrow the selection, WPL's BookMatch form is composed of three key questions. The first two questions deal with the clients' reading history and life context.

> Tell us about a book you read recently that you enjoyed.
> Tell us a little about your current interests.

These open-ended questions allowed clients to comfortably provide the information necessary for the librarian to generate recommendations without feeling the sense of pressure attached to needing to come up with a "favorite" book. At WPL, we added a further question that helped to guide our selections.

Is there an author that you particularly dislike? Who? Why?

This question helps librarians hone their thinking and can be a fun way to encourage discussion. People tend to be vocal about their dislikes, and asking them their opinion in this way can provide valuable insights into elements that do not appeal. The form can either be written out by the clients or employed as a guide for an interactive RA interview. At WPL, we attempt to offer as many options as possible to promote our services, including e-mailing a list of suggestions to a client based on the information contained in the form.

One of the most successful facets of BookMatch has been in the generation of further reference transactions simply through positioning the reference librarian in a clear service role. By leaving the structured setting of the reference desk, the librarian is able to change the social rules of the library interaction and encourage engagement that exceeds the client's expectations. According to a July 2008 OCLC report titled *From Awareness to Funding: A Study of Library Support in America*, clients who perceive the library as "transformational" are much more likely to support increases in funding (DeRosa & Johnson, 2008). This study confirms what we have seen at WPL—when libraries surprise their clients and surpass expectations libraries become an integral and valued part of their communities. BookMatch has served as a focal point for interface between service and programs at WPL and proved a valuable tool to promote reference services.

Thinking Beyond the Desk

As we have seen with BookMatch, leaving the reference desk to offer specialized services to library clients is a winning strategy. But what about leaving the library? Director of Colorado's Douglas County Libraries, Jamie LaRue, has questioned the traditional paradigm of reference librarianship, advocating that it is time to step out from behind the desk and into the communities that we serve. Instead of staffing desks, LaRue believes that reference librarians should focus their time on the difficult reference questions, providing expert assistance when needed and engaging in "community reference work" through active engagement with organizations and individuals who may not be aware of library resources (LaRue, 2008).

The programs that we have implemented at WPL and the service goals that we have articulated have led us to re-evaluate and redefine our model of public services. In September 2008, we took the next step. Eliminating the traditional departmental boundaries between reference and circulation, WPL Director Barbara Brattin and Public Services Manager Sarah Landeryou spearheaded the creation of two new departments. Instead of circulation and reference, WPL now delivers integrated client services through a public services department and the circulation of materials through a materials management department. Public service specialists have undergone intensive training in all aspects of desk assistance and client account management. They can assist a client in finding a book, using the Internet, and getting a library card. This new model allows us to provide the same level of service at each of our desks, dispensing with the need to send clients to different places for different kinds of assistance. By training paraprofessionals as the front-line service providers, we maximize the amount of time librarians may spend on collection development, extensive research assistance, RA, and community development. While we are still in the early stages of implementation of these sweeping changes, we are already seeing impressive results in a dramatic rise in service statistics and greater awareness of the library as a community resource.

Training Reference Librarians for the Future

If reference librarianship is to weather the transition to an information society, we must be creative and resourceful in both the services we offer and their delivery. Despite all of the talk about the impact of broader access to information on the library, it takes only a glance around WPL to realize that many libraries are thriving. People crave the community space that libraries provide and need our help to navigate the complex world of information in creative ways. This renaissance requires a strong emphasis on reference from the institutions that are training the librarians of the future. A clear understanding of the role of the reference librarian as an educator and research resource within the community is vital to the new professionals who will become the leaders of the new reference paradigm.

Librarianship boasts a long professional history, and most clients hold firmly entrenched perceptions of who librarians are and what they do. We must demonstrate that we can use our professional traditions in innovative ways that offer value to our communities. By identifying opportunities to partner with other organizations, step out from behind the desk and provide entertaining yet edifying service and programming, we can give our clients the community space that they desire.

References

Breivik, P. S., & Gee, E. G. (1989). *Information literacy: Revolution in the library*. New York: American Council on Education.

Brown, J. S., & Duguid, P. (2000). *The social life of information*. Boston: Harvard Business School.

DeRosa, C., & Johnson, J. (2008). From awareness to funding: A study of library support in America. Retrieved October 15, 2008, from www.oclc.org/reports/funding/fullreport.pdf.

LaRue, J. (2008). Who needs reference librarians? Retrieved October 8, 2008, from www.libraryleadership.net/LaRue031708.asp.

Library Research Service. 2007 Colorado Public Library annual report [Data file]. Retrieved from www.lrs.org/pub_stats.php.

Pearl, N. (2007). Doorways to enjoyment: Providing excellent reader's advisory service. Presented at Colorado Association of Libraries Conference, November 8, Denver, Colorado.

Reference and User Services Association. (2004). Guidelines for behavioral performance of reference and information service providers. Retrieved April 13, 2009, from www.ala.org/ala/mgrps/divs/rusa/resources/guidelines/guidelinesbehavioral.cfm.

Saricks, J. G., & Brown, N. (1989). *Readers' advisory service in the public library* (1st ed.). Chicago: American Library Association.

Swett Green, S. (1876, October). Personal relations between librarians and readers. *Library Journal, I*, 74–81.

Wilkinson Public Library. (2008). Adult services statistics [Data set]. Telluride, CO: Author.

C H A P T E R 18

You Bought It, Now Sell It: Creating a Reference Renaissance in the Public Library by Marketing Collections and Services

Bernadine Goldman, Lizzie Eastwood, and Karen Long

Overview

This chapter details and examines the initiatives of two New Mexico public libraries in marketing their reference collections and services to increase their relevancy in the Internet era. Los Alamos County Library System integrated heretofore separate print and electronic reference collections into keyword areas without altogether abandoning the Dewey Decimal System. Staff created many engaging displays of reference materials. Farmington Public Library packaged their reference delivery methods into one convenient unit called Just Ask, incorporating in-person, telephone, e-mail, and instant messaging avenues. Marketing to library staff as well as to patrons was very important to both initiatives. Though it is early for definitive answers, in-house usage of reference books and patron satisfaction with recommended Web sites have clearly increased the relevance of the reference collection in Los Alamos. Similarly, patron usage of the Just Ask Web site and the instant messaging service have increased the relevance of reference services at Farmington. Continuing efforts to improve usage are ongoing in both libraries.

Introduction

Since the start of the third millennium, reference librarians have been warned of their irrelevance. As Steve Coffman stated, "There can be no doubt that reference librarians, as we know them—those of us who sit behind desks for five or six hours a day...waiting for people to walk up and ask us questions—those reference librarians are toast" (Anhang & Coffman, 2002, p. 51). However, there is also no doubt that reference collections in both print and electronic formats and reference services in terms of enhanced technologies are today providing us with an unprecedented wealth of resources with which to satisfy our patrons' informational and recreational needs, if only our patrons would realize it. As John Barnes of Gale/Cengage has stated, "Our greatest challenge is reaching users to raise their awareness of the credible, accurate reference resources available..." (Polanka, 2008, p. 130). This chapter showcases the initiatives of two New Mexico public libraries in reaching out to patrons and meeting them on their own terms by merchandising reference collections and services.

Marketing Collections

Los Alamos County Library System is located in Los Alamos, New Mexico, a town of almost 19,000 residents. The library system, which consists of a central library and one branch, is a crown jewel of the town and is well supported by the community. Los Alamos is a company town, home to Los Alamos National Laboratory, many of whose workers commute to Los Alamos and use the public library, swelling its service area to a population of 25,000. The local population is highly educated (over one-third have a graduate degree) and technologically oriented. The community holds the library to very high standards. The print reference collection is mainly housed at the central library, Mesa Public Library, and consists of some 6,000 volumes. The library also provides access to 85 separate databases.

The Problem

Print materials continue to form the core of the public library reference collection. In the Subject Listings to the *2008 Library Journal Reference Supplement*, 320 publications are listed. Of these, 61 percent are available in print format only, and yet we see that neither staff nor patrons turn first to print materials to answer their reference questions. The Internet is easily available, either at home or at the local public library, and it is easy to type search terms into Google, getting results quickly if unevenly. Information on the Internet may be more current than that in print materials. Furthermore, it is impossible to search a book by keyword, forcing us to think about the correct term for the subject in question and to use the book's index.

Reference e-books represent an improvement in terms of convenience in that patrons can access them remotely and can search them by keyword. Yet they too are static files, published in PDF form, and they are vulnerable to becoming outdated. At this point, they get little usage in our public library.

Online databases share the advantages of searchability and can be as current as the Web, but they require some patience in learning their best applications and can be very expensive. They require constant marketing to give a good return on investment. Databases are forever changing, and staff must be sure to monitor the databases for these changes so that they can properly instruct patrons on how to use them. This can be a tall order as libraries acquire more and more databases, although assigning specific staff members to watch one or two databases each and report changes back to other staff members may keep anyone from feeling overwhelmed by the rate of change. Most important, library staff need to remember that we have the databases and which ones are best suited to answer which types of questions.

The Opportunity

At the same time as this problem has come to the forefront, the idea of marketing for the public library has arisen. Most recent public library conference programs contain presentations on marketing the circulating collection, usually by arranging it on a retail model and trying to minimize the influence of classification schemes such as the Dewey Decimal Classification (DDC). The sanctity of the reference collection has no doubt saved it from these mildly subversive ideas, but this sanctity has also prevented people from using it as the solid and well-considered resource that it is.

Inspired by both the stories of merchandising success at the 2008 Public Library Association Conference and by the call at their PLA/3M Leadership Institute to be bold and to experiment, the reference staff discussed the possibility of rearranging the print reference collection into subject categories while not entirely abandoning DDC. In addition, we planned to post in these subject areas lists of our relevant subscription databases and the Reference and User Services Association (RUSA) recommended Web sites for information on these subjects. Our goal was to make sure that all users of the reference collection are aware of all the resources available and are introduced to them all in one place.

The Initiative: Integrating and Marketing the Reference Collection

In order to achieve this goal, three staff members formed a project team and decided to rearrange the physical reference collection to reflect more of the keyword way people are thinking about information retrieval today—the Internet search engine factor. We also planned to integrate the different types of reference material formats by placing signs and lists of online resources next to the books, thus selling our reference collection as a complete package. Our plan "focused on creating a user-centered arrangement of information regardless of format" (Dickinson & George, 2006, p. 167). We envisioned a hybrid reference collection with "seamless access to resources regardless of format" (Levrault, 2006, p. 21). With this in mind, it made sense for us to start offering patrons the content we have in the way that they prefer to get it.

Integrating the reference collection was easier said than done, with one part being virtual and one part being physical. Having decided to organize the collection by keyword, we faced the problem of deciding which of various possible keywords would get the greatest number of hits. We could only imagine the tagging clouds for each book. This issue brought to mind the section heading "Everything Has Its Places" from the book *Everything Is Miscellaneous* (Weinberger, 2007, p. 23).

Rather than abandoning the DDC entirely, we brought subjects together where Dewey had separated them. Books on aging from the medical and the sociology section were placed together in the sociology section; books on public health were moved to the medical section to join other health materials; books on weapons were moved from the technology and sports sections to join their companions in the military section; and books on jobs and companies where people might seek jobs were joined. In doing so, we sometimes discovered that we had two editions of the same book classified in two different call numbers because of changes in DDC that had taken place through the years. We were thus able to weed an entire cart of books and free up much-needed space in our reference collection. We did not remove the DDC numbers from the spine labels and relabel the books, as this was a pilot project, and we did not want to impose extra work on our technical services staff until we were sure it was necessary.

End-of-range signs with DDC numbers were replaced by signs with subject keywords. Shelf label signs were placed where each new topic started on the shelves. This new arrangement gave us the freedom to decide that no longer would attractive new reference books be shelved on the bottom, away from notice, just because that's where they fell in the DDC arrangement. Older sets such as *Essay and General Literature Index* were moved to the bottom and new books with attractive covers were placed on top, some with covers facing out. Additional new books were displayed on easels and on a handsome display shelf no longer needed in another part of the library.

We checked all the RUSA Best Free Reference Web Sites lists, keeping the sites that were still operational and free and classifying them into the same keywords we had used for the books. We then laminated and posted signs with these Web site listings near the related books. We also added onto the Web site signs the applicable online databases and e-book titles in our collection, allowing us to tap into the cross-marketing potential of our arrangement and to highlight all of our resources. This helped both staff and patrons to focus informational searches. We designed a new brochure with the RUSA Best Free Reference Web Sites for distribution to our patrons, and we are in the process of adding these to our Web site.

Though reference staff has not yet taken the step of allowing our reference books to circulate, we have put up signs offering to copy ten pages free for patrons. We have the same policy on our online catalogs that connect to our databases. We are hoping this gives people the "permission" they seem sometimes to need even to consider looking at reference books. All of this was done in the spirit of adventure. Most of the collection was rearranged in one weekend, and the Web sites/e-books/databases posters were placed during the following week.

Reactions

During the next few months, we felt free to rearrange what seemed to be hindering rather than helping people's use of the collection. We had so many books on display, for instance, that people who tried to consult reference books had no place to put them down in order to read them. Remedying this situation was quite easy, by cutting down on the number of display books.

While some staff found this new arrangement liberating and empowering, it was mystifying for some of our long-term staff members who had struggled to learn DDC, were now comfortable with it, and were not able to adjust easily to the keyword way of thinking when it comes to print materials. To help with this issue, we created a list of all of the subjects in their shelf order and put in the exact titles of the most used books in their new places in the order. We were resistant to creating this list at first, but we decided that perhaps it would serve as an interim measure to help staff adjust to a new way of thinking. We may also place additional spine labels on each book with the relevant keyword. We have welcomed staff suggestions for alternative arrangements, where they feel a different subject placement would serve users better.

Everyone loves the displays, and patrons have been especially appreciative of the new arrangement, with one patron remarking that we had "doubled the value of the library." There has been much interest in the listings of reliable Web sites, and much more browsing of beautiful reference books, some of which we have had for years while they have gone unnoticed. For instance, staff has repeatedly brought the *Dictionary of Imaginary Places* back to our area from other parts of the library. Before this project, it had languished on the shelf since 2000. It is clear that we have introduced reference books as recreational reading, and we are now considering establishing a comfortable seating area near the reference shelves.

For the first time, everyone is talking about the reference collection. The impacts on budget (almost none, as most of our materials were already in the library) and staff time have been minimal compared to the thought-provoking staff reactions and to the rejuvenation of a stodgy collection. We encourage others to experiment with the venerable reference collection. We also benefited from the support of our library director, who sends some staff to attend conferences each year and who considers the application of a new idea gained at these conferences to be a good return on investment.

Assessment

Our main goal was to make sure that all users of the reference collection are aware of all resources available and are introduced to them all in one place.

Though we are certain that everyone is noticing our reference collection, we would like to assess if this new awareness has resulted in an increase in its usage.

Our means of statistically based assessment are imperfect. We cannot measure the checkouts of reference books, as we do not allow them to be checked out. However, we can measure the in-house use, and to that end we placed collection baskets throughout our reference shelves imploring patrons not to shelve their materials but to place them in the baskets for us to tally. We do not get full compliance with this request, but it does provide us with some numbers. We can thus compare the six-month period May–October 2008 with the same period in 2007 (see Table 18.1).

Our reference checkout statistics, as extracted from our Horizon catalog, provide two measures: Reference Out-House (OH), reflecting usage where patrons must identify themselves and ask staff to provide the materials, usually from behind the reference desk, and Reference In-House (IH), reflecting the usage of general reference books by staff and patrons. Although overall use of reference books increased by only 5.9 percent, in-house use of reference books increased a significant 17.2 percent.

Even with these encouraging results, the reference team is continuing to explore ways to better market an integrated reference collection and to keep our resources relevant and foremost in our own and our patrons' minds.

Marketing Services

Farmington Public Library has served a multicultural community in the Four Corners area since 1921, comprised of a cultural climate that includes Spanish speakers and a diverse Native American population that includes the Navajo and Ute tribal nations. Since its inception, the library and its community have grown to over 100,000 people served by a collection of almost 200,000 items. After moving into a new, 50,000 square foot building in 2003, the library won New Mexico's Best New Building award for Interior and Best Lighting. Farmington

Table 18.1. Reference Collection Usage, 2007 and 2008

2007	May	June	July	August	September	October	Totals
Out of House	30	36	35	45	28	31	205
In House	119	109	131	82	108	144	693
2008	May	June	July	August	September	October	Totals
Out of House	25	23	17	26	24	24	139
In House	92	127	131	172	172	118	812

Public Library is unique in that it is a large, state-of-the-art facility housed in a relatively rural area; its community base includes the city of Farmington, with its population of roughly 40,000, and also the surrounding towns of Aztec, Bloomfield, and Shiprock. The entire branch system is made up of almost 200 employees who serve the main library as well as the libraries located in the other three towns.

Merchandising Reference Services

In taking a look at what role the library's reference desk will play in the twenty-first century, the Adult Services staff at Farmington Public Library sought ways to increase usage of our reference services, which include face-to-face reference transactions, telephone reference interviews, e-mail correspondence, and instant messaging (IM). In late 2007, when IM was first implemented, we set up a plan to repackage all four services into in one convenient unit, allowing us to reach our users at their point of need instead of waiting for them to come to us. In meeting this end, there have been many strategies that have proven most effective.

Make It Memorable

Our objective was to design a marketing initiative that would entice as many people as possible. This necessitated the design of an eye-catching Web page that would identify all four services in one convenient location, and library Web sites are frequently highlighted as an important resource for marketing virtual reference programs (MacDonald, van Duinkerken, & Stephens, 2008).

Adult Services staff members met to determine how we would devise an easily accessible and user-friendly Web site, which in turn spawned the discussion of a memorable logo, an icon that patrons could click on to access the page. It was decided that a logo in the shape of a puzzle piece with the slogan "Puzzled? Just Ask!" would have the best chance of sparking interest. Space and convenience issues on the Web page necessitated the shortening of the slogan to *Just Ask*, and thus the Just Ask puzzle piece was born. We put the logo in as many locations as possible to ensure both patrons and staff would see it. It has been found at the reference desk, worn by staff members, seen on the library's homepage, and, of course, featured on the Just Ask page, viewable at www.infoway.org/reference/justask.asp.

Promote Internally to Staff

Farmington Public Library does not have a lot of signage because we have encouraged our staff to act as "human signs" when talking with patrons. For this reason, it was more effective for our institution to promote Just Ask internally before introducing it to the public. To ensure staff members were on board, we used different methods to show the functionality of the service.

SHOW, DON'T TELL

To introduce Just Ask to staff, we held hands-on demonstration sessions within each department. We modeled the custom-cut puzzle piece pins we had purchased for staff to wear, showed them how to access Just Ask from the library's home-page, and demonstrated the usability of the Just Ask page by instant messaging a librarian through our interactive chat widget. Once staff saw firsthand what the Just Ask pins represented, they were better able to explain it in a way that made sense to patrons.

DEMONSTRATE THE FUNCTIONALITY AND RELEVANCE OF THE SERVICE

We also encouraged staff to promote our instant messaging feature through pro-motional items called Cordmen, little plastic figurines used to hold headphone cords. Each Cordman has our IM username on it to encourage people to add us as a buddy. It has been important for us to convey to staff that they need to demonstrate what the Cordmen represent instead of just handing them to patrons without explanation. Cordmen were thus placed behind the service desks to enable staff members to start a conversation with patrons about IM and Just Ask.

REVISIT AND REITERATE AS NECESSARY

Once a service has been successfully implemented, it is helpful to periodically revisit promotional avenues with staff members. A prime opportunity to rein-force Just Ask occurred when staff members would gather every day about 15 minutes before opening for what we have dubbed "The Daily Show." We devised weekly trivia questions for staff that connected Just Ask with "Daily Show" announcements. As an example, one question involved finding out what the Cherry Blossom Festival celebrated, and a prize of free tea was given to the first staff member who approached with the correct answer while wearing his or her Just Ask pin. This encouraged staff to wear their pins, sparked their awareness of Just Ask, and provided them with further incentives to promote the service to patrons.

Promote Externally to Patrons

Once staff was on board, we concentrated on external promotion using the fol-lowing strategies.

KNOW YOUR AUDIENCE AND MEET THEM AT THEIR POINT OF NEED

Since we knew that college students could benefit from virtual reference services, we sought ways to reach this target demographic. Our local community college has its own radio station, and it proved a reliable medium. We highly recommend local radio interviews with librarians. Such opportunities allow us to do something both memorable and out of the ordinary and to ensure that library products and services will be better remembered outside of library walls. People are more likely to use a service when it becomes a necessity. For this reason, the timing of pro-motion is essential in meeting patrons at their point of need. Since our main radio audience was students, we waited until finals week to advertise Just Ask. Not surprisingly, we saw a large surge in use at a time when students were more likely to ask reference questions.

KEEP IT SIMPLE

We included an announcement of Just Ask in our monthly e-mail to teachers, since another target demographic included K–12 schools. When constructing these announcements, it is important to keep the syntax and diction as simple and direct as possible in order to make the message more memorable. To get the word out to the general public, we made similar announcements in our library newsletter and printed quick blurbs on our self-check receipts.

PROVIDE INCENTIVES TO USE LIBRARY SERVICES

As a public library, we reach out to the families in our community through what are known as "Prime Time" sessions. In these gatherings, we provide the incentive of a free dinner to discuss how the library can benefit them as a community. Each session includes calling the reference desk on speakerphone, library "commercials," and story readings for children. Due to the wide scope of "Prime Time," each host wore a Just Ask pin and gave out Cordmen to guests. A couple of hosts even opted to demonstrate the Just Ask page. Similar demonstrations of this nature were also given to our local Rotary Club. In essence, Farmington Public Library aims to provide incentives for potential patrons to use services by focusing on *their* needs and making the library about *them*.

Assessment

With any new initiative, it is important to monitor progress. Since October 2007, we have been measuring the use of Just Ask via IM, seen in the Table 18.2.

The exchanges classified under "IM" represent patron communication with the desk via instant messenger applications such as America Online (AIM), Yahoo, and Windows Live. The "Plugoo" interactions represent a different demographic who chose the interactive Plugoo chat widget, an Internet-based window that allowed them to communicate instantly via the library's Web page. The table indicates that the latter method was preferred. Surges in IM use, such as those seen in November and March, occurred after we revisited our Just Ask promotion efforts and reintroduced the service to staff. Due to the recent nature of this project, we are still in the process of exploring other methods of assessing its effectiveness.

Conclusion

These two projects, and the way they have been marketed, showcase two different initiatives that are producing similar results in terms of an upswing in usage of reference collections and services, with proven appeal to their communities.

Table 18.2. Comparison of IM to Plugoo Use by Time of Day, Late 2007–Early 2008									
	9 a.m.–11 a.m.		11 a.m.–1 p.m.		1 p.m.–3 p.m.		3 p.m.–5 p.m.		5 p.m.–9 p.m.	
DATE	IM	Plugoo	IM	Plugoo	IM	Plugoo	IM	Plugoo	IM	Plugoo
Oct. 2007	0	1	0	1	1	1	2	2	0	4
Nov. 2007	2	3	0	5	2	2	0	5	1	4
Dec. 2007	0	3	0	1	0	2	0	2	0	4
Jan. 2008	1	2	0	2	0	1	2	0	0	0
Feb. 2008	1	0	0	3	1	2	0	0	1	1
Mar. 2008	0	3	0	0	0	0	1	1	1	2
Apr. 2008	0	1	1	0	0	0	0	1	0	1
May 2008	0	1	1	1	0	6	0	6	0	3
Jun. 2008	0	1	1	3	0	2	0	4	1	2
Jul. 2008	0	3	0	3	2	5	6	7	0	2
Aug. 2008	1	3	0	1	0	5	2	4	1	5
Sep. 2008	0	1	0	2	2	1	0	2	0	1
TOTAL	5	22	3	22	8	27	13	34	5	29
Grand Total: 168									

References

Anhang, A., & Coffman, S. The great reference debate. *American Libraries*, *33*(3), 50–54.

Dickinson, J. B., & George, S. E. (2006). The Ames Library: A model for collection integration. In A. Fenner (Ed.), *Integrating print and digital resources in library collections* (pp. 167–179). Binghamton, NY: The Haworth Press.

Levrault, B. R. (2006). Integration in academic reference departments: From print to digital resources. In A. Fenner (Ed.), *Integrating print and digital resources in library collections* (pp. 21–36). Binghamton, NY: The Haworth Press.

MacDonald, K. I., van Duinkerken, W., & Stephens, J. (2008). It's all in the marketing: The impact of a virtual reference marketing campaign at Texas A&M University. *Reference & User Services Quarterly*, *47*, 375–386.

Polanka, S. (2008). Off the shelf: A view from the top. *Booklist*, *104*, 130.

Subject Listings. (2007). *2008 Library Journal reference supplement*, *132*, 13–58.

Weinberger, D. (2007). *Everything is miscellaneous: The power of the new digital disorder*. New York: Times Books.

Staff Development and Training

CHAPTER 19

Utilizing New Staff Training Initiatives to Develop and Implement Reference Competencies at the University of Nevada, Las Vegas Libraries

Victoria Nozero and Sidney Lowe

Overview

Building on an orientation program established by the University of Nevada, Las Vegas (UNLV) Libraries' Human Resources unit for all new employees, the Research and Information Department developed a training and orientation program for new employees who participate in the reference desk service pool. A task force composed of service pool members created a checklist of expectations that led to a new mission statement and core values for the department as well as a time line for training new employees. The use of a staff wiki to provide access to the expectations, time line, and other resources is explored. Assessment mechanisms, adjustments to the program, and future plans are detailed.

Introduction

The University of Nevada, Las Vegas is located on a 350-acre campus and is classified in the category of a high research activity university by the Carnegie Foundation for the Advancement of Teaching. UNLV is an urban commuter institution of 28,000 students, 3,300 faculty and staff, and offers more than 220 undergraduate, master's, and doctoral degree programs ("Best Colleges," 2008). Lied Library, the 300,000 square-foot main campus library at UNLV, opened for business in January of 2001, replacing an outdated and much smaller facility.

Like many new academic libraries, it was designed to be not only an attractive and comfortable space for students but also the place for UNLV's faculty and students to access information resources and services for their research and learning, both in person and virtually.

At Lied Library, providing services to meet the needs and expectations of a new generation of techno-savvy users included implementing chat and e-mail reference, acquiring electronic databases across the curriculum, and establishing two full-service reference desks on separate floors of the library. The reference service pool is a diverse group of 30 members comprised of librarians, para-professionals, students, and volunteers from library departments outside of the public service realm. The skills and experiences of these individuals vary widely, and previous training efforts primarily consisted of a combination of on-the-job learning by "shadowing" at the reference desk and informal guidance from experienced reference staff.

Process

Soon after moving into Lied Library in 2001, the Human Resources unit worked with supervisors to develop an orientation checklist for supervisors of new employees. Similar to checklists developed by other libraries, included in UNLV Libraries checklist were activities to be completed prior to the arrival of the new employee, such as preparation of the workspace, installation of phone lines, obtaining an e-mail account and appropriate keys, and acquisition of necessary office supplies (Rogers, 1994). Also included in the checklist are various policies and procedures that need to be imparted to new employees, such as leave policies, holidays, and annual evaluations. In addition, supervisors are to discuss performance expectations and introduce the new employee to their colleagues in their own units and to other colleagues in other departments and divisions. For librarians, the checklist includes meetings with the Library Faculty Moderator, Tenure and Promotion Committee, and Merit Advisory Committee. Meetings with the campus Human Resources staff to explain and select health and retirement benefits are required for both librarians and support staff.

After the creation of a staff wiki in 2007, separate orientation pages for support staff and librarians were created that explain the different policies that apply to each category of employee. Links to relevant staff and campus Web pages are also provided. Supervisors are expected to socialize new employees into the culture and values of the organization. As described by Ballard and Blessing (2006), successful socialization into the organization "may indicate a new employee's job satisfaction and influence his or her longevity in the organization" (p. 240).

However, the orientation for new employees is very generic and intended for all new employees, regardless of their position in the libraries' organizational structure or their responsibilities. The progressively complex levels of knowledge and skills needed to provide excellent user services necessitated a new emphasis on staff development for the Research and Information (R&I) Department of Lied Library. After five new entry level librarians and staff were hired within a period of two years, the department identified the need for a more formalized orientation program to include organized and consistent basic training in reference services and resources for its new employees. Ballard and Blessing (2006), citing an article by Claudia Reinhardt (1988), go on to say that organized and consistent orientation programs have been shown to "prevent performance problems, instill positive attitudes about the organization, and pave the way for better communication between the supervisor and the new employee" (as cited in Ballard & Blessing, 2006, p. 241). Certainly these are all goals an organization has in mind when a new employee is hired. Orientation programs, if they are well thought out, relevant, objective, and consistent can make the socialization of new employees successful for both the employees and the organization.

There were additional motivations for the growing movement toward an orientation initiative. Results from the national LibQual survey indicated that there were perceived patron service weaknesses to be addressed, particularly in the area of "knowledgeable staff." R&I management decided to address this gap between user expectations and perceptions first through a better orientation program for new employees.

The New Staff/Volunteer Training Task Force, composed of volunteers from the service pool, was formed to organize an orientation program. The charge of the task force included several elements, and its underlying principle was that the desk staff were expected to be customer oriented and also to be knowledgeable about UNLV, the libraries, and its policies and information resources. The group was charged with preparing a checklist of the skills and knowledge base expected of new R&I service pool members. The pool consists of several categories of staff that provide reference services, and it was initially thought that there should be a separate checklist for each staff category. The task force was also charged with recommending methods for training new service pool staff to acquire the skills and knowledge defined in the checklist and for developing an objective means to determine when participants reached the desired levels of competency.

The task force began meeting regularly to work on its assignment, and it started by breaking down the components of the charge and then dividing the labor among its members. A literature review was conducted for benchmarking other academic libraries in the area of orientation to identify and adopt the best practices. Contacts were made with other libraries, who shared their reference checklists, standards, and competencies, and the group began to develop the UNLV Libraries' checklist of expectations for its new employees. As members of the task force began to work on the checklist, it became apparent that the group's charge should be amended to reflect the realities of our organization.

Although there are several categories of staff that work on the two reference desks, the differences between services provided at each of the service desks were greater than the differences of expectations between staff categories. The separate desks are distinguished principally by their physical surroundings. The first floor R&I desk is centrally located in a high traffic area close to the library's Information Commons and the noncirculating reference stacks, and it also shares space with the Computer Help Desk. Reference questions range from quick directional and informational queries to in-depth research assistance, and desk staff also handle overflow computer help questions. The second floor desk is situated near the current and bound periodicals, government publication stacks, and the majority of the library's microform collections with their scanner/printer stations. Much of the patron service at this desk includes hands-on assistance with these unique tools and materials. The task force members decided that it would be more beneficial for new employees to work from *one* expectations checklist with sections for each of the two desks listing the fundamental skills for *all* categories of staff. Additional sections of the checklist included resources, policies, customer service, and equipment and facilities. A copy of the R&I Department's general checklist for participation in the service pool is provided as Table 19.1.

The checklist was at first the primary product of the task force's efforts, but there was an unexpected outcome in the evolution of their work process. As the customer service component of the checklist was developed, the need for clarifying

Table 19.1. Research and Information Service Pool Expectations			
Resources	**Policies**	**Customer Service**	**Equipment and Facilities**
Be aware of key library services and collections of the Lied Library and the UNLV branch libraries.	Know how to find the UNLV Libraries' policies and procedures, including those of the various library departments.	Adhere to the American Library Association's Guidelines for Behavioral Performance of Reference and Information Service Providers (RUSA Reference Guidelines). These can be found at www.ala.org/ala/rusa/rusaprotools/referenceguide/guidelinesbehavioral.htm.	Know the basic functions of the R & I desk telephones, including transferring calls, forwarding, and retrieving and deleting voicemail messages.
Possess a general working knowledge of the location and accessibility of libraries' electronic, media, and print resources.	Know the location of Computer Guest Use Policy and Guidelines.	Acknowledge patrons who are waiting for assistance.	Have basic knowledge and locations of copiers, printers, and scanners.
			(Continued)

Table 19.1. Research and Information Service Pool Expectations *(Continued)*			
Resources	**Policies**	**Customer Service**	**Equipment and Facilities**
Be able to navigate the UNLV Libraries' Web site to retrieve information.	Be able to locate resources or make appropriate referrals when library policy issues arise.	Know where to find subject/liaison librarian contact information on the libraries' Web page.	Know how to use the print system to "push" print jobs for patrons when necessary.
Know how to locate and search databases linked from the homepage of the UNLV Libraries' Web site.	Be aware of the current policy regarding guest researchers, visiting faculty, and unaffiliated patrons with specific research needs.	Know the basic functions of chat reference, e-mail reference, and where to enter statistics data.	Be familiar with and follow the established procedures for reporting technical problems and/or equipment malfunctions.
Know how to locate course reserves, both physical and electronic reserve materials.	Know that any patron specifically requesting government information must be given access to both print and onlIne government publications.	Know where the off-desk reference statistics database resides and how to enter statistics data.	Know when and how to contact UNLV Libraries' security staff.
Be able to conduct basic and modified searches on the libraries' online catalog.		Provide referrals and/or directions to other service points when R & I is not the appropriate contact.	
Know how to find information on style guides for citing references (APA, MLA, and Chicago).			
Know the locations of print and electronic handouts and flyers.			
Have the ability to use Pharos Remote to send print jobs to printers.			
Meet with the designated computer help desk trainer to learn the basics of the computer help desk operations, public computers, and FAQs.			

Note: This table presents the basic skills and knowledge expectations for all participants in the UNLV Libraries' Research and Information Service Pool. After an initial orientation and training period, all participants in the UNLV Libraries' Research and Information Service Pool are expected to have full competency in each category.

the department's vision emerged. A new mission statement was written, vetted with the service pool and disseminated to staff and patrons by placing it on the departmental Web page, and the task force also developed a set of core values that characterized its underlying service principles. The task force believed that a clear statement of the mission and core values of the department that was shared with employees at an early stage in their tenure with the organization was an important element in the socialization of new employees.

In addition to the checklist, the task force also developed other training tools. An orientation plan and timeline was developed that was divided into a set of training sessions designed so that the new employee would learn new processes in a logical sequence of learning. One task force member worked on a frequently asked questions (FAQ) knowledge base, and another developed a referral List. The latter was a list of identified library "experts" in specific subject areas for in-depth research assistance or who were responsible for specific library tasks or processes for patron referrals from the reference desk.

As the group worked on the new employee orientation plan, it became clear that these training tools would also be useful for experienced service pool members as well as other library staff. The UNLV Libraries' staff wiki was an excellent place to house the checklist and other tools, so a department wiki was created. The department's orientation and training documents were posted on the wiki, along with links to useful resources such as video clips of reference interviewing techniques and the American Library Association's Reference and User Association's *Guidelines for Behavioral Performance of Reference and Information Service Providers* (Ward et al., 2004). Since wikis allow for relatively easy editing, it was simple for the task force to contribute additional tools and to update them as needed. In addition, use of the wiki allowed access to all service pool members for maintaining their own skill levels.

The training and orientation tools of the task force were tested by three new employees, and the group was interested in evaluating the results of their efforts. In his library training guide, Bruce Massis (2004) lists key questions that an evaluation team should ask participants to determine the effects of the training program. Some of these are the following:

- Is the training content accurate and relevant to the participants' jobs?
- Is the training information presented well by the instructor?
- Is the training timely (not too early or too late)?
- Did the participants retain what they learned?
- Are the participants applying what they learned back on the job? If not, why?
- Do the work processes allow the participants to apply what they learned? (p. 58)

The initial assessment efforts of the R&I Department included creating an orientation completion checklist on a spreadsheet that would allow for trainers and new employees to check off and date their assigned tasks and objectives. Upon completion, new staff were then interviewed to assess their competency level and orientation experience. This feedback approach was valuable for modifying future training initiatives, and there was much room for improvement. For example, the timeline has been changed to allow related items to be grouped together in a more coherent manner, the spreadsheet has been made available to the new employees, and staff changes have required changes in trainers.

In measuring the success of a training program, the question of retention of the content is an important one. Massis referred to Hermann Ebbinghaus's work in evaluation and learning theory when he stated that "people forget 90 percent of what they learn in a class within thirty days" (as cited in Massis, 2004, p. 59). He then stressed the vital importance for staff training program participants to immediately apply what they have learned in their work setting (Massis, 2004). To reinforce the information new employees are receiving through the formalized orientation program, new R&I staff begin shadowing at the service desks with experienced librarians in order to see what they have learned in action.

Retention of information is a driving force for future R&I Department training and orientation initiatives. The UNLV Libraries' R&I task force plans to add a requirement to its orientation program that provides for recertification of the entire service pool on a regular basis. An ongoing training program is being developed that includes online modules, library guides and tutorials, hands-on training sessions, regular maintenance of the service pool's core competencies, and additional resources for the wiki pages.

Conclusion

While the process followed in creating the Research and Information Department's orientation program was time consuming and difficult, the benefits far outweighed these concerns. First, involving staff at an early stage allowed the task force to address some issues that had long been of concern to management, such as the development of core values and application of the expectations to all staff, not just new hires. However, one major obstacle has been discovered: it is difficult to maintain the same momentum over a long period of time, especially when a project is outside the regular job responsibilities of those involved. Another issue confronted by management has been the slowdown in the hiring of new staff. Keeping an orientation program vital and effective when no new staff is being hired is a major challenge. To address some of these concerns, department and division managers are now looking at ways to provide training to new and continuing staff using self-paced tutorials and/or screencasting.

As is true of any staff training program, new staff orientation is not static or ever really complete. It is inherently a program that needs constant and systematic review and revision. We do feel, however, that our process of involving staff early in the development of staff expectations and a consistent orientation/training program is beneficial to everyone involved and can be effective in socializing new staff and providing research assistance and customer service that meets or exceeds user expectations.

References

Ballard, A., & Blessing, L. (2006). Organizational socialization through employee orientations at North Carolina State University Libraries. *College & Research Libraries*, *67*(3), 240–248.

Best colleges: University of Nevada–Las Vegas. (2008, November 3). *U.S. News & World Report*. Retrieved April 17, 2009, from http://colleges.usnews.rankingsandreviews.com/college/items/2569.

Massis, B. E. (2004). *The practical library trainer*. Binghamton, NY: The Haworth Press.

Reinhardt, C. (1988, June). Training supervisors in first-day orientation techniques. *Personnel*, *65*, 24, 26, 28.

Rogers, S. L. (1994). Orientation for new library employees: A checklist. *Library Administration & Management*, *8*(4), 213–217.

Ward, D., et al. (2004). *Guidelines for behavioral performance of information service providers*. Chicago: American Library Association. Retrieved April 16, 2009, from http://ala.org/ala/mgrps/divs/rusa/resources/guidelines/guidelinesbehavioral.cfm.

Additional Readings

Block, K. J., & Kelly, J. A. (2001). Integrating informal professional development into the work of reference. *The Reference Librarian*, *34*(72), 207–217.

Hacker, C. A. (2004). New employee orientation: Make it pay dividends for years to come. *Information Systems Management*, *21*(1), 89–92.

Weingart, S. J., Kochan, C. A., & Hedrick, A. (1998). Safeguarding your investment: Effective orientation for new employees. *Library Administration & Management*, *12*(3), 156–158.

CHAPTER 20

Reference Training through a Co-mentoring Program

Louise Klusek and Christopher Tuthill

Overview

While many reference training programs focus on mentoring or coaching, Newman Library's program for new reference librarians is built on a co-mentoring model that encourages collaboration, mutual support, and reflection on day-to-day encounters at the reference desk. Mentoring has a long history of helping new employees transfer knowledge, manage their careers, and develop other job-related skills. Research by Kram (1985) showed that peer mentoring achieves many of the same goals as traditional mentoring and is more likely to be available to professionals. New mentoring models, as outlined in Piktialis and Greenes (2008), include group-based approaches such as peer group mentoring and facilitated group mentoring. Our program is led by a group of peers of varying ages, experience, and educational background, and is facilitated by the head of reference. In peer group mentoring, peers with similar learning needs are brought together and mentor one another. Our focus is on the development of reference librarianship skills and the fostering of relationships among working professionals new to the field. This chapter gives an overview of the program, outlines its structure, and includes outcomes based on interviews and a written survey from the members of the program.

Like many other academic libraries, Newman Library at Baruch College historically did not have a formally structured program of reference training for newly hired librarians. In 2006 when we needed to integrate a group of new librarians into our staff, we decided to establish a training program with a twofold focus: the development of librarianship skills and the fostering of relationships among working professionals new to the field. We developed a program based on "co-mentoring" or peer-group mentoring, a teaching and learning model that is different from both the top-down mode of supervisor and subordinate and the one-on-one relationship of mentor and mentee. In peer group mentoring, peers with similar learning needs are brought together and mentor one another. They set the learning agenda and share their knowledge. All members are givers and receivers in a relationship where they are guides for one another.

We also decided that ours would be a facilitated group. Because our peer group would consist of new librarians, they would meet in a group led by a facilitator, the head of reference, who would guide the learning process.

Introduction

Mentoring has a long history in the business world going back as far as the apprenticeship model where the mentor was trainer and role model. The key purpose was to facilitate the transfer of knowledge. As broadly and traditionally defined,

> Mentorship is a dynamic, reciprocal relationship in a work environment between an advanced career incumbent (mentor) and a novice (mentee) aimed at promoting the career development of both. Mentoring encourages a mentee to manage his own career growth, maximize his potential, develop his skills, and improve his performance. (Piktialis & Greenes, 2008, p. 47)

A framework for understanding mentoring relationships in the workplace was first described in an influential study by Kathy E. Kram published in the book *Mentoring at Work* (1985). Kram identified the functions served in a mentoring relationship and outlined the phases a typical mentorship followed. Kram's study of the traditional mentoring relationship also found that many new professionals reported the importance of peers to their career development. In a subsequent study of the role of peers, Kram and Isabella (1985) found that peer mentoring provided an alternative to traditional mentoring, achieved many of the same objectives, and was more likely to be available to professionals. Peer mentoring resulted in an increased sense of competence and confidence in the participants' professional roles (Kram & Isabella, 1985). In addition, peer mentoring facilitated a wide range of career-enhancing and psychosocial functions including some that were not found in traditional mentor-mentee relationships. Psychosocial roles pertain to the interpersonal aspects of mentoring. The role of peers in these aspects mirrors that of traditional mentors in providing confirmation, emotional support, and personal feedback. The role of peers in career-enhancing functions is different because it focuses on information sharing and job-related feedback rather than providing sponsorship, protection, exposure, or coaching—the commonly recognized functions of a mentor.

Today the traditional one-on-one mentoring relationship is no longer the only mentoring model. New approaches to mentoring are being promoted in response to changes in the workplace that often include a flatter management structure that encourages teamwork and collaboration. Characteristics of the new generation of workers, called the Millennials or Generation Y, who want constant feedback and prefer learning that is team based, also encourage new mentoring models. Piktialis and Greenes (2008) delineated the ways in which knowledge transfer methods in today's companies are influenced by differences in learning styles among generations. The report suggests that mentoring relationships no longer need to be hierarchical but can be modeled on a group-based approach that has generations working together. Two popular approaches outlined in the report are peer group mentoring and facilitated group mentoring. In peer group mentoring, groups of self-directed and self-managed individuals set their own learning agenda so that they benefit from the knowledge, expertise, and experience of one another. In a facilitated group, the members share a mentor who provides direction and feedback.

Literature Review

An Association of Research Libraries (ARL) survey (Wittkopf, 1999) looked at the characteristics of 113 formal mentoring programs in academic libraries. They found that the primary purpose for mentoring programs was to provide guidance for reappointment, tenure, and promotion. Knowledge transfer or training was not identified as a goal in any of the programs. The study also did not identify any program where peers mentored professional staff.

Our examination of the literature on mentoring in academic libraries found that there has been little research on the use of peer mentoring for knowledge transfer or training. Dankert and Dempsey (2002) wrote a case study of the peer-to-peer reference training program at DePaul University, but its focus seemed to be on facilitating communication among campus libraries. Peer mentoring in academic libraries has most often been studied in terms of peer coaching, a practice borrowed from the field of education and frequently used as a training model by teachers in secondary education. Peer coaching is often focused on changing specific behaviors or helping a partner achieve specific performance goals. Also, coaching is usually applied in a partnership, not a group setting. A few studies in academic library settings report on peer coaching in reference: to raise awareness of behaviors specific to the reference interview (Arthur, 1990), and as a formative assessment technique in reference teaching (Vidmar, 2005).

Our Program of Co-mentoring

Prior to 2006, Newman library provided a training program for new librarians that was probably typical of many programs at small-sized to medium-sized academic libraries. New librarians shadowed more experienced librarians at the reference desk, met with the head of reference to discuss the library's mission and reference philosophy, and worked through rules and practices posted in our reference wiki, our online reference handbook. Librarians also attended an in-house professional development seminar each January, and a portion of every division meeting was devoted to some type of training, usually a demonstration of a new database or a discussion of a best practice. When several retirements meant that we would start the new school year with a group of new librarians, we knew we couldn't give them the one-on-one attention and coaching that had been the usual practice. We took the opportunity to develop a formal training program specifically designed to meet the special challenges that new librarians would be certain to meet working in reference at the library of an urban public university in the center of Manhattan offering both graduate and undergraduate degrees, chiefly in business but in a variety of other fields as well. The multiplicity of curricular offerings at Baruch (in the Zicklin School of Business, the Weissman School of Arts and Sciences, and the School of Public Affairs) requires multifaceted library-reference support. That said, the fact that about 80 percent of our 11,000 undergraduates are business majors and our largest graduate programs are also in the Zicklin School of Business means that all of our librarians, regardless of their educational background, need a basic knowledge of the sources and methods of business research.

Goals of the Program

What was most important to us in developing goals for our training program were two developmental functions known to be fostered by peer mentoring: information sharing and emotional support. Since we would be working with librarians who were just establishing their careers rather than ones at midcareer, we did not want a mentoring program that focused on leadership skills. Neither were we concerned with mentoring for tenure or promotion because our library system had several programs in place to address issues of tenure and to support research and publication. We wanted to give new librarians the opportunity to build knowledge and skills and do it in a collaborative environment. We knew that new librarians needed on-the-job training in the behavioral standards of reference: approachability, interest, and listening/inquiring skills. They also needed to develop a thorough knowledge of the library's sources and collections and the confidence to know how to approach complex research questions inside and outside of their areas of subject expertise. And because our reference philosophy statement emphasizes the importance of being "teaching librarians," we wanted our new librarians to understand how students learn and how librarians teach at a reference desk.

We did not lose sight of the necessary focus on knowledge transfer essential to any effective mentoring program. But with co-mentoring we established an equally serious focus on constructing and developing peer relationships. What are co-mentors? Co-mentors are close colleagues in a mutual mentorship. Co-mentors engage in dialogue and form networks (Rymer, 2002). Five librarians formed the original co-mentoring group in the spring semester of 2007. There were large differences in the age and experience of the members. There were recent MLS graduates new to the profession as well as experienced librarians who were new to Newman Library. The range of reference experience also varied widely. Librarians came from all divisions of the library, and some were new to reference, being specialists in metadata, cataloging, and archives. Only one, our new business librarian, reported having much experience with the kinds of business questions we get at Baruch. Other librarians had advanced degrees in fields as diverse as art history, geography, computer science, and English.

Structure of the Program

How is the co-mentoring program structured? The group meets every two weeks for an hour with the head of reference for an informal, semistructured discussion or activity. Typically the discussion covers approaches to types of reference questions, reviews of new reference sources, or practices for teaching in a reference context. The focus is on the reference transaction as American Library Association's Reference and Users Services Association (RUSA) (2007) has recently defined it: "Reference transactions are information consultations in which library staff recommend, interpret, evaluate, and/or use information sources to help others meet their particular information needs." The immediate goal is to have the librarians share information that would help them perform well in information consultations whether at the reference desk, in a student conference, or in e-mail or chat reference.

Before each meeting, members write an essay about a recent personal experience in reference. These essays can be about "success stories," difficult situations, unresolved research queries, or musings on alternative approaches to a question or questioner (see Appendix 20.1). The guiding principle is to encourage reflection about reference events and to share interesting experiences. These essays, sometimes read aloud by volunteers, drive the agenda of many of the meetings. Situations described in the essays often lead the group to analyze alternative approaches or compare sources. At other times they form the basis of an extended case study that is used to discuss best practices. The essays also prompt co-mentoring sessions that are structured as formal instruction where subject specialists from inside or outside the group are invited to teach or make a presentation.

The group determines the length of time we devote to a subject. We have tackled several subjects in depth over two or more meetings. One example was our exploration of issues related to accounting literature. After a member wrote an essay on the problems of helping students with a class assignment dealing with the subject of financial audits, we invited our accounting librarian to talk to us about the accounting literature and how auditing standards, as well as other accounting norms, are set. Following that session, one of our group librarians prepared a demonstration of key accounting databases. The final meeting dealing with this subject entailed a working session on a typical student assignment. In another ad-hoc unit of multisession meetings, we worked through various approaches to a frequent student assignment: the company/industry case study. For this we read Michael Porter's articles on the theory of five forces that drive competitive strategy, worked through our own SWOT (strengths, weaknesses, opportunities, and threats) analysis, and reviewed several business databases in depth including Standard and Poor's NetAdvantage and Euromonitor's GMID (Global Market Information Database).

Role of the Facilitator

Our peer mentoring program is a facilitated one, with the head of reference as the group facilitator. The main reason why we chose the facilitator model, and made a supervisor the facilitator, is that research shows that supervisor support influences whether employees take advantage of learning opportunities and apply new learning on the job (Tannenbaum, 1997). The facilitator has many roles, most obviously the planning role of providing structure, although this must be accomplished in large part through the direction and input of the members. But his or her principal role is active, ad-hoc intervention: to stimulate discussion, to be the "learning leader," and to encourage active participation by all the members of the group. The facilitator should be ready to initiate active learning methods including setting up teams or pairing members to lead discussion sessions. She should encourage brainstorming by the group. In one of our sessions about how to research the e-garbage industry, the employment of active-intervention techniques by the facilitator led to a wide ranging discussion of the best ways to identify industry experts, local environmental organizations, and government agencies.

In addition to setting the structure and operating as a catalyst for discussion, the facilitator, in our case, also promotes the sharing of group discoveries with the entire reference staff by encouraging members to post their experiences on the library's reference blog, Reference at Newman. In addition, the facilitator schedules meetings, acts as an interface and promotes the program with library administration, and ensures that the objectives of the program are being met in such a manner as to satisfy the stated goals of the college administration for the library.

Outcomes: The Program from the Point of View of the Participating Librarians

In order to assess how the co-mentoring program was working, one of the authors, a member of the peer group, interviewed all of the participants in individual open-ended sessions and by written questionnaire (see Appendix 20.2). We wanted to find out how the members felt about the program, and we also wanted to see if any of the career-enhancing or psychosocial functions that are typical of peer mentoring were realized in our co-mentoring group. We found that all the members cited the career-enhancing function of information sharing as one of the main benefits of the program. Many, but not all, of the members reported that they appreciated the personal feedback and the friendships that developed. All of the members, in one way or another, expressed that they were pleased that the program gave them a mechanism by which to gauge their progress in relation to that of their colleagues. As one librarian said, "The exercises and discussion allowed you to compare and gauge where you are in relation to your peers." This was echoed by another librarian who said the meetings "helped you to see how you were doing in relation to everyone else." Another librarian noted that the program allowed her to "learn from experienced colleagues how to interpret and answer reference questions. It motivated me to extend my knowledge and abilities." Other members said that "it was good to hear about others' experiences" and that "the program, as well as working with these colleagues at the desk, helped us to become friends."

Even for librarians who joined the co-mentoring group with previous reference experience, the program proved useful. These librarians reported that they were exposed to sources that they would not have otherwise used, and in some cases were not familiar with at all. Databases that were mentioned by librarians as being new to them, as well as being particularly helpful, included EDGAR I-Metrix, a database of SEC filings and financial data, and RIA Checkpoint, a tax research database. Librarians also singled out the sessions on how to read a 10-K report, how to conduct a SWOT analysis, and the introduction to GAAP (generally accepted accounting principles) and the accounting literature as particularly beneficial. They reported satisfaction that they were able to use in their work at the reference desk what they had learned in the mentoring program. Several reported that their anxiety at working with business questions decreased as the semester progressed and they became more familiar with using the sources introduced in the group sessions.

The members commented on not only what they had learned but on how they had learned. The essays written and discussed in the sessions "helped reinforce what we were doing at the desk," according to one librarian. They said the group work was "very helpful" and that "the group work would sometimes focus on an essay question or a new resource [allowing] us to collaborate on questions in an informal, collegial setting." All of the librarians mentioned the reference blog as a tool that helped them keep current. One librarian noted that his having been encouraged to follow up questions with blog posts "helped us share as much information as possible." In summary, as one librarian wrote, "If I encounter a reference question that has been discussed in our sessions, I feel more confident and comfortable. More importantly, it [the program] helped me develop strategies and approaches when I encounter typical or difficult reference questions. It helped me make good judgments."

Outcomes: The Program from the Point of View of the Facilitator

The facilitator looked at the program from a slightly different angle. She appreciated the emphasis that the program put on reference and the development of reference skills. It gave her a venue to meet regularly with her new staff. She saw how the program encouraged librarians to value reflection on their day-to-day reference experiences, as librarians were eager to discuss reference situations with her inside and outside of the biweekly meetings. This showed that members had internalized the value of continuous learning in the workplace. More concretely, she saw an increase in postings to the library's reference blog as well as librarians reporting that they used the blog as a knowledge base.

The facilitator also saw the staff build a network of relationships. The sharing, supportive climate of the program seemed to spill over to a more positive work environment at the reference desk where librarians took learning seriously and were eager to share their knowledge with others. Teamwork became the norm.

Conclusion

We are now in our fifth semester of the co-mentoring program. We see the practical results of the program in the confidence and expertise shown by our new librarians in reference consultations. We are encouraged that the members report that the program has fostered a sense of community and mutual support.

Where do we go from here? All of the librarians who started with the group in its first year are still members, and we have added two new librarians. As retirements of experienced reference staff continue, and as new librarians arrive at Baruch, one hopes that "graduates" of our present co-mentoring program will naturally fill teaching and leadership roles to help the new arrivals. When learners help one another to learn, they become teachers, and over time they can become facilitators. It is our expectation and hope that our mentoring program will self-replicate and grow, eventually making reference service an operation of mind where teaching and learning become indistinguishable from one another.

References

Arthur, G. (1990). Peer coaching in a university reference department. *College & Research Libraries*, 51(4), 367–373.

Dankert, H. S., & Dempsey, P. R. (2002). Building reference strengths through peer training. *Reference Services Review*, 30(4), 349–354. doi:10.1108/00907320210451358.

Kram, K. E. (1985). *Mentoring at work: Developmental relationships in organizational life*. Glenview, IL: Scott Foresman.

Kram, K. E., & Isabella, L. A. (1985). Mentoring alternatives: The role of peer relationships in career development. *The Academy of Management Journal*, 28(1), 110–132. Retrieved November 6, 2008, from http://search.ebscohost.com/login.aspx?direct=true&db=buh&AN=4377106&loginpage=Login.asp&site=bsi-live.

Piktialis, D., & Greenes, K. A. (2008). *Bridging the gaps: How to transfer knowledge in today's multigenerational workplace.* New York: The Conference Board.

Rymer, J. (2002). Only connect: Transforming ourselves and our discipline through co-mentoring. *The Journal of Business Communication, 39*(3), 342–363. Retrieved November 6, 2008, from http://search.ebscohost.com/login.aspx?direct=true&db= buh&AN=7256702&loginpage=Login.asp&site=bsi-live.

Tannenbaum, S. I. (1997). Enhancing continuous learning: Diagnostic findings from multiple companies. *Human Resource Management, 36*(4), 437–452. doi: 10.1002/(SICI) 1099-050X(199724)36:4<437::AID-HRM7>3.0.CO;2-W.

Vidmar, D. J. (2005). Reflective peer coaching: Crafting collaborative self-assessment in teaching. *Research Strategies, 20*(3), 135–148. doi: 10.1016/j.resstr.2006.06.002.

Wittkopf, B. J. (1999). *Mentoring programs in ARL libraries: A SPEC kit.* Washington, DC: Association of Research Libraries.

Appendix 20.1. Essays from the Participants

Finding Primary Sources

A student came to the desk, looking for primary sources about Joseph Stalin of all types: books, correspondence, diaries, speeches, videos, photos, etc. I searched CUNY+ by author "Joseph Stalin," and got 15 records. Some of them are correspondence, some are books written by Stalin, and other records are not primary resources.

Stalin, Joseph, 1879–1953
Stalin, Joseph, 1879–1953—Correspondence

I also searched the databases Academic Search Premier and History Abstracts by author "Joseph Stalin" and found speeches and addresses by Stalin such as "Protect Armed Forces and Defensive Power," "Russia's War Achievements," etc. from "Vital speeches of the day." I used a search engine and typed "Stalin, primary sources" for online primary sources.

We found some photographs at the New York Public Library digital gallery (http://digitalgallery .nypl.org/nypldigital/index.cfm). Another Web site, "Joseph Stalin Biographical Chronicle," includes photos, audio speeches, and other primary sources (www.stel.ru/stalin).

Some tips I gave to the student for primary sources:

1. Search historical persons as authors rather than subjects (example, Stalin, Joseph).
2. If you do not have the name of an individual, search the library catalogs by topic and add the appropriate subheading to the subject heading: correspondence, diaries, interviews, personal narratives, speeches, etc.
3. Do a word search on your topic, limiting the results to items published during the relevant time frame.
4. Examine and understand the purpose of the Web site before relying on the information provided by a Web site.

Hunting for the Numbers: Census and Demographic Data

I had a visit from a graduate student yesterday who was looking for demographic data. She is in a marketing class and was scoping out a neighborhood in Brooklyn to find an appropriate place for opening a business. She was quite resigned, as she had searched Google thoroughly and could find only reports that she would have to buy, and they were much too expensive. Was there any-place else she could go?

Could this be the cliché library example of the student who thinks the sum of the world's knowl-edge (at least the stuff worth looking at) is trapped underneath the blinking Google search box? That was my initial thought, as I put the question to her, "Who would create demographic data?" Once we answered this, I was able to guide her to the sources—the U.S. Census Bureau, who initially collects and compiles the data, and the NYC Department of Planning, who processes the data and recompiles it for New York neighborhoods (as the census bureau wouldn't release data specifically for these areas). She expressed surprise when we went to the NYC page, as she had gone there frequently to get building permit data (she works in construction) but would have never thought to look for population data there. We also paid a visit to the NYC Department of Health's homepage, where they compile census and health survey data for all of the neighbor-hoods in the city.

Our next stop was Google Earth, as we wanted to see what businesses were in this area. Now, it was my turn to be surprised. She said that this source was no good. The data was too old, three or four years out of date. I tried explaining that the software came out three years ago, but that the imagery and layers do get updated periodically. She was unconvinced: "Look, the (whatever it was called) shopping mall was missing. This can't be any good!" Something with the word Google attached wasn't any good? So she was evaluating the information she was searching through. Then why rely on Google as the first stop for finding census information?

(Continued)

Appendix 20.1. Essays from the Participants *(Continued)*

Here's a possible answer. This particular student was from Eastern Europe. In the world of census data, the United States is somewhat of an anomaly. Most datasets produced by the U.S. federal government are free, open access, public source. You don't have to pay a dime, and you can use it however you want. This is not the case in many other countries, and I would suspect this is not the case in many nations in Eastern Europe. As recently as a few years ago, Canada was charging its citizens for certain parts of its census data, and redistributing it in any way was illegal.

After considering this, I made a mental leap back to a few days before this one, when I received a question from a professor. He had some students out looking for data on religious affiliation in the census, and they returned telling him that this information was not available. He found this hard to believe, so he gave me a ring to confirm that the data was in there, somewhere, and that the students just couldn't find it. He was surprised when I told him it was against the law for the U.S. government to collect this kind of information (instead, a consortium of statisticians from various faiths within the United States meet and compile their own census, which is available from the Association of Religious Data Archives) . Why was he surprised? Well, other countries collect this information, including India, the country where he is from.

So there's an issue. Baruch is one of the most diverse academic communities in the country, and has students from over 160 countries, countries where demographic information is collected differently—different variables and time frames, or sometimes the data is public or available for a fee or not available at all. The freewheeling data world of the United States is quite foreign to many of these international students and émigrés who would have little knowledge of what the U.S. Census Bureau collects and provides and how vital statistics are compiled here. So the Google-info literacy matter may be at work here to some extent, but there's also the issue of international students and faculty becoming acclimated to numeric data sources, providers, and issues in this country. A crash course in the U.S. census (at the very least) may be in order.

Data Sources Mentioned in This Essay

NYC Department of City Planning,
    Reference Section
www.nyc.gov/html/dcp/html/subcats/
    resources.shtml

NYC Department of Health, Community Profiles
www.nyc.gov/html/doh/html/data/data.shtml

U.S. Census Bureau
www.census.gov

ARDA, Association of Religious
    Data Archives
www.thearda.com

Narrowing a Topic

A student approached the reference desk looking for sources to support a research paper on mobile communications. At this point, he admitted, the topic was very broad; it was up to him to find a specific aspect of the topic to research for his paper. First the student asked if Factiva would be a good place to start. The librarian suggested Factiva could be useful for a more specific search. In order to narrow the otherwise broad topic, the librarian guided the student in searching "wireless communications" or "mobile communications" in the FAITS (Faulkner's Advisory for Information Technologies Studies) database and Business Source Premier. In light of the search results, the student decided to focus his paper on the social aspects of wireless communication devices like cell phones and Blackberries. The suggested topics in the sidebar of Business Source Premier proved helpful in narrowing the search. Eventually, the librarian and student searched Factiva. The topic had narrowed to the role wireless communications in terrorism. The librarian constructed a search query using the wildcard asterisk and the "atleast" function. Here is the search query: [hlp=(wireless or mobile) and hlp=(terroris*) and atleast3 terroris*]. The student paid close attention to the query construction and took notes as the librarian explained the process. They then searched CUNY+ for books, using broad subject terms "technology and history" with a focus on

(Continued)

Appendix 20.1. Essays from the Participants *(Continued)*

finding the most recent publications. The desk was not busy, so this interaction lasted about 15 or 20 minutes. The student walked away from the desk with a list of articles and a few call numbers for appropriate books. Judging from his interest level and note-taking, I think he also understood how to search databases more effectively after the interaction.

I found this reference interaction interesting for a few reasons. The student approached the reference desk with a vague idea of a topic and was keen to use the reference interview to help narrow it down. He initially allowed the availability and quantity of information for certain topics to influence his choice. However, there were a lot of specific results for social aspects of mobile communications. Although not many apparent resources for the role of mobile technology in terrorism were available, the student found an interest in the topic and a few sources. So the search ended with a specific topic and several sources for the student.

Literary Criticism on Specific Poems
A student I met during a course-related lecture for a section of ENG 2150 was having trouble finding criticism on a poem by Edmund Spenser (1552–1599) that the student claimed was titled "My Love Is Like to Ice." He said a librarian had already worked with him at the desk for a while and was unable to find any criticism. I had just finished doing some nosing around and thought I'd share what I learned (which I hope will be instructive not just for this one particular poem but as a general approach when searching for criticism of a single poem). First, I found that the proper title of the poem is actually "Sonnet 30," although informally the poem is often known as "My Love Is Like to Ice," which happens to be the start of the first line, "My love is like to ice, and I to fire . . ." It is worth knowing that it is common for poems, especially numbered sonnets, to be known by the first line; scholars, though, will typically refer to such poems by their official or real titles. I also discovered that the poem was published in Spenser's lifetime in a collection known as *Amoretti*.

It is the official title of the poem (or the title of the book-length collection where the poem first appeared) that you will want to use as part of your search, not the informal title of the poem. I suggested in an e-mail to the student that he search for articles in Literature Resource Center and Academic Search Premier with this query: SPENSER AND (AMORETTI OR SONNET 30). For criticism in books, I recommended a slightly different query in the catalog: SPENSER EDMUND AND CRITICISM. I directed him to look through the tables of contents and the indexes in those books for references to "Amoretti" or "Sonnet 30."

Appendix 20.2. Survey of Participants

1. Please describe your library work experience before coming to Baruch. Did you work in reference before coming here? If so, in what type of library?
2. Did the reference mentoring program help you answer questions that you would not have been able to otherwise or that you were struggling with? Are there any specific questions or reference transactions that come to mind?
3. How well did you think the training helped you prepare for work at the reference desk? Did it encourage you to follow up with patrons or work more at answering difficult questions? Did it help you keep current with new sources?
4. Is there a session that you remember best, or a source that you remember using that has been particularly useful?
5. Did the program promote a sense of collaboration in the department? Did you find that the experience helped keep you motivated? Did it challenge you to extend your knowledge or abilities?
6. Please describe your impressions in the mentoring program. Overall, how would you describe the experience?
7. Were there any negative aspects of the program that you can think of?

About the Editors and Contributors

Marie L. Radford, PhD, is Associate Professor in the Department of Library and Information Science at the Rutgers University School of Communication and Information in New Jersey. Previously, she was Acting Dean of Pratt Institute's School of Information and Library Science in New York City. She holds a PhD from Rutgers University and an MSIS from Syracuse University. She gives frequent keynote speeches and scholarly papers at national library and communication conferences and publishes widely in academic journals. Radford was the coprincipal investigator of an Institute of Museum and Library Science–funded project "Seeking Synchronicity," evaluating virtual reference services. She has authored and edited several books, including *Conducting the Reference Interview*, Second Edition, with Catherine Sheldrick Ross and Kirsti Nilsen (Neal-Schuman, 2009); *Academic Library Research: Perspectives and Current Trends* with Pamela Snelson (Association of College and Research Libraries, 2008); and *Virtual Reference Service: From Competencies to Assessment* (Neal-Schuman, 2008). She directs the online Virtual Reference Bibliography (http://vrbib.rutgers.edu), blogs at Library Garden (http://librarygarden.net), and her Web site is at: http://comminfo .rutgers.edu/~mradford.

R. David Lankes, PhD, is director of the Information Institute of Syracuse and an associate professor in Syracuse University's School of Information Studies. Lankes has always been interested in combining theory and practice to create active research projects that make a difference. Past projects include the ERIC Clearinghouse on Information and Technology, the Gateway to Education Materials, AskERIC, and the Virtual Reference Desk. Lankes's more recent work involves how participatory concepts can reshape libraries and credibility. This work expands his ongoing project to understand the integration of human expertise in information systems. His Web site is at: http://quartz.syr.edu/rdlankes/index.php.

* * *

Stephanie Alexander is Social Sciences Reference and Instruction Librarian at the University of Colorado at Boulder. She earned her master of science in information degree from the University of Michigan and a bachelor's degree in mass communications from the University of California at Berkeley. She provides general reference services and bibliographic instruction at Norlin Library, the main humanities and social sciences library on the Boulder campus. She also serves as the library liaison to the Sociology and Communication Departments and the School of Journalism and Mass Communication, and she is responsible for collection development in those areas. She currently cochairs the Association of College and Research Libraries Anthropology and Sociology Section's Instruction and Information Literacy Committee. In addition to her interest in improving access to instructional materials online, she is working on a research project evaluating the effectiveness of the content of library instructional guides.

Lisa A. Ancelet is Head of Reference Services at Albert B. Alkek Library, Texas State University–San Marcos. She earned a MSIS from the University of Texas, Austin, in December 2003 and became Head of Reference at Alkek Library in May 2009. Her day-to-day duties include managing department operations to providing leadership and vision in planning delivery and assessment of reference services. Ancelet is also the team leader/developer of the library Web site. Prior to her promotion in May, Ancelet was Virtual Reference Services Librarian. She plays an instrumental part in developing the use of emerging technologies and Web 2.0 tools for reference services, campus outreach, information literacy instruction and Web development at Alkek Library. She is a member of the Emerging Technologies Committee at Alkek. Due in part to the work with the Virtual Reference Task force at Alkek, one of the early initiatives setting into motion the innovative approach to service implementation at Alkek, Ancelet was awarded Outstanding New Librarian from the Texas Library Association New Members Round Table in 2006. She has been a member of American Library Association, Association of College and Research Libraries, and Texas Library Association since 2001 and was recently in the American Library Association Emerging Leaders Class of 2008. She is currently Cochair of the Association of College and Research Libraries, Instruction Section, Instructional Technologies Committee, member of the American Library Association Committee on Literacy and is on the editorial board of *College & Research Libraries News*.

Susan Beatty is Head, Information Commons, at the University of Calgary, Canada. She has extensive experience in managing customer service in both academic and public libraries. Her main responsibility is coordinating the delivery of reference service and technical support in the Information Commons. Beatty has presented at international conferences in Hong Kong, New Zealand, United States, England, and Scotland.

Wayne Bivens-Tatum is General and Humanities Reference Librarian and Selector for Philosophy and Religion at the Princeton University Library, Princeton, New Jersey, and he a lecturer in the Princeton Writing Program. He holds an MS in library and information science and a MA from the University of Illinois at Urbana–Champaign. He frequently writes and speaks on issues of technology and librarianship and blogs at http://academiclibrarian.net.

Kay Ann Cassell, PhD, is Lecturer and Director of the MLIS Program in the Department of Library and Information Science, School of Communication and Information, at Rutgers University in New Jersey, where she teaches reference and collection development. She is the author of several books including *Reference and Information Services in the 21st Century*, Second Edition, with co-author Uma Hiremath (Neal-Schuman, 2009), and *Developing Reference Collections and Services in an Electronic Age* (Neal-Schuman, 1999). Cassell is also the editor of the quarterly journal *Collection Building*. She is active in the Reference and User Services Association of the American Library Association, Association for Library and Information Science Education, and International Federation of Library Associations.

Yit Chin Chuan is a Senior Librarian at the Lee Kong Chian Reference Library, the National Library of Singapore. He has been working in the library service for more than ten years covering Public Libraries and Service Development. More recently, Chuan has been taking care of Science and Technology subjects for Reference Services.

Helen Clarke is currently Head Collections Services and Electronics Resources Librarian at the University of Calgary, Canada. Helen is also chair of the Taylor Family Digital Library Collections team (one of the Implementation Teams of the new Taylor Library) and is leading a review of collections for the new library at the University of Calgary.

Virginia Cole, PhD, has held the position of Reference and Digital Services Librarian at Olin, Cornell University's humanities and social sciences library, since 2001. In 2005, she also became Cornell's Medieval Studies Bibliographer. She holds a master's degree in teaching and a PhD in medieval history from the State University of New York at Binghamton. Her previous publications focused on medieval poverty. Currently, her research interests are virtual reference and user research behaviors.

Lynn Silipigni Connaway, PhD, is Senior Research Scientist at OCLC Research. Her research projects include data mining WorldCat and other library data and studying information-seeking behaviors to facilitate library decision making. She coauthored the fourth edition of *Basic Research Methods for Librarians.* Connaway was the coprincipal investigator of an Institute of Museum and Library Science–funded project evaluating virtual reference services and the coinvestigator of another Institute of Museum and Library Science–funded study investigating information-seeking behaviors of academics. She has published and presented in numerous scholarly and professional venues. Previously she was on the graduate faculty at the University of Denver and the University of Missouri, Columbia.

Lizzie Eastwood has worked professionally in libraries since 1993. When she moved to the United States from the UK in 2000 she earned her MLIS from Dominican University in Illinois. She has worked in many diverse libraries with many different roles, including interlibrary loan librarian in a physics laboratory and an information officer for a charity working to support those with arthritis. Lizzie has worked in the Reference section of the Los Alamos County Library System since 2004. Her special interest and passion is in consumer health information, and she regularly reviews consumer health titles in *Library Journal.*

Lorrie Evans is currently Head of Library Instruction at the Auraria Library, which serves the University of Colorado Denver, Metropolitan State College of Denver, and the Community College of Denver. Through single and multisession workshops, a semester-long graduate course, and online services, she reaches a diverse population of students in the library instruction program. Current projects include program development in the area of curricular integration. She has been actively involved with reference and instruction in academic libraries for 20 years. Previously Lorrie was a reference librarian at the University of Denver and a part-time psychology instructor and librarian at James Madison University. Research interests include decision making during the research process for new and more experienced searchers. She holds a master of library science degree from the University of Maryland and a master of science in cognitive psychology degree from Kansas State University.

Reference Renaissance

Lorin Flores Fisher is Information Literacy Coordinator at Albert B. Alkek Library, Texas State University–San Marcos. She graduated from the University of North Texas, earning a MLS in 2000 and began at Texas State University–San Marcos in early 2001 as Reference/ Instruction Librarian. Her duties include coordinating the Information Literacy and Instruction program and leading a team of instruction librarians at Alkek Library, encompassing various tasks including scheduling classes, teaching classes, designing learning activities, and leading informal training sessions for colleagues and instruction session assessments. She is very interested in new and emerging technologies, new forms of literacy, gaming, virtual worlds and their effect in libraries, student learning, information literacy, and assessment. Throughout her time at Texas State, she has been heavily involved in various projects and initiatives to implement new technologies at Alkek Library, both for reference and instructional uses. She has had a prominent role in the development of the Alkek Library Wiki, production of library tutorials on Alkek's YouTube site, and is the lead author of the Alkek Library Information Literacy Blog. She chairs Alkek Library's Emerging Technologies Committee and is a member of the "Dream Team" developing the Texas State University Second Life campus presence. She is also a volunteer reference librarian at Info International, the Second Life Library in Second Life.

Jennifer Gerke is Electronic Government Information Librarian at the University of Colorado at Boulder. She earned her master of science in library science degree from Indiana University, her master of English from Washington University in St. Louis, and bachelor's degree in English and computational science from Hollins University. She provides general reference services in Norlin Library as well as bibliographic instruction for classes related to political science (with whom she is the library liaison), international area studies, and government publications. She is also responsible for collection development in political science and international area studies. She is currently active in American Library Association's Government Documents Roundtable. In addition to an interest in integrating government resources into library resources such as guides and instruction, she is completing a research project evaluating the ways library patrons use materials available in both print and electronic formats.

Bernadine Goldman is Assistant Library Manager at Los Alamos County Library System. She earned her master of library science degree at the University of British Columbia and her master of public administration degree at the University of New Mexico. In a long career in public and academic libraries, she has served as head cataloger, interlibrary loan librarian, children's librarian, branch manager, and reference and information services manager before accepting her current position in 2007. Her present responsibilities include implementing the unification of library public services, library collection development, and library staff development. She has presented programs at several New Mexico Library Association conferences as well as at the Internet Librarian conference. She is a continuing mentor in the American Library Association's New Members Roundtable Mentoring Program.

Glynn Harmon, PhD, is Professor and Graduate Advisor in the School of Information at the University of Texas at Austin. His research interests involve modeling the cognitive processes of information seekers and query generation (including unconscious cognition and the impact of short-term human memory); the acceleration of personal, professional and scholarly discovery; and education for information studies. He has published monographs on human memory and its relation to the formation of knowledge systems and on real estate information systems. His journal articles and book chapters have addressed the scope and nature of information, information science and professionalism, and the Memex and World Encyclopedia. He is currently coauthoring a book on Nobel laureate discovery patterns in physiology and medicine and articles on the acceleration of discovery. His professional service includes research in information retrieval, reference and library work, and as instructor and researcher at the University of Texas at Austin, where he served twice as interim dean. Prior to entering the information field, he served as a Navy pilot and naval communications administrator, education officer, and Russian interpreter. He holds BA and MA degrees in public administration from the University of California at Berkeley, MS and PhD degrees in information science from Case Western Reserve University, and an MBA from Southwest Texas State University.

Mary Kickham-Samy, a librarian at Macomb Community College in Warren, Michigan, is the quality control manager and training coordinator for the Michigan Virtual Reference Collaborative. She is also a doctoral student in Instructional Design and Technology at Old Dominion University in Norfolk, Virginia. In addition to holding a master's degree in library and information science from Wayne State in Detroit. Mary also has a master's degree in teaching English as a foreign language from the American University in Cairo, Egypt, where she taught for over 22 years.

Louise Klusek is Associate Professor and head of reference at the William and Anita Newman Library at Baruch College in New York City where she has worked for the past five years. Previously she was a Research Associate and Assistant Vice President in the libraries of Salomon Smith Barney and Citigroup in New York City. She is the library liaison to the department of Management and the Weissman Center for International Business. She holds an MLS from the University of Pittsburgh and an MBA from Temple University.

Hannah Kwon is a PhD student in library and information science at the School of Communication and Information at Rutgers University. Her research interest is people's narrative descriptions of information needs, particularly as they function representationally and interactionally to situate individuals in relation to their information needs and the process of information seeking. A former reference librarian, she is also interested in how narrative methods can be used in the process of community analysis to uncover the information needs of unserved and underserved "thought communities."

Kathryn Lage is Map Librarian at the Jerry Crail Johnson Earth Sciences and Map Library at the University of Colorado at Boulder. She is responsible for providing reference services, bibliographic instruction, collection development, and managing all aspects of access to digital and print cartographic resources. She holds a BA degree in American Studies from the University of California, Santa Cruz, and an MLS degree from San José State University in California. Kathryn recently completed collaborative digital projects to provide online access to collections of historical aerial photographs of Colorado's Front Range and of Sanborn Fire Insurance maps of Colorado. Her research interests include methods of access to and delivery of digital geospatial data and the library's role in organizing and providing access to digital cartographic information. She is active in the Western Association of Map Libraries and is a representative to the Cartographic Users Advisory Council.

James LaRue has been the director of the Douglas County Libraries since 1990. He is the author of *The New Inquisition: Understanding and Managing Intellectual Freedom Challenges* and has written a weekly newspaper column for over 20 years. He was the Colorado Librarian of the Year in 1998, the Castle Rock Chamber of Commerce's 2003 Business Person of the Year, and in 2007 won the Julie J. Boucher Award for Intellectual Freedom.

Sarah Lawton came to librarianship from a background as a bookseller in an independent bookshop. Her emphasis on customer service and innovative programming inform her work as a reference librarian and Teen Services Manager at Wilkinson Public Library in Telluride, Colorado. A 1999 graduate of Macalester College, Sarah received her BA in sociology. She was a 2009 American Library Association Emerging Leader and received her MLIS from the University of Wisconsin–Milwaukee in August 2009. She is a member of the American Library Association Literacy and Outreach Services Advisory Committee and the Marketing and Public Relations for Reference Services Committee of Reference and User Services Association's Reference Services Section.

David W. Lewis is Dean of the Indiana University–Purdue University Indianapolis University Library and Indiana University and Assistant Vice President of Digital Scholarly Communications. He has a BA in history form Carleton College and an MLS from Columbia University. He came to Indiana University–Purdue University Indianapolis in 1993 as the Head of Public Services and has been the Dean of the University Library since 2000. In 2009 he accepted the additional responsibility of Assistant Vice President Digital Scholarly Communications to advance Indiana University's programs in digital scholarship and to "recapture the scholarly record." Lewis has written over 30 articles and book chapters on topics ranging from reference services to the management of libraries to scholarly communication (see http://idea.iupui.edu/dspace/handle/1805).

Karen Long has worked as an Adult Services Librarian at the Farmington Public Library in New Mexico since she received her MLIS in the summer of 2007. In her time at Farmington Public Library, she has implemented instant messaging reference, managed the rollout of a comprehensive promotional initiative covering electronic, print, and in-person reference called Just Ask, organized information literacy sessions for local community college business students, and staged a successful family gaming event. Through these and other programs, she enjoys helping patrons by making the library and its resources as user-friendly as possible. Karen writes reviews for *Library Journal* and a blog about writing in libraries.

Sidney Lowe is currently serving as the Head of the Research and Information Department for the University Libraries at the University of Nevada, Las Vegas. She is responsible for administering the research and information services provided at Lied Library. Lowe also manages the libraries' government information resources and serves as the liaison librarian to University of Nevada, Las Vegas's Political Science Department. She spent many years as a paraprofessional library employee before earning her MLIS from the University of

North Texas in 2004. Lowe earned her BA in sociology from the University of California, Santa Barbara, and also holds a master's degree in public administration from the University of Nevada, Las Vegas.

Nina McHale is Assistant Professor, Web Librarian at the Auraria Library in Denver, which serves the University of Colorado Denver, Metropolitan State College of Denver, and the Community College of Denver. She has experience in both reference and systems, and prior to coming to Auraria she held academic positions at Howard Community College (Columbia, Maryland) and Georgetown University. Her research interests include emerging technologies, usability testing, user-centered design, and Web accessibility. Nina holds an MA in Arthurian literature from the University of Wales Bangor as well as a joint MA/MSLS in English and library science from the Catholic University of America.

Lilia Murray received her MLIS from the University of North Carolina at Greensboro. She is Assistant Professor/Reference Librarian at Murray State University in Murray, Kentucky. In addition, she serves as the library liaison to the Art & Design, Modern Languages, Music, and Theatre Departments.

Judy Ng is the Deputy Director of the National Reference and Special Libraries, the National Library of Singapore. She has 22 years of library experience and is currently overseeing the Lee Kong Chian Reference Library and 13 government libraries. She had served in different postings and had experience in running the public libraries as well as reference library. She is involved in the development of collaborative reference services at the National Library. Judy received a master's degree in library and information science from the University of Western Ontario, Canada.

Victoria Nozero, JD, currently serves as Director of Research and Education at University of Nevada, Las Vegas's University Libraries. Her responsibilities include overseeing the Collection Management, Instruction, and Research and Information Departments and three branch libraries. Prior to her appointment as director in October 2007, Nozero was Head of Research and Information Department in Lied Library at University of Nevada, Las Vegas for eight years. Before coming to University of Nevada, Las Vegas, Nozero was employed by Aspen Systems Corp., Rockville, Maryland, for whom she served as project manager at the U.S. Department of Interior and U.S. Department of Labor Headquarters Libraries. Nozero received her MSLS from the Catholic University of America in Washington, DC, and a BA in history from the University of California, Los Angeles. She also earned a JD from George Washington University.

Mary Pinard is Public Services Librarian at the Sacramento County Public Law Library. She received a BA in history from Northwestern University and an MLIS from the University of Texas at Austin. After a short stint with a small state agency library, Pinard joined the reference staff at the Sacramento County Public Law Library in 2002. In this position, she provides reference services to attorneys, self-represented litigants, and the general public; works with a team of staff members to update and maintain the library's Web site; and teaches classes on legal research topics to attorneys and the general public. Pinard has served as the editor of Northern California Association of Law Libraries' newsletter,

NOCALL News, since 2005, and as Co-Coordinator of California's AskNow Law Service since 2007. She has also served as Webmaster for both the American Association of Law Libraries Copyright Committee and the Council of California County Law Librarians.

Ivy Lee Huey Shin is Senior Librarian at the Lee Kong Chian Reference Library, the National Library of Singapore. Upon receiving her MSc in information studies from the Nayang Technological University of Singapore, she joined the public libraries working as an adult and young people librarian before moving on to the National Library to specialize in reference and research services. Shin's research interests include virtual reference and collections development.

Karen Sobel has been Assistant Professor and Reference and Instruction Librarian at the Auraria Library, which serves the University of Colorado Denver, Metropolitan State College of Denver, and the Community College of Denver, since January 2008. She is currently coteaching a LibGuides-based online library skills course open to all students at the University of Colorado Denver. She holds a master of science in library science degree and a master of arts in English degree from the University of North Carolina at Chapel Hill. Her interests include instruction for first-year college students, development of online educational materials, and assessment of learning during library instruction.

Ralph Stahlberg is Reference Librarian at the Los Angeles Law Library in Los Angeles, California. He received a BA in history from the University of California, Santa Barbara, in 1980 and a master of librarianship from the University of Washington in 1983. He began his library career as Assistant Librarian at the King County Law Library in Seattle and has been with the Los Angeles Law Library's Reference Department since 1988. With nearly 1,000,000 equivalent volumes, the Los Angeles Law Library is the largest public law library in the United States. Stahlberg's duties at the library include providing reference service to a diverse group of users, which includes attorneys, librarians, court personnel, self-represented litigants, and the general public. The library staff responds to reference questions in person and by phone, e-mail, mail, and live chat. Stahlberg also teaches public research classes as part of the library's training programs and participates in collection development. He is a member of American Association of Law Libraries and of the Southern California Association of Law Libraries. Southern California Association of Law Libraries honored Stahlberg with their Chapter Service Award in 1999 for his archival service to the association. He was part of the original group of participants in California's AskNow Law Service and has served as Co-Coordinator for the group since 2004.

Carla J. Stoffle has been Dean of Libraries and Center for Creative Photography at the University of Arizona since 1991. She is the author of three books and more than 50 major articles and chapters about academic librarianship. Stoffle also has participated in over 100 presentations, workshops, and panels from 1972 to the present. She was Acting Director of the University of Arizona's School of Information Resources and Library Science from 1999 to 2001. Stoffle currently serves as Amigos Library Services Trustee and an American Library Association Councilor at Large. She is former Chair of the Greater Western Library Alliance Board of Directors and the Center for Research Libraries Board of Directors as well as a past president of the Association of College and Research

Libraries. Stoffle received the American Library Association's 2002 Elizabeth Futas Catalyst for Change Award and was named the 2000 Arizona Librarian of the Year.

Feili Tu, PhD, is Assistant Professor in the School of Library and Information Science at the University of South Carolina. Tu received her PhD from Texas Woman's University and an MLIS from Louisiana State University. Her area of expertise in both research and teaching is in health informatics and health sciences librarianship with a strong academic background and experience in reference and information services, especially virtual reference services.

Christopher Tuthill is Assistant Professor and information services librarian at Baruch College in New York City. He has been at Baruch since January 2008, when he began attending the reference training program. He teaches an information research course for undergraduate students and serves as library liaison to the English department. Previously he has worked as a librarian at the University of Maine and Queens Borough Public Library. He holds an MLS from the State University of New York at Albany and an MA in English from State University of New York at Binghamton.

Amy VanScoy is Associate Head, Research and Information Services at North Carolina State University Libraries. She shares responsibility for managing reference and digital reference services. VanScoy coordinates reference staff training and assessment of user instruction and has significant supervisory responsibilities. In previous positions at North Carolina State University Libraries, VanScoy was Assistant Head, Research and Information Services and Librarian for Undergraduate Research. VanScoy is also a doctoral student at the University of North Carolina at Chapel Hill. Her research focuses on the personal theories of academic reference librarians. She has the MLIS from the University of Alabama and the MA in French from Indiana University. VanScoy enjoys opportunities to guest lecture at local library and information science programs and recently developed a for-credit course for honors students concerning the social and economic aspects of information. A frequent presenter at national and local conferences, VanScoy has published in the areas of digital reference, diversity, and undergraduate instruction.

Lynn Westbrook, PhD, is Associate Professor in the School of Information and the Center for Women and Gender Studies, the University of Texas at Austin. Her research interests include the role of mental models in reference work and information seeking, the nature and quality of digital reference transactions, domestic violence survivors' affective and cognitive behaviors and their adaptive information use patterns, and electronic information service development. She has published monographs on identifying and analyzing user needs, interdisciplinary information seeking in women's studies, qualitative evaluation methods for reference services, and paper preservation. Her professional experience includes reference and bibliographic instruction work and public services administration at the University of Georgia and the University of Michigan. Before coming to the University of Texas, she served on the faculty and was Interim Director at the School of Library and Information Studies at Texas Women's University. She holds a MA in library science from the University of Chicago and a PhD in Information and Library Studies from the University of Michigan at Ann Arbor.

Andrea Wright is Science Reference Librarian in the Thomas Cooper Library at the University of South Carolina. She received her MLIS from School of Library and Information Science at the University of South Carolina and BS from Furman University in Greenville, South Carolina. Her areas of interest include virtual reference services and instruction with a special emphasis on science, technology, and mathematics.

Index

Page numbers followed by the letter "f" indicate figures; those followed by the letter "t" indicate tables.

Handwritten: 11 60452 Ref 006.60 Re #25—